MOBILE INFORMATION SYSTEMS

IFIP – The International Federation for Information Processing

IFIP was founded in 1960 under the auspices of UNESCO, following the First World Computer Congress held in Paris the previous year. An umbrella organization for societies working in information processing, IFIP's aim is two-fold: to support information processing within its member countries and to encourage technology transfer to developing nations. As its mission statement clearly states,

> IFIP's mission is to be the leading, truly international, apolitical organization which encourages and assists in the development, exploitation and application of information technology for the benefit of all people.

IFIP is a non-profit making organization, run almost solely by 2500 volunteers. It operates through a number of technical committees, which organize events and publications. IFIP's events range from an international congress to local seminars, but the most important are:

- The IFIP World Computer Congress, held every second year;
- Open conferences;
- Working conferences.

The flagship event is the IFIP World Computer Congress, at which both invited and contributed papers are presented. Contributed papers are rigorously refereed and the rejection rate is high.

As with the Congress, participation in the open conferences is open to all and papers may be invited or submitted. Again, submitted papers are stringently refereed.

The working conferences are structured differently. They are usually run by a working group and attendance is small and by invitation only. Their purpose is to create an atmosphere conducive to innovation and development. Refereeing is less rigorous and papers are subjected to extensive group discussion.

Publications arising from IFIP events vary. The papers presented at the IFIP World Computer Congress and at open conferences are published as conference proceedings, while the results of the working conferences are often published as collections of selected and edited papers.

Any national society whose primary activity is in information may apply to become a full member of IFIP, although full membership is restricted to one society per country. Full members are entitled to vote at the annual General Assembly, National societies preferring a less committed involvement may apply for associate or corresponding membership. Associate members enjoy the same benefits as full members, but without voting rights. Corresponding members are not represented in IFIP bodies. Affiliated membership is open to non-national societies, and individual and honorary membership schemes are also offered.

MOBILE INFORMATION SYSTEMS

*IFIP TC8 Working Conference on
Mobile Information Systems (MOBIS)
15–17 September 2004
Oslo, Norway*

Edited by

Elaine Lawrence
University of Technology Sydney, Australia

Barbara Pernici
Politecnico di Milano, Italy

John Krogstie
SINTEF and Norwegian Institute of Science and Technology, Norway

 Springer

Library of Congress Cataloging-in-Publication Data

A C.I.P. Catalogue record for this book is available from the
Library of Congress.

ISBN 978-1-4419-3562-5   e-ISBN 978-0-387-22874-7   Printed on acid-free paper.

Printed in the United States of America.

9 8 7 6 5 4 3 2 1

springeronline.com

Contents

Contents

Preface

Mobility is perhaps the most important market and technological trend within information and communication technology. With the advent of new mobile infrastructures providing higher bandwidth and constant connection to the network from virtually everywhere, the way people use information resources is predicted to be radically transformed. Over the last years, a new breed of information systems, referred to as mCommerce systems or mobile information systems, has appeared to address this emerging situation.

In 2000, the IFIP 8.1 WG decided to look into establishing a task group to look closer at this area, and the idea was adopted and extended by IFIP TC8 the following year. After the arrangement of several workshop, this task group has been the driving force behind the arrangement of MOBIS (IFIP TC 8 Working Conference on Mobile Information systems) held in Oslo, Norway, 15-17 September 2004.

The objective of the working conference was to provide a forum for researchers and practitioners interested in planning, analysis, design, construction, modification, implementation, utilization, evaluation, and management of mobile information systems to meet, and exchange research ideas and results. Specifically, we tried to use the working conference to

- Clarify differences and similarities between the development of mobile vs. more traditional information systems
- Investigate organizational impact of mobile information systems
- Investigate mobile commerce applications combined with the advantages of mobile communications technologies

- Evaluate existing and newly developed approaches for analysis, design, implementation, and evolution of mobile information systems.
- Investigate technical issues and the constraints they pose on mobile information systems functionalities and design

The conference would not have been made possible without the assistance of many people. We received over 40 papers which were peer reviewed by a minimum of two reviewers and 19 full papers and 6 short papers were accepted. We are indebted to the program committee members and additional reviewers for preparing thorough reviews in a very tight schedule. The authors are thanked for their efforts in making an excellent scientific contribution to this new and challenging field. Finally, IFIP, TC8 officers and Dataforeningen have been instrumental for the success of the event.

June 2004

Elaine Lawrence, Sydney
Barbara Pernici, Milano
John Krogstie, Oslo

Conference Committee

General Chair
Prof. Dewald Roode
University of Pretoria
South Africa

Program Co-Chairs
Prof. Barbara Pernici
Politecnico di Milano, Italy

Dr. Elaine Lawrence
University of Technology Sydney
Australia

Organizing Chair
Prof. John Krogstie
SINTEF and Norwegian Institute of Science and Technology
Norway

Program Committee
Luciano Baresi, Italy
Boualem Benatallah, Australia
Richard Baskerville, USA
Gordana Culjak, Australia
Jashir Dhaliwal, Norway
Chiara Francalanci, Italy
Manfred Hauswirth, Switzerland

Jan Pries Heje , Denmark
Jo Herstad, Norway
George Giaglis, Greece
Garrick Jones, UK
Ravi Kalakota, USA
Karl-Heinz Kautz, Denmark
Steven Kelly, Finland
Christen Krogh, Norway
Michel Leonard, Switzerland
Binshan Lin, USA
Heiko Ludwig, USA
Kalle Lyytinen, USA
Ralf Muhlberger, Australia
Erich Neuhold, Germany
Erik Gøsta Nilsson, Norway
Andreas L. Opdahl, Norway
Lim Ee Peng, Singapore
Wolfgang Prinz, Germany
Siggi Reich, Austria
Gustavo Rossi, Argentina
Matti Rossi. Finland
Keng Siau, USA
David Simplot, France
Guttorm Sindre, Norway
Mikael B. Skov, Denmark
Kari Smolander, Finland
Robert Steele, Australia
Marie Thilliez, France
Jari Veijalainen, Finland
Antony Wasserman, USA
Jens Wehrman, Germany

CONTRACTS FOR DEFINING QOS LEVELS
IN A MULTICHANNEL ADAPTIVE INFORMATION SYSTEM

M. Callea, L. Campagna, M.G. Fugini and P. Plebani
Politecnico di Milano - 20133 Milano Italy

Abstract: Multichannel Information Systems provide a way to invoke the same service through several channels. In this way, even if the functionality provided by the service is independent of the actual channel, the quality varies according to the particular devices used by the service consumer. In this context, this paper presents a frame for the creation and management of contracts formalizing the agreement, in terms of quality of service, between an *e*-Service provider and an *e*-Service consumer in a multichannel adaptive information system. In particular, the work relates to some of the existing modelling languages for QoS, such as QML, WSLA and XQoS, and presents some extensions to WSLA able to deal with a multichannel environment. The presented model is validated by a prototype developed to support creation and subscription of contracts. The prototype application allows a *provider* to publish others regarding *e*-Services with desired QoS parameters, and a *consumer* to subscribe a contract with the negotiated QoS levels.

Keywords: multichannel systems; quality of service; contract; adaptivity.

1.   INTRODUCTION

The first efforts in the field of Service Oriented Computing (SOC) mainly focused on the definition about how an *e*-Service could be built, deployed, and invoked. As a consequence, different standards or standard proposals are now available, and different platforms are able to provide a set of *e*-Services mainly through the Web [Alonso et al., 2003]. Starting from this scenario, most recent researches concentrate on possible extensions of the Service Oriented Architecture (SOA) where the coordination, composition, and management of *e*-Services are also considered [ACM,

2003]. Besides such conceptual extensions, starting from the consideration that the Web Service technology is an instantiation of the SOA, it is very interesting to consider other kinds of extensions in order to define how an *e*-Service can be provided through several channels using for example a Smartphone or a PDA. In this way, if the same *e*-Service can be exploited through several channels, and it is up to the user to switch among available channels according to his current needs. In particular, in this work, we focus one expressing these multichannel requirements in terms of the quality of the delivered *e*-Service, in order to allow the user to change the *e*-Service delivery mode when he realizes that the current quality level is not adequate.

According to various proposals currently available to define the QoS, this paper deals with the need of models and methods that allow the specification of quality levels in Multichannel Information Systems. In particular, in the Italian MAIS project [MAIS Team, 2003], multichannel systems are regarded as able to provide an *e*-Service on different channels having different technological characteristics, such as diverse delivery times, responses, or simply different data rendering, depending on the used protocols, networks, and devices. On the other hand, Adaptive Systems are regarded as able to analyze the network and to suggest the user the most convenient way (e.g., the most suitable receiving device, or the most suitable transmission mode) to receive and use the e-Service, while maintaining an adequate quality level.

In this paper, we present the model studied in the MAIS project for specifying the QoS in Multichannel Adaptive Information Systems. In this model, a user looking for an *e*-Service around the network is interested not only in functional aspects, but also in non-functional aspects of the *e*-Service, such as response time, security and integrity of transactions, or costs, which can be grouped under the term of *Quality of Service* (hereafter QoS) aspects. The paper is organized as follows. After a brief analysis on some existing QoS modelling languages presented in Section 2, Section 3 describes the proposed Quality model, whereas Section 4 presents an extension to WSLA to cover aspects of multichannel systems. Section 5 outiline the basic features of the prototype developed on the basis of the presented model and finally Section 6 draws conclusions.

2.   RELATED WORK

QoS is currently considered as an important topic in several research communities and a lot of work had been done to provide a definition. For this reason, nowadays several languages and specifications are available in telecommunication [ITU, 1994; ITU, 2001; Crawley et al., 1998; Huston,

2000], middleware [Zinky et al., 1997; Marchetti et al., 2003], and information system communities [Frølung et al, 1998; Keller et al., 2002; Exposito et al., 2003]. Concentrating on a subset of such specifications, proposals like QML, WSLA, and XQoS, capture the main aspects to be taken into account in the definition and management of the QoS and, to this aim, we present an overview of these three languages in the following subsections.

2.1   QML (Quality of Service Modelling Language)

QML [Frølung et al, 1998] tries to model the QoS as independent as possible of the specific domain where the service operates. For this reason, QML relies on the definition of QoS parameters organized according to the concepts of the object-oriented paradigm. QML specification lists a set of elements that each QoS document should consider in order to provide a good specification about the quality. In particular:

- QoS specification should be syntactically separated from the other portions of service specification, such as interface definitions;
- it should be possible to specify both the QoS properties required by the user and the QoS properties about the service provisioning;
- there should be a way to determine how the QoS specification can match the user QoS requirements;
- it should be possible to redefine and to specialize an existing specification, analogously to what inheritance mechanisms do in object-oriented programming.

According to these requirements, QML provides three main abstraction mechanisms for QoS specification: *contract type*, *contract*, and *profile*. While a contract type defines the dimensions that can be used to characterize a particular QoS aspect, a contract is an instance of a contract type and represents a particular QoS specification. In particular, a contract type defines a collection of dimensions, each associated with a range of allowed values. A contract redefines these constraints according to given needs. A profile associates the contracts to the service interfaces operations, operation arguments, and operation results.

QML does not specify either how QoS can be enforced and monitored nor the way to distribute responsibilities among the involved actors.

2.2   WSLA (Web Service Level Agreement)

WSLA [Keller et al., 2002] is an XML-based, extensible language used to define a contract between a Web Service provider and a Web Service user. Analogously to QML, WSLA defines QoS levels according to a set of different quality parameters; differently from QML, WSLA considers also the responsibility about quality monitoring and enforcement. A WSLA document is composed of three main sections:

- *parties description*: who is involved in the contract;
- *service definition*: what are the parameters describing the QoS, what are the metrics related to them, and, for each parameter, who is in charge of monitoring the values;
- *obligation:* the range of values the parameters have to respect, and the action to be undertaken in case of violation.

Due to its native purpose, WSLA is strictly related to Web Service provisioning and has no mechanisms to specify the QoS in case the same service is provided through a channel different from the Web.

2.3   XQoS (XML-Based QoS Specification Language)

XQoS [Exposito et al., 2003] defines the QoS on both the user's and provider's standpoints; moreover, the language is basically oriented to multimedia services. At the user's side, the parameters are bound to the human perception of a service, whereas at the provider's side these parameters are bound to the communication services used to provide the service. This specification relies on a formal model represented by Time Stream Petri Nets [Diaz et al. 1994] for multimedia systems.

Even if XQoS is strictly related to a particular class of applications, i.e. multimedia, the provided modelling concepts about elements composing a multimedia service are useful for multichannel systems.

3.   QUALITY MODEL

In the MAIS project, the problem of defining QoS is one of the main topics since the definition of what quality means and how it can be measured and monitored during service provisioning enables system designers and providers/users to properly define the concept of "adaptivity". Figure 1 sketches the quality model adopted in MAIS [Marchetti et al., 2004] on which the contract needs to be based. In particular, this model represents how the channel can influence the quality, as perceived by the user, with respect to the quality, as provided by the system. Hence, the model consists of (i) a *system model*, defining objects (*e-Service* , *network,* and *device*) and actors (*e-Service provider, network provider, device provider*, and *user*), and of (ii) *a set of roles and rules* enabling the association between quality information, expressed by quality parameters, and objects.

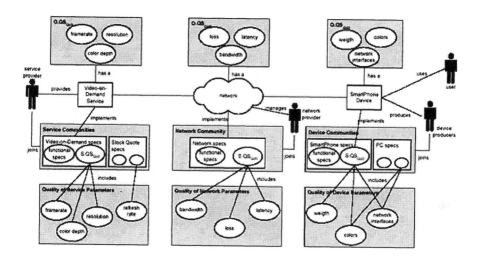

Figure 1. MAIS Model

The *<network, device>* pair represents the *channel* able to connect the *e*-Service provider and user. In particular, given an *e*-Service, the *e*-Service provider, by selecting the networks and the devices, defines a set of channels through which the *e*-Service can be invoked. Simple examples of channels are: < 802.11; PDA >,<Modem; PC >,<802.11; PC >,<GSM; Smartphone>.

In order to attach quality information to the objects, the model introduces *quality parameters* in the form of *<name; admissible value>* pairs, where *name* represents a unique parameter identifier, and *admissible value* represents the range of values suitable for the parameter. To normalize the possible different interpretations of concepts related to quality, the model introduces the *community* as a group of providers who propose a specification for a group of objects with relevant common characteristics. Hence, we have an *e-Service community* for groups of *e*-Services providing the same functionality (e.g. hotel reservation service, video on demand service), a set of *network communities,* and *device communities.* The communities declare both the *functional specifications* and *the set of quality parameters* they consider as relevant. All the providers who intend to implement the relative object will refer to such specifications.

To clarify the model, consider an example regarding a video-on-demand *e*-Service, allowing a user to receive video-streams on different devices, e.g., PCs, cable TVs, or SmartPhones. Both the functional and quality features of this class of *e*-Service are specified by the *user community* of the video-on-demand *e*-Service. In particular, the quality of this *e*-Service can be characterized by quality parameters such as *framerate, colordepth,* and *resolution.* Analogously, suppose that a *network community* defines the quality of a generic network according to the *bandwidth*, *latency* and *jitter* quality parameters, whereas the *devices community* introduces the *videoresolution* and *colordepth* parameters. For each parameter, the communities also define the range of admissible values. Once a provider decides to implement an object, he has to define the quality according to the parameters specified by the communities related to the object. This means a possible restriction of the range of allowed values of quality parameters describing the *e*-Service, obviously respecting the guidelines of the *e*-Service communities. For example, if the video-on-demand *e*-Service community has defined the range [*5fps...40fps*] as admissible values for *framerate*, the *e*-Service provider, on the basis of his available computational resources, can restrict such range to, say, [*5fps...20fps*], that is, to the value he is actually able to provide for the *e*-Service.

So far, the quality has been defined from the provider's perspective. Considering the *e*-Service user's perspective, we observe that, in general, the quality perceived by the user is possibly different from the quality perceived by the provider [Khirman and Henriksen 2002]. In fact, the network and the device both affect the *e*-Service exploitation. In the MAIS quality model, this influence is captured by a set of *quality rules* that make explicit the relationship between the different quality parameters, in order to compute the *quality of experience*, i.e., the actual quality perceived by the *consumer*.

The quality rule *framerate**colordepth*resolution=*K**bandwidth, for example, states the relationship among one of the network parameters, i.e., the bandwidth, and the *e*-Service quality parameters. In this way, it is possible to compute the minimum and maximum values for *framerate*, allowed from the user side. By identifying and executing the quality rules for all the QoS parameters, the user gets the basis for deciding the most suitable execution channel.

4.   WSLA EXTENSION

The quality model described above enables providers and user to set up a *contract*, intended as a formal document where two parties set up an agreement, in our case about provisioning and usage of an *e*-Service. As a basis, such document should contain: i) the data identifying the contracting parties, ii) the object of the contract, iii) the general conditions of agreement, and iv) the responsibilities and penalties in case of violation. These aspects are properly captured by the WSLA language described above. However, some extensions are needed, in particular with concepts belonging to QML and XQoS suitable to describe the quality in a multichannel environment, rather than in Web Service environments only.

The first kind of extension we propose for WSLA introduces some attributes to the *ServiceLevelObjective* and *ActionGuarantee* tags which represent the admissible values of quality parameters, and the actions to be taken in case of agreement violation. In particular, the *order* attribute, which can be *increasing* or *decreasing*, states how the quality varies with respect to an increasing value of the quality parameters. This specification is needed since the order depends on the semantics of parameters; for example, for the response time, the higher the value the lower the quality, whereas, for the throughput, the higher the value the higher the quality.

As for channel definition, a second extension we propose for WSLA is the introduction of the *device* and *network* attributes; now, the contract is suitable to specify a particular quality level, which depends on the selected channel. This extension supports the not only the description of an *e*-Service through the available channels but also the comparison of different quality values, in order to enact the more suitable adaptation strategies for *e*-Service provisioning.

The last kind of extension regards the introduction of two new kinds of *domains* in WSLA: the *set domain* and the *enumerated domain*. In both cases, a quality parameter must hold one of the values belonging to the domain; however, for the first domain, a quality parameter can assume one or more values at the same time, whereas for the second domain, the parameter can hold one value only.

Now, in the next paragraphs, we are ready to describe how the proposed extensions are used, and then how the main sections composing a contract are structured in WSLA.

4.1 The Parties

One of the most important parts of the contract is the description of the actors, called *parties*, of the agreement, i.e., the *provider* and the *consumer*. In addiction, a third party, called *guarantee*, is introduced to control and guarantee the contract terms between the two parties. In our case, the third party is the actor that measures, or is enabled to retrieve from a log file, the quality parameters values, and compares them against the values specified in the contract. Indeed, depending on the nature of the contract and on the role of the parties, the contract can also consider the provider or the user as a guarantee. If the guarantee, during the monitoring activity, measures a value outside of the range of admissible values, he notifies the *exception* to the two involved parties, as shown in Figure 2: here each party is defined by its name, address, and by information about actions to be possibly taken in case of violation notification.

```
<Parties>
   <ServiceProvider name="myProvider">
      <Contact>
         <Street>21 Rome st</Street>
         <City>Milan</City>
      </Contact>
      <Action name="notification" partyName="myProvider"
      xsi:type="WSDLSOAPActionDescriptionType">
      <WsdlFile>notification.wsdl</WsdlFile>
      <SOAPBindingName>VideoOnDemandBindingName</SOAPBindingName>
      <SOAPOperationName>VideoOnDemandOperationName</SOAPOperationName>
      </Action>
   </ServiceProvider>
   <ServiceConsumer name="...">

      ...
   </ServiceConsumer>
   <SupportingParty name="...">

      ...
   </SupportingParty>
</Parties>
```

Figure 2. Parties section of the contract

4.2   Service definition

For each *e*-Service, a set of quality parameters is attached to its definition as shown in Figure 3. Such parameters are defined by: a measure unit, a metric, the data type, and the indication of parties that can provide, read, and manage these data. Here, the Operation tag states how to find and to invoke the *e*-Servicee referring to a WSDL specification. The Schedule tag holds the date of validity of the contract, while *SLAParameter* is the object storing information about the QoS parameters. Each *SLAParameter* has a *Metric* that can be simple, or composite. For a simple metric, its measure is provided directly by a measurement system; hence, in the contract, the location of this measurement system is written. For a composite metric, this section shows how data can be aggregated in order to compute the metric.

```
<ServiceDefinition>
   <Operation name="GetVideo" xsi:type="wsla:WSDLSOAPOperationDescriptionType">
      <WsdlFile>servicefile.wsdl</WsdlFile>
      <SOAPBindingName>VideoOnDemandBindingName</SOAPBindingName>
      <SOAPOperationName>GetVideo</SOAPOperationName>
      <Schedule name="MainSchedule">
         <Period>
            <Start>06/02/2004</Start>
```

```
       <End>06/02/2005</End>
     </Period>
     <Interval>
        <Second>1</Second>
     </Interval>
  </Schedule>
  <SLAParameter name="Bandwidth" type="float" unit="Kbps">
     <Metric>Bandwidth</Metric>
     <Communication>
        <Source>Provider</Source>
        <Pull>Provider</Pull>
        <Push>Provider</Push>
     </Communication>
  </SLAParameter>
  <Metric name="Bandwidth" type="float" unit="Kbps">
     <Source>Provider</Source>
     <MeasurementDirective resultType="float" xsi:type="wsla:Counter">
        <MasuremementURI>http://MeasurementService.com/</MasuremementURI>
     </MeasurementDirective>
  </Metric>
  <SLAParameter name="...">
     ...
  </SLAParameter>
  <Metric name="...">
     ...
  </Metric>
  ...
  </Operation>
</ServiceDefinition>
```

Figure 3. Service Definition section of the contract

4.3 Guarantee terms

This section of the contract glues the parties to a particular *e*-Service also considering the possible delivering channels of an *e*-Service . Here, it is important to notice that while the set of QoS parameters strongly depends on the provided *e*-Service, the admissible values perceived by the user strictly depend on the channel used by the *consumer*. To fulfil this mismatching visions, the *guarantee party* must monitor what the user perceives rather than what the system provides; hence, for each *<device, network>* pair, i.e. for each channel, a specific WSLA portion specializes the quality parameters by defining: a) the range of allowed values, b) the order of the allowed values, c) the party which has to take over in case of contract violation, and d) the agreement validity time.

Here, the actual values are computed starting from what the provider offers, according to the identified quality rules for the considered channels.

In particular, Figure 4 indicates, in the *ServiceLevelObjective* tag, the range of allowed values of each QoS parameter, the related device, and the network interface. For each *e*-Service level, an *ActionGuarantee* object and information about how notification actions can be invoked are included. In the example, the '*' symbol means that all the involved parties have to be informed of a possible violation.

5.   A PROTOYPE APPLICATION FOR CREATING CONTRACTS

According to the specification described above, we built a prototype (Figure 5) for contract definition and management in a multichannel environment. The provider represents the actor in charge of formulating and offering the *e*-Service through a set of channels. The consumer uses the *e*-Service; the selection of the channel is driven by the selection of the device.

The contracts representing the agreement between the user and the provider, and defined before an actual *e*-Service invocation, are stored in the *Contract Repository*. The *Monitoring System* is responsible for measuring the QoS perceived by the consumer, for extracting contracts from the Contract Repository, and for comparing the values written in the contracts with the measured values. In case of agreement violation, the Monitoring System invokes a set of suitable notification services acting on behalf of the provider and consumer.

As a sample scenario for the prototype, we refer to a Video-on-demand *e*-Service which provides to the users a set of video clips related to soccer matches. As discussed above, the quality of provided clips is affected not only by the provider but also by the selected channel. In fact, although a provider is able to broadcast images and clips with a high resolution, a user with a SmartPhone will not be able to fully appreciate the high resolution, since the device has a limited screen size. The same occurs for the network that, due latency and the bandwidth values, can even block the video broadcasting.

```
<Obligation>
    <ServiceLevelObjective device="Computer" name="SLBandwidth" network="802.11b"
    order="Increasing">
        <Obliged>Provider</Obliged>
        <Validity>
            <StartDate>06/02/2004</StartDate> <EndDate>06/02/2005</EndDate>
        </Validity>
        <Expression>
            <Predicate xsi:type="Greater">
```

```
            <SLAParameter>Bandwidth</SLAParameter>
            <Value>350</Value>
        </Predicate>
    </Expression>
    <Expression>
        <Predicate xsi:type="Less">
            <SLAParameter>Bandwidth</SLAParameter> <Value>500</Value>
        </Predicate>
    </Expression>
    <EvaluationEvent>NewValue</EvaluationEvent>
</ServiceLevelObjective>
<ActionGuarantee name="GDNBandwidth">
    <Obliged>*</Obliged>
    <Expression>
        <Predicate xsi:type="Violation">
            <ServiceLevelObjective>SLBandwidth</ServiceLevelObjective>
        </Predicate>
    </Expression>
    <EvaluationEvent>NewValue</EvaluationEvent>
    <QualifiedAction>
        <Party>*</Party>
        <Action actionName="*" xsi:type="Notification">
            <NotificationType>Violation</NotificationType>
            <CausingGuarantee>SLBandwidth</CausingGuarantee>
            <Network>802.11b</Network>
            <Device>Computer</Device>
            <SLAParameter>Bandwidth</SLAParameter>
        </Action>
    </QualifiedAction>
    <ExecutionModality>Always</ExecutionModality>
</ActionGuarantee>
<ServiceLevelObjective name="..." >
    ...
</ServiceLevelObjective>
<ActionGuarantee name="..." >
    ...
</ActionGuarantee>
...
</Obligation>
```

Figure 4. Obligation section of the contract

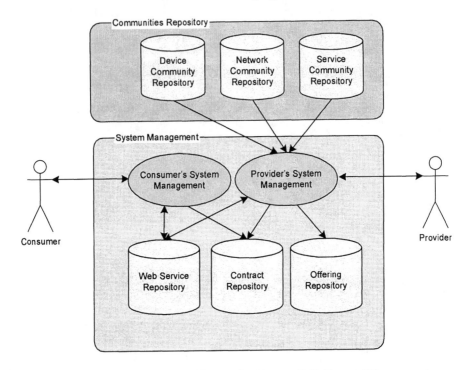

Figure 5. General Prototype Architecture for Contract Definition and Management

In order to avoid unavailability, the MAIS project is studying methods to provide a set of adaptation strategies able to allow the user to switch among different channels. Actually, channel switching can also be influenced by the user preferences. For example, the user can start watching the clips on one device, the PC, and complete the vision on the SmartPhone, e.g., because he is on travel.

The overall structure supporting quality information described in the community specifications, and the object implementations are shown in Figure 6. All of the documents are specified in XML, basically due to portability and ease of use reasons. The System Management module has three associated repositories, where the *e*-Services used by the application, the offers of the providers, and the contracts subscribed by consumers are stored. The *Provider's System Management* refers to the *Communities Repository* in order to obtain the specifications defined by the community needed to implement an object compliant to them. Otherwise the *Consumer's System Management* use *e*-Service Repository to retrieve the offers of the providers, to compare them and, once on of them is selected as the effective provider, to define and store the contract in the Contract Repository.

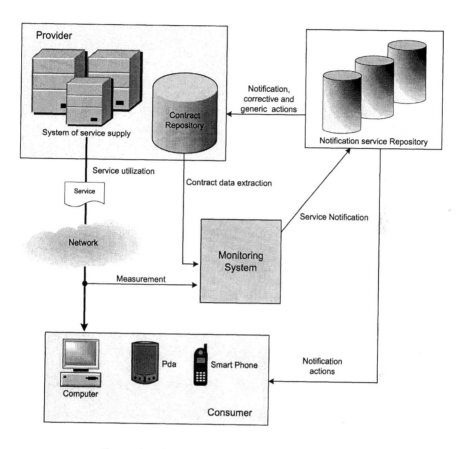

Figure 6. Reference Architecture for Quality in MAIS

6.   CONCLUDING REMARKS AND FUTURE WORK

This paper has presented a model for creating QoS contracts in a multichannel adaptive environment, and an application supporting the creation and management of such contracts. Our approach relies on some of the existing approach available in the literature, and provides a syntactic extension to WSLA to capture some basic peculiarities of a multichannel system. The paper has presented some extensions to WSLA, a quality model, and a prototype supporting quality contracts creation and management.

Currently, the prototype is able to manage the interaction between provider and user in the contract definition phase; the main prototype extension regards the *monitoring aspects*. To this aim, we are investigating on the way the quality values can be captured, checked, and reasoned upon.

Besides the monitoring functions, a set of e-Service able to run-time react to the quality changes is needed. Moreover, these e-Services can be used by the other systems composing the MAIS platform as a trigger for the adaptation strategies needed by the overall MAIS architecture.

REFERENCES

ACM 2003, Communications of the ACM, Special Issue: Service-Oriented Computing, Vol. 46, n.10, October 2003.

Alonso 2003, Alonso, G., Casati, F., Kuno, H., Machiraju, V., Web Services: Concepts,Architectures and Applications (Data-centric Systems & Applications). Springer-Verlag, 2003.

Crawley et al., 1998, Crawley, E., Nair, R., Rajagopalan, B., and Sandick, H., A framework forQoS-based Routing in the Internet. Internet Engineering Task Force - RFC 2386, 1998.

Diaz et al. 1994, Diaz, M., Súnac, P., Time Stream Petri Nets - A Model for Timed Multimedia Information, in Proceedings of 15th International Conference of Application and Theory of Petri Nets 1994 Zaragoza, Spain, LNCS v.815, Springer-Verlag, 1994.

Exposito et al.2003, Exposito, E., Gineste, M., Peyrichou, R., Snac, P., Diaz, M., XQoS: XML-BasedQoS Specification Language. Proc. 9th International Conference on Multi-Media Modeling, Taiwan, January 2003.

Frølung et al. 1998, Frølung S., Koistinen, J., QML: A Language for Quality of Service Specification, Tech. Rep. HPL98-10, HP Labs, HP Software Technologies Laboratory, 1998.

Huston, 2000, Huston, G. Next Steps for the IP QoS Architecture. Internet Engineering Task Force RFC 2990. 2000.

ITU 1994, International Telecommunication Union (ITU), Terms and definitions related to quality of service and network performance including dependability. ITU Recommendation E.800 (08/94), 1994.

ITU 2001, International Telecommunication Union (ITU), Communications Quality of Service: A framework and definitions. ITU Recommendation G.1000 (11/01), 2001.

Keller et al. 2002, Keller A., Ludwig, H. The WSLA Framework: Specifying and Monitoring Service Level Agreements for Web Services. Technical Report RC22456(W0205-171), IBM Research Division, T.J. Watson Research Center, 2002.

Khirman and Henriksen 2002, Khirman S., and Henriksen, P., Relationship Between Quality-of-Service and Quality-of-Experience for Public Internet Service, In Proceedings. of the 3rd Workshop on Passive and Active Measurement, Fort Collins, Colorado, USA, March, 2002.

MAIS Team 2003, The MAIS Team, MAIS: Multichannel Adaptive Information Systems, http://black.elet.polimi.it/mais/documenti/pdf/mais.pdf, 2003.

Marchetti et al. 2004, Marchetti C., Pernici B., Plebani P., A Quality Model for Multichannel Adaptive Information Systems, Proc. 13rd International World Wide Web WWW Conference (WWW 2004), New York City, NY, May 2004.

Zinky et al., 1997, Zinky, J.A., Bakken, D. E., and Schantz, R.E., Architectural support for quality of service for CORBA objects, Theory and Practice of Object Systems, 1997, vol. 3(1).

ACTION, INTERACTION AND THE ROLE OF AMBIGUITY IN THE INTRODUCTION OF MOBILE INFORMATION SYSTEMS IN A UK POLICE FORCE

Dr David Allen and Professor T. D Wilson
Leeds University Business School, The University of Leeds, Leeds, LS2 9JT

Abstract: Mobile wireless computing has been identified as a critical new application of information technology; however, only a few case studies are available focusing on the organisational or social issues related to the deployment of these technologies. This paper provides a rich description of the situated activities of a particular set of mobile workers (police officers) during the implementation of mobile wireless laptops. The paper describes two implementations of one type of technology in a single organisation. The implementations took very different trajectories; in one the technology was resisted and eventually withdrawn while in the other it was embraced and embedded into working practices. The paper clearly demonstrates how ambiguity, over time, influenced the trajectory of the implementation process in the different sites. The paper explores the use of an alternative theoretical approach to the use of technological frames to understand ambiguity and implementation of technology: Strauss's Theory of Action. Using Strauss's concept of trajectory the paper demonstrates the importance of understanding the relationship between ambiguity and the implementation of mobile information technology.

Key words: Mobile Information Systems, Police, Ambiguity

1.   INTRODUCTION

Mobile computing has been heralded as the next major paradigm in personal computing (Okoli, Ives et al. 2002). It is unsurprising, therefore, that over the last two years there has been a rapid growth in the literature and research relating to the technical and commercial aspects of the application of mobile devices (Siau, Ee-Peng et al. 2001). A number of researchers, however, have indicated that there are 'few studies of the *use* of these mobile devices' Wilberg (2001)). (Kakihara and Sørensen 2002) have pointed to the pressing need for further theoretical and empirical work in this area. In particular, there is a need for IS research to be actively involved in studies where technologies are being built and tried out – before they reach the marketplace (Lyytinen and Yoo 2002). This paper provides one such empirical study approaching the research from an alternative perspective: mobile informatics (Dahlbom and Ljungberg 1998; Kakihara and Sørensen 2002; Nulden and Lundin 2002), or analysing the use of mobile devices in a particular setting.

The paper analyses the implementation of a mobile office solution in two sites in a large UK police force (Surrey Police Force). This presents an intriguing case: one where the implementations in the two sites took very different trajectories; in one the technology was resisted and eventually withdrawn while in the other it was embraced and embedded into working practices. As the research progressed it became clear that the role of ambiguity during the process of implementation was particularly significant. In attempting to understand this, the researcher turned to the body of work about how people make sense of ambiguity (multiple meanings) created by the implementation of IT. There is only a small amount of literature which focuses on the collective creation and shaping of interpretations for understanding and enacting IT (Henfridsson 2000). Much of this work draws upon sense-making perspectives and also utilizes a cognitive perspective.

One of the most influential works in this area is that of Orlikowsi and Gash (1994) who introduced the idea of technological frames. They described these as schema used by actors to interpret technology, arguing that when there is ambiguity or difference between individuals' technology frames the implementation will be more problematic. Henfridsson (2000), however, argues that this work places too much emphasis on the reduction of ambiguity between different stakeholders' assumptions, beliefs and values about a technology. He points out that the work of Ciborra and Lanzara (1994) indicates the importance of ambiguity in stimulating innovation and learning and he puts forward an alternative approach, suggesting that ambiguity can be managed most effectively when there is a transition between states of ambiguity about the use and role of the technology and states of common sense where there is no ambiguity. Indeed, he argues that ambiguity should be created around technologies in order to make the most of IT adoption. In contrast, Davidson's (2002) research, from a quantitative and positivist perspective, reinforces and develops Orlikowski and Gash's use of technological frames, and identifies four frame domains that are pertinent during the information systems development (ISD) process. She indicates that repeated shifts in salience between two specific technological frames (related to the business value of IT and IT delivery) can disrupt the information systems development process. In common with the earlier work of Orlikowski and Gash, Davidson seems to argue that, by recognizing (and therefore reducing) ambiguity, the process will be improved: "...if shifts in frame salience are recognized and explicitly acknowledged, ISD participants may be better able to manage" (Davidson 2002:353). Barrett (1999) develops Orlikowski and Gash's work in another direction augmenting their socio-cognitive approach with 'structural culture' (Thompson 1990; Thompson 1995) from a critical perspective. Barrett argues that a key reason for low levels of EDI adoption is an incongruence of cultural assumptions among different sub-cultures. Mantovani and Spagnolli, (2001), working from within Actor Network Theory, add another dimension to the debate by indicating that the existence of ambiguity about norms and technology is particularly useful at the start of the implementation of a technology, because it allows the expression of different interests of actors involved in the implementation. They also argue that the ambiguity associated with norms and technology will naturally be reduced during the process of implementation as 'shared lines of interpretation crystallise.' (Mantovani and Spagnolli 2001:317)

While the findings of these approaches are useful and relevant, it could also be argued that they place too much emphasis on socio-cognitive structures determining and shaping action and too little emphasis on the way socio-cognitive structures are contested and shaped over time. As Ciborra stated, in understanding IT implementation there is a need to bring back into the picture the situation of the actor (Ciborra 1999). While this seems to be acknowledged in IS research, it is achieved, mainly, by the introduction and adaptation of ideas from cognitive psychology (c.f. Tan and Hunter 2002). While providing a useful and interesting contribution, the application of socio-cognitive theory can be criticized on a number of grounds:

- It fails to acknowledge the emotional aspect of organizing (Fineman 1996; Ciborra 1999).
- The cognitive view has only recently achieved widespread acceptance in organizational studies (Hodgkinson and Sparrow 2002) and, therefore, the language of cognition is still diffuse and conflicting. Walsh (1995) identified more than 90 terms related to cognition in the language of management theory. Translation from its use in organizational studies to information systems or information management should be undertaken cautiously.
- Cognitive theory has developed in a behaviourist tradition (positivistic and nomethetic), but it is being used in an interpretive (ideographic)

tradition in the field of information systems (Orlikowski and Gash 1994). Some researchers point to this use in ideographic frameworks as positive, but it has been criticised in the mainstream management literature. Tan and Hunter (2002), for example, cite the work of Daniels, Johnson, and de Chernatony (1994) as a useful route for IS researchers to follow, but this work has been roundly criticized by mainstream cognitive researchers in management (Hodgkinson 2002) as theoretically confused.

- Socio-cognitive approaches are used from an interpretative perspective, but are operationalised in a way that suggests that cognitive structures are impermeable and create action; whereas we argue that structures are constantly created and recreated in action.

The first section of the paper presents a brief background and context to the case study. The second section presents the theoretical position and methodology. The next section presents a description of the initial sense-making about the introduction of the technology in two sites, analysing them through the lens of the temporal and spatial aspects of mobile work. It also provides an analysis of the relationship between new information behaviour enabled by the technology and power relations. This section identifies the initial commonality of opinion and a common trajectory of the implementations in the both sites. The fourth section goes on to describe the way sense-making about the implementation and the trajectories of the implementation diverged. The paper concludes with a discussion of the results and their implications for research and practice.

1.1   Background to the Implementation

Police forces in the UK are at radically different stages of development in their use of information systems (O'Dowd 1998; Povey 2001). With strong support from the UK Government they are now placing more emphasis upon the use of technology to support all aspects of their work. The intention is for many aspects of their operations to be transformed by 2005. This has been labeled 'e-policing' (Povey 2001), a key aspect of which is mobilising information (Povey 2001) to make it available to officers wherever they are working through the use of mobile phones, mobile data terminals and mobile computing devices (wireless laptops and Personal Data Assistants (PDAs)). One of the leading forces in the UK in the deployment of mobile systems is Surrey Police, which is based in the south of England, sharing a boundary with London. Its area of operation includes urban and rural areas and involves the management of a number of varied policing environments, from Heathrow Airport to rural villages.

This paper discusses the implementation of a specific mobile technology: the Surrey Police Remote Officer and Vehicle EnviRonment (ROVER) units. ROVER is essentially a laptop computer with a GSM mobile phone modem allowing officers in any location to access the Force intranet, the Surrey Police Information and Knowledge Environment (SPIKE). This gives officers access to police-specific software (such as national databases of legal information or information on holders of firearms) and generic software (e-mail or word processing software) from a laptop with wireless access to the organisation's intranet. It is important to note that this police force had mobilised its own network environment; thus, the officers were not faced with a new interface or new software. Two implementations were studied: the first was in a small town with uniformed patrol officers, the second was a larger town with plain-clothes detectives.

2. THEORETICAL POSITION AND METHODOLOGY

At the start of the project (October 2000) very little research on the use of mobile wireless technologies was available and no empirical research was located on the organisational aspects of their use in the police. The objective of the research, therefore, was to explore the situated activities of these mobile workers, to produce a rich description of the implementations.

While aware of the research on adoption and assimiliation of information systems (c.f., Gallivan 2001), the primary approach in the IS literature has been through the use of the Technology Acceptance Model (TAM) (Adams, Nelson et al. 1992; Agarwal 2000; Venkatesh 2000). In this research we wished to take a different approach. Much of the TAM literature focuses on the individual level and is nomothetic and positivistic. In contrast this research project focused on the group level and works from within an interpretive framework: drawing on interactionism, pragmatism and utilizing ideographic tools.

In an attempt to place more emphasis on the interaction between structure and action over time, and to illuminate the contested and changing nature of structures, Strauss's (1993) Theory of Action is used here. In particular, four concepts are drawn upon: trajectory, trajectory phasing, trajectory projection, and orders. Trajectory refers both to the course of any observed phenomenon as it evolves over time and the actions and interactions contributing to its evolution. Strauss uses the term to encompass both a predetermined course of action and interaction in ways that are unanticipated and not entirely manageable. He argues that researchers and those involved in the interaction can distinguish phases in the trajectory of a phenomenon. He illustrates this point by drawing on his earlier work (Glaser and Strauss 1968) where the phase of 'they are dying' was identified by those involved in the trajectory of terminal illness. The term technological trajectory has been used in a similar way by Jenkins and Floyd (2001). The third concept used in this paper is that of trajectory projection. This refers to a vision of the expected course of interaction, which may or may not be shared by the actors. Strauss also identifies "orders", defined as analytic abstractions that summarize what the actions and interactions involved in a phenomenon are intended to achieve. The orders used here are: temporal order, spatial order, work order, informational order and technological order. The term "temporal order" (Strauss 1993) is used to refer to the frequency, scheduling, pacing, duration and timing of actions. The term "spatial order" refers to "how objects are arrayed in given spaces; how actions take place or are supposed to take place in certain spaces; the symbolism associated with various spaces" (Strauss 1993: 59) "Work order" refers to the way in which work is organised. Informational order refers to the flow of information between actors. The final order, "technological order", refers to the organisation of technological artefacts and the routines that surround them

We hold that the Theory of Action and the concepts of 'trajectory' and 'orders' are particularly useful in research on mobile data applications. The point must be stressed that the term 'mobile data' is not entirely adequate, since in the police applications, it is the person who is mobile, while, especially in the case of thin-client systems, the data remain on the server until pulled by or pushed to the user. The temporal order is critical in police work where the rapid availability of information in a stop-and-search event may make the difference between a successful arrest and a need to let the suspect go free, or where the scheduling of actions in response to an incident may make the difference between the effective and ineffective use of people. The spatial order is also highly relevant, as the police officers are continually on the move from one location to another either on foot or in police vehicles and some of the spaces they occupy have greater or lesser degrees of symbolism associated with them. A suspect on the street, a public place, is subject to less pressure than the same person in a police car, or removed to a cell in a police station. From a police perspective, the more sure and the more rapid the transfer from one to another can be made, the better.

The discussion is based on qualitative data from the study of the implementation of ROVER over a twelve-month period. Although data gathering techniques included the analysis of project documentation and observation, the primary method used was semi-structured interviews. Respondents included senior police officers in Police Headquarters (who had approved the implementation), senior police officers involved at a Divisional Level in the implementation (and who had requested the implementation), IT Services (including the IT Support Officer, those involved in offering training on the system, the Knowledge Manager involved in the process of implementation and the Director of IT Services). Individual interviews were also conducted with the senior staff in both police stations (Inspectors and Sergeants) and most officers involved in using the technology. The more junior police officers were interviewed either in focus-group and/or individual interviews.

Observation of working practices and information behaviour also took place, but only in the Police Stations. This was a condition of gaining entry for the research. A limitation on the findings was that observation of use of the technology 'in the field' could not be undertaken. This issue is being addressed in further studies in other police forces.

Karahanna, Straub, and Chervany (1999) note that few research projects have dealt with pre-adoption and post-adoption beliefs and attitudes in IT implementation. The data collection for this research project was undertaken in three distinct stages. The first stage was before the implementation, where attitudes and expectations of the implementation were discussed. The second stage was two months after implementation, to gauge initial reactions and to understand how the technology was being used and had influenced working practices. Finally, the last data collection visit took place twelve months after the implementation to understand how the technology was shaped during the implementation and how the innovation had shaped organisational practices. The case study presented below is the authors' interpretation of the data collected through this process.

3. IMPLEMENTATION: INTIAL STAGE OF THE TRAJECTORY

The initial stage of the trajectory was characterised by a lack of ambiguity over the implementation of the technology. The impetus for the initiation of the ROVER came not from the Information Management or Information Technology Service in the police force, but from the users and, in particular, Senior Operational Officers in the Uniformed Division. When interviewed, these senior officers had a clear vision for the future trajectory of the implementation: it would increase operational efficiencies by changing the working practices of officers; in particular it would influence spatial and work orders. They described this through the metaphor of reducing the "yo-yo effect": a process by which police officers had to return numerous times during the day to the police station to communicate or process information before returning to the field. It was believed that, if the number of times the officer had to return was reduced, officers would 'stay out on the street' for longer periods and so increase the visibility of uniformed police (an important objective set for them by Central

Government). They also wanted to shape informational orders: there was a hope that the ROVER would enable a more effective approach to policing by providing information when and where police officers need it; thereby supporting an intelligence–led, pro-active style of policing.

The initial implementation in both sites, was perceived in a positive manner by the officers involved. Officers gave accounts that indicated that they felt more informed, made better use of existing internal information resources and had located new external sources. They also felt that their external communication had improved and, critically, they felt that the use of the ROVER helped create a perception in the public that a higher quality of service was being delivered. The two implementations of the ROVER seemed to take similar trajectories: at both sites it was initially reported as extremely successful, gaining support from senior managers, uniformed officers and plain clothes detective officers. The way the technology was perceived to have shaped behaviour initially can be seen through the accounts illustrating three key elements which changed after the implementation: the changes in temporal, spatial, information, and work orders.

3.1   Temporal Order

A number of researchers have argued that the 'network society' is characterised by the decline of any rhythm or cycle of life, either biological or social (Castells 1996). While the relationship between time and technology is a contested one (Frissen 2000), information systems researchers have presented a sophisticated perspective of the influence of technology on time (Lee 1999; Lee and Liebenau 2000; Orlikowski and Yates 2002), particularly in the area of IS development (Nandhakumar 2001). In both implementation sites accounts that identified the impact of the implementation on the temporal order of actions were identified. One example of this is the way uniformed officers reported that they could change the way they input and updated crime reports on the crime information system (CIS). They could, for example, input information while it was 'fresh in their minds' whilst they were on patrol. A probationary, uniformed officer noted that, using the traditional approach, he could accumulate three or four reports in his notebook as he was sent from incident to incident. It could then be perhaps 24 hours later before he was able to update the system. Using ROVER, information could be input into CIS in 'real time' and it was said that information entered would not only be more 'up-to-date', but would also be more comprehensive and accurate. Another PC stated:

"I use it quite a lot - linking up when I am a passenger in a car looking at current jobs and my workload, doing checks on vehicles rather than doing it over the air, updating crime reports at the scene. It is very useful for that, I can go in, do the update while I am standing there talking to them and if they ask any questions I have got it at my fingertips. I don't have to do it from memory and I can give them the relevant numbers." (Uniformed PC)"

Similarly, CID Officers described the way they were using the technology to overcome temporal and spatial issues. One officer noted the way it enabled him to become better informed and more focused when called out to an incident, allowing him to access the force system into which crimes were stored after being reported by the public (the ICAD):

"The only time I take it home is when I'm on call. The advantages are at 3 o'clock in the morning you get a phone call, the control room only through necessity only ever give us three lines: 'It's such and such an incident, there's a bloke in custody and it happened in .....' 'Oh great, what about this?' 'Don't know!' You are talking to people third hand. So what you can do ... look at the actual ICAD as well as get a feel for the job before you actually speak to anyone."

In the initial phase of the implementation, account of the use of the technology to overcome temporal barriers was common in both implementation sites, and was supportive of the implementation.

3.2   Spatial Order

The spatial concept of location is one which, as Healey and Reeves (2001) point out, is the most intuitive framework for understanding mobile work. The role of information technology in making it possible for spatially or organizationally distant parties to communicate has been a recurring theme in much of the literature on CSCW (DeSanctis and Monge 1999). It is unsurprising, therefore, that recent work on mobile technologies and mobile work practices identifies it as a key dimension of mobile work (Kakihara and Sørensen 2001; Kakihara and Sørensen 2002).

Much of the language that legitimised the implementation of the ROVER emphasised the spatial order of action. Officers described the way they could use the ROVER to be 'informed' at remote locations and, therefore, work faster and more effectively. One officer described how he used the system in the Police office in the Crown Court. He was able to use ROVER to find information to resolve questions put to him and thereby 'appear more professional'. He stated:

"They were asking me questions, the defence were coming up with items and the prosecution were saying that they wanted this, this, and this. And instead of my rushing off for hours and trying to find someone to ask, I would just turn this on and answer it within a couple of minutes...it speeded the whole process up."

Most of the officers interviewed noted the importance of the mobile data link, stating that they were often working in environments (often outside the area covered by the police force) where they were unable to get access to a landline. A number of the officers told how they could use the ROVER in locations where radio contact was difficult.

Accounts about the use of the technology to overcome spatial barriers seemed to permeate early discourses within both sites, reinforcing the perception of a rapid internalisation, use and acceptance of the technology within the organisation.

3.3   Information Order

The use of the wireless laptops augmented existing information channels (e.g., police radio) and allowed police officers direct access to remote databases. This removed existing information intermediaries (such as control room operators) who had provided the only form of access to information held in police databases via the police radio. The control room operator plays a key role in most police forces; they take calls from the public, enter the information into police information systems and call officers on the radio in order to dispatch them to a respond to calls. They also play a pivotal role in the information gathering by the police officers as they provide the only remote access to police information systems. The police officers would use a shared radio system to contact the control room operators, therefore, conversations could be overheard by other officers (peers and superiors).The use of the ROVER units, therefore, moved the information behaviour of officers in the field from a position where information seeking and use was observed, shared and reliant up a third person to a position where it was closed to observation and individual. Officers, particularly younger officers who feared looking foolish in the eyes of their team, or censure from their sergeant for asking too many questions or taking up too much time on the radio said that they were more likely to search for information directly using the ROVER units. The relationship between control operators and patrol officers can sometimes be strained because of their differing reward systems and objectives. The control operators often have competing demands on their time and are evaluated on the speed with which they deal with a call. The patrol officers, on the other hand, require information with a high degree of accuracy and depth. The use of the ROVER units to bypass the control operators was seen as particularly useful, and was reported to improve the effectiveness and safety of officers. It seemed that officers were much more likely to search for information on the mobile terminal than by using traditional channels, precisely because it was not observed: officers' information seeking was not exposed to the comment and scrutiny of senior officers. It was also clear that they became more active information gatherers; rather than waiting to be informed, they used the technology to scan their environment and look for information, or reports to which they could add their information. This was particularly true whilst officers were working on nights or during quiet periods on patrol. One young officer said he used the technology to access the Police National Legal Database (a repository of information about police legal powers):

> "I used PNLD when I was out. It gets a bit embarrassing when you don't know the law. If you have got it to hand, before you pop in the house to speak to them you can just think look it up on PNLD and I will be up to speed, you are more aware of your power to deal with things."

This was particularly important as it reinforced the police officer's core values: the need to be seen by the public to be informed and enabling officers to understand the limits of their own powers (such as the power of arrest).

4. IMPLEMENTATION: DIVERGENCE AND CRYSTALISATION OF TRAJECTORIES OF INTERPRETATION

The initial reactions to the implementation were similar, but, as the implementation continued the trajectories diverged. By the end of the project many (if not most) of the uniformed officers had stopped using the technology. One officer noted:

> "It made my life easier not to get the laptop out of the bag".

This change in attitude was particularly puzzling because at the start of the project uniformed officers were all very supportive of the technology. One officer noted:

> "People were initially very keen, very into it, changing their desk tops and got it all sorted. It was a neat bit of kit."

The resistance was such that the project with the uniformed officers was abandoned. However, the detective officers remained enthusiastic, actively using the technology. One detective commented in an interview that: "It would have to be a very big bloke that comes and takes my computer off me." Another stated that she though the technology was "… fantastic and I would now hate to be without it, I've quickly got used to the flexibility of it." The following text analyses the sense-making as conflicting interpretations of the technology developed, were contested and began to converge upon a dominant perspective and "crystallize in shared lines of interpretation" (Mantovani and Spagnolli 2001:317) this dominant perspective was represented in the renegotiation and interpretation of the perceived impact of the technology.

4.1   The Implementation in the Uniformed site

The implementation in the uniformed police station was characterised by a high degree of ambiguity about acceptable use of the technology, ambiguity about the permanence of the implementation, and ambiguity about the reasons for the implementation. Ambiguity was present because different interpretations were supported at the same time (Weick 1995). Without objective criteria given for the implementation the officers relied upon professional values to make sense of the situation, using these values to extrapolate from the data available. It is significant that the officers read from the facts according to their professional value system, divergence in sense-making being linked to the existence of different sets of values. This will be discussed further in the next section of the paper. As the implementation progressed the technology was increasingly perceived as threatening a particular set of officers' values. The role and nature of the implementation became highly ambiguous. McCaskey (1982) identifies characteristics of ambiguity as: multiple, conflicting interpretations, different value orientations and political and emotional clashes. The Uniformed site became one in which discourses about ambiguity and anxiety (Baruch and Lambert 2002) rapidly dominated.

4.1.1   Work Order and ambiguity;

This ambiguity was demonstrated by one officer in his discussion of his use of the technology. As already noted, the system allowed officers to use the technology to change their information behaviour and their work practices. For example, one officer noted that use of the technology allowed him to park his car and access his e-mail from wherever he was:

> *"Promoted my pulling up and using it to see, pulling up on nights and saying to myself 'is there anything about' and using the terminal – quickly check my mails to see what was going on at 2.00am in the morning."*

While this sort of behaviour was seen as beneficial to the officer and his team, there was still a great deal of ambiguity about the acceptability of these behaviours. The same officer, for example, went on to say that he was concerned what the reaction of his senior officers would be to his remote use of the technology.

> *"I felt that if a governor pulled up next to me, I would think – what do I say? I am checking my e-mails, using CIS, PNLD etc [I was] worried that I would be seen as a bit of a skiver [i.e., avoiding work]".*

The ambiguity about the new behaviours was compounded by ambiguity over the permanence of the implementation. Organisational history is important in that the contextual conditions and work itself has a history (Strauss 1993:89). History can become embodied within work, in routines and norms, and thereby be rendered invisible. For example, as work evolves over time, routines, behaviour and attitudes are woven into work order and remain, often after their origins are forgotten. These routines are 'black-boxed' and are only questioned when the work order is challenged and sense-making Weick (1995) occurs. During sense-making the past is interpreted and reinterpreted by actors in order to make sense of change in the work order. When the technology is implemented it begins to challenge embedded routines, as the technology enables the actors to evolve new routines and behaviour with the technology. As the implementation progressed, confidence in the implementation was affected as officers drew on accounts of the past implementations to understand the current implementation.

This police force has a particularly proactive and innovative Information Technology Service which is at the vanguard of changes to the use of information technology in the police service and is recognised as one of the most technologically advanced in the UK. It has a history of testing and developing technologies in the field. Officers drew on their understanding of the past implementations of technology when making sense of the ROVER units. Crucially, operational staff saw the earlier use of laptops as unsuccessful. Although the case reported in this paper was the first deployment of wireless laptops the force had attempted a limited deployment of laptops on other occasions, one PC noted:

"I have had two laptops before this one in the last year and they have been absolutely useless"

This particular station seems to have the status of a 'test bed' for some of this organisational and technological change. While this has positive implications because the staff took pride in this reputation, on the other hand many of these changes seemed to have been ephemeral in nature. The project was seen as just another experiment. The experimental status was also reinforced by the IT service who, recognising the relatively low cost of implementation and the fact that they were the first police force (and indeed one of the first organisations UK wide) to mobilise their whole intranet in this way, used the term 'experiment' to reduce risk, to involve the officers, and, therefore, to reduce resistance to the technology. This had the effect of increasing ambiguity about the implementation: in many ways it made it easy and acceptable for officers to stop using the technology.

As the implementation proceeded this ambiguity was compounded by an increasing concern about why the technology was being implemented. The uniformed officers felt that the operational future of their station (and therefore of their team) was in question. Officers interpreted the messages that they were given about the implementation by their senior officers as indicating that the successful implementation of the technology would lead to their Police Station being closed. One officer noted:

"I was sure that they also meant it to assist us with our job as well...we weren't sold on this. The American thing was sold a lot, that you can have your RV [meal break] outside, almost that you could almost not use the police stations anymore."

The American model of policing was explained as being one in which officers left the station in the morning and only returned at the end of their shift. To facilitate this, officers could take meal breaks outside the station in named restaurants. This would be a significant change in culture for officers in the force who, up to this point, were not allowed to eat in a public restaurant while wearing a uniform. This fear of dramatic changes to working practices and insecurity about the future of the police station created a general sense of insecurity, which limited innovative use of the technology.

Furthermore, the technology was interpreted as threatening the core values of the police officers: attacking their existing constructions of identity. The station culture in the uniformed patrol officers could almost be described as one of a 'siege mentality'. The impression gained was that the station was extremely hierarchical, and that the PCs were heavily reliant upon each other and their senior staff for guidance and support. There was a clear sense that their world-view was very much 'us against the world'. This was put to us as, 'if you offend one of us you offend all of us'. The impression was conveyed that the management style in action (as opposed the espoused management style) was a 'traditional' command and control approach based on 'rank determining role' and the restriction of the questioning of orders. This had a significant impact on the way officers were encouraged to use the system, as there was a mismatch between the espoused culture (the vision for policing offered by the Headquarters) and the culture in action as demonstrated in the station. One officer noted,

> *"In training I was told that the prevention was the most important part of side of the job; if you prevent it you will not have to respond to it. But it hasn't been happening like that because we have been busy and we haven't got the manpower.... We get tasked by three different sources... and they ask too much... [we] end up doing the reactive rather then the investigative, pre-crime work...You really don't get time."*

Officers, initially, seemed to project their own expectations on to the technology. For some, ROVER was seen as a mechanism by which they could return to 'traditional' ways of policing. One officer, for example, noted that the implementation of technologies in the police force had led to them 'losing focus' and that this technology should help them get back to 'how it was and how it should be'. However, as the implementation progressed it became clear that the implementation of ROVER, rather than facilitating a return to the past, actually enabled new forms of work. This resulted in some officers feeling threatened by the technology. ROVER provided access direct access to the Surrey Police Information and Knowledge Environment (SPIKE), this is a rich information environment supportive of reflective and preventative police work. Although ROVER allowed access to information needed in responsive modes (what was referred to as *fast- time*) or use within conflict situations, it was not ergonomically designed to function effectively in these environments. While ROVER supported the mission of the force as a whole was not explicitly designed to support the values of the patrol officers. Indeed, it was increasingly seen as deeply threatening to the values and working practices of the uniformed officers.

4.1.2　Spatial Order and ambiguity;

The development of a strong team ethos based on face-to-face, peer-to-peer information sharing was highly valued. One officer noted,

"We are all very young in service, so we need people who have more experience so that we can sit and socialise with them and ask how would you deal with this...if you can sit face to face you can explain the thing more effectively".

The officers, therefore, placed a great deal of importance on co-location. This value was seen as being directly threatened by the implementation of ROVER. The senior officers in the station seemed to take a particularly close role in mentoring and managing the tasks undertaken by PCs. The inspector, for example, stated that she spent more time in the Constable's Report Room than in her own office. Senior officers stressed the importance of this face-to-face interaction in training their staff, but the author also gained the impression that there was a strong sense that this was also a mechanism by which they could control the behaviour of subordinates. Indeed, fear of loss of control was a key factor that influenced some of the officers' reaction to the technology. Officers expressed the concern that by using the technology they would have less control over their subordinates:

"There was fear that you would be out there on your own (because we are single crewed) for eight hours. I wouldn't be able to supervise people, lot of probationers, I wouldn't be able to go out with them and see what they are doing, because I would never see them. They used to come back regularly and I would say what are you doing now and someone would say, 'I have just been to this job and this happened'. So I would know what was going on. That wouldn't happen with the new system."

The issues of loss of control were also raised during the process of implementation. Initially, the implementation of ROVER was requested by the senior officer responsible for the station; however, as the implementation progressed senior officers in the station became increasingly concerned that they were losing control over the process of implementation and the ways in which the technology was being used. This was expressed through concerns about the communication of fault reporting and ideas about the use of the technology.

During the implementation and initial use of the technology sense-making was (as Weick (1995) argues sense-making inevitably is): driven by as plausibility rather than accuracy. The implementation became a battle ground of values, the discourses which finally dominated being those which were most socially acceptable and credible within the group. Although this particular implementation was abandoned, users in other police stations have requested access to the technology and alternative modes of delivery of the mobile information to uniformed officers are being explored. The police station which had been the site of the implementation was closed and the officers redeployed elsewhere.

4.2   The Plain Clothes Detectives

In contrast to the unformed case, the implementation in the Detective Branch reduced ambiguity about the intention and use of the technology. The technology was also rapidly linked to the detective's values. These officers valued their independence and ability for autonomous decision-making: these were seen as being supported by the implementation of ROVER. In particular, the ROVER units were utilised in a way which supported the detectives spatial, temporal and work order. One of the ways in which this manifested itself was through descriptions of how ROVER had influenced the temporal and spatial order of the mechanism by which officers were able to make decisions on how to respond to a call out. A 'call-out' was a situation where they would be asked to move to an incident and manage it (at any time of day or night). One officer stated that, in the past, they had to respond to all call-outs, often not being needed when they responded. By using ROVER they could often resolve the issues from home:

"It has given me a lot more flexibility in when I attend the Police Station or should I be called out. Do I actually have to leave my home or can I deal with it from home?"

Most officers noted that they worked over and above the normal shift hours. However, by using the ROVER they could perform any extra work as and when they wished:

"I do work 8 hours everyday, but it means that I can choose when I do extra and where I do the extra. It means I can see my daughter before she goes to bed and do a little bit afterwards if required. That's the usage I get from it."

The implementation of the technology did not threaten to change their existing work order with regard to social face-to-face interaction; rather it was seen as augmenting their existing working patterns, adding a further dimension rather than fundamentally changing working patterns. Thus, they saw ROVER as enabling greater communication between officers working on the same case, but working on different shift patterns. The temporal aspect of the implementation was one which was stressed by most of the officers interviewed, the way the technology influenced the traditional rhythms of police work was supportive of making individual police officers visibly more effective. One officer, for example, described how, when working on a rape case he was able to search on the Internet for information on drug rape.

The interpretations about the technology seemed to crystallize around these positive accounts. As ambiguity was reduced officers seemed more ready to invest in peer-to-peer support. A significant element of the learning that took place during the implementation, for example, seemed to be based on peer-to-peer support. Officers described this as spreading expertise. Activities like:

> *"...Doing mail merge for another officer, showing how to use the spreadsheet database for a stolen property enquiry."*

This learning seemed to be taking place on a one-to-one basis, based on example. Officers who had taken on the units early in the implementation played an active role in this. The telling of stories of successful or unsuccessful use of ROVER was the main mechanism by which individuals' located people with relevant experience.

> *'If we are trained and know what to do, the uses we find will be conveyed by word of mouth.'*

The computer services also managed the implementation process in the CID site slightly differently; in particular they placed heavy emphasis on factors which would reduce anxiety and ambiguity. For example, they identified a single 'enthusiast' for the technology and gave her a ROVER unit for three months before roll-out. This officer acted as an advocate for the roll-out and as an unofficial, first line help-desk when the ROVER units had been deployed. They also reviewed her use of the technology and supported her dissemination of 'best practice' in the use of ROVER to her team. They also based an IT support technician in the CID office in order to provide a rapid response to technical problems with the ROVER units and to and help users if they encountered difficulties.

5.   CONCLUSION

Both these implementation sites characterise situations where individuals in a community attempt to make sense of the implementation of a technology which was (on first view) relatively simple and unthreatening. The implementation was of a generic laptop technology with wireless access to the existing intranet service. This allowed members of the organisation to access sources of information through an interface with which they were already familiar. It is important to note that this was not the study of the introduction of a totally new mobile technology, with a new interface, functionality or information sources: this case provides the story of the mobilisation of the familiar and of the pre-existing technology and information sources. It is also interesting in that this implementation was to support already mobile workers: the aim was not to create discontinuous change in working practices but to augment and enable to evolution of existing working practices. Its implementation was also in an organisation in which structural and cultural norms valued obedience and rule following: it could rationally expected that in this environment resistance to the technology would be limited.

As the trajectory of the implementation unfolded it became clear that the ROVER units enabled officers to re-order their actions and behaviours in new and unexpected ways. In the uniformed site this became the basis of the development high levels of ambiguity about ROVER leading finally to resistance and the rejection of the ROVER units. Where high levels of ambiguity are present the sense-making process around information technology becomes, as Weick (1995) notes, based on the enlargement of small cues, interacting to flesh out hunches and of interpreting and reinterpreting the past and driven by plausibility rather than accuracy. This also emphasises the relevance of the work of Henfridsson (2000) and Mantovani and Spagnolli (2001) on the importance of understanding the relationship between ambiguity created by the implementation of information technology and the sense-making process. In the Detective site, where there was less ambiguity about possible effects of the implementation on spatial, temporal and work orders, the systems was embraced and embedded into existing work practices. The paper clearly demonstrates how ambiguity, over time, influences the trajectory of the implementation process.

The primary contribution of this research is to provide a rich description of the situated activities of these mobile workers: a description which demonstrates the complexity of the social and organisational issues related to the mobilisation of information technology. This is novel not only in the perspective taken but also on the nature of the technology implemented. The technology implemented was the mobilization of the whole information environment (from e-mail to specific and specialised applications). Much of the earlier work on mobile technologies focuses on the application of specific and new mobile technologies which fit a particular task (Wiberg 2001).

REFERENCES

Adams, D. L., R. R. Nelson, et al. (1992). "Perceived usefulness, ease of use and usage of information technology: a replication." MIS Quarterly 16(2): 227-247.

Agarwal, R. (2000). Individual acceptance of information technologies. Framing the domains of IT management: projecting the furture threough the past. R. W. Zmud. Cincinnati: OH, Pinnaflex Press: 85-104.

Barrett, M. I. (1999). "Challenges of EDI adoption for electronic trading in the London Insurance Market." European Journal of Information Systems 8: 1-15.

Baruch, Y. and L. Lambert (2002). Organizational Anxiety: Applying psychological metaphor into organizational theory. The 4th International Conference on Organizational Discourse:

Word-views, Work-views and World Views.

Castells, M. (1996). The Rise of the Network Society. Malden, MA, Blackwell.

Ciborra, C. U. (1999). "Notes on Improvisation and Time." Organizations. Accounting, Management and Information Technologies 9: 77-94.

Ciborra, U. C. and G. F. Lanzara (1994). "Formative contexts and information technology: understanding the dynamics of innovation in organsiations." Accounting, Management and Information Technologies 4(61-86).

Dahlbom, B. and F. Ljungberg (1998). "Mobile Informatics." Scandinavian Journal of Information Systems 10(1/2): 227-234.

Davidson, E., J (2002). "Technology frames and framing: a socio-cognitive investigation of requirments determination." MIS Quarterly 26(4): 329-358.

DeSanctis, G. and P. Monge (1999). "Introduction to the special issue: Communication processes for virtual organizations." Organization Science 10(6): 693-703.

Fineman, S. (1996). Emotion and organising. Handbook of organization studies. S. R. Clegg, C. Hardy and W. R. Nord. London, Sage: 543-565.

Frissen, V. A. J. (2000). " ICTs in the rush hour of life." Information Society 16: 65-75.

Gallivan, M. J. (2001). "Organizational Adoption and assimilation of complex technological innovations: development and application of a new framework." The DATA BASE for Advances in Information Systems 32(3): 51-85.

Glaser, B. and A. Strauss (1968). Time for dying. Chicago, Aldine.

Harris, S. G. (1994). "Organizational culture and individual sensemaking: A schema based perspective." Organizational Science 5(3): 309-321.

Healey, P. G. T. and A. J. Reeves (2001). Mobility and Participatory Status. Interventions in the social, cultural and interactional analysis of mobility, ubiquity and information & communication technology, Cumberland lodge, windsor, uk.

Henfridsson, O. (2000). "Ambiguity in IT adaptation: making sense of First Class in a social work setting." Information Systems Journal 10(2): 87-104.

Hodgkinson, G. P. (2002). "Comparing Managers' Mental Models of Competition: Why Self-report Measures of

Belief Similarity Won't Do." Organization Studies 23(1): 63–72.

Hodgkinson, G. P. and P. R. Sparrow (2002). The competent organisation. Buckingham: UK, Open University Press.

Jenkins, M. and S. Floyd (2001). "Trajectories in the Evolution of Technology: A Multi-level Study of Competition in Formula 1 Racing." Organization Studies 22(6): 945–969.

Kakihara, M. and C. Sørensen (2001). Mobility Reconsidered: Topological Aspects of Interaction. IRIS'24, Ulvik, Norway, University of Bergen.

Kakihara, M. and C. Sørensen (2002). Mobility: An Extended Perspective. Thirty-Fifth Hawaii International Conference on System Sciences (HICSS-35), Big Island, Hawaii., IEEE.

Karahanna, E., D. W. Straub, et al. (1999). "Information technology adoption accross time: a cross-sectional comparison of pre-adoption and post-adoption beliefs." Managment Information Systems Quarterly 23(2): 183-213.

Lee, H. (1999). "Time and information technology: Monochronicity, polychronicity and temporal symmetry." European Journal of Information Systems **8**(1): 16-26.

Lee, H. and J. Liebenau (2000). "Temporal effects of information systems on business processes: focusing on the dimensions of temporality." Accounting, Management and Information Technologies **10**(3).

Lyytinen, K. and Y. Yoo (2002). "Research Commentary: The Next Wave of Nomadic Computing." Information Systems Research **13**(4): 377-388.

Mantovani, G. and A. Spagnolli (2001). "Legitimating technologies: ambiguity as a premise for negotation in a networked institution." Information Technology & People **14**(3): 301-320.

McCaskey, M. B. (1982). The executive challenge: managing change and ambiguity. Marshfield: MA, Pitman.

Nandhakumar, J. (2001). "Managing time in a software factory: termporal and spatial organisations of IS development activities."

Nulden, U. and J. Lundin (2002). Introduction to the Mobile Informatics Mini-Track. Thirty-Fifth Hawaii International Conference on System Sciences (HICSS-35), Big Island, Hawaii., IEEE.

O'Dowd, D. J. (1998). Beating Crime: HMIC Thematic Inspection Report 1998. http://www.homeoffice.gov.uk/hmic/beatcrim.htm, Her Majesty's Inspectorate of Constabulary.

Okoli, C., B. Ives, et al. (2002). The Mobile Conference Information System Unleashing Academic Conferences with Wireless Mobile Computing. 35th Hawaii International Conference on System Sciences - 2002, Big Island, Hawaii.

Orlikowski, W., J and D. C. Gash (1994). "Technological frames: making sense of information technology in organizations." ACM Transactions on Information Systems **12**: 174-207.

Orlikowski, W. J. and J. Yates (2002). "It's About Time: Temporal Structuring in Organizations." Organization Science **13**(6).

Povey, K. (2001). Open all hours: A thematic inspection report on the role of police visibility and accessibility in public reassurance. London, Her Majesty's Inspector of Constabulary: 1-191.

Siau, K., L. Ee-Peng, et al. (2001). "Mobile Commerce: Promises, Challenges, and Research Agenda." Journal of Database Management.

Strauss, A. (1993). Continual permutations of action. New York, Aldine De Gruyter.

Tan, F. B. and M. G. Hunter (2002). "THE REPERTORY GRID TECHNIQUE: A METHOD FOR THE STUDY OF COGNITION IN INFORMATION SYSTEMS." MIS Quarterly **26**(1): 39-57.

Thompson, J. B. (1990). Ideology and modern culture: critical social theory in the era of mass communication. Cambridge, Polity Press.

Thompson, J. B. (1995). The media and modernity: a social theory of the media. Cambridge., Polity Press.

Venkatesh, V. (2000). "Determinants of Perceived Ease of Use:Integrating Control, Intrinsic Motivation,

and Emotion into the Technology Acceptance Model." Information Systems Research **11**(4): 342-365.

Walsh, J. P. (1995). "Managerial and organizational cognition: notes from a trip down memory lane." Organization Science **6**(3): 280-321.

Weick, K. (1995). Sensemaking in organisations. London, Sage.

Wiberg, M. (2001). <u>Collaboration on the move: An empirical study of mobile work at Telia Nära</u>. 24th Information Systems Research Seminar in Scandinavia (IRIS 24), Ulvik in Hardanger, Norway.

TOWARDS A SERVICE-ORIENTED ARCHITECTURE
FOR MOBILE INFORMATION SYSTEMS

K. Rehrl, M. Bortenschlager, S. Reich, H. Rieser, R. Westenthaler
Salzburg Research, Jakob-Haringer Strasse 5, 5020 Salzburg, Austria

Abstract: Although hardware and networking infrastructures have evolved over the years and people are able to connect their devices to mobile networks and exchange information, we argue that the missing glue to enable the true potential of mobile information systems lies in the seamless integration of wireless infrastructures with existing wired infrastructures. In our paper, we present the service-oriented middleware *Asomnia*, which adapts traditional service-oriented concepts in order to cope with requirements arising from mobile computing challenges.

Key words: service-oriented architecture; mobile service environment.

1.   INTRODUCTION

With the emergence of mobile information technologies, we are continuously heading towards Mark Weiser's vision of ubiquitous computing (Weiser, 1991). Mobile end user devices and wireless connection technologies allow for an anytime, anywhere vision (Kleinrock, 1996) and recent developments (Ferscha and Vogl, 2002; Garlan et al., 2002; Strang, 2003; Waldo, 1999) show remarkable approaches towards mobile computing. However, these developments often face the problem to strive towards mobility in a rather isolated way. Mobile technologies are exploited in order to achieve similar functionality as in wired infrastructures, although capabilities of mobile devices or wireless connection technologies are rather limited and the limitations are not considered to disappear in the upcoming years. Thus we argue, that mobile information systems only can reach their expected advantages and user acceptance trough integration with existing wired infrastructures, i.e. the full value of mobile computing can only be gained by making use of the advantages of a wired infrastructure such as reliability, availability, bandwidth, richness in capabilities in conjunction with the benefits of wireless technologies such as mobility, ad-hoc connectivity or context awareness (Banavar et al., 2000; Banavar and Bernstein, 2002; Raatikainen et al., 2002).

In this paper we argue for a service-oriented middleware (SOM) called *Asomnia* (*A Service-Oriented Middleware* for ambie*Nt Information Access*) as an approach for bridging the gap between the wired and wireless world. The paper starts with an overview of the main concepts and characteristics of existing service-oriented architectures (Section 2). In Section 3 we continue with a discussion on the characteristics considering pervasiveness and we state requirements for pervasive service-oriented architectures. Section 4 describes the architecture of *Asomnia* and in Section 5 we show two example applications. Section 6 gives an overview of related work and compares existing systems. We finish with a summary and conclusions (Section 7).

2.   CHARACTERISTICS OF SERVICE-ORIENTED ARCHITECTURES

In order to describe requirements concerning service-oriented architectures for mobile information systems, in this section we first want to give an overview of characteristics of existing service-oriented architectures. (Bieber and Carpenter, 2001; McGovern et al., 2003; Strang, 2003) describe that services and service-oriented architectures deal with the issue of designing and building systems by using heterogeneous network addressable software components. Thus, service-oriented architectures are architectures that can be characterised by certain properties like being built of loosely coupled components or allowing for broad interoperability. Looking at the historical evolution, the term "service" has been used in many different architectures reaching from transaction monitors in the early 1990s to today's client-server architectures and web service architectures. Following the evolution process, service-oriented architectures have reached a degree of development where the basic concepts have been widely accepted and a set of properties for each concept has been defined to provide a more detailed characterisation of these architectures.

Typically, a service-oriented architecture consists of the following main concepts or any derivations of these (Bieber and Carpenter, 2001; Hashimi, 2003; Pallos, 2001; McGovern et al., 2003; Newmarch, 2000): **Service components (services), Service contracts (interfaces), Service containers**

(contexts), Service connectors (transports), Service discovery (registries).

Service Components or simply services are defined by network addressable software components. One characteristic, that is still open in service-oriented architectures, is the *granularity* of these service components. Fine-grained or micro (Strang, 2003) service components have the advantage to allow for improved reusability because of the atomic nature, but suffer from the disadvantage of being difficult to organise. Coarse-grained or macro services provide good encapsulation of functionality (e.g. information hiding), but are limited in their reusability. Hence, one trend in the conception of service components is to make the service components adaptable, which means that services can either be used in fine-grained or coarse-grained manner. Another important characteristic is the *mobility and on-the-fly deployment* of service components (Waldo, 1999), which also has an impact on the dynamic nature of applications built on the service components. Technically, the mobility of service components has been enabled with the advent of mobile code techniques (Gosling et al., 1996; Meijer and Miller, 2001). Another widely adopted characteristic is the *location transparency* of service components (Foster et al., 2002), which allows for a location independent service provision and hence assists the virtualisation of resources (Kagal et al., 2001).

One characteristic concerning **Service Contracts** or **Interfaces** is whether the service contract is *public or published* (Fowler, 2002). Typical representatives for architectures with published contracts are CORBA (OMG, 1991, JiniWaldo, 1999 or Web Services W3C, 2002), public service contracts are often used together with message or event-based systems like *Hermes* (Pietzuch and Bacon, 2002). Another characteristic of service contracts is how the contract is described (e.g. the description language used for the interface). Examples are the IDL of CORBA, Java interfaces used by Jini or WSDL used by Web Services. The choice of description language has great impact on *interoperability* issues of the architecture.

Service Containers deal with the issue of providing a common execution software environment for service components in order to achieve a high degree of modularity. Service containers can differ in the execution mode for services, meaning that execution of a single service as well as execution of multi services within one container is possible. We characterise containers by their execution modes as *single service containers* and *multi services containers*.

Service Connectors are used for exchanging messages between service components (Hashimi, 2003; Pallos, 2001. According to Stevens, 2002), interoperability is one of the crucial characteristics of service-oriented architectures. Beside the definition of universal interfaces, interoperability can be reached by choosing flexible service connectors. Service connectors are typically capable of various transport protocols and payload formats for messages (Bieber and Carpenter, 2001; Stevens, 2002). Thus, we consider the capability for *various transport protocols* and *various payload formats* as a main characteristic for service-oriented architectures.

Service Discovery is another important concept for service-oriented architectures and as shown in (Bettstetter and Renner, 2000), various approaches exist. One important characteristic of the different approaches is the aspect of *dynamic service discovery* which is strongly related to the spatial focus of the architecture. Wide area service-oriented architectures like Web Services, CORBA or DCOM rather use more static discovery mechanisms like UDDI or CORBA trader, local area service-oriented architectures like Jini or MOCA (Beck et al., 1999) provide more dynamic discovery mechanisms which allow for services appearing and disappearing dynamically within little time periods. Another characteristic closely related to the dynamic aspects of service discovery can be described by the *hierarchy* of registries. Central registries imply a hierarchical network structure, whereas distributed registries (Beck et al., 1999) provide a flat network structure and are therefore also applicable to P2P networks. Closely related to the distributed mode is the characteristic of *autonomous discovery*, which describes whether the service-oriented architecture is dependent on central registry services or individual services are able to find each other autonomously.

In the next Section we will discuss adaptations of service-oriented architectures for mobile information systems.

3.   REQUIREMENTS FOR PERVASIVE SERVICE-ORIENTED ARCHITECTURES

Service-oriented architectures have their origin in the 1990s and have shown their power in wired infrastructures like LANs or WANs. However, since the main characteristics are historically grown and mainly targeted to wired environments, existing service-oriented frameworks often lack the possibility to adapt to non-wired environments (OMG, 1991; Eddon and Eddon, 1998). This is also true for a group of recent developments (van Steen et al., 1999; Foster et al., 2002; W3C, 2002), especially designed for the use in wide area network applications like the WWW. Another group of more recent developments (Kindberg et al., 2002; Beck et al., 1999; Strang, 2003; Waldo, 1999) addresses aspects of mobility (Mattern and Sturm, 2003; Satyanarayanan, 1996); however, the integration with existing infrastructures and the adaptation of proven service-oriented concepts is often neglected. Thus, in this Section we want to describe important requirements addressing the necessary adaptations of service-oriented middleware for the use in mobile information systems.

3.1   R1 Overcome Heterogeneity by using Adaptive SOM

Heterogeneity in pervasive environments can be manifold, it can result in incompatibilities of devices, system platforms, communication networks or applications. Today's applications are typically developed for specific device classes and system platforms (Saha and Mukherjee, 2003), which leads to an increasing number of different versions of the same application. Adaptive middleware can bridge the gap between heterogeneous devices, system platforms and communication networks. As stated in Section 2, service-oriented middleware is traditionally well suited to overcome heterogeneity in wired networks and therefore can also solve incompatibility issues in pervasive environments. Service containers will enable device and platform portability, different service connectors allow for heterogeneous communication networks and universal service contracts reduce incompatibility issues between different applications. New challenges of heterogeneity in pervasive environments arise from mobility issues (Banavar and Bernstein, 2002; Henricksen et al., 2001; Satyanarayanan, 1996) and have to be addressed by the middleware.

3.2   R2 Integration of existing Computing Infrastructure and Computing Components

By now, applications on mobile devices are poorly integrated with existing computing infrastructures and computing components (Mattern and Sturm, 2003. As stated in Banavar et al., 2000), a mobile device should be a portal into an application or data space and not a repository for custom software components. In order to generate real added value for mobile users, existing computing infrastructure and computing components have to be integrated smoothly into mobile environments. For instance, wrappers or proxies can be used in order to integrate existing infrastructure for providing added value. To combine services to a portal view, as stated in (Banavar et al., 2000), is also a widely adopted user interface concept in service-oriented environments.

3.3   R3 Service-Oriented Architectures should incorporate a View on People, Places and Things

According to (Kindberg et al., 2002), nomadic people, places they enter and computerised things in these places are crucial to mobile computing environments and therefore have to be considered in the computing infrastructures. Service-oriented architectures typically only deal with virtual resources such as service components, which have no connection to the physical world. To be adapted to pervasive environments, service components and service containers have to be semantically modelled (Banavar and Bernstein, 2002) under consideration of the hosting device (things), the location of the hosting device (places) and the current user (people). Thus, service provisioning has to come along with a conceptual model for managing devices in certain locations, groupings of services on devices or at locations and adoption to user profiles.

3.4   R4 Consideration of Mobility Aspects in Service-Oriented Architectures

Traditional service-oriented architectures typically do not consider mobility aspects. According to (Satyanarayanan, 2001), important issues include *mobile networking, mobile information access, support for adaptive applications* and *location and context sensitivity*. Service-oriented architectures are able to provide assistance in mobile networking and mobile information access through dynamic service discovery (Banavar et al., 2000) and reaching a certain level of autonomy for devices (Strang, 2003) (disconnected operation, caching of data). Support for adaptive applications is provided through on-the-fly deployment, laissez-faire or lazy loading of services (Satyanarayanan, 1996; Beck et al., 1999) and task-centred user interface services (Banavar et al., 2000). Based on the characteristics and requirements, in the following Sections, we give an overview on the system architecture and example applications of *Asomnia*.

4.   SYSTEM ARCHITECTURE

The main goal of the system architecture was to overcome the deficiencies of existing service-oriented architectures as described above.

4.1   Network Structure

The network structure is designed as a 2- layered network scheme with hierarchy, where the first layer, the global domain, basically represents a highly reliable and available backbone managed by a central registry service and providing basic system services. The global domain consists of one central authority, a well known central registry, which hosts configuration settings of devices and services in the backbone as well as the current sub domains building up the second layer of the *Asomnia* network. Devices and services in each sub domain have access to a local registry, which is either well known by devices or found via network multicast. This allows mobile devices to register in currently available sub domains and is therefore considered as a crucial requirement for pervasive environments. Moreover, the sub domains can be organised according to physical places, which allows for inherent location awareness of devices (cf requirement R3). The 2-layered hierarchy allows for consistency as well as scalability of the system structure.

4.2   Service Discovery

The 2-layered hierarchical registry system allows for dynamic registration of mobile devices. Based on the concept of local registries, mobile devices and services in the sub domain can find currently available devices and services in this domain (cf R4). Whereas typical service-oriented architectures do not consider location and characteristics of hosting devices, we consider (mobile) devices and places (sub domains) as important to be modelled in a mobile environment (Kindberg et al., 2002) (cf R3). In contrast to wired infrastructures, where devices are rather homogeneous and differ only little, mobile computing focuses on a huge variety of heterogeneous devices with greatly differing functionality. Moreover, an increasing set of pervasive services will be closely tied to certain devices (e.g. sensor devices) and places, where these devices are available. Thus, we argue, that our registry system allows for location aware discovery of devices as well as services virtually representing the functionality of these devices (cf R3). Moreover, our hierarchical registry system allows to combine the benefits of wired backbone infrastructures and wireless infrastructures within one middleware (cf R2).

4.3   Service Containers

Service containers in *Asomnia* provide a basic runtime infrastructure for services and fulfil the basic characteristics of portability and reuse of common functionality. However, to go a bit further, *Asomnia* uses service containers, which, depending on the executing device, are able to adapt to different roles. On wired devices, the service container adapts to the role of a single service container, i.e. each service on a device is running in its own service container, whereas on wireless, less powerful devices, the container adapts to the role of a multi service container (Fig. 1).

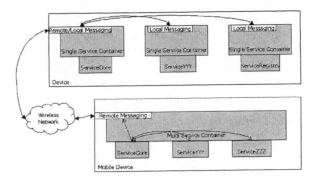

Figure 1. Single Service Container and Multi Service Container

Local and remote communication is handled by a local service broker called the *ServiceCore*. This approach ensures a maximum degree of reliability in wired infrastructures and reduced resource consumption on less powerful devices (cf R2, cf R4).

4.4 Devices and Service Components

Service components in *Asomnia* are typically rather coarse grained software entities. However, in order to allow for reusability, we have developed a concept for coarse grained services to be built of fine grained functional units (FU) (Fig. 2).

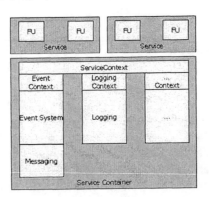

Figure 2. The layered architecture consists of functional units (FU), service components and the service container

Functional units are typically not visible from outside but are encapsulated in the service component to follow object oriented principles. New service components can be composed of a set of functional units at design time, applications can be composed of service components at runtime leading towards adaptive applications (cf R4).

To address the requirement R3, we not only focus on service components, but also on modelling devices. Physical devices typically provide a collection of services, utilising the device's functionality. A device together with the service components is registered in the registry system. Thus, in order to deal with devices and services, any device needs to be controlled by a controller service i.e. *ServiceCore* (Fig. 1). The *ServiceCore* is the first service which is started for each device, and is used for management functionality. This includes starting and stopping of services on the device, registering the device at the registry system or maintaining the leases (Waldo, 1999) for the device. Additionally, the *ServiceCore* is responsible for remote communication, i.e. it is a kind of communication broker for the device. Registering devices in addition to services and providing one access point to the device has a few advantages:

- Easier management at the overlay network level (easier configuration of network and devices)
- Easier management at the network level (since all devices only communicate via the port of the *ServiceCore*, only this port has to be known to other devices and opened in the firewalls)
- Reaching a certain degree of autonomy of devices (cf R4)
- Services have a strong relation to devices and thus can also be related to places (cf R3).

4.5 Service Contracts

Asomnia uses a non-validated event exchange based on an XML-based event hierarchy together with an event description similar to (Pietzuch and Bacon, 2002). Currently we use the event hierarchy in a public way, future developments will focus on establishing explicit semantics by using a common ontology. Events can easily be serialised to messages and can be delivered either synchronously or asynchronously, which enables store and forward delivery upon network disconnection (cf R4).

4.6 Service Connectors

As described above, *Asomnia* uses event-based communication. Events allow for efficient delivery of information to other services either asynchronously or synchronously. Asynchronous event delivery is mostly used on mobile devices, whereas on wired infrastructures, synchronous delivery is the first choice due to the high level of availability and reliability in case that sender an receiver are both online. For reliable asynchronous communication on mobile devices we use store and forward delivery: For network communication we use messages, which are events encoded according to an exchangeable payload format (*Formatter*). The messages are sent via exchangeable transport protocols (*Transport*). Both concepts allow for greater flexibility and are typically not provided by other service-oriented systems like Jini or MOCA. In our approach, for example, the default encoding for the wired environment may be XML, which allows for easier interoperability. However, for mobile devices, the XML-conversion may be to cumbersome, thus, an additional binary *Formatter* can be provided, which allows for higher performance in event encoding.

To sum up, since payload format and transport protocols are exchangeable, we are able to provide interoperability between heterogeneous devices on the network layer (Bluetooth, WLAN, infrared connection) as well as on the platform layer. It is possible with *Asomnia* to run each service in a different platform even on the same device.

5.   PROTOTYPE AND DEMONSTRATION

According to the system architecture described in the previous Section we have implemented a prototype based on the .net Framework and the .net Compact Framework. In our prototype application scenario, a user with a PDA carries along a Powerpoint presentation and wants to take advantage of an existing video beamer equipment in a meeting room for presentation (cf R3). The user's PDA has access to the *Asomnia* enabled environment and after establishing a personal area network connection via Bluetooth or WLAN, the device automatically finds the local *Asomnia* registry by IP-multicast and starts to register itself. After the registration, the user is informed about available devices and services and uses the presentation control service running on the PDA in order to find the appropriate video beamer device and the proxy service which gives access to the Powerpoint application (cf R1). Upon connection to the service, the user starts uploading the presentation to the beamer device for getting immediately access to the slides from the PDA. During the presentation, the user can randomly jump to the different slides and is able to fully control the presentation on the PDA. If there would be a printer accessible from the computing environment, the presentation control service on the PDA would adapt to the situation (cf R4) and offer a possibility to print out slides. Due to the wireless connection of the PDA and the integration with existing infrastructures (cf R2), the user gets a feeling of pervasiveness and having control over the surrounding environment.

6. RELATED WORK

Our approach towards a mobile service-oriented middleware shares similarities with other work. In the following we will briefly highlight the most relevant ones.

The main goal of the (Heywow framework Strang, 2003), developed by the German Aerospace Center, is to provide location based information to mobile users. Heywow focuses mainly on service discovery and service description for services executed on mobile devices. Discovery and execution take into account the users' context. *Asomnia* differs from Heywow in two main aspects. We use exchangeable service connectors, i.e. transport protocols and payload formatters, since we argue, that HTTP transport and XML-parsers cannot be assumed for all kinds of mobile devices.

(Jini Waldo, 1999) provides a service oriented architecture for building distributed systems. It is based on the distributed computing mechanisms of sockets and remote method invocation (RMI). The intention is to offer a network plug and work mechanism where new services can join a network of other services and where service requestors can search for and use them (Newmarch, 2000). In contrast to *Asomnia*, even local communication between services is done via the lookup service (LUS) and therefore mobile devices can not reach autonomy. Furthermore, Jini assumes a Java Virtual Machine and provides only one type of service connectors, which results in rather few possibilities to integrate mobile devices.

TheWeb Services protocols (W3C, 2002) allow software services in a WWW environment to be deployed, discovered and accessed. Web Services are well suited for wired environments, but due to their rather static nature and resource consuming service containers less viable for low processing power devices in pervasive scenarios. The registry used with Web-Services - UDDI - is kind of static and not well suited for the dynamic requirements of mobile systems.

The *Open Grid Services Architecture* (OGSA) (Foster et al., 2002) by the Global Grid Forum builds on Web Services and provides a higher-level concept of services for grid computing infrastructures. In *Asomnia* we make use of plugable service connectors similar to the Web Services approach, however, we use lightweight service containers and dynamic registries.

CoolTown (Kindberg et al., 2002) offers a web model for supporting nomadic users and does this by tying web resources to physically present objects. The project strongly emphasis on common standards, however, it does not provide an architecture for a service-oriented middleware.

MOCA (Beck et al., 1999) provides a service framework that supports the development and execution of applications with a special focus on mobile computing devices. Basically, the concept is similar to Jini. The service registry, however, is located and maintained at each participating device, which results in more flexibility with respect to mobility and in independence from a central entity. MOCA is fully implemented in Java and each device requires a JVM to be able to participate, which both restrict this framework regarding technology independence issues.

Some other systems or architectures influenced our work. The most important ones are JXTA and Bluetooth. JXTA (Gong, 2001) is a standard protocol set for a pure Peer-to-Peer (P2P) infrastructures. The mobile extension of JXTA called JXME (JXTA, 2003) seems to be appropriate for pervasive scenarios, however, due to the lack of central authorities in P2P systems, administrative and configuration issues are more complex. Bluetooth (Naveen and Yen, 2002) is a technology specification targeted to establish a standard to interconnect devices with a special focus on mobile devices. The Bluetooth stack spans a great variety of functionality ranging from hardware issues like radio frequency (RF) and coding schemes, basic software issues like addressing and network management, up to a sophisticated service discovery mechanism called the Service Discovery Protocol (SDP). Although SDP and service-oriented concepts are closely related to our work, Bluetooth is a hardware oriented low level protocol and thus considered to be rather an underlying technology compared to *Asomnia*.

A comparative overview of related work according to Section 2 is provided in the characteristics matrix (Table 1).

Table 1. Characteristics matrix (- not supported, + basic support, ++ full support)

	Heywow	Jini	OGSA	CoolT.	MOCA	ASOMNIA
Components: Granularity	+	+	++	-	+	-
Components: Mobility	+	++	-	-	+	++
Components: Transparency	+	++	++	++	+	+
Contracts: Interoperability	-	+	++	+	-	+
Contracts: Published	-	++	++	-	+	-
Containers: Portability	-	+	++	+	+	++
Containers: Service execution	+	+	n.a.	+	+	++
Connectors: Protocols	-	-	++	-	-	++
Connectors: Payload formats	-	-	++	-	-	++
Service discovery: Dynamic	++	+	-	-	++	++
Service discovery: Hierarchy	++	-	+	-	-	++
Service discovery: Autonomy	++	-	-	-	+	+

7. SUMMARY AND CONCLUSION

In this paper we have argued that there is a growing need for seamless integration of wireless and existing wired computing infrastructures. Existing developments in service-oriented middleware have mainly focused on characteristics important for wired infrastructures (e.g. taking advantage of always available and reliable infrastructures) and do insufficiently cope with the requirements arising from pervasiveness, such as dealing with certain aspects of mobility (e.g. increasing heterogeneity and resource poverty of mobile devices, location awareness or error-prone wireless networks). To overcome these limitations, in our approach we propose a service-oriented middleware targeted to adapt the historically grown and well proven characteristics of service-oriented architectures in order to cope with the forthcoming challenges of pervasive environments. Our architecture addresses the differences of wired and wireless infrastructures using the concept of adaptive service containers and hierarchical registries. In conclusion, we believe that *Asomnia* provides a step towards a service-oriented architecture for seamless integration of wireless and wired computing infrastructures.

REFERENCES

Banavar, G., et.al. (2000). Challenges: an application model for pervasive computing. In *Proceedings of the 6th annual international conference on Mobile computing and networking*, pages 266–274. ACM Press.

Banavar, G. and Bernstein, A. (2002). Software infrastructure and design challenges for ubiquitous computing applications. *Communications of the ACM*, 45(12):92–96.

Beck, J., Gefflaut, A., and Islam, N. (1999). Moca: a service framework for mobile computing devices. In *Proceedings of the 1st ACM international workshop on Data engineering for wireless and mobile access*, pages pp. 62–68, Seattle, Washington, United States. ACM.

Bettstetter, C. and Renner, C. (2000). A comparison of service discovery protocols and implementation of the service location protocol. In *Proceedings of Sixth EUNICE Open European Summer School - EUNICE 2000*, Twente, Nederlands.

Bieber, G. and Carpenter, J. (2001). Introduction to service-oriented programming (rev. 2.1).

Eddon, G. and Eddon, H. (1998). *Inside Distributed Com.* Microsoft Press.

Ferscha, A. and Vogl, S. (2002). Pervasive web access via public communication walls. In *Pervasive Computing, Springer LNCS 2414*, pages pp. 84–97, Zurich, Switzerland.

Foster, I., Kesselman, C., Nick, J. M., and Tuecke, S. (2002). The physiology of the grid: An open grid services architecture for distributed systems integration. Draft 5, Mathematics and Computer Science Division, Argonne National Laboratory and Department of Computer Science, University of Chicago and Information Sciences Institute, University of Southern California and IBM Corporation.

Fowler, M. (2002). Public versus published interfaces. *IEEE Software*, Vol. 19(2):18–19.

Garlan, D., Siewiorek, D., Smailagic, A., and Steenkiste, P. (2002). Project aura: Toward distraction -free pervasive computing. *IEEE Pervasive Computing*, 4:pp. 22–31.

Gong, L. (2001). Project JXTA: A Technology Overview. http://www.jxta.org/project/www/docs/jxtaview 01nov02.pdf.

Gosling, J., et.al. (1996). *The Java Language Specification*. Addison-Wesley.

Hashimi, S. (2003). Service-oriented architecture explained. *O'Reilly ONDotnet.com*.

Henricksen, K., Indulska, J., and Rakotonirainy, A. (2001). Infrastructure for pervasive computing: Challenges. In *GI Jahrestagung Vienna*, pages 214–222.

JXTA, P. (2003). JXTA for J2ME. http://jxme.jxta.org.

Kagal, L., Korolev, V., Chen, H., Joshi, A., and Finin, T. (2001). Centaurus: A framework for intelligent services in a mobile environment. In *Proceedings of the International Workshop on Smart Appliances and Wearable Computing (IWSAWC)*.

Kindberg, T., Barton, J. J., Morgan, J., Becker, G., Caswell, D., Debaty, P., Gopal, G., Frid, M., Krishnan, V., Morris, H., Schettino, J., Serra, B., and Spasojevic, M. (2002). People, places, things: Web presence for the real world. In *MONET 7(5)*, pages 365–376.

Kleinrock, L. (1996). Nomadicity: Anytime, anywhere in a disconnected world. In *Mobile Networks and Applications 1*, pages 351 – 357.

Mattern, F. and Sturm, P. (2003). From distributed systems to ubiquitous computing - the state of the art, trends, and prospects of future networked systems. In Klaus Irmscher, K.-P. F. E., editor, *Proceedings of KIVS 2003*, pages pp. 3–25. Springer-Verlag.

McGovern, J., Tyagi, S., Stevens, M., and Mathew, S. (2003). *Java Web Services Architecture*. Morgan Kaufmann.

Meijer, E. and Miller, J. (2001). Technical overview of the common language runtime. *MSDN*.

Naveen, E. and Yen, D. C. (2002). Bluetooth Technology: A strategic Analysis of its Role in global 3G wireless Communication Era. *Computing Standards and Interfaces*, 24

Newmarch, J. (2000). *A Programmer's Guide to Jini Technology*. Springer-Verlag.

OMG (1991). The common object request broker: Architecture and specification. Technical report, Object Management Group (OMG), OMG Document Number 91.12.1

Pallos, M. S. (2001). Service-oriented architecture: A primer. *eAI Journal*, pages 32–35.

Pietzuch, P. R. and Bacon, J. M. (2002). Hermes: A distributed event-based middleware architecture. In *Proceedings of the 1st International Workshop on Distributed Event-Based Systems (DEBS'02)*.

Raatikainen, K., Christensen, H. B., and Nakajima, T. (2002). Application requirements for middleware for mobile and pervasive systems. *ACM SIGMOBILE Mobile Computing and Communications Review*, 6(4):16–24.

Saha, D. and Mukherjee, A. (2003). Pervasive computing: A paradigm for the 21st century. *IEEE Pervasive Computing*, pages pp. 25–31.

Satyanarayanan, M. (1996). Fundamental challenges in mobile computing. In *Proceedings of the 15th annual ACM symposium on Principles of distributed computing*, pages 1–7. ACM Press.

Satyanarayanan, M. (2001). Pervasive computing: Vision and challenges. IEEE Personal Communications.

Stevens, M. (2002). Service-oriented architecture introduction. *developer.com*.

Strang, T. (2003). Towards autonomous context-aware services for smart mobile devices. In Chen, M.-S., editor, *MDM 2003 (4th International Conference on Mobile Data Management)*, volume LNCS 2574, pages pp. 279–292, Melbourne, Australia. Springer.

van Steen, M., Homburg, P., and Tanenbaum, A. S. (1999). Globe: a wide area distributed system. *IEEE Concurrency*, 7:pp. 70–78.

W3C (2002). Web services activity. http://www.w3.org/2002/ws/.

Waldo, J. (1999). Jini technology architectural overview. Technical report, SunMicrosystems, 901 San Antonio Road, Palo Alto, CA 94303 U.S.A. Available as http://www.sun.com/jini/whitepapers/architecture.html.

Weiser, M. (1991). The computer for the 21st century. *Scientific American*, 265(3):66–75.

A TASK-BASED FRAMEWORK FOR MOBILE APPLICATIONS TO ENHANCE SALESPERSONS´ PERFORMANCE

Chihab BenMoussa
Turku Centre for Computer Science,Lemminkäisenkatu 14 A
FIN-20520 TURKU, FINLAND

Abstract: The paper suggests a framework for mobile applications aimed at supporting salespersons` tasks for greater performance when they are operating within a highly mobile work environment. To do so the paper starts by providing a review of mobile technologies characteristics in terms of mobile devices, connectivity and mobile applications. After deriving a set of propositions, the paper offers some concluding remarks and suggests areas for future research

Key words: Mobile technologies; Salespersons performance; salespersons tasks; task technology fit.

1.   INTRODUCTION

The role of the professional selling has expanded and changed dramatically in recent years. Instead of merely selling products, today's sales persons are expected to serve customers as consultants who offer expert advice on improving customer's life style or making their business operations more profitable. They operate like micro marketing-managers in the field. Buyers are becoming increasingly skilful at obtaining value of their expenditures. Salespersons now usually deal with professional buyers or purchasing agents who base their buying decisions on the representative's delivery of quality and service and how the product will affect their company's profit. Such rapidly growing sophistication of professional buyers and their increasing access to information will continue to challenge salespersons to find new sources and faster methods of obtaining information despite their constant move. Additionally, the unique nature of selling with its mobility requirements, time demand, psychological strain, work-related role stress and performance orientation continue to put unusual pressure on salespersons.

The advent of access to services through mobile and wireless devices has resulted in a fast growing of a number of mobile applications and service. Mobile (or wireless) applications, despite being different in their nature, they share a common characteristic that distinguishes them from their wire-line counterpart: They put the user at the centre of information and communication through the provision of location specific information, personalization, immediacy, and service availability (Durlacher, 2001). These characteristics would enable the development of innovative mobile applications to support firms´ salespersons for greater performance despite their high work mobility. How and which mobile applications can support these frontline ambassadors in their sales efforts are key questions facing a number of stakeholders including sale managers today.

The paper suggests a task-based framework for developing mobile applications to support salespersons` tasks when they are operating within a highly mobile work environment. To do so the paper starts by providing a review of mobile technologies characteristics in terms of mobile devices, connectivity and mobile applications. After deriving a set of propositions, the paper offers some concluding remarks and suggests areas for future research

2.   MOBILE TECHNOLOGIES OVERVIEW

A complex, interconnected set of technologies provides the basis on which mobile applications and services can be built. Similar to traditional information systems (IS), mobile technologies can be reviewed according to three dimensions: mobile devices corresponding to the hardware in IS, network connectivity and applications (software).

2.1   Mobile Devices

Mobile technologies bring back to discourse the issues associated with devices that can be used to access and utilize IS functionality. Laptop PCs have extended IS functionality by enabling workers to bring their digital work with them whenever they were going. Gradually smaller devices have been developed. Personal Digital Assistant (PDA) such as Psion, Palm and

Windows CE based palm tops, and operating systems such as WinCE, EPOC and PalmOS have emerged for mobile users. Smartphones, a combination of a mobile phone and a PDA have increasingly become popular and hold a great promise. They include versions of Nokia communicators, Handspring Treo, smartphone devices form vendors such as Orange, Samsung and AT&tT Wireless version (www.synchrologic.com).

For the purpose of this paper, a mobile device is any device connected to the Internet or other networks through wireless networking using any standard wireless communication protocol. They include such devices as laptop PCs, Tablet PCs, PDAs, smartphones and WAP enabled phones.

Mobile devices can be assessed according to the three dimensions: usability, capability and cost. Usability includes such characteristics as portability, micro-mobility, display and input characteristics. Portability as determined by the device's weight and size is a significant usage factor for the mobile workforce. Device's micro-mobility as describes by Luff and heath (1998) is inherent in the physical objects in that they may be moved about and be shared between people to support communication (i.e. during a meeting).

Device's capability include such characteristics as processing power, amount of local storage, battery life, available connection options, location-awareness and security factors (see for example, Tarassewich et al. 2002, Ovum 2003, synchrologic 2003 for discussions of open issues).

The device 's cost factor includes procurement cost, support and add-in cost. Add-in cost is the cost resulting from adding other functionality to an existing type of device such as a cell phone. An example is mobile software applications that add processing and other functionality to cell phones (Gebauer et al., 2002)

Mobile devices differ in terms of their usability, capability and cost characteristics. Such differences give raise to tradeoffs particularly between device capability and device usability. For instance a Laptop Pc offers some good features in terms of processing power, memory, display and input /output characteristics, but they are often awkward to use on the move. Indeed, a laptop is able to receive a document anywhere that a network can be established with computers back at the office. However once the document is received, the laptop cannot be spatially reoriented at the micro-level, during a face-to-face meeting in a way that a PDA or a smartphone allows. Additionally, The Laptop's procurement and maintenance cost are far high compared to PDAs or smartphones.

2.2   Connectivity

In addition to mobile devices, networking support is crucial to support a mobile workforce without constant physical access to stationary IS. Mobile and wireless networks are experiencing significant progress in the form of wireless local area network (WLAN), Satellite-based Networks, Wireless Local Loops, Mobile Internet Protocol and Wireless Asynchronous Transfer Mode Network (see for example Varshney 2002 for more details about such technologies). One emerging technology is bluetooth, a short-range, point-to-multipoint data transfer, which provides low cost short-range radio link for wireless connecting.

Distinguishing factors for network connectivity include Network capacity (i.e. bandwidth), geographic network availability and connection fees. Significant efforts are in course to enhance mobile and wireless network' bandwidth. In addition, developments in mobile middleware platforms contribute in optimising for low bandwidth, intermittent connections as well as the amount of processing required at the mobile device.

Network availability, including roaming across multiple networks and the mobile user location's environment (outdoor, indoor, underground); might be a significant functionality factor for mobile applications and services, in particular those supporting an on the move workforce. An example is location based mobile applications and services, which rely on positioning technologies such as GPS and Cellular positioning technologies. The positioning accuracy of such technologies depends on whether the user is in an indoor environment (i.e. a building), a rural or dense urban area. (BenMoussa, 2004).

Current developments in wireless and mobile connectivity in the form of the third generation mobile communication systems (3G) hold a great promise in providing a faster and reliable access time to users and reducing the total cost of access and transfer of data across multiple networks. Some firms started developing 4G technologies and global standards. NTT DoCoMo, Inc. announced in 2003 plans for a field trial of 4G mobile communication systems.

2.3   Applications

Although mobile technologies such as mobile phones and PDAs were first developed as consumer products rather than business solutions, a number of innovative companies have adopted those technologies as enablers for their process innovation' initiatives (Kakihara et al. 2003). Traditionally, the use of mobile technologies in business environment has been concentrated in supporting sales process and logistics (i.e. the cases of

Fritto-lay, UPS). The introduction of wireless digital networks has made it possible to transfer data cost effectively and potentially increase the added value of mobile applications through the provision of location sensitive information.

The paper categorizes mobile application and services into the three functional categories: the connective, the interactive and the proactive mobile application and services. The following outline the three analytical categories of mobile application and services.

2.3.1   Connective mobile applications

Connective mobile applications involve basically a mobile and a wireless client accessing a centralized service. An example of connective mobile applications includes accessing wirelessly Intranet functionality via a mobile device. The user sends information requests to the server, which in turns serves, the relevant information back to the user. Another example is accessing wirelessly a WAP or I-mode site.

2.3.2   Interactive mobile applications

Mobile interactive applications support the generation of information through communication between people. Obviously the best example of interactive mobile applications is the mobile phone itself (Sorrensen et al., 2002). The SMS functionality supports short text messages can also be considered interactive mobile applications. As is the instant messaging services, such as ICQ, AOL, and MSN messenger service for pocket PC 2002. Other examples of interactive mobile applications include e-mail systems and Awareware supporting mutual awareness through synchronous or asynchronous modes of awareness employing visual or verbal media.

2.3.3   Proactive mobile applications

Proactive mobile applications are aimed at supporting mobile users in responding proactively to potential changing environmental trends. Based on the user's situational context and changing environment, the service provider delivers content without receiving a request from him/her. An indicative example of mobile applications could be the use of mobile wireless client in managing the supply chain allowing dispersed actors to interact with the parameters governing the supply chain and respond proactively to potential malfunction (i.e. lost or delayed orders).

3.   FRAMEWORK FOR MOBILE APPLICATIONS TO SUPPORT SALESPERSONS TASKS

The paper now suggests three propositions for developing mobile applications aimed at supporting salespersons for greater performance.

✓ Categorising salespersons tasks by the areas that might be affected by mobile technologies,

✓ Fitting mobile technologies characteristics with salespersons´ task requirement in order to increases the applications´ chance to succeed,

✓Involving actively the salespersons in the design, development and implementation of mobile applications can increase the success chance of such applications.

3.1   Categorizing Salespersons Tasks by the Areas of Mobile Support

The paper suggests that categorising salespersons tasks based on the areas that mobile technologies can support, would provide a rich resource in terms of delivering a targeted support to salespersons in order to handle the tasks at hand. Salespersons tasks can thus constitute the point of departure in terms of developing salespersons´ mobile applications. Using tasks as unit of analysis for supporting knowledge workers in general has been emphasised by many authors (Hackman, 1969; Druckar, 1999; Byström, 1999; Perry et all, 2001, luff and Heath, 1998). For instance, Druckard points out that understanding knowledge workers´ tasks is the first requirement in tackling knowledge workers ´ productivity. One reason for this, Druckard said, stems form the fact that unlike manual work, knowledge work does not program the worker. (Luff et all, 2000) have shown that the misunderstanding of the mature of tasks that workers perform can be problematic and lead to technologies being used in unexpected ways. For example they describe a situation in which a mobile device was introduced onto a building site to replace a paper allocation sheet used to record the amount of time workers spent on particular aspects of a job. The system was supposed to provide a mobile resource for the workers to help them monitor problems as they occur and to support in situ discussion with other people on the site. What happened in actual use however differed form the intent. Instead of being used as a communication tool to support the mobility of the worker around the site, it was used primarily as a data documentation device. This occurred because the device impeded certain important features of collaborative work practices of the workers and the other workers when on the site.

The paper proposes the following categorisation of salespersons tasks based on the review of the determinants of salespeople performance and the characteristics of mobile technologies.

3.1.1 Information tasks

Mobile technologies can enable salespeople to collect and have access to information irrespective of their locations, which would have an impact on the areas of prospecting and customer relationship management.

In prospecting, salespersons can be supported by having access anywhere and anytime to customize the list of prospects together with additional information about customer's buying history, real time orders, and latest events in the customer's business, which may enable them to qualify prospects and apply target selling.

In the field, mobile technologies can also enable salespersons to obtain up-to date information about the prospect and use it during the sales call to adapt to sales situations and to overcome objections. In addition, Mobile technologies can give the sales force the ability to check the availability and prices of any products, and thus deliver feasible promises. Salespersons can also configure products to reflect customers needs and wants, while with the customer, by having access to communication with the company's technical specialist. Furthermore, awareness of salespersons' location can enable useful information about the customer to be delivered to them so that they can reflect it during their sales call.

3.1.2 Interaction Tasks

Information contained in sales call, expenses and calendar reports from salespersons is vital to sales managers´ ability to both adapt their marketing strategies and manage salespeople. Mobile technologies can help sales persons in reporting such information any time and irrespective of their locations. Also, ubiquitous access to e-mails and corporate data by salespersons may enable them to make themselves readily available to interact with their accounts and address their problems and question, which would have a positive impact on their customer orientation. Indeed the customer requires, in today's highly competitive world, timely and accurate information, fast response to questions and the ability to work with salespersons that can provide these things (Engel et all, 2000). In addition mobile technologies would make it possible to salespersons, irrespective of their locations, to seek support from both their colleagues and managers should they face an unexpected challenging sales problem.

3.1.3   Planning Tasks

Mobile technologies can enable salespersons to better manager their time and reorganize their contacts irrespective of their locations so that they can focus on the most profitable accounts and use their dead time more productively. This time generally occurs between tasks and between meetings, in which salespersons usually have little control over the resources available to them. For instance, pharmaceutical sales reps often visit doctors to provide them with information on what is available as order brochures on products in which the doctor is interested. Frequently the doctor is not available and the representative wants to find a nearby alternative contact. If there is no alternative contact to visit, then the time for waiting for the doctor to become available may turn to be dead time for the sales representative. With mobile technologies, the sales rep can turn this dead time into a productive one by performing non-selling tasks such as completing and sending expense reports to her company, preparing invoices or writing and sending thanks letters to customers. These reduce the time that sales reps have to spend in the office to perform routine tasks and thus allow them to spend more time selling. Indeed, despite the problems associated with laptop computer in terms of carrying behaviour, weight and booting time, Hewlett Packard found that salespeople using laptop computers spent 27 percent more time with customers, earned 10 percent more sales and achieved three times the productivity of sales reps who did not use laptops (Taylor, 1987). Using dead time more efficiently may occur in a variety of locations (i.e. trains, airports, airplanes, hotels rooms, office buildings, etc).

3.2   Fitting Salespersons´ Task Requirements with Mobile Technologies characteristics

After reviewing mobile technologies characteristics in terms of devices, processing and network connectivity, the paper suggested a categorisation of salespersons tasks based on the areas that can be affected by mobile technologies, the paper derived three categories of salespersons tasks: information tasks, interaction tasks, planning tasks and mobile tasks. The paper now suggests that each of the above mentioned category of tasks has specific requirements in terms of mobile technologies characteristics, and that a fit between mobile technologies characteristics and the requirements of the tasks with respect to content, processing, device portability, device micro-mobility, retrieval and location based alerts can support the success of salespersons ´mobile applications in terms of achieving the expected benefits. Figure one refers to a framework of mobile applications to support salespersons´ tasks when they are operating within a mobile work environment.

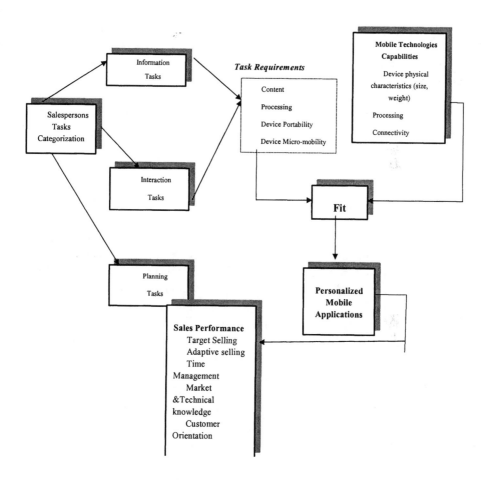

Figure 1: Fit between salespersons task requirements and mobile technologies capabilities as enabler of the success of mobile applications to support salespersons performance

The paper proposes that salespersons perform a variety of tasks with different purposes, which impose requirements that cannot fit the characteristics of a specific mobile device. For instance a laptop is able to receive a document anywhere that a network connection can be established with a computer back at the office. But once the document is received, the laptop cannot be spatially reoriented at the micro-level, for example during a face-to-face interaction in a way that a PDA or a smart phone can allow. Additionally a mobile phone can be appropriate for alerts and notification to support information tasks as well as simple interaction tasks (i.e. inventory checking, price inquiry or product inquires) but difficult to use it for interaction tasks involving a data processing or complex information analysis such as reports on customers´ business or key accounts profitability.

In contrast the laptop, given its size and functionality can support salespersons in performing such tasks. However for alerts and notifications, laptop might not be an adequate medium given their size, weight and booting requirement.

The tasks also impose requirements in terms of the content. For instance information tasks require an adaptation of the content so that it can fit with other requirements such as device portability or micro-mobility and thus make the information relevant to the situation faced by the salesperson. Content about products, market or prospects´ business should be adapted so that they can fit with the portability characteristics of mobile phones or PDAs and thus they can be used at the moment of relevance (i.e. during customer interaction).

Travel is a key component of salespersons´ work. Studies have shown that before the trip, workers face unpredictability with respect to the nature of information and artefact that they need during a trip. (Perry et all. 2000). As a result, they plan ahead to take thinks that they just feel they would need. The purpose is to make sure that documents and information are available in the appropriate form when and where needed to support unanticipated information and communication need. In theory laptops can support this type of impromptu document access because they offer the potential flexibility to open unanticipated documents from hard disk or over network connections. However Perry et al. 2000 behaviour study of 17 mobile professionals from a variety of professions (management personnel, sales staff, consultant, medical workers, civil servant and media) revealed that while 70% of the participants they studied have access to a laptop, only about a half took them to the trip and those participants bringing their laptop do not necessarily take them to meeting. Furthermore according to such a study, the use of connected laptops to access information was hindered because laptops themselves were subject to planning (should they be taken or not). This was due to the laptop carrying behaviour (i.e. size, weight, risk of theft) conflicts with potential use in supporting unanticipated documents and communication needs.

3.3   Involving Salespersons in Applications´ Design, Developments and Implementation

The paper suggests that the real benefits of developing mobile applications to support salespersons´ tasks come from their use in actual selling and customer interaction. Therefore salespersons should be encouraged to use such application. This raises the need of the acceptance of such applications by salespersons. The paper proposes that involving salespersons in the design, development and implementations of such applications can insure good information of the applications' design, which in turn can have a positive impact on the quality of support the applications provide. Delone and Mclean (1992) model supports this proposition. DeLone and McLean believe that the information technology system' quality, together with the quality of information will lead to the utilisation of the information technology. This utilization then leads to an individual impact resulting in an organizational impact. They also point out that utilisation also interacts with user satisfaction. Additionally, involving actively salespersons in the different stages of applications development process might lead to new innovative ideas in terms of the use of the new technologies that salespersons can come up with based on their experience.

CONCLUSION

The paper has proposed a framework for mobile applications to support salespersons tasks .The paper suggested a categorisation of salespersons tasks based on the areas that can be affected by mobile technologies. The paper then derived three categories of salespersons tasks: information tasks, interaction tasks and planning tasks. The paper also suggests that each of the above mentioned category of tasks has specific requirements in terms of mobile support and that a fit between mobile technologies characteristics and the requirements of the tasks in terms of content, processing, device portability, device micro-mobility, retrieval and location-based alerts can increase the success of salespersons 'mobile applications in terms of achieving the expected benefits. The paper also proposes that involving actively salespersons in the design, the development and implementation of the applications can increase the chances of developing high quality application; which in turn would affect positively their acceptance by salespersons and thus their use during sales situations.

It is worth mentioning that the use of mobile technologies may result in some consequences that salespersons may not welcome. Perhaps the most immediate drawback of extensive use of mobile technologies by salespersons is the problem of "information and interaction overload". In addition, some salespersons may perceive mobile applications and services as threat of their freedom in the field and thus may be reluctant to adopt them.As the acceptance of mobile applications and services by salespersons goes beyond the scope of this paper, future research is needed to both address acceptance issues associated with mobile applications and services and translate the rapid development of mobile technologies into innovative and value adding solutions for the sales force.

REFERENCES

Amabile, Teressa (1983). The social Psychology of Creativity: A componential conceptualisation ". Journal of Personality and Social Psychology, 45 (August) 357-376.

Anderson R, (1995). Essential of personal selling: the new professionalism. Prentice Hall, NJ

BenMouss Chihab (2004)."Supporting salespersons through location based mobile applications and services". IFIP World computer congress,

Behrman D, Perreault W (1984). The role stress model of the performance and satisfaction of industrial salespersons. Journal of marketing. Vol.48 (Fall 1984), 9-12-

Boles, Johnston, Hair (1997). Role Stress, Work-Family Conflict and Emotional Exhaustion: inter-relationships and effects on some work-related situations. Journal of personal selling &sales management. Volume XVII, number 1 (winter 1997, Pages 17-28)

Churchil, G., Ford, N., Hartley, S., Walker, O. (1985), The Determinants of Salesperson Performance:

A Meta-Analysis, Journal of Marketing Research, 12, May, 130-118.

Davenport T, (1993). Process innovation: Reengineering work through information technology. Harvard business school press. Boston, USA.

Daft R and R.h Lengel (1986) "organizational Information Requirements, Media Richness, and structural design "Management Science 36 (6), 689- 703

Drucker, P. Knowledge-worker productivity: The Biggest challenge", California Management Review 41 (Winter 1999): 79-94.

Dubinsky, Alane J., Roy D. Howell, Thomas N, Ingram, and Danny N.Bellenger (1986)"Salesforce Socialization" Journal of Marketing, 50 (October), 192-207

Durlacher Research Report, 2001. M-commerce Durlacher Research Institute (April, 2000) available at http://www.durlacher.com

Goodhue D, and Thompson R. (1995). "Task Technology Fit and Individual Performance". MIS Quarterly.

Girard, K (1998) "Stats not good for sales technology" Computer world 32, 14 (April 6), 29

Good D. J and R.J Schultz (1997) "Technological Teaming as a marketing strategy" Industrial marketing management 26, 5 (September) 413-412

J. L. Funk "Key Technological Trajectories and the Expansion of Mobile Internet Applications" proceeding of Stockholm mobility Roundtable 2003

Kakihara, M. and C. Sørensen (2003). Mobile Urban Professionals in Tokyo: Tales of Locational, Operational, and Interactional Mobility. In *Proceedings of the 2nd Stockholm Mobility Roundtable.* Stockholm, Sweden

Kotler, Philip (1994), Marketing Management: Analysis, Planning, Implementation and Control, 8 ed., Prentice Hall, NJ

Paul Luff, Christian Heath (1998), Mobility in collaboration. Proceedings of the 1998 ACM conference on Computer supported cooperative work

Paul Markovits (1988), "Direct selling is alive and well", sales and marketing management, August PP 76-79

.Marshall, Greg W., Moncrief, William C. and Felicia G. Lassk (1999), The Current State of SalesForce Activities, Industrial Marketing Management, 28, 87-98.

Robert F.Vizza and T.E,. Chambers, (1971) Time and Territorial Management for the Salesman, The sales executive club of NewYork), p 97

Thayer Taylor, (1987) " Hewlett- Packard gives sales reps a competitive edge" Sales and marketing management, pp 36-37

Peterson, G,S (1997) High impact sales force automation. St Lucie press, Boca Raton Fl

Sichel, DE, (1997). The computer Revolution, Brookings Institute, New York, NY.

Sujan, H., Weitz, B., Kumar, N. (1994), Learning Orientation, Working Smart, and Effective Selling, Journal of Marketing, 58, July, 39-52.

Sujan, H., Weitz, B.A., and M. Sujan (1988), Increasing Sales Productivity by Getting Salespeople to Work Smarter, Journal of Personal Selling and Sales Management, August, 9 19.

Sulek, J., Maruchek, A. (1992), A Study of the Impact of an Integrated Information Technology on the Time Utilization of Information Workers, Decision Sciences, 23, 1174-1191.

Tarasewich, P., R. C. Nickerson, and M. Warkentin (2002) "Issues in Mobile ECommerce",*Communication of the AIS* 8, pp. 41-64.

Taylor, TC (1993) "Getting in Step with computer age" Sales and marketing managemen, 145, 3 (March), 52-59.

Thetyi, O (2000) "Radical Makeovers: How three companies use strategic planning, Training, and Support to Implement Technology on a Grand Scale" Sales and Marketing Management 152, 4 8April) 78- 88

Weitz, B., Sujan, H, Sujan, M. (1986), Knowledge, Motivation and Adaptive Behavior: A Framework for Improving Selling Effectiveness, Journal of Marketing, 50, 174-191.

Skiba, Brian, Johnson, Mairi, Dillon, Michael (2000) "Moving in mobile media mode".Lehman Brothers, 2000, http.// www.entsoftware.com

Schafter S. (1997) "Supercharged sell"Inc technology supplement 19, 9 (June 14) 100-106

Varshney, U., and R. Vetter (2001) "A Framework for the Emerging Mobile Commerce Applications", Proceedings of the 34th Hawaii International Conference on System Sciences.

CONCEPTUAL MODELING OF STYLES FOR MOBILE SYSTEMS
A layered approach based on graph transformation

Reiko Heckel[1] and Ping Guo[2]

[1]*University of Dortmund, Germany(on leave from University of Paderborn), reiko@upb.de;*
[2]*University of Paderborn, Germany, Intl. Gradrate School of Dynamic Intelligent Systems,*
ping@upb.de

Abstract: When designing a mobile application, we have to be aware of the properties and facilities of the target platform. At a conceptual level, this platform can be specified by a style, defining the structures and operations available to applications. In this paper, we use an UML-like meta model for the structural aspect and graph transformation rules over its instances to specify the dynamics of a style of mobile systems. The model is layered to separate clearly the software from the hardware and the geographic view of the system.

Keywords: mobility; QOS; meta modeling; graph transformation.

1.   INTRODUCTION

Already today, the majority of computing devices is mobile. They include, besides smart cards with limited capabilities, laptops, handheld computers, and mobile phones, all equipped with communication and computation power beyond that of stationary computers a few years ago. In order to manage the resulting logic complexity of applications, conceptual modeling techniques are required like for the development of "stationary" software.

In addition, mobility creates new and diverse concerns. As stated in [19], mobility is a "total meltdown" of the stability assumed by distributed systems, the main differences being caused by the possibility of roaming and wireless connection [21]. Roaming implies that, since devices can move to different locations, their context (network access, services, permissions, etc.) may change, and that mobile hosts are resource limited, for example, in computation power, memory capacity, and electrical power. Wireless connections are generally less reliable, more expensive, and provide smaller bandwidth, and they come in a variety of different technologies and protocols. All this results in a very dynamic software architecture, where configurations and interactions have to be adapted to the changing context and relative location of applications.

In order to provide continuous service to mobile devices, or compensate for the lack of it, a number of different solutions have been developed. Telecom systems like GSM, GPRS, or UMTS use handover protocols to provide continuous connectivity. Mobile IP extends seamless IP connectivity to mobile hosts. Besides, there exist middleware platforms supporting mobility at the application-programming level like J2ME, a reduced version of J2EE for resource-limited devices with support for wireless communication, and Wireless CORBA which supports terminal mobility through CORBA bridges and handover protocols.

However, even with dedicated middleware it is not possible in general to completely hide the consequences of mobility from the application which has to be aware of, and able to react to, changes in its context given by its current location, quality, cost, and type of available connections, etc. What is more, the amount of context information required and available to the application greatly varies, depending on the employed infrastructure so that, in the end, not every intended application scenario may have a meaningful realization on any given platform. That means, developers have to take into account the properties of the infrastructure they are using, not only for the final implementation, but also already at a conceptual level during requirements analysis.

In this paper, the conceptual modeling of *styles of mobile systems* is proposed as a way of capturing the properties of a certain class of mobile computing platforms. Such conceptual models consist two parts: a structural model given by UML class diagrams whose instances represent the valid system configurations, and a dynamic model given by transformation rules over these instances, specifying the operations of the style. Graph transformation systems [20] shall provide the underlying formal model and operational semantics.

Graphs provide a popular model for a variety of structures, including network topologies and software configurations. Their evolution can conveniently be specified by graph transformation rules that manipulate the graphs by means of pattern matching and rewriting. Such specifications have a formal operational semantics, can thus be executed by tools and analyzed for certain properties.

In order to employ graphs and graph transformations for our purposes, the different interpretations of their vertices as components, devices, areas, etc. and their edges as connectors, network connections, neighborhood relations, etc. have to be defined. This is done by a meta model consisting of three interconnected layers, structured by means of packages.

Rules formulated over this meta model shall describe a style of mobile systems given by a set of basic actions that can be invoked or observed by the application. This is comparable to the specification of an architectural style by graph transformation rules [14, 13, 6], but for the fact that the scope is not limited to the software architecture. Then, a mobile application scenario, expressed as a sequence of such basic actions, can be analyzed for its realizable in the style by constructing an execution of the corresponding rule sequence, either by means of a model checker or interactively with the help of a graph transformation tool. This aspect, however, is beyond the scope of this paper.

The paper is organized as follows. In Section 2, we introduce a basic style of mobile systems following the three-layered structure discussed above. In Section 3, this basic model is extended by taking into account quality-of-service information. An example is presented to illustrate this aspect. Section 4 discusses related work and Section 5 concludes the paper.

2. A BASIC STYLE OF MOBILE SYSTEMS

We give a conceptual model that captures the basic structures and operations typical to nomadic networks. Our conceptual model consists of two parts, a structural meta model represented by UML class diagrams and a dynamic model given by graph transformation rules.

2.1 Meta Model

Following [11], we use a meta model structured into three packages. This allows us to separate different concerns, like software architecture, distribution, and roaming, while at the same time retaining an integrated representation where all elements of a concrete model are presented as vertices of the same graph, i.e., an instance of the overall meta model. Based on this uniform representation, the different sub-models can be related by associations between elements belonging to different sub-models.

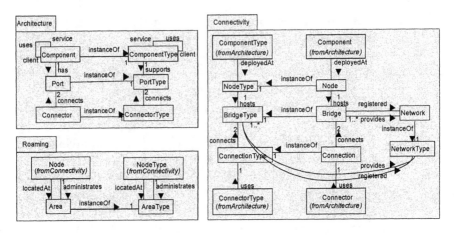

Figure 1. Architecture, Connectivity and *Roaming* package

Our basic style of mobile information systems is focused on the roaming and connectivity of mobile hosts, i.e., hosts can change location and possible connections may vary according to their relative location to each other. Naturally, architecture and behavior of applications depend on the connectivity and location of their host computers. Our three-layered meta model captures these relations in the three packages *Architecture*, *Connectivity* and *Roaming* to present different viewpoints of the systems.

The Architecture package in Fig. 1 defines the architectural view, containing both a definition of an architectural model (meta classes *ComponentType, ConnectorType, PortType*) as well as of an individual configuration (meta classes *Component, Connector*, and *Port*), related by the meta association *instanceOf*.

The Connectivity package in Fig. 1 presents the distributed view of the system in terms of the concepts *Node, Bridge,* and *Connection,* paired as above with corresponding type-level concepts. A node is a (real or virtual) machine, accessible through bridges via connections. The typing means that we can distinguish, for example, between Ethernet, WLAN, or GSM-based connections, or between different kinds of machines like PCs, laptops, cell phones, etc. The package uses the elements *Component, ComponentType* from the Architecture package to be able to specify deployment using the *deployedAt* association. Bridges on client nodes need to be registered with a network in order to build up connections. Moreover, they are typed (e.g., an Ethernet bridge cannot connect to a GSM network). Bridges on server nodes provide network access to registered clients. A Connection is a physical network link that delivers communication services to Connectors at the software level.

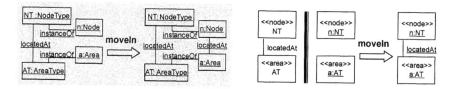

Figure 2. Transformation rule *moveIn*: meta model-based presentation (left)
and UML-like concrete syntax (right)

The Roaming package in Fig. 1 defines the location and mobility of Nodes
in terms of *Areas*, i.e., places where Nodes can be located. An area is
defined by an administrative domain, like a cell managed by a GSM base
station, or a Wireless LAN domain. Thus, there are different types of areas
that may be overlapping. An area can have an administrative Node who
serves the connections in this Area. This node does not need to be located
inside the same area. We do not separate mobile from stationary hosts at this
level. A node is mobile if it changes its location to a different area, a fact that
is part of the dynamics of the model. This allows the added flexibility of
considering, e.g., a laptop that does not move as a stationary device.

2.2 Rules

Based on the integrated representation of the different views in a single
meta model, we can define the rules governing movement and connectivity
as graph transformation rules typed over the corresponding package(s). The
basic operations of the style include *moveIn, moveOut, register, deRegister,
connect, disconnect* and *handOver*. Due to space limitations, operations
moveOut, register, deRegister and *disconnect* are omitted. *moveOut* and
disconnect are dual to *moveIn* and *connect*, respectively. The *register*
operation is responsible for subscribing a bridge on a client node with a
network, so that the client gets permission to connect via this bridge.
Operation *deregister* is, again, the dual.

In the left of Fig. 2 the *moveIn* rule is shown. According to its pre-
condition, expressed by the pattern on the left-hand side, there should be a
Node n and an Area whose types NT and AT should be connected by a
locatedAt link. That means the node is of a type that is supported by the area,
like a cell phone in a GSM cell. In this case, the rule can be applied with the
result of creating a new *locatedAt* link between the two instances. This is
expressed in the post-condition of the rule shown on the right-hand side. The
dual operation *moveOut*, specifying the deletion of a *locatedAt* link, is
omitted here.

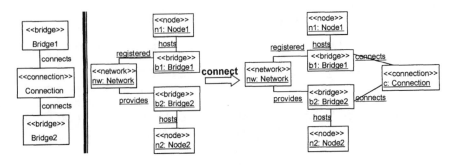

Figure 3. Transformation rule *connect*

In order to simplify the notation, we use a UML-like concrete syntax with separation of type and instance level and stereotypes to denote meta types. The corresponding presentation of the *moveIn* rule is shown in Fig. 2 on the right. The types declaration is separated from the actual rule by the black vertical line. The instanceOf relation is expressed in the standard way as *instance : Type*, while stereotypes like <<node>> represent meta types Node and NodeType.

Connecting is the act of building a network connection between two nodes through their bridges. The precondition of the rule in Fig. 3 requires the existence of a corresponding connection type between the two bridge types. Moreover, bridge b1 has to be registered with network nw provided by bridge b2. As postcondition, the desired connection c:Connection and its links are created. The dual rule *disconnect* for deleting a connection is, again, omitted.

These rules, as well as the following one, are typical for nomadic networks where a fixed infrastructure provides wireless connectivity to the mobile devices. Examples of such systems include mobile phone networks (GSM, GPRS, UMTS) or Wireless LAN.

Handover procedures are unavoidable in mobile system in order to realize seamless connectivity across different access points. At the physical link level, this means to preserve the connection between the moving terminal and its infrastructure [2], providing the same type of connectivity or switching from one type of connectivity to another as infrastructure coverage changes [4]. In higher-level protocols, like Wireless CORBA, one needs to support continuous object connectivity, using handover and tunneling between different bridges on the physical link layer. We give a handover rule typical for nomadic networks, where a fixed infrastructure provides connectivity to mobile hosts.

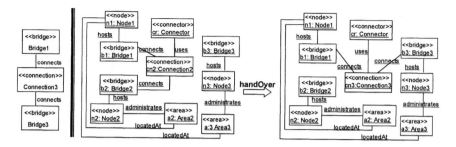

Figure 4. Transformation rule *handOver*

The rule shown in Fig. 4 explains how to maintain connectivity between administrative domains. It requires that node n1 is located in two areas served by two administrative nodes n2 and n3. Connector cr uses connection cn2 between bridge b1 and b2. The connection is replaced by cn3 of type Connection3 that, according to the types declared on the left, is permitted between bridges of type Bridge1 and Bridge3. The uses relation of the connector is transferred to the new connection.

3.   TOWARDS A QOS-AWARE STYLE

In this section, we indicate a possible extension of our model towards a style of systems that are aware of quality-of-service (QoS) properties, requirements, and their matching. Different applications may have different QoS requirements, and the degree to which this aspect is transparent varies greatly in different systems. For example, [17] discusses the pros and cons of application-transparent vs. application-aware adaption to changes of QoS properties. Therefore, the handling of QoS is an important aspect to be modeled as part of a style of systems.

Without aiming at a complete model of this aspect, we want to demonstrate how the behavior of the operations of our style can be controlled by QoS properties. We present a basic model of QoS in mobile systems, again consisting of a static meta model and graph transformation rules. Then we illustrate the concepts by an example.

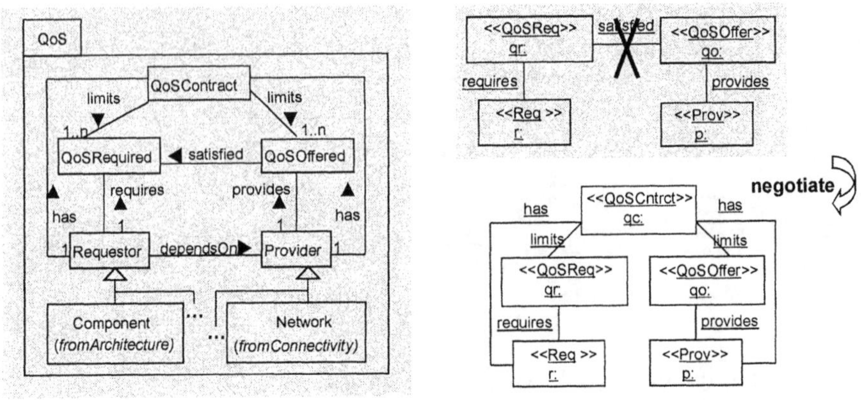

Figure 5. QOS package and transformation rule *negotiate*

3.1 Meta Model

The QoS package in left of Fig. 5 defines the basic concepts of QoS, i.e., requirements *QoSRequired* of service Requestors, properties *QoSOffered* offered by Providers, a dependency relation between Provider and Requestor, and a satisfaction relation between offered and required properties. The roles of Provider and Requestor can be played by any entity of the model, e.g., Network, Component, Connection, etc. A *QoSContract* is the result of a negotiation between Requester and Provider in case the offer does not meet the requirements, putting a lower limit to the first and an upper limit to the latter.

This quite general structure is a simplified version of the meta model of the UML profile for QoS [18]. An important difference is that, in our case, QoS is dealt with at the instance level, i.e., at run-time. For example, in [10] the authors stress that the major impact of mobility on QoS is due to the dynamic changes in the context of applications, and platforms like [17] monitor QoS changes at run-time to inform or adapt their applications. This does not exclude the specification and matching of QoS properties at the type level, but the instance-level is mandatory.

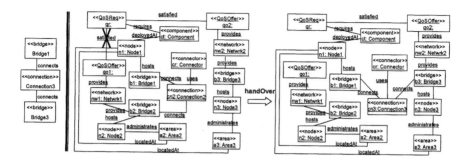

Figure 6. handOver rule with QOS

3.2   **Rules**

The effect of a negotiation between the QoS requester and provider when the offered QoS does not satisfy the requested QoS is defined by the rule *negotiate*. Since we consider QoS only at the instance level, the corresponding objects are labeled like *qo*: without type, but with stereotype <<QoSOffer>> referring to the meta type. The pre-condition of the rule in Fig. 5 on the right contains a negative application condition, represented by the crossed-out link, which makes sure that the rule is only applicable if the QoS requirements are not satisfied.

Note that match making in our model is abstracted through the *satisfies* association, while the detailed conditions for satisfaction and the protocols for negotiation are left open for possible refinements of the model towards a concrete platform.

As an example of how QoS may affect the behavior of operations of our style consider the extended *handOver* rule in Fig. 6. The idea is that the selection of the new bridge to connect to may depend on the QoS requirements of the application component as well as on the actual properties of available bridges. Both can, moreover, change over time.

Then, if the current network does not satisfy the current requirements, the responsible bridge will hand over to a bridge of a network where the requirements are satisfied. According to the left-hand side of the rule, it can only be applied if the quality of the current network is not satisfactory.

3.3   **Example**

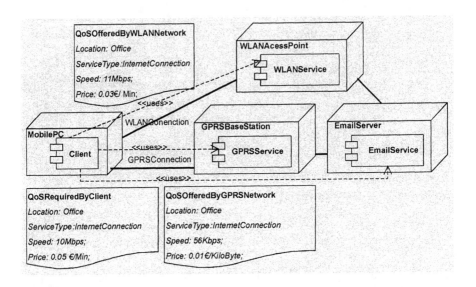

Figure 7. Application scenario with QOS (deployment diagram)

Let us conclude this section by giving an example for how to use our conceptual model in a concrete application. Assume a mobile PC equipped with Wireless LAN and GPRS cards, hosting a component that needs to access an Email server on a stationary host. We suppose that we have two areas for movement: the office and outside. Wireless LAN and GPRS networks are both available in the office, while outside only GPRS is available. Because of the higher speed and cheaper price, the system should use the Wireless LAN whenever available. However, when the user moves from the outside area to the office, the Email connector based on GPRS should not be interrupted while the underlying connection changes to Wireless LAN. The different QoS requirements and offers of the component and the two available networks are shown in the deployment diagram of Fig. 7.

This situation can be represented as an instance of the meta models introduced in this and the previous section. It should be clear that, being in the office, rule handOver in Fig. 6 will allow us to connect to the Wireless LAN, but not to the GPRS network. Fig. 8 shows a part of the configuration of the scenario before and after the application of this rule.

In the upper part of Fig. 8, the mobilePC has just moved from outside into the office. The lower part represents the configuration where the

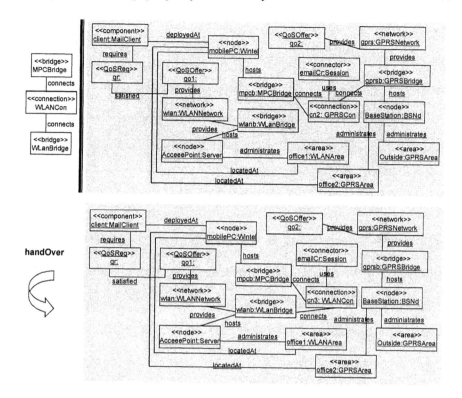

Figure 8. Configuration of the scenario before and after handover

mobilePC has been connected to the Wireless LAN network, while the Email connection has been be reserved.

4.   RELATED WORK

The general idea of modeling classes of systems with common structural and behavioral characteristics by a combination of meta modeling and graph transformation is due to [14], where it has been applied to software architecture styles. For distributed systems, [13] argues that rules should be strictly local, covering only the operation of a single component, while global effects should be achieved by synchronization. This restriction, however, does not apply to the high-level specification of operations at the system level.

A number of different process calculi have been proposed to describe the interaction and movement of mobile processes, mostly by extending the πcalculus [16, 12, 9]. In order to express runtime properties of mobile systems, some of these calculi have been complemented by logics [7, 15].

Apart from the fundamentally different appearance and style which, in our opinion, makes them harder to grasp for the average software engineer than our meta model-based approach, these process calculi with their associated logics have a complementary focus: They provide means for programming mobility in terms of the processes driving individual components or devices, rather than for its high-level conceptual modeling in terms of global pre- and post-conditions. In this sense, our model defines requirements, e.g., for handOver, while the actual protocol implementing the operation is more easily specified (and verified) in a process calculus.

Closer to our approach are some of the techniques proposed by the AGILE project [5], extending existing specification languages and methods. UML class, sequence, and activity diagrams are extended be features to describe how mobile objects can migrate from one host to another, and how they can be hosts to other mobile objects. In particular, their stereotypes <<mobile>> or <<location>> are not unlike our <<node>> and <<area>>. Graph transformation systems are proposed as a means to give an operational semantics to these extensions.

Other extensions are based on architectural description languages, like the parallel program design language CommUnity [3, 5]using graph transformation to describe the dynamic reconfiguration; Klaim as a programming language with coordination mechanisms for mobile components, services and resources; the specification language CASL as a means for providing architectural specification and verification mechanisms.

While Klaim and CASL are, again, more programming and verification-oriented, the approaches based on UML and CommUnity are at a level of abstraction similar to ours. However, the goals are different: Our focus is to model a style of mobile applications, e.g., corresponding to a certain mobility platform, while the focus in the cited approaches is on the modeling of applications within a style more or less determined by the formalisms. Indeed, being based on a meta model, our approach can easily specify styles exhibiting all kinds of features like QoS (as demonstrated above) or more sophisticated aspects of context awareness, handOver operations within one or between different networks, etc.

Finally, our three-layered approach provides a clear separation of the different views of software architecture, connectivity, and mobility, which is required in order to specify a physical phenomenon, like the loss of a signal, in relation with the intended reaction of an application or middleware platform, like the transfer of ongoing sessions to a new connection.

5. CONCLUSION

In this paper, we have presented a basic example for a style of mobile systems to illustrate how such styles can be defined using meta models and graph transformation. Not tailored towards a particular platform, the model reflects the properties of so-called nomadic networks, where mobile devices are supported by a fixed infrastructure. An extension towards QoS-dependent behavior of such systems is sketched and illustrated by an example.

In the future, we intend to use conceptual models like the one presented here as a means for classification, comparison, and improvement of mobility platforms. Moreover, the formal background of graph transformation systems can be exploited to analyze properties of systems by simulation.

Based on the operational semantics of graph transformation, a scenario represented by a trace of operations can be validated by executing the model starting from an initial configuration. Support for the execution of graph transformation systems is available, e.g., in tools like Fujaba [1] or PROGRES [22]. A major requirement here is a good visualization of configurations, since the meta model-based representation is not concise enough for larger examples.

REFERENCES

[1] From UML to Java and Back Again: The Fujaba homepage. www.upb.de/cs/isileit.
[2] I. Akyildiz, J. Mcnair, J. H, H. Uzunalioglu, and W. Wang. Mobility management in next-generation wireless systems. Proceedings of the IEEE, 87:1347– 1384, 1999.
[3] A. Lopes, J. Fiadeiro, and M. Wermelinger. Architectural primitives for distribution and mobility. In Proc. 10th ACM SIGSOFT symposium on Foundations of software engineering (FSE 2002), pages 41 – 50, Charleston, South Carolina, USA, 2002. ACM SIGSOFT.
[4] G. Alsenmyr, J. Bergstrm, and M. Hagberg. Handover between WCDMA and GSM, 2003.
[5] L. Andrade, P. Baldan, and H. Baumeister. AGILE: Software architecture for mobility. In Recent Trends in Algebraic Development, 16th Intl. Workshop (WADT 2002), volume 2755 of LNCS, Frauenchiemsee, 2003. Springer-Verlag.
[6] L. Baresi, R. Heckel, S. Thöne, and D. Varró. Modeling and validation of service oriented architectures: Application vs. style. In P. Inverardi and J. Paakki, editors, Proc ESEC 2003: 9th European Software Engineering Conference, pages 68–77, Helsinki, Finland, September 2003. ACM Press.
[7] L. Caires and L. Cardelli. A spatial logic for concurrency (part I). Information and Computation, 186(2):194 – 235, November 2003.
[8] L. Cardelli and A. Gordon. Anytime, anywhere. modal logics for mobile ambients. In 27th ACM Symposium on Principles of Programming Languages, pages 365–377. ACM, 2000.

[9] L. Cardelli and A.D. Gordon. Mobile ambients. In Foundations of Software Science and Computation Structures: First International Conference, FOSSACS '98. Springer-Verlag, Berlin Germany, 1998.

[10] D. Chalmers and M. Sloman. A survey of quality of service in mobile computing environments. IEEE Online Communication Surveys, 1(2), 1999.

[11] R. Heckel and G. Engels. Relating functional requirements and software architecture: Separation and consistency of concerns. Journal of Software Maintenance and Evolution: Research and Practice, 14(5), 2002. Special issue on Separation of Concerns for Software Evolution, edited by Tom Mens and Michel Wermelinger.

[12] M. Hennessy and J. Riely. A typed language for distributed mobile processes. In Proc. ACM Principles of Prog. Lang. ACM, 1998.

[13] D. Hirsch and U. Montanari. Consistent transformations for software architecture styles of distributed systems. In G. Stefanescu, editor, Workshop on Distributed Systems, volume 28 of Electronic Notes in TCS, 1999.

[14] Le Métayer, D. Software architecture styles as graph grammars. In Proceedings of the Fourth ACM SIGSOFT Symposium on the Foundations of Software Engineering, volume 216 of ACM Software Engineering Notes, pages 15–23, New York, October 16–18 1996. ACM Press.

[15] S. Merz, M Wirsing, and J. Zappe. A spatio-temporal logic for the specification and refinement of mobile systems. In Mauro Pezzé, editor, Proc. Fundamental Approaches to Software Engineering, 6th International Conference (FASE 2003), volume 2621 of LNCS, pages 87–101. Springer-Verlag, 2003. [16] R. Milner, J. Parrow, and D.Walker. A calculus of mobile processes. Information and Computation, 100:1–77, 1992.

[17] B.D. Noble, M. Satyanarayanan, D. Narayanan, J.E. Tilton, J. Flinn, and K.R.Walker. Agile application-aware adaptation for mobility. In Proc. of the 16th ACM Symposium on Operating Systems Principles, pages 276–287, 1997.

[18] OMG. UML profile for modeling quality of service and fault tolerance characteristics and mechanisms, 2002. http://www.omg.org/docs/realtime/03-08-06.pdf.

[19] G.-C. Roman, G. P. Picco, and A. L. Murphy. Software engineering for mobility: A roadmap. In A. Finkelstein, editor, Proc. ICSE 2000: The Future of Software Engineering, pages 241– 258. ACM Press, 2000.

[20] G. Rozenberg, editor. Handbook of Graph Grammars and Computing by Graph Transformation, Volume 1: Foundations. World Scientific, 1997.

[21] M. Satyanarayanan. Fundamental challenges in mobile computing. In Symposium on Principles of Distributed Computing, pages 1–7, 1996.

[22] Andy Schürr, Andreas J. Winter, and Albert Zündorf. PROGRES: Language and environment. In Hartmut Ehrig, Gregor Engels, Hans-Jörg Kreowski, and Grzegorz Rozenberg, editors, Handbook on Graph Grammars and Computing by Graph Transformation: Applications, Languages, and Tools, pages 487–550. World Scientific, Singapore, 1997.

A MULTIMODAL CONTEXT AWARE MOBILE MAINTENANCE TERMINAL FOR NOISY ENVIRONMENTS

Fredrik Vraalsen, Trym Holter, Ingrid Storruste Svagård, and Øyvind Kvennås
SINTEF ICT, N-7465 Trondheim, Norway

Abstract: Maintenance workers in the oil and process industry have typically had minimal IT support, relying on paper-based solutions both for the information they need to bring into the field and for data capture. This paper proposes *a mobile context aware system for maintenance work* based on electronically tagged equipment and handheld wireless terminals with a multimodal user interface. Particular attention has been given to voice interaction in noisy industrial scenarios, utilising the PARAT earplug. A proof-of-concept demonstrator of the system has been developed. The paper presents the demonstrator architecture and experiences gained through this work.

Key words: Mobile systems; maintenance; multimodality; context awareness; noise robustness; automatic speech recognition; electronic tags.

1.   INTRODUCTION

The process industry has implemented elaborate maintenance procedures to maximize production throughput and minimize downtime due to uncontrolled failures. Estimates show that for critical equipment, unplanned corrective maintenance costs on average three times more than planned maintenance work. Furthermore, estimates show that in process industry today, only about 65% of the total maintenance work hours are spent on actual repair work. The remainder is spent on preparations, searching for documentation, applying and waiting for work-permits, reporting etc. (SINTEF 2002). Another problem reported by our user group, described in chapter 2, is that the documentation of historical maintenance work is often not satisfactory. This is attributed to the process itself being cumbersome, and that the workers lack the incentive for it. The potential for quality improvement and cost reductions related to maintenance work seems obvious.

Mobile and wearable computers supporting maintenance and inspection tasks have been subject to attention from both researchers and suppliers for some years, such as for aircraft inspections and maintenance (Ockerman and Pritchett 1998)(Siegel and Bauer 1997), train maintenance (Siewiorek et. al. 1998) and maintenance of buildings and technical installations (Ailisto et. al. 2003)(Stäger et. al. 2003). A common focus has been increased efficiency and accuracy compared to paper-based approaches. Other focus areas include hands-free operation through the use of voice commands and heads-up displays (Ailisto et. al. 2003), context aware systems (Ockerman and Pritchett 1998), self-diagnostic systems and sensor networks (Stäger et. al. 2003) and remote collaboration through the use of wireless communication (Ockerman and Pritchett 1998)(Siewiorek et. al. 1998).

This paper presents a scenario based on the process industry. We propose a mobile maintenance support system designed specifically with a focus on multimodal user interfaces (Comerford et. al. 2001)(Huang et. al. 2001) suitable for hands- and eyes-free operation. Such interfaces offer the user freedom to use a combination of modalities depending on the specifics of the task or environment (Oviatt et. al. 2000). An unsolved problem in this field is the fragile performance of speech recognition in noisy environments (Cole et. al. 1995), making deployment in process industry challenging due to the potentially severe noise levels (Tempest 1985). This problem is addressed through the use of the PARAT earplug (Aakervik 2000)(*NACRE* 2004), an intelligent device designed for hearing protection, speech recognition and human-to-human communication in noisy environments.

The approach proposed here also utilises context information from electronic tags on equipment to automate equipment identification and facilitate onsite access to data in a backoffice maintenance system through wireless communication.

The remainder of this paper is organised as follows: Chapter 2 discusses the user requirements that form the background for the system design. A scenario and an overview of the proposed mobile system are presented in chapter 3. Chapter 4 describes the design and implementation of the proof-of-concept demonstrator. The paper closes with a discussion in chapter 5 and conclusions and future work in chapter 6.

2. USER REQUIREMENTS

The maintenance scenario and related user requirements were studied through a series of informal meetings with offshore personnel from a major oil company that were experienced with maintenance, both managers and field workers. The following were perceived as the most important areas for improvement:

1. Access to data: Retrieval of background maintenance data often involves searches in large paper-based archives. This process is time consuming, and too often the required material can not be found.

2. Quality of maintenance data: The quality of historical maintenance data is often substandard, and such data is thus of little help. One manager stated that "solutions that could lower the documentation threshold *just a little bit*, and make the workers report *some* more of their findings, would be a big improvement".

3. Information flow and work-processes: Work-orders and work-permits are most often paper-based. This process often introduces long delays as the documents travel between the involved parties.

4. Access to personnel: When a situation requires expert support, delays occur while waiting for such help. If advice could be given from a remote location, these delays could be avoided. In an offshore setting, this even opens for locating key personnel onshore, from where they could support multiple installations.

Based on this input, use cases were developed describing detailed user-system interaction and corresponding system response for a range of activities. The use cases were presented to the users for feedback and the system design was adjusted accordingly. The most important aspects of the user feedback can be summarized as follows:

- Mobile access to maintenance data such as work and safety procedures is a good idea. It is particularly important as it is a trend, especially offshore, that the personnel must be able to service an increasing number of different types of equipment, and the maintenance worker may not necessarily be an expert on all the equipment that he or she services.

- Many maintenance workers have little experience with mobile terminals. Thus particular emphasis must be put on usability and reliability aspects of the solutions. Including well known functionality and user interfaces (like mobile telephony) into the device could be a way to increase user acceptance.

- Hands-free operation of the device is required to make it simpler to document and report findings for work situations where the hands and/or eyes are busy.

- Electronic tagging of equipment is perceived as a good idea for several reasons. Most importantly it simplifies the equipment identification process and is less error prone and cumbersome than manual identification.
- The maintenance application must allow the worker to document irregular findings whenever and wherever he or she discovers them.

There are a number of user requirements beyond this, which our user group did not focus on. Most important among these were information security and safety requirements, such as ATEX (ATEX 1994). In our proof-of-concept demonstrator we chose not to focus on these issues. Human-to-human communication aspects (e.g., remote collaboration with experts) were also kept outside of the scope of work.

3. SYSTEM CONCEPTS AND OVERVIEW

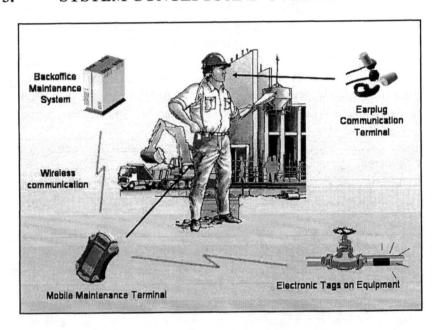

Figure 1. Conceptual overview

Figure 1 shows a conceptual overview of our suggested maintenance system. The following is a scenario that illustrates the system vision:

Maintenance worker Baker approaches gearbox GB-13-407 in area A30 for a routine inspection, in accordance with the work order just downloaded to his mobile maintenance terminal. As he approaches, his terminal communicates with the radio tag on the gearbox and verifies that Baker is at the right device. Before Baker can start the inspection, the system prompts him to read through a new safety procedure that recently has been implemented. He also takes a brief look at the maintenance log, downloaded in real-time from the backoffice maintenance system. Before he rolls up his sleeves and goes to work, he activates the application's speech mode by tapping the screen and puts the terminal in his belt. Audio prompts received through the earplug terminal guides him through the inspection procedure, one step at a time. The earplug eliminates the strong background noise and captures his commands and annotations flawlessly, allowing him to navigate through the check list and document his work with his hands free. At one point during the inspection he requests to see a technical diagram for guidance. He temporarily halts the procedure and inspects the diagram on the screen, before returning the terminal to his belt. On completion of the work, a report is compiled. Baker signs the report and is ready for the next work order on his list.

The rugged mobile terminal runs a dedicated maintenance application which communicates wirelessly with the backoffice systems. Electronic tags labelling the equipment provide context information and enable the application to present the user with information and services relevant to the current maintenance task (Dey 2001). The user can interact with the application in different ways based on preference or requirements of the current environment or task, and noise-robust speech recognition solutions facilitate hands-free operation even in harsh industrial environments. Services offered by such a system would typically include:

- Administrative tasks, such as work scheduling
- Display information about equipment, e.g. design schematics and maintenance logs
- Work support, interactively guiding the user through the maintenance process
- Log the performed tasks and measurements
- Automatically generate and transmit maintenance reports and notifications
- Cooperative maintenance work, e.g. on-line communication with experts

The system can also help improve safety by ensuring that procedures are followed, e.g. by handling work permits and including safety steps in the interactive maintenance guide.

The UML class diagram in Figure 2 shows a platform independent[1] view of the main maintenance system components. The maintenance application consists of components performing tasks such as generating reports and identifying equipment based on the tags. It can also contain a number of user

---

[1] Independent of implementation strategy, e.g. programming language or physical distribution

interface components, which may in turn rely on other components, e.g. for speech recognition and text-to-speech synthesis. A controller orchestrates the various components.

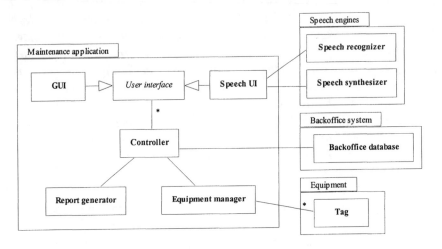

Figure 2. Main system components

4.   SYSTEM DESIGN AND IMPLEMENTATION

A demonstrator was implemented to show the core functionality of the maintenance system described in chapter 3. The main components of the demonstrator, their interrelationships, and their physical distribution are shown in the UML deployment diagram in Figure 3. The diagram is a platform specific realisation of the design in Figure 2. The remainder of this chapter discusses aspects related to the implementation of this design.

4.1   Development environment

The mobile device we have chosen for the demonstrator is an iPAQ 5450 PDA, as it contains most of the desired features, most notably built-in WLAN (802.11b) and Bluetooth for wireless communication and equipment identification, as well as support for connecting an external microphone. In addition, the iPAQ provides ample expansion capabilities through the use of various expansion jackets. The iPAQ is running Pocket PC 2002.

The mobile maintenance application has been implemented mainly in Java, using the Java 2 Micro Edition (J2ME) Personal Profile, and is running on the IBM J9 Virtual Machine. Some low-level features are implemented in

C/C++, described in more detail below. The backoffice maintenance system is a simple mock-up to allow testing of the mobile maintenance application. It consists of an Apache web server which provides the maintenance application with maintenance data, e.g. work orders and equipment technical data, and a simple server that receives and processes maintenance reports.

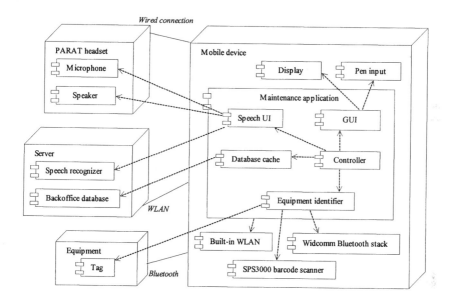

Figure 3. Maintenance system components and their physical distribution

4.2   Demonstrator functionality

The maintenance application initially displays an overview of current work orders. Selecting a work order, the user can view the work order details, such as maintenance procedure descriptions and equipment technical data, as shown in Figure 4, in addition to performing administrative tasks such as checking and requesting work permits. Once the user has selected a work order, he or she can start the inspection. The interactive maintenance guide is similar to a wizard dialog, consisting mainly of a sequence of questions with predefined answers, illustrated in Figure 5. The user can also attach comments to each maintenance inspection step in the form of free-text comments or audio recordings. Once the inspection is completed, the user is presented with a report summary for confirmation before sending the report to the backoffice maintenance system via the wireless network.

The maintenance application offers a multimodal user interface with support for speech-based input and output in addition to a GUI with pen-based input. The user can switch freely between the two modalities, allowing him or her to select the most suitable interaction method. One of the advantages of using speech input is that the user has both hands available for other tasks. This is even more important due to the small size of mobile devices, which often means that tactile input is cumbersome to use. The device also offers speech output for certain parts of the application. It is sometimes argued that speech output is impractical due to the amount of information (Ailisto 2003)). We find however, that during the wizard dialog, the amount of information is fairly small, and thus speech output is advantageous because it also allows *eyes-free* operation of the application.

One of the main obstacles to using interfaces based on speech technology is the fragile performance of speech recognition in noisy environments (Cole et. al. 1995). In the next section we describe how we aim to mitigate this problem.

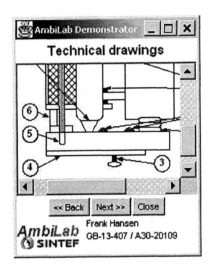

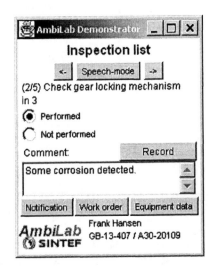

Figure 4. Equipment technical data   *Figure 5.* Inspection wizard

4.3   The PARAT communication terminal and automatic speech recognition

PARAT (Personal Audio/Radio Active Terminal) (Aakervik 2000)(*NACRE* 2004) is an intelligent hearing protector and audio interface for communication systems. A principle sketch is shown in Figure 6. An earplug with a seal sits in the ear. In a quiet environment the sound captured by the outer microphone is reproduced unaltered by the loudspeaker on the inside of the earplug. When the noise becomes severe, the transmission from the outer microphone is processed and gradually reduced.

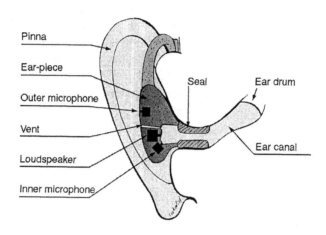

Figure 6. The PARAT earplug

The primary purpose of the inner microphone is to capture the user's voice in a manner that is robust against even strong ambient noise, and can be used both for voice communication and speech recognition purposes. This approach to speech recognition is complementary to the main-stream research in noise-robust speech recognition over the last few years, and has been shown to be successful (Strand et. al. 2003). Noise-robust speech recognition research has to a large degree been focusing on signal and feature compensation methods, driven through the ETSI Aurora initiative (*ETSI* 2004). The approach described here on the other hand focuses on the signal acquisition level.

For speech recognition we use Sprex ANSR (*Sprex* 2004), a network-distributed speech recognition system. Some initial processing of the speech input is done locally, e.g. to identify conversation end-points, before the processed data is transferred over the wireless network to a server where the actual recognition is performed. The results, i.e. the recognized phrases, are then returned to the client where they are used to generate the relevant UI events.

Given the fairly simple dialog structure and limited number of speech prompts, we have chosen to use pre-recorded speech for speech output. This gives better speech quality than a text-to-speech synthesis running on the PDA or on the network, of course at the cost of lower flexibility. The pre-recorded speech files are stored locally on the PDA.

4.4   Tag solution

In our application, tags serve the purpose of identification only; hence no data will be stored in the tags except for the ID of the object. Thus several tag types could be applied; both passive (no battery) and active (battery-powered) tags would serve the purpose.

The actual implementation offers three different methods, illustrating the choice and flexibility possible among tagging schemes. The primary method is using the built-in Bluetooth communication to read the unique Bluetooth address of a Bluetooth tag, deriving the equipment ID through a database lookup. This method illustrates active tags and the fact that objects can be identified without visibility to the physical tag. This approach enabled us to use readily available technology (Bluetooth is embedded in the iPAQ 5450, Bluetooth tags are easily acquired and protocol stacks exist), hence reducing implementation time and risk. The drawback is the limitations of battery life time, requiring batteries to be replaced at regular intervals.

To overcome the potential problem of battery life time, the demonstrator also supports scanning barcode-based IDs using the Symbol SPS3000 barcode scanner. Bar code scanning is an extremely cheap and extensively used technology, and virtually no maintenance is required. However, bar code scanning requires visibility which may be hard to satisfy in an industrial process plant.

Finally, as a supplement to Bluetooth and bar code scanning, the user can manually enter the ID. This is important as a fallback solution, both because deployment of new technology may be gradual and electronic tags may thus not always be available, and for robustness in case the Bluetooth or barcode solutions are not working.

Although not implemented in the demonstrator, other tagging methods would also be adequate in our application, in particular RFID, which solves both the problem of battery life time and visibility. RFID tags will be the subject of future extensions of the demonstrator.

4.5   Communication with backoffice system

The maintenance application uses the built-in WLAN to communicate with the backoffice maintenance system. As a constant network connection is assumed by the chosen speech recognition solution, there is no functionality that enables off-line work for the user in the current demonstrator. However, we do cache information related to the current work task locally, e.g. technical diagrams, mainly for efficiency reasons. This is most likely not a reasonable choice in a real production setting, but in this demonstrator the primary concern was to exhibit speech recognition and control.

XML (Extensible Markup Language) is deployed for information exchange between the backoffice system and mobile terminal. XML defines the structure of documents through the use of DTDs (Document Type Definitions) or XML Schema, but leaves the meaning or *semantics* up to the user and application. Practically all application content, i.e., work orders, inspection lists, equipment data, maintenance reports, etc., is defined in the form of XML documents with accompanying DTDs. This simplifies the procedure of adjusting the application in response to requirements changes and was found very useful. Furthermore, XSL (eXstensible Stylesheet Language) transformations can be used to translate between different XML formats and to other textual or binary data formats, facilitating integration with a wide variety of third party systems.

4.6   Implementation experiences

A number of low-level features of the PDA OS and hardware lack Java APIs in the J2ME Personal Profile, e.g. the Bluetooth stack. The AveLink Bluetooth Suite (*Atinav* 2003) provides a Java Bluetooth API (JSR-82 2004) implementation for J2ME, however this was not yet available for the iPAQ 5450 at the time of implementation. Instead, we used the Widcomm Bluetooth SDK (*WIDCOMM* 2003) for the iPAQ 5450 to implement a subset of the Java Bluetooth API using C++ and Java Native Interface (JNI). This solution provides us with a level of portability, allowing us to easily move the application to different platforms which provide the Java Bluetooth API. Similar solutions have been used for other low-level functionality, e.g. recording and playback of sound.

The use of Java and XML has made it simple to adapt the demonstrator to new and changing requirements. The portable nature of Java has also enabled a more rapid develop-test cycle, as we were able to develop and test most of the application (excluding the device specific functionality) on a regular PC before deploying it on the actual PDA. Testing on the PC was much faster, both as transferring updates to the PDA incurred an overhead and as the lower processor and communication performance on the PDA leads to more time-consuming testing. Furthermore, by utilising software design patterns such as MVC (Krasner and Pope 1998) and Mediator (Gamma et. al. 1995) we achieve a degree of decoupling which enables us to replace individual components without changing the rest of the system.

Accessing low level features through native code turned out to be a feasible workaround until implementations of the necessary Java APIs are available on the PDA. However, much of the device specific functionality was not covered by the standard Windows CE/Pocket PC API, and finding and acquiring the necessary development documentation and SDKs for the device specific features can be both time consuming and costly, if they are available at all.

5. DISCUSSION

Although limited, our user requirements studies indicate that usability is a prerequisite for successful introduction of mobile work support in maintenance and operations. Similar observations have been done by previous studies (Ockerman and Pritchett 1998)(Siegel and Bauer 1997)(Ailisto 2003). The users focus on hands- and eyes-free operation, and speech technology is thus a key component. We believe that the suggested multimodal interface with the PARAT earplug has the potential to meet these requirements. Preliminary tests show that it improves noise robustness compared to standard solutions and its unobtrusive form-factor ensures that it will not interfere with the physical activities involved in maintenance work.

Tags were introduced into the system concept to provide context awareness. The user's position relative to the equipment is verified, giving automated and error-free identification of equipment. With radio tags in particular, this can be achieved with no active intervention from the user. Other approaches to positioning are often promoted for safety reasons, to monitor the whereabouts of personnel in critical situations. This has not, however, been the focus of our study.

Another advantage of active radio tags is the possibility of local data storage. One way to exploit this possibility is to store the maintenance log on the tag, which will always follow the equipment. This would be an advantage especially for equipment that is moved around, or even sent away for service and repair. The main drawback of active tags is the fact that they require power supply, and effective schemes for this must be devised before this is a realistic option.

Bluetooth tags were chosen to demonstrate the concept of radio tags in the demonstrator. The same functionality could have been achieved with RFID, but Bluetooth tags were chosen due to the easy availability of devices and components.

WLAN was chosen for wireless communication much for the same reasons. It also seems to be a realistic future choice in our application scenario, due to the low cost of infrastructure and use, high bandwidth, and satisfactory range. WLAN security has also improved over the recent years.

For scenarios where geographical distance is an issue, GPRS would in many cases be a realistic option.

Probably the most important issues related to introducing this kind of new technology, are the required organizational and procedural changes. For the technology to have the desired effect, the implications on all levels of the organisation have to be considered carefully. It is very unlikely that this process will succeed unless the users are motivated for the change, and the key will be to involve the users in the further stages of implementation.

6. CONCLUSIONS AND FUTURE WORK

This paper describes user requirements, design and implementation for a mobile maintenance support system targeting process industry environments. The feedback from a focus group working on the user requirements showed clearly the importance of hands-free operation of the mobile device, and emphasis has thus been put on noise-robust speech recognition, facilitated by the PARAT ear-plug communication terminal.

The proof-of-concept demonstrator described in detail in this paper is based on context awareness through electronic tagging of equipment and a mobile maintenance terminal with wireless communication with a backoffice maintenance server. Initial tests of this approach validate its usability.

In the next stage of this work, our goal is to have a pilot implementation and evaluation, based on further development of the demonstrator, in a real scenario and with real users. Potential application areas are offshore and onshore process installations, but also other kinds of applications areas will be considered.

REFERENCES

Ailisto, H., Haataja, V., Kyllönen, V. and Lindh, M. (2003) 'Wearable context aware terminal for maintenance personnel', In: *Proceedings of The European Symposium on Ambient Intelligence (EUSAI 2003)*, Nov. 3-4 2003, Elsevier Science, Eindhoven, The Netherlands

Cole, R. et. al. (1995) 'The challenge of spoken language systems: research directions for the nineties', *IEEE Transactions on Speech and Audio Processing*, vol. 3, Jan. 1995, pp. 1 – 21

Comerford, L., Frank, D., Gopalakrishnan, P., Gopinath, R. and Sedivy J., (2001) 'The IBM Personal Speech Assistant', In: *Proceedings of IEEE International Conference on Acoustics, Speech, and Signal Processing (ICASSP 2001)*, May 2001, Salt Lake City, Utah

Dey, K. (2001) 'Understanding and Using Context', *Personal and Ubiquitous Computing*, vol. 5, pp. 4-7

Gamma, E., Helm, R., Johnson, R. and Vlissides, J. (1995) *Design Patterns – Elements of Reusable Object-Oriented Software*, Addison-Wesley

Huang X. et. al. (2001) 'MIPAD: A Multimodal Interaction Prototype', In: *Proceedings of IEEE International Conference on Acoustics, Speech, and Signal Processing (ICASSP 2001)*, May 2001, Salt Lake City, Utah

Krasner, G. E. and Pope S. T. (1998) 'A cookbook for using the model-view controller user interface paradigm in Smalltalk-80', *Journal of Object-Oriented Programming*, vol. 1, August/September 1998, pp. 26-49

Ockerman, J.J. and Pritchett, A.R. (1998) 'Preliminary Investigation of Wearable Computers for Task Guidance in Aircraft Inspection', In: *Proceedings of The Second International Symposium on Wearable Computers (ISWC '98)*, Oct. 19-20 1998, Pittsburgh, PA, pp. 33-40

Oviatt, S. et. al. (2000) 'Designing the User Interface for Multimodal Speech and Pen-Based Gesture Applications: State-of-the-Art Systems and Future Research Directions', *Human-Computer Interaction*, vol. 15, pp. 263—322

Siegel, J. and Bauer, M. (1997) 'A Field Usability Evaluation of a Wearable System', In: *Proceedings of The First International Symposium on Wearable Computers (ISWC '97)*, Oct. 13-14 1997, Cambridge, Mass, pp. 18-22

Siewiorek, D., Smailagic, A., Bass, L., Siegel, J., Martin, R. and Bennington, B. (1998) 'Adtranz: A Mobile Computing System for Maintenance and Collaboration', In: *Proceedings of The Second International Symposium on Wearable Computers (ISWC '98)*, Oct. 19-20 1998, Pittsburgh, PA, pp. 25-32.

SINTEF (2002), *Offshore Reliability Data Handbook (OREDA)*, 4th ed, Det Norske Veritas, Norway

Strand, O. M., Holter, T., Egeberg, A. and Stensby, S. (2003) 'On the feasibility of ASR in extreme noise using the PARAT earplug communication terminal', In: *Proceedings of IEEE Workshop on Automatic Speech Recognition and Understanding (ASRU 2003)*, December 2003, IEEE, Virgin Islands, USA

Stäger, M., Junker, H., von Waldkirch, M., Tröster, G. (2003) 'Using Wearables in Maintenance: A Modular Test Platform', In: *Proceedings of TCMC 2003: Workshop on Wearable Computing*, Mar. 11-12 2003, Graz, Austria

Tempest, W. (1985) Noise in Industry, in: Tempest, W. (ed) *The Noise Handbook*, Academic Press, New York, pp. 179-194

Aakervik, A.-L. (2000, Dec. – copyright date) "An earplug passes the word", (*Gemini*), Available: http://www.ntnu.no/gemini/2000-06e/09_1.htm (Accessed: 2004, May 25)

"ANSR – Action-oriented, Network-distributed Speech Recognition", (2004 – copyright date), (*Sprex*), http://cassandra.sprex.com/ansr/, (Accessed 2004, May 25)

"ATEX Directive 94/9/EC: Equipment and Protective systems intended for use in potentially Explosive Atmospheres", (1994, Mar. 23 – copyright date), (*European Union*), Available: http://europa.eu.int/comm/enterprise/atex/ (Accessed 2004, May 25)

"Aurora – Distributed Speech Recognition", (2004, May 25 – last updated), (*ETSI*), Available: http://portal.etsi.org/stq/kta/DSR/dsr.asp, (Accessed 2004, May 25)

"aveLink Bluetooth", (2003 – copyright date), (*Atinav*), Available: http://www.atinav.com/bluetooth/index.htm (Accessed 2004, May 25)

"JSR-82: Java APIs for Bluetooth", (2004 – copyright date), Available: http://www.jcp.org/en/jsr/detail?id=82 (Accessed 2004, May 25)

"Natural Communication in Rough Environments", (2004, Jan 30 – last updated), (*NACRE*), Available: http://www.nacre.no (Accessed 2004, May 25)

"WIDCOMM: Bluetooth Connectivity Solutions", (2003 – copyright date), (*WIDCOMM*), Available: http://www.widcomm.com/Products/bluetooth_comm_software_btce.asp (Accessed 2004, May 25)

WORKFLOW PARTITIONING IN MOBILE INFORMATION SYSTEMS

Luciano Baresi, Andrea Maurino, and Stefano Modafferi
Politecnico di Milano, Dipartimento di Elettronica e Informazione, piazza L. Da Vinci 32 - I20133 - Milano Italy, baresi, maurino, modafferi@elet.polimi.it

Abstract: The increasing success of wireless technologies is sustaining the diffusion of mobile information systems, but the youth of the underlying technology and its peculiar characteristics are impacting the development of such systems. For example, the execution of business processes in such a context must cope with the variable and fluctuating bandwidth available to the different devices. This leads the designer to stress the independence of each actor -- by minimizing interactions and knowledge sharing -- to increase the reliability of the whole system.

To this end, the paper proposes a rigorous approach for partitioning the execution of BPEL workflows on sets of portable devices, that is, the infrastructure of mobile information systems. The approach abstracts BPEL processes into attributed graphs and uses a graph transformation system as rules to split single workflows into meaningful sets of related processes. The paper presents such rules and exemplifies them on a case study in the cultural heritage domain.

Key words: Mobile information systems; distributed workflows; partitioning rules.

1. INTRODUCTION

In these years, mobile technologies are deeply changing our way of leaving. The more these technologies become reliable and widely available, the more business scenarios use them. New wireless technologies, like Bluetooth or Wi-Fi, are creating the technological backbone for mobile information systems (MobIS): The structure of these systems is not fixed and all business processes must be able to deal with nomadic actors and dynamic changes. It is true however that the youth and limitations of these technologies still impact the systems that run on them: Roaming, frequent disconnections, and security holes [Gaertner and Cahill, 2004; Vaughan-Nichols, 2003], along with the variable bandwidth offered by the wireless medium, must be taken into account to design and implement reliable mobile systems. The execution of a business process in a mobile environment - with different devices connected through different network technologies - needs new strategies with respect to the traditional solutions adopted for centralized workflows. These solutions rely on a single engine that knows and controls all system resources, but mobility demands for decentralized executions carried out by a federation of heterogeneous devices. All these requirements lead to a new strategy that stresses the independency among actors - to minimize the necessity of interaction and knowledge sharing - and thus increases reliability.

This paper tackles the problem by proposing formal partitioning rules to transform a unique workflow into a set of federated workflows that can be executed by different engines. This is the typical scenario where different devices contribute to the enactment of the whole process by executing a fragment and synchronizing with the others. The paper builds upon the approach described in [Maurino and Modafferi, 2004] for transforming BPEL processes and paves the ground to the release of an automatic slicing engine for the run-time partitioning of business processes.

Partitioning rules exploit the UML profile for BPEL [Thatte, 2003], to abstract workflows as attributed graphs (i.e., stereotyped activity diagrams), and graph transformation theory [Baresi and Heckel, 2002] to formally specify the steps that lead to the separate workflows (i.e., the set of graphs). The rules are implemented by using AGG (Attributed Graph Grammars, [Beyer, 1992]) as supporting tool for both modeling and validation. Two other results of the paper are the validation of the proposed rules and its application to a case study in the cultural heritage domain.

The paper is organized as follows. Section 2 introduces graph transformation to set the basis of this work. Section 3 describes the partitioning rules identified for moving from centralized to decentralized workflow executions. Section 4 applies the rules on an example process taken from the risk management in the cultural heritage domain. Section 5 summarizes the related work on decentralized workflow models and Section 6 concludes the paper.

2.   GRAPH TRANSFORMATION

Before describing our partitioning rules, we introduce graph transformation [Baresi and Heckel, 2002] as the formal background needed to understand them.

A *typed graph transformation system* $G = \copyright TG, C, R\rangle$ consists of a type graph TG, a set of structural constraints C over TG, and a set R of rules $p\colon L\phi$ R over TG. The type graph defines the types of nodes and edges that can be used to create graphs. The set of structural constraints identify constraints on how nodes and edges are linked, and rules state how graphs can be modified. In particular, a graph transformation rule $r\colon L\phi R$ consists of a pair of *TG-typed* instance graphs L, R such that the intersection $L∩R$ is well-defined (this means that, e.g., edges which appear in both L and R are connected to the same vertices in both graphs, or that vertices with the same name have the same types, etc.). In other words, the left-hand side L defines the pre-conditions that must hold on the graph to enable the rule while the right-hand side R describes the post conditions, that is, the modifications on the graph after applying the rule. The application of a graph transformation rule comprises three steps:

- We find an occurrence o_L of the left-hand side L in the current graph G (the BPEL process, in our case).
- We remove all the vertices and edges from G which are matched by $L \setminus R$. The remaining structure $D := G \setminus o_L (L \setminus R)$ must be a legal graph: no edges are left dangling because of the deletion of their source or target vertices. In this case, the dangling condition is violated and the application of the rule is prohibited.
- We glue D with a copy of $R \setminus L$ to obtain the derived graph H. We assume that all newly created objects, links, and attributes get fresh identities, so that $G∩H$ is well-defined and equal to the intermediate graph D.

Usually, rules must be composed to perform significant transformations. Thus, a transformation sequence $s = (G_0 \overset{p_1(o_1)}{\Rightarrow} \ldots \overset{p_n(o_n)}{\Rightarrow} G_n)$ in G, briefly $G_0 \overset{s}{\Rightarrow}_G^*$ G_n, is a sequence of consecutive transformations using the rules of G such that all graphs $G_0, \ldots, G_n$ satisfy the topological constraints.

In this paper, we concentrate on AGG (Attributed Graph Grammars, [Beyer, 1992]) to model and validate our rules. AGG allows users to specify complex structures as graphs and exploits the Java type system to associate attributes with values. It also supports layered rules where layers fix the application order among rules. The interpretation starts with level zero rules and then moves to higher ones. Besides pre and post conditions (left- and right-hand side graphs), AGG also supports negative application conditions, that is, sub graphs in the left-hand side that must not exist to enable the rule.

Additionally, rules can embed conditions on attribute values in the form of boolean Java expressions.

3. PARTITIONING RULES

The Business Process Execution Language for Web Services [Thatte, 2003], hereafter BPEL, provides an XML notation for specifying the behavior of businesses based on Web Services. A BPEL process is defined in terms of its interactions with the partners that provide services, require services, or participate in a two-way interaction with the process.

In this paper, we do not present the XML representation of these processes, but we adopt an extended version of the UML profile for automated business processes, described in [Gardner et al., 2003], to render workflows as stereotyped UML activity diagrams and thus attributed graphs. Translation rules are summarized in Table 1.

Table 1. Guidelines for the translation

BPEL Primitive	Graph Element
Basic Activities	Basic activities are rendered as `Activity` nodes. Each of these nodes has an attribute `device`, which stores the name of the device that controls the activity, a `type`, equal to `normal`, and a `name` equal to the one of the UML activity.
Links between activities	Links are rendered as edges of type `follow` between `Activity` nodes.
Structured activities	Structured activities are rendered with two special purpose `Activity` nodes. Their attributes `type` and `name` have the same values and are equal to `Start<Name>` and `End<Name>`, where `<Name>` is the type of the corresponding UML structured activity (e.g., `Loop` or `Switch`). Each structured activity is also associated with a number, which is assigned to the variable value of the two added `Activity` nodes.

Partitioning rules operate on such an abstract representation to create the set of cooperating workflows. The application of partitioning rules - and the execution of disconnected operations - requires the workflow meet the following requirements: (1) The control of the execution of a specific task can be assigned to a single device; (2) The `StartLoop` and `EndLoop` nodes of `While` structured activities must to be assigned to the same device; (3) The `Start` node of `Pick`, `Switch`, and `While` structured activities is in charge of evaluating the condition; (4) The workflow has no global variables and all the variables are passed as parameters between different actors. If all requirements are met, the partitioning process starts identifying where to partition the workflow and how to maintain the execution flow across structured activities. Then it defines the sub workflows by creating local views.

Rules are organized in layers that govern their applicability. Rules that belong to "low" layers are applied before those of "high" layers. Within each layer, rules can be triggered in a non deterministic way.

The lowest-level rules (layer 0) are devoted to synchronizing (delegating) the execution flow between two activities of a Sequence that are executed by different devices. Fig. 1(a) shows the AGG rule **AddDelegate** that synchronizes Sequences split on different devices. The rule can be applied if there is an Activity node (either simple or structured), controlled by an actor A_1 followed by another Activity node controlled by a different actor A_2. The right-hand side of the rule introduces two new special Activity nodes where the former is controlled by A_1, and the latter by A_2. These two nodes add a pair of invoke/receive activities to forbid the second activity to start before the completion of the first one. Notice that this rule is also able to partition Sequences that belong to Flow activities. The delegation (synchronization) is described by the delegate arc between the two newly introduced Activity nodes.

The main problem with partitioning structured activities, like Switch or Pick ones, is to be sure that all devices involved in such activities follow the same branch. In fact, while in Flow activities all branches are executed in parallel, in Switch activities only one branch is executed. Consequently, rules of layer 1 identify all the controllers involved in the structured activity while rules of layer 2 add a Flow activity before any Switch (resp. Pick) node to communicate the chosen branch to the other controllers.

Fig. 1(b) shows the rule **StartSwitch** (layer 1) that identifies Switch nodes. The right-hand side of the rule identifies the beginning of a Switch activity. Notice that the existence of the rule **AddDelegate** ensures that there is always an Activity node controlled by the same device as the one controlled by the StartSwitch node. Rule **AddStartSwitch** (layer 1), not shown here, marks all activities directly connected to StartSwitch nodes with isSwitched arcs. Each arc is enriched with two attributes: device and value. The former represents the device that controls the switch; the latter identifies the specific switch controlled by the device.

Starting form these isSwitched nodes, four further rules (layer 2) mark all activities involved in the Switch activity. Fig. 1(c) shows one of such rules. This rule is applied when a node with an isSwitched arc follows another node without such an arc. The right-hand side adds a new isSwitched arc to the latter node.

Similarly, the rules that belong to layers 1 and 2 deal with `Pick` structured activities. These rules are very similar to the ones described for `Switch` activities and are not shown here for lack of space. The partitioning of `While` activities is slightly more complex. The number of iterations is not known a-priori and the variables that control the loop can be updated by any actor involved in the activities that belong to the loop.

Consequently, like for other structured activities, we introduce a `Flow` activity before the `StartLoop` node, with the goal of communicating to the other devices involved in the `While` activity if the condition is satisfied. We also add another `Flow` activity before the `EndLoop` node to communicate to the other devices if the loop condition is still satisfied.

After suitably decorating `Switch`, `Pick` and `While` activities, the rules at layer 3 address the problem of partitioning them. These rules add special purpose activities to notify the branch followed by the execution of a given structured activity. Rule **RemoveSwitchArc**, shown in Fig. 1(d), describes it. The rule is activated when there is at least one activity marked with an `isSwitched` arc whose attributes device and level are equal to those of the `StartSwitch` node. If the left- hand side is matched, the right-hand side adds two new `Activity` nodes between the `Flow` activities created by the rules at layer 1. The last set of rules (layer 4) removes extra arcs added in layer 1. Fig. 1(e) shows the rule for removing `isSwitched` arcs.

After extending the host graph (BPEL process), we can create the local views to decentralize the workflow execution. By "local", we mean that each actor only knows its tasks, i.e., its sub-workflow. More details about local views in business processes can be found in [van der Aalst and Weske, 2001]. To create views, we set the context in terms of the actor (device) for which we want to produce the view and apply the following rules: (1) We remove all activities whose execution is not controlled by the current actor; (2) We translate all structured activities, with the exception of `Sequences`, that do not include local activities into `Sequences` with no tasks.

For example, Fig. 1(f) shows the rule **RemoveOtherDevice** that implements the first rule. The left-hand side is applied as long as we find a node not controlled by the specific device. The right-hand side removes that node and adds a direct arc to fill the hole, that is, between the two tasks before and after the removed one. Notice that even if the whole workflow is composed of one task only, it is always connected to the nodes that correspond to the start and end of the workflow. The rule that corresponds to the second bullet is not presented here.

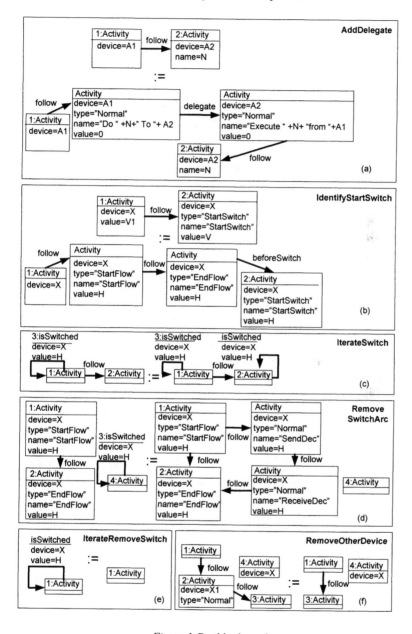

Figure 1. Partitioning rules

3.1 Validation

The feasibility of the described transformation depends on the assumptions that:

- Partitioning rules define a graph transformation system that exposes a functional behavior, i.e., is confluent and terminates;
- The execution flow of the original workflow is preserved. This means that the local process views do not alter the global execution.

The first assumption is mandatory to ensure that the actual transformation does not depend on the order with which we apply rules (confluence) and does not enter infinite loops (termination). In other words, even if we apply the same set of rules in a different order, we obtain the same result. The second assumption is needed to preserve the original "behavior" even if we move from centralized to decentralized execution. We can check the first hypothesis by exploiting the critical pair analysis capabilities supplied by AGG. The set of critical pairs represents precisely all potential conflicts: Given two rules p1 and p2, there exists a critical pair if and only if p1 may disable p2, or p2 may disable p1. If no conflicts exist between any pair of rules the graph transformation system has a functional behavior [Hausmann et al., 2002].

After designing our rules, we used AGG to check all possible pairs in the same layers, that is, all pairs of rules that could potentially be in conflict: After some modifications all layers do not present conflicts.

As to the second hypothesis, currently we do not have a formal way to prove that partitioning does not alter the execution flow. We are conducting experiments with formal models that allow us to analyze the execution traces in the two cases (i.e., centralized and decentralized execution), but currently our proof is based on the observation that partitioning rules only add activities to synchronize the different sub-workflows, which do not alter the execution flow. Even the rules that create the local views do not modify the execution flow because they create a view of the process by deleting those elements that are controlled by other devices and filling the holes with empty sequences.

Besides these two observations, our confidence is supported by the results obtained on several case studies. One of them is presented in the next section.

4.   EXAMPLE APPLICATION

This section demonstrates the application of our rules on a significant case study in the cultural heritage. Interested readers can refer to [Maurino and Modafferi, 2003] for more details on the example.

Italy probably hosts one of the widest and most significant cultural heritages in the world. Unfortunately, this abundance is in danger of destruction because of the many earthquakes, high density of population and, like all industrialization countries, high pollution. All these aspects impose the definition of an administrative and scientific instrument to manage and protect the huge cultural heritage. In 1990, the Italian government began a project to realize the risk map of cultural heritage (MARIS).

In this case study, we consider that the MARIS system can be improved by using cooperative mobile information systems in the data acquisition phase. The goal of this map is to create a complete repository of the state of all cultural heritages in a given region. In particular the risk map aims at allowing users to process data regarding territorial danger factors and vulnerability conditions of monuments and helping local and state administrations improve their decision-making processes for conservative interventions.

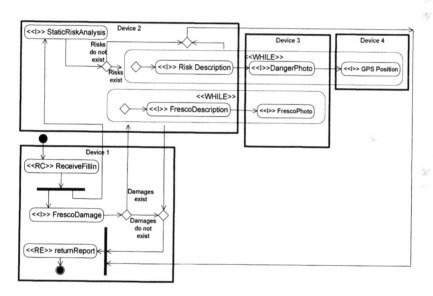

I = Invoke, RC = Receive, and RE = Reply

Device 1	Device 2
ReceiveFillIn receives the card that the team has to update. The completion of this task activates the Flow activity.	***StaticRiskAnalysis*** evaluates the number of external damages in the analyzed site.
FrescoDamage evaluates -- and if needed describes -- the damages on the frescos of the church.	***FrescoDescription*** supplies a textual description of damages on frescos.
ReturnCard returns the filled card after terminating all branches of the Flow activity.	***RiskDescription*** describes the risks from a given static problem in the site.
Device 3	**Device 4**
DangerPhoto takes a picture of the static risk.	***GPSPosition*** determines the exact GPS position of the static risk.
FrescoDamagePhoto takes a picture of the damage on frescos.	

Figure 2. The process with its portions assigned to the devices

Since we concentrate on the data acquisition phase, we consider that we have to define a risk level associated with each site and create a site description card to fully describe it. All data must be stored electronically and consequently the data acquisition is facilitated by the use of mobile devices like laptops, PDAs, or smart phones.

The whole process for managing the cultural risk map is composed of several sub/processes, some of them executed in parallel. The one presented here defines how to describe a given cultural site through a site description card (hereafter, card). The card is composed of a number of items and changes according to the specificities of what is described (e.g., a church, an archeological site, or an historical building). Fig. 2 shows a simplified process for filling in a card for a Romanic church, where we foresee the use of four devices.

The first step for partitioning the workflow of Fig. 2 is its translation into an AGG Graph. This is only a problem of using the right format: For example, the activity diagram can be saved as an XML/XMI file and then converted into a GXL file. XMI (XML Metadata Interchange) is the OMG standard XML format to exchange UML models. GXL is the XML-based language used by AGG to describe graphs.

Then AGG applies iteratively the rules described in Section 3 to decorate the workflow and then create the sub-workflows. For example, we can apply rule **AddDelegate** to the `StartController` of the `Flow` activity and the `StaticRiskAnalysis` activity to introduce two new tasks as shown in Fig. 3.

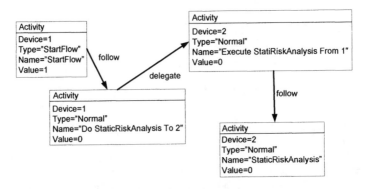

Figure 3. Example application of rule AddDelegate

The last step is the definition, for each device, of the local view of the workflow, which for the sake of brevity are super-imposed onto the workflow directly in Fig. 2.

5.   RELATED WORK

The opportunities given by workflow distribution have been thoroughly studied in the field of business process design in the last ten years. The main goal of this research is the cooperation/integration among different companies, that is, among different workflows. This problem reappears nowadays with mobile information systems and the problems that come with them. In [Jablonski et al., 2001], the authors present a comparison among the different approaches to distribution. Cross-Flow [Grefen et al., 2000] provides high-level support to work- flows in dynamically-created virtual organizations. Virtual organizations are created dynamically by contract-based match-making between service providers and consumers. In Agent Enhanced Workflow [Judge et al., 1998], the agent-oriented solution presents the interesting aspect of building execution plans using a goal approach. Event-based Workflow Process Management [Eder and Panagos, 1999] includes an event-based workflow infrastructure and addresses time-related aspects of process management. The main feature of ADEPT [Reichert and Dadam, 1998] is the possibility of modifying workflow instances at run-time.

In MENTOR [Muth et al., 1998], the workflow management system is based on a client-server architecture. The workflow is orchestrated by appropriately configured servers, while applications are executed on the client sites (where applications may in turn issue requests to other servers, no matter of the fact that the application is invoked within a workflow or not). In enterprise-wide applications, workflows may span multiple autonomous organizational units. Consequently, heterogeneity and scalability impose an approach in which a large workflow can be partitioned into a number of sub-workflows (e.g., based on organizational responsibilities) handled by different servers. It considers the workflow as a statechart that reflects the control flow among activities and uses orthogonal rules to partition it.

The METEOR (Managing End to End OpeRations [Anyanwu et al., 2003]) system leverages Java, CORBA, and Web technologies to support the development of enterprise applications that require workflow management and application integration. It enables the development of complex workflow applications that involve legacy information systems, are geographically distributed, and span multiple organizations. It also provides support for dynamic workflow processes, error and exception handling, recovery, and QoS management. Exotica [Mohan et al., 1995] is characterized by the possibility of disconnected operations. It does not permit complete decentralization because it maintains a central unit and all operations obey a client/server paradigm. WISE [Alonso et al., 1999] exploits the Web for its engine and offers an embedded fault handler. WAWM [Riempp, 1998] focuses on the problems related to workflow management in wide area networks. Mobile [Jablonski and Bussler, 1996] is developed to support inter-organizational workflows and is strongly based on modularity. This characteristic alleviates change management and also allows users to customize and extend aspects individually.

The analysis of these proposals suggests two different and dual approaches to the problem of workflow coordination. The first approach supports the integration of autonomous and preexisting workflows and it aims mainly at the coordination of different and independent actors.

The second approach supports the decomposition of single workflows to support its autonomous execution by means of different engines. Cross-Flow, Agent Enhanced Workflow, Event-based Workflow process Management, Adept, WISE and WAWM belong to the first approach. Mentor, Exotica and Mobile belong to the second class.

Described systems also offer three different solutions to the definition of partitioning and allocation rules. The first solution proposes specific definition languages (Cross-Flow, Agent enhanced workflow, Mentor, Exotica). The second solution proposes the extension of workflow languages with distribution rules (Cross-Flow, ADEPT, WISE, WAWM, Mobile). The third solution does not consider the language for distribution rules (Event-based, workflow Process Management). Cross-Flow belongs to more than one class because the distribution rules are split into several parts.

Our delegation model supports disconnected components, like Exotica, the independence of workflow engines, like MENTOR, and the possibility of modifying the workflow instance at run-time, like ADEPT.

Moreover, we argue that the mobile environment needs a language strongly oriented to the automatic execution, like BPEL, but we also demand for lightness, which is a mandatory feature if the system runs on portable devices in ad-hoc networks. As far as the definition of rules is concerned, our approach defines partitioning rules, but does not define allocation rules. It demands them to the specific business process and application domain.

6.   CONCLUSIONS AND FUTURE WORK

The paper presents an approach for partitioning the execution of BPEL processes onto a network of mobile devices. The approach produces an overall execution model that is "equivalent" to the centralized one, but supports disconnected components and independent workflow engines.

Partitioning rules are specified using a graph transformation system and implemented using a special-purpose tool called AGG. In this paper, we demonstrate that these rules do not alter the execution flow by means of sound observations and the presentation of a case study. The complete demonstration is part of our future work. We are also working on making presented rules more robust and on analyzing the transactional behavior of partitioned sub-workflows.

The final goal is the definition of an automatic engine for the run-time partitioning of workflows to execute them on a federation of mobile devices.

6.1.1   Acknowledgments

This work has been partially funded by the Italian Project MAIS (Multi-channel Adaptive Information Systems) [MAIS_Consortium, 2002].

References

Alonso, G., Fiedler, U., Hagen, C., Lazcano, A., Schuldt, H., and Weiler, N. (1999). WISE: Business to business e-commerce. In RIDE, pages 132--139.

Anyanwu, K., Sheth, A., Cardoso, J., Miller, J., and Kochut, K. (2003). Healthcare enterprise process development and integration. Journal of Research and Practice in Information Technology, 35(2).

Baresi, L. and Heckel, R. (2002). Tutorial Introduction to Graph Transformation: A Software Engineering Perspective. In proc. of the First International Conference on Graph Transformation (ICGT 2002), volume 2505 of Lecture Notes in Computer Science, pages 402--429. Springer-Verlag. Barcelona, Spain.

Beyer, M. (1992). AGG1.0 - Tutorial. Technical University of Berlin, Department of Computer Science.

Eder, J. and Panagos, E. (1999). Towards distributed workflow process management. In proc. of the Workshop on Cross-Organizational Workflow Management and Co-ordination, San Francisco, USA.

Gaertner, G. and Cahill, V. (2004). Understanding link quality in 802.11 mobile ad hoc networks. Internet Computing, 8:1:55 -- 60.

Gardner, T. et al. (2003). Draft UML 1.4 profile for automated business processes with a mapping to the BPEL 1.0. IBM alphaWorks.

Grefen, P., Aberer, K., Hoffner, Y., and Ludwig, H. (2000). Crossflow: Cross-organizational workflow management in dynamic virtual enterprises. International Journal of Computer Systems Science & Engineering, 15(5):277--290.

Hausmann, J. H., Heckel, R., and Taentzer, G. (2002). Detection of conflicting functional requirements in a use case-driven approach: a static analysis technique based on graph transformation. In proc. of the International Conference on Software Engineering, pages 105--115.

Jablonski, S. and Bussler, C. (1996). Workflow Management: Modeling Concepts, Architecture and Implementation. International Thomson.

Jablonski, S., Schamburger, R., Hahn, C., Horn, S., Lay, R., Neeb, J., and Schlundt, M. (2001). A comprehensive investigation of distribution in the context of workflow management. In proc. of the International Conference on Parallel and Distributed Systems ICPADS, Kyongju City, Korea.

Judge, D., Odgers, B., Shepherdson, J., and Cui, Z. (1998). Agent enhanced workflow. BT Technical Journal, (16).

MAIS_Consortium (2002) (http://black.elet.polimi.it/mais/). Mais: Multichannel Adaptive Information Systems.

Maurino, A. and Modafferi, S. (2003). Challenges in the designing of cooperative mobile information systems for the risk map of Italian cultural heritage. In proc. of the 1st Workshop on Multichannel and Mobile Information Systems, held in conjunction with the International Conference on Web Information Systems Engineering, 2003, Roma.

Maurino, A. and Modafferi, S. (2004). Workflow management in mobile environments. In proc. of the International Workshop on Ubiquitous Mobile Information and Collaboration Systems UMICS, Riga, Latvia. To appear.

Mohan, C., Alonso, G., Gunthor, R., and Kamath, M. (1995). Exotica: A research perspective of workflow management systems. Data Engineering Bulletin, 18(1):19--26.

Muth, P., Wodtke, D., Weisenfels, J., Dittrich, A. Kotz, and Weikum, G. (1998). From centralized workflow specification to distributed workflow execution. Journal of Intelligent Information Systems, 10(2):159--184.

Reichert, M. and Dadam, P. (1998). Adeptflex - supporting dynamic changes of workflows without losing control. Journal of Intelligent Information Systems, 10(2):93--129.

Riempp, G. (1998). Wide Area Workflow Management. Springer, London, UK.

Thatte, S. (2003). Business process execution language for web services. www-106. ibm.com/developerworks/webservices/library/ws-bpel/.

Vaughan-Nichols, S.J. (2003). The challenge of Wi-Fi roaming computer. IEEE Computer, 36:7:17--19.

Van der Aalst, W. M. P. and Weske, M. (2001). The P2P approach to interorganizational workflows. In Proc. of the Conference on Advanced Information Systems Engineering CAiSE, pages 140--156, Interlaken, Switzerland.

AN APPROACH TO MULTIMODAL AND ERGONOMIC NOMADIC SERVICES
A research experience and a vision for the future

Marco Riva and Massimo Legnani

Cefriel, via Fucini 2 - 20133 Milano (Italy), {surname}@cefriel.it
Tel.: +39 0223954 203 - +39 0223954 210
Fax: +39 0223954 403 - +39 0223954 410

Abstract: The technological evolution in the last few years in the field of devices and network infrastructure and the consequent diffusion of mobile devices have produced the need to allow different ways to use a Web hypertext. Since mobile applications are generally used on small devices with reduced capabilities, there is the need for services able to make the most of the resources available. Two possible approaches to this problem are the multimodal and the ergonomic delivery of hypertexts. In this article we propose a solution for these two approaches.

Key words: multichannel; multimodal; context aware; nomadic; ergonomic; hypertext.

1.   INTRODUCTION

Over the last few years Web applications have evolved in different ways, becoming richer, more interactive and more usable.

From the interactivity point of view it is possible to see a transition from simple static to transactional Web sites, where users may perform complex e-commerce operations like buying something or paying taxes and on without moving from their homes.

Another, even more important, revolution has been made in the field of devices. At the beginning of the history of the Web it was only possible to navigate the Web using a personal computer with a browser. It is possible to name this phase the "table Web", since users needed a table or a desk for their pc. As time passed, smaller devices were introduced and the Web became the "handbag" Web and then the "pocket Web". The Web had become movable.

The third factor of innovation is due to telecommunications: newer technologies have been introduced, allowing wider connectivity and higher bit rates. Nowadays devices are able to manage different kinds of networks (GPRS, UMTS, Wi-Fi) being able to stay connected while moving, as the context changes. Not only can the devices connect to networks, but also they are even able to communicate with each other creating personal area networks (PANs). It is then possible to use Web applications on a taxi, on a train, or even while walking. The Web has become "nomadic"[1].

With such technological changes it is necessary to allow different ways to use a Web application. Referring to the Web applications made to be used from a PC with a browser, we can observe a growing interest in the field of usability attempting to simplify the user experience of Web applications.

When talking about nomadic applications the problems and the situations involved are very different from the ones reported in the case of a "traditional" Web navigation. Mobile applications are generally used on small devices with different features and different capabilities and in a context that can vary very rapidly. The technological development has driven improvements in everyday user's life but the exasperated trend towards nomadic and mobile device miniaturization has led to many problems to both the uses and the service developers. The problems are mainly due to the interaction modes with the services. Displays, for example, may be very small, and keyboards are not suited to insert long text. Features that are advantages when talking about mobility, weight and smallness, may become drawbacks when the user needs to use the device.

To improve accessibility and usability to hypertext content, but also to simplify the user-service interaction new access channels, like for example voice control or DTMF (dual-tone multifrequency), were introduced. Moreover, new service adaptation technologies were proposed to adapt contents and services to the user's terminal and device characteristics.

Web applications, developed and delivered as hypertext are now accessible every time and everywhere. The Web has become so big that today it is the best way to find services and contents to solve everyday problems, but also for work, leisure and to meet other people connected to the Internet.

---

[2] Due to the arguments treated, in this article the terms "nomadic" and "mobile" are considered as synonyms.

However, is today the interaction with Web applications natural? Why don't we try to improve the interaction with services and contents, like for example as in a man-to-man communication?

Man to man communication uses different modes to communicate: voice for long text, visual interaction for images, gestures to improve the communication.

Multimodal delivery of hypertexts offers a possible solution to these kinds of problems. The possibility to interact with the device using different modes allows the user to send inputs and receive outputs in the way he feels more natural and adequate to the service he is using, to its preferences, and to the situation in which he is.

Services with multimodal access may then cover a fundamental role in the future development and success of the Web applications intended for heterogeneous devices.

Different market researches [2] have shown that multimodal services may improve everyday life of service users, increase the user satisfaction and become a competitive advantage for the firms proposing them.

To achieve these goals, a new framework, M^3L [3], has been studied and developed. This framework allows "multimodal hypertext" definition and delivery. Since at the moment only text and voice technologies are available, our multimodal solution only deals with these two modalities. The framework has been designed to be "open" and it may be easily extended adding other interaction modalities. Now it is possible to define a hypertext in which we can specify content that has to be spoken, shown, or both. The same is valid for the input and navigation between pages: we can specify which input is to be completed by voice, by text or pointing, or both.

The user can interact with the service using the best mode for the specific part of the content, as decided at design-time by the hypertext designer.

However, may the designer foretell the best interaction mode at design-time? This is true for standard web applications, where users access the Web contents and services using a PC in their office or at home. But this is not true for a nomadic or mobile user [4]. This kind of user may be in different situations, where one mode is better than another; this is not predictable at design-time, but the best time to make this selection is at run-time. For a nomadic user not only the best interactive modes need to be selected at run-time but also content, hypertext navigation [5] and presentation need to be adapted at run-time to the situation the user is in. An hypertext, able to be adapted at run-time, depending on the delivery environment properties surrounding the user, its preferences and the device being used to improve usability and service's agreeable, is called "ergonomic hypertext".

To adapt a service to the delivery environment we need to know the context information. New technologies for context capturing are available and in the future more a more are going to be available.

Context aware services are sensitive to the state of the context in which they are used. Context awareness is a possible solution to improve the delivery of hypertext on small mobile and nomadic devices. Context-awareness is also one of the most important factors enabling the creation of ergonomic services.

According to what we said, an ergonomic service is also able to select the best interaction mode depending on the situation in which it is delivered. This property is very important for Web services and content created for a nomadic user.

The approach to multimodality and to ergonomic service followed in this work is focused on the following main assertions:

- The service must be written once and automatically deployed and supplied
- The service model has to be simple and easy to translate into XHTML
- The adaptation of contents, presentation, and hypermedia structure must be made server-side so that no particular requirement must be imposed on the client devices. This approach is different from multimodal client-side like SALT [13] or X+V[14] [15] in which the client has to support specific and often proprietary technologies
- The proposed solution must work with today available standard technologies (XHTML, voiceXML, HTML, WML, etc) and devices (PDA, Mobile Phone, Laptop, Smart Phone, etc.)
- The user may use one or more devices by different access modes. This is not possible in client side solution like x+v or SALT.
- The framework must be an open framework, so that it is possible to improve the framework with the new technologies that will be available.

This document describes the results of our research activities and the architecture of the prototype we built to demonstrate the validity of the approach.

This paper is organized as follows: in the first section we describe the M^3L language, that we have defined for the writing of multimodal services and the multimodal delivery framework that we have developed to deliver the multimodal hypertexts written with M^3L. We then describe the ergonomic delivery platform and the eML language, for the delivery of ergonomic services. It must be noted that the main aim of this paper is to describe the multimodal solution while the ergonomic aspects of the problem are mainly introduced to show how the proposed solution may be simply used in the nomadic and ergonomic contexts. The final section of the paper contains our conclusions.

2.   MULTIMODAL DELIVERY

There are different definitions of the term "multimodal", but in this paper we adopt a W3C (World Wide Web Consortium) [6] derived one:

"Multimodal interaction will enable the user to speak, write and type, as well as hear and see using a more natural user interface than today's single mode browsers"

With the term "multimodal" then, we mean the possibility to interact with a service using different modes. As a consequence, a multimodal service must be able to support different input and output modes.

In our work, as input modes, we refer to the voice and to the keyboard of a mobile device (PDA or smartphone); voice, audio, written text and images have been chosen to be the output modes. This choice has been made considering the capabilities and characteristics of the devices available on the market. Actually, the modes supported by the devices are the ones listed above.

Anyway, when richer devices will be available, it could be possible to consider other interaction modes, like gestures and haptics, for example.

The solution that we propose for the multimodal delivery of hypertexts allows writing services once. The service is then automatically delivered to the user allowing him the use of different interaction modes.

The solution that we propose for the multimodal delivery of hypertexts is thought to be used in the situations where the hypertext is the same independently from the delivery channels, so that it is possible to write a service once. This solution is not suited to write services where the contents or the structure must be different on the different channels.

The integration of our solution with a methodology (and related tools) for the design of hypertexts [7] that considers different site views for different channels may anyway solve the problem. An example of such a methodology is WebML [8] (and WebRatio).

The main goals of our multimodal delivery platform are:

- The user must be able to interact with the service using the most natural interaction mode.
- Different channels must be used to offer a service to the wider set of users.
- The hypertext creator must define an intrinsic multimodal service to improve service usability and service pleasantness

The framework built allows:

- The access to the services using market available devices.
- The use of currently available delivery technologies. No specific software is needed onboard the device.

2.1   Approach

Our approach to multimodality starts from the experience with multichannel frameworks.

In a multichannel environment, the user must be able to use the same application using different channels (but only one at a time). It is then possible, for example, to use the same service both from a Web browser running on a desktop PC and from the microbrowser of a mobile phone and from a telephone connected to a voice gateway.

A new multichannel markup language [9] was defined. This language is used to write new services (existing ones may be anyway simply manually translated). Every multichannel document written in this language carries extra information about the objects contained, like their essentiality for the overall document comprehension.

The multimodal solution described here starts from our multichannel work, introducing the possibility to use in a coherent and synchronized way the different interaction modes supplied by different channels. It is possible to use a single device (supporting different modes) or even different devices each supporting a subset of the interaction modes.

The same device (or different devices) may then access the same multimodal service using one or more different channels that must be synchronized and coherent while with the multichannel approach only a channel at a time is used.

A new multimodal markup language, called M^3L, has been defined. This language is aimed at writing hypertexts.

The M^3L language allows writing a service that can be delivered using at the same time multiple interaction modes. A prototype shows the integrated "vocal" and "visual" interaction modes being used to deliver web hypertexts. The language offers to the developer a set of attributes and elements that allow to:

- Select the better interaction mode to present the different contents
- Define the modes that can be used to interact with the service
- Force the user to input data only availing of specific mode(s). For example, it is possible to force the user to insert his password only by keyword.

M^3L has been derived from XHTML, adding new elements and attributes. Those elements are used to manage the synchronization of the inputs from the user (essentially during forms definition) and to allow the developer to choose the best interaction mode to deliver the outputs.

2.2   Implementation

Figure 1 shows the architecture of the multimodal delivery platform built: the two modes supported (vocal and visual) are managed using two different channels that are simultaneously open.

The framework proposed here allows a user to interact with both a graphic interface (visual mode) and a vocal one. Those interfaces may be accessed by adequate browsers, able to interpret HTML and VoiceXML documents.

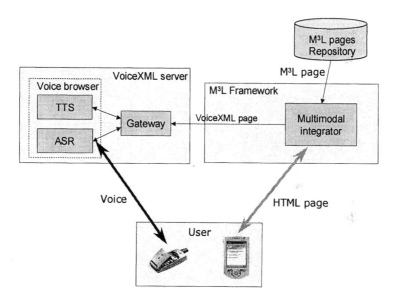

Figure 1. Proposed architecture

The *multimodal integrator* is the core of the multimodal framework we built because it manages the overall operation logic of the system and integrates the inputs coming from the different channels and modes connected. The integrator determines the outputs to send to the user and manages the synchronization between the different channels.

The multimodal integrator is completely written in the Java language and can be installed on any platform supporting the J2EE technology.

The process followed by the integrator to deliver contents to the user is here briefly described:

- At the first request, the multimodal integrator creates a new user's session and sends back to the voice server the VoiceXML initial document. It then creates an applicative session that is necessary to synchronize the different modes used.

- When the user connects to the system with an HTML browser (or with a phone to the voice server) the multimodal integrator asks to the user to login; then takes the current session and finds the M^3L document to be delivered. After that it applies to the M^3L document a set of XSLT transformations thus obtaining the VoiceXML and HTML pages. The multimodal integrator then creates a finite state machine from the M^3L page requested by the user. This machine synchronizes the inputs and outputs coming from and directed to the user on the different channels.
- The pages just created (or part of this) are sent to the browsers that will interpret them.
- The multimodal integrator waits for requests coming from one of the channels in use. These requests may be updating requests, requests of a new M^3L page, requests carrying data inserted by the user or commands.
- Depending on the requested operation, the multimodal integrator sends the updated page or the new page requested or the page resulting by the execution of the command or update requested.

The *M^3L repository* is the container of the multimodal services and contents.

The *voice server* is the component that allows the vocal communication between the user and the service. It receives the VoiceXML documents generated by the multimodal integrator for the communication with phones, interprets them and manages the vocal interaction with the user. A TTS (text-to-speech) is used to generate the speech to the user, while an ASR (Automatic Speech Recognition) is used to manage the speech of the user and then to collect input data. The IBM WebSphere Voice Server SDK was used, but every VoiceXML compliant voice browser may be used. The voice server enables the vocal interaction allowing the transmission of the voice over ordinary PSTN or GSM networks. As an alternative, it is possible to directly send the VoiceXML file to the client as long as it has an adequate vocal browser.

2.2.1   The M^3L language

The M^3L language was defined as a set of XHTML modules [10]. New tags have been inserted and among them the most important ones are:
- <label> that associates a label to the different input tags available in the language (as in HTML 4.01 specification);
- <menu> that allows to create link groups, that is to say menus. Grouping anchors is important relating to the voice channel since the reading of a long list of links would be very boring for the user.

The new language specifies even a set of new attributes associated to the elements of a page. Those attributes allow the service developers to select the preferred (or compulsory) delivery or input mode.

The *out* attribute allows specifying which modes can be used to deliver to the user the content of an element. This attribute is made available to any tag that contains information to be presented to the user.

The *mode* attribute, instead, specifies the modes that a user can use to input data. It is then associated to form fields and, relating to our base framework, may have three possible values: "text" to indicate that the user can use a keyboard, "voice" to indicate that the user may use his voice and "all", to say that every known input mode may be used (this values may be extended to support new interaction modality).

The multimodal integrator analyzes these attributes during the transformation from M^{3}L into the two VoiceXML and HTML documents.

If, for example, the <p> tag has the "out" attribute set to "visual", the text contained will be delivered only with a visual mode (a screen, for example).

2.2.2   Problems solved by the proposed framework

The design of a multimodal delivery platform for hypertexts requires the resolution of different problems. These problems are essentially due to the use of different channels and modes at the same time.

The need to line up the different channels is the most important problem in the multimodal delivery, since it is necessary to offer to the user the sensation to dialog with the same service even when using different devices. Synchronization has the objective to align the data flows sent or received by the different channels used at the same time.

It is possible to separately deal input (from the user to the service) and output (from the service to the user) synchronization problems. The data inserted by the user in the form fields, the navigation commands and the page change requests are managed by a component in the multimodal integrator that generates and maintains the information about the data inserted by the user.

The founding idea of the synchronization mechanism implemented in our framework consists in the extrapolation of a set of tasks from the M^{3}L document being processed. The sequence of tasks reproduces the steps that must be performed to complete the service distribution. For any input the user must give to the platform, the system creates a task that will be completed by the user with the insertion of the requested information. Only the available/allowed modes may be used. Once a task is completed, the system processes the next one requesting again the insertion of the needed information. The insertion may be performed only with the modes that are allowed in the M³L document (with the *mode* attribute).

The multimodal integrator manages this process extracting the flow of tasks directly from the M³L document and then generating a finite state machine memorized on the server.

Depending on the collected data and on the reached state, the multimodal integrator determines both if the data insertion is completed and the correct VoiceXML dialog to send.

3.   ERGONOMIC MULTIMODAL DELIVERY

According to the definition from IEA (International Ergonomics Association) [11] ergonomics is the scientific discipline concerned with the understanding of interactions among humans and other elements of a system, and the profession that applies theory, principles, data and methods to design in order to optimize human well being and overall system performance.

We consider ergonomics to be the science that studies the relationships between man, machine and environment to obtain the best mutual adaptation.

Therefore, in our case, an ergonomic service must be able to adapt its presentation, contents and navigation to the status of the context that is to the delivery environment, user preferences and device features.

Being our ergonomic solution an evolution of the multimodal research activities, the channels and the modes considered are the same described for the multimodal delivery.

Ergonomic hypertexts are enabled by a framework that has been built to develop and deliver applications able to adapt themselves to the context, thus becoming more appealing as the situation changes. An ergonomic service can automatically propose different interaction modes, different contents and adequate graphical layouts as the context changes.

3.1   Approach

As described above, M³L allows specifying the modes to be used to deliver every single part of the contents of an application. With the same approach it is possible to specify which modes can be used to input data, from the user to the service itself.

The choice of the modes that best fit the user's needs in M³L is made at "design time", when the service is created, but since it is possible to use the service in very different situations, the "design time" forecasts may be wrong. If, for example, the vocal mode is chosen to input the information for a search engine, the service cannot be used when the user is in an extremely noisy environment.

There is the need to design a solution for the adaptation of the service and of the interaction modes to the state of the environment in which the user may be. This can be achieved selecting at "run-time" the best interaction mode(s) between the user and the service itself.

The next step is to introduce ergonomic features in the multimodal platform.

This platform may be very useful in every application requesting a great amount of interaction between the user and the machine, like information kiosks (at the airport, at the station, in a public building). Typical goals of the platform are:

- Simplifying the creation and use of applications usable [12] by people with disability.
- Reaching a wider set of users
- Increase the usability of the service
- Increase user satisfaction

There are two main concerns that have to be solved in order to achieve these objectives and then allow the ergonomic creation of services:

- Define a model for the description of context information. This model must be abstract enough to be independent from the measurement (capturing) systems (like environmental sensors, body sensors and so on).
- Define the model of an "ergonomic service". This model must describe a service that can perceive the context information available.

The approach followed to make an ergonomic service is to support a static service, placing side by side a set of active ECA (Event Condition Action) rules. These rules can make the service reactive to the available context information since allow to specify:

- An "event" part, used to catch changes in the context status
- A "condition" part, where a set of predicates allow to choose the activation of the rule, on the basis of the information related to the event occurred
- An "action" part, where the actions to be taken are listed. These actions must be done only if the rule is activated.

We designed a new XML language aimed at writing "adaptable" services. This language was named eML (ergonomic Markup Language) and it is thought to write Web hypertexts that can react to context changes by ECA rules.

eML allows describing the parts that compose a service, the elements that make up the parts of the service and the actions that may be applied to the elements.

The language is composed of a passive and a reactive section. The passive section describes the non-ergonomic aspects of the service and is composed of:

- Contents: the information exchanged between the user and the service
- Navigation: navigation paths available to reach the contents
- Style: styles applied to the page
- Layout: the structure of the page

On the other side, the reactive section of the language is used to express the rules that make the service reactive to changes in the context (events).

The general idea of our approach is shown in figure 2.

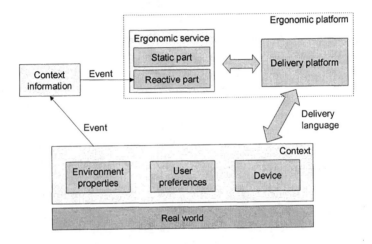

Figure 2. the approach to ergonomic services

4.   RELATED WORK

To improve the results of our recent research activities, we are working on different approaches to improve user-service interaction and hypertext delivery mechanism.

The first activity is to try to define "design methodologies" and "development tools" able to create ergonomic nomadic services, accessible by different "channels" also simultaneously (multimodal ergonomic services for Nomadic and mobile users).

The second activity is to improve the multimodal technologies available, putting together different approaches available for multimodal delivery of content. In this activity we propose a service model and a set of related tools to select the multimodal system available to the user in the specific situations the user may be and using available devices. If the user, for example, has a SALT capable browser (client side approach to multimodality) we can deliver the modeled services as a "SALT" service. On the contrary, if the user has two devices (for example a mobile phone and a video-text guide), we provide the services in M^3L like mode, delivering the voice part to the mobile phone and the visual part on the visual terminal.

Another active work is the MAIS project. We are trying to put together a data intensive hypertext methodology (WebML and a WebML run time, like WebRatio) with the multimodal delivery ergonomic system presented here. The primary goal is to improve methodologies, and provide tools to simplify the design and implementation of multimodal adaptive services.

Finally we are working on the Nomadic Media project, that aims at integrating advanced interaction modes like gesture and haptics with classic interaction modes (voice, video, text, etc) to provide the best available value added service to a Nomadic User.

5. CONCLUSIONS

In this paper we described the M^3L framework and language that support the creation and the delivery of multimodal hypertexts. In addition we mentioned the eML language for the delivery of ergonomic hypertexts.

M^3L provides an easy way to write and delivery newly made multimodal services while eML allows writing and deploying ergonomic services.

Starting from our previous experience, we demonstrated that, with simple extensions (a few attributes and tags) to the XHTML language, it is possible to create very powerful and automated multimodal and ergonomic applications, only using currently available technologies (devices, standard, etc.).

We are now working on the extension of the data intensive methodology WebML, which is our proposal for adaptive hypetext modeling; eML is the language defined to write ergonomic services. The language defined for the final (multimodal) delivery is M^3L.

It is then possible to model a data-intensive hypertext application using WebML* and then make it ergonomic and context-aware specifying its implementation and a set of active rules using the eML language. An eML service may be delivered to the final user by the M^3L multimodal framework proposed here.

This solution is suited even for the multimodal and ergonomic delivery of contents to persons with disabilities.

The typical problems of disabilities, in fact, may be solved with the eML & M^3L solution when considering that all the people have, more or less, disabilities, depending on the specific situation they are. A person with disabilities has specific needs, as anyone else has, and thus, considering the disability as a part of the context, it is possible to define a set of adaptive rules with eML to adapt the service to the specific needs of a person with disabilities like it is possible for the person that hasn't disabilities.

Even if this approach does not allow solving all the accessibility problems of all the people with disabilities (like, for example, cognitive disability where contents have to be different), the union of the multimodal ergonomic delivery with the "site view" approach of WebML may be suited for most cases.

REFERENCES

[1] Leonard Kleinrock - Nomadic Computing - an opportunity - January 1995.
[2] Comverse - Comverse And The Yankee Group Announce Preliminary Results From User Research Into Multimodality - 19 February 2002 (http://63.64.185.200/news/news_big.asp?cat=65&newsid=247)
[3] Marco Riva, Massimo Legnani, Maurizio Brioschi - Multimodalità nella fruizione dei servizi - 07 October 2003. MAIS report 7.1.1
[4] M. Weiser - The Computer for the 21st Century - November 1991
[5] Andrew Dillon - Designing usable electronic text: ergonomic aspects of information usage - 1994
[6] W3C Activity - Multimodal Interaction Activities (http://www.w3.org/2002/mmi/) – 2002
[7] Niels Erik Wille - Hypertext concepts: A historical Perspective - November 2000.
[8] Stefano Ceri, Piero Fraternali, Aldo Bongio – Web Modeling Language (WebML): a modeling language for design Web sites – WWW9 Conference May 2000 - http://www.webml.org/webml/upload/ent5/1/www9.pdf
[9] Massimo Legnani, thesis "CDI-ML: Channel and Device Independent Markup Language", October 2000
[10] W3C Recommendation - Modularization of XHTML - 10 April 2001. Available online at http://www.w3.org/TR/xhtml-modularization/
[11] IEA (International Ergonomics Association), "The Discipline of Ergonomics", http://www.iea.cc/ergonomics/, August 2000
[12] Maurizio Boscarol - Che cos'è l'usabilità dei siti web – novembre 2000 - http://www.usabile.it/012000.htm
[13] SALT – Salt forum (http://www.saltforum.org) – 2002
[14] W3C Note - X+V – XHTML + Voice Profile 1.0 (http://www.w3.org/TR/xhtml+voice/) - 21 December 2001
[15] VoiceXML forum - X+V – XHTML + Voice Profile 1.2 http://www.voicexml.org/specs/multimodal/x+v/12/spec.html - 16 March 2004

TOWARDS HIGHLY ADAPTIVE SERVICES FOR MOBILE COMPUTING*

Alessandra Agostini[1], Claudio Bettini[1], Nicolò Cesa-Bianchi[2], Dario Maggiorini[1], Daniele Riboni[1], Michele Ruberl[3], Cristiano Sala[3], and Davide Vitali[1]

[1]DICo, University of Milan, Italy
[2]DSI, University of Milan, Italy
[3]B Human Web Factory, Milan, Italy

Abstract: The heterogeneity of device capabilities, network conditions and user contexts that is associated with mobile computing has emphasized the need for more advanced forms of adaptation of Internet services. This paper presents a framework that addresses this issue by managing distributed profile information and adaptation policies, solving possible conflicts by means of an inference engine and prioritization techniques. The profile information considered in the framework is very broad, including user preferences, device and network capabilities, and user location and context. The framework has been validated by experiments on the efficiency of the proposed conflict resolution mechanism, and by the implementation of the main components of the architecture. The paper also illustrates a specific testbed application in the context of *proximity marketing*.

1.   INTRODUCTION

The continued growth in the amount of content and the number of information services available on-line has made effective personalized content delivery a hot research topic. Considering the increasing capabilities

* This work has been partially supported by Italian MIUR (FIRB "Web-Minds" project N.RBNE01WEJT_005)

of mobile infrastructure and device hardware, mobile devices will probably become the most common clients for on-line information systems. User-orientation and personalization in mobile information systems has been recognized as a major research challenge [20]. Indeed, due to the heterogeneity of these devices, new aspects should be taken into account for effective adaptation, among which device capabilities and status (e.g., screen resolution, battery level, network available bandwidth). Mobility also leads to a much wider variety of user contexts including but not limited to spatio-temporal data (e.g., location, speed, direction), and social setting situations (e.g., business meeting, home, shopping). If known by the service provider, this data can be extremely valuable for adapting content delivery. In our framework, we extend the notion of *profile* data to include all the information that can contribute to achieve an effective adaptation.

Current approaches to mobile oriented adaptation are still quite limited. In most cases, they are technically based on transcoding, and conceptually based on the assumption that device capabilities can be deduced by the HTTP request headers. Moreover, most approaches assume that user profile data is available server-side. We believe that, despite a lot of information can be gathered server-side, either explicitly given by the user or deduced by historical data on interactions with the same user, this information cannot include many of the relevant aspects we have mentioned above. In our view, profile data is naturally distributed and should not be forced to be stored and managed only server-side. In our framework, each source of profile data (e.g., user, network operator, service provider) has an associated trusted profile manager, which is typically running on a wired infrastructure, and that can communicate with other profile managers. Hence, profile data can be stored and managed locally and selectively made available to service providers. It is the responsibility of service providers to access the portion of profile data needed for the services they are delivering. User profile data can be made available to a new service provider by simply allowing access to the user profile manager. This model, by storing and managing profile data at the source, also avoids consistency problems upon updates of profile attributes (consider e.g., spatio-temporal or social setting information). Upon each user request the service provider profile manager is responsible for querying the necessary profile managers and aggregating profile data. This task includes solving conflicts due to different values provided by different entities for the same attribute. The introduction of profile managers also implies the adoption of a standard formalism for the representation of profile data, enabling the interoperability among the various entities.

In order to achieve enhanced personalization, our framework also allows users and service providers to augment the profile attributes with policies; that is, rules that set or change certain profile attributes based on the current values of other profile attributes. Clearly, the introduction of policies makes it possible to have, once more, conflicting attribute values, even considering only policies from the same entity (service provider or user). For this reason, the policy evaluation mechanism defined by the framework includes a quite involved conflict resolution technique.

The main contribution of this paper is the presentation of the architecture of our framework, first from a logical point of view, and then from an implementation point of view, in terms of a software architecture. Finally, in this paper we present a test case with an *adaptive proximity marketing* application used to validate our prototype on a real domain. A theoretical and experimental study on the soundness and efficiency of our conflict resolution mechanism has also been performed that validates our approach in terms of performance and scalability, but details are beyond the scope of this paper. For lack of space, we cannot include in this paper the discussion of two relevant issues: 'intra-session' adaptation, and privacy. We just mention here that we devised a distributed trigger mechanism for the former, and adopt access control techniques [3, 16] for the latter.

The rest of the paper is structured as follows: In the following section we give an overview of the framework logical architecture illustrating the formalism used to represent profiles and policies, the role of the main modules and the techniques used for conflict resolution. In Section 3 we illustrate how each component of the logical architecture has been implemented in the corresponding software architecture. Section 4 presents a testbed application used to demonstrate the system prototype. Section 5 discusses related work and Section 6 presents future research directions.

2. ARCHITECTURE

In this section we describe the logical architecture of our framework, starting with a list of requirements that have driven the design process. We then present its main components as well as the issues related to profile and policy representation and management.

2.1 Requirements

Based on an analysis of a large spectrum of Internet services that would benefit from adaptation, of the data required for implementing highly adaptive services, of the infrastructure that is available now and will available in the near future, as well as of the issues of data privacy and accessibility, we have identified the following set of requirements. (*i*) A representation formalism is needed for the specification of a very broad set of profile data, which integrates device capabilities with spatio-temporal context, device and network status, as well as user preferences and semantically rich context; (*ii*) A representation formalism is needed for the specification of policies, which can dynamically determine the value of some profile data or presentation directives based on other values, possibly provided by different entities; (*iii*) Vocabularies and/or ontologies should be defined in order for different entities to share terms for the specification of profile attributes; (*iv*) The architecture should support the distributed storage and management of profiles and policies, with information stored and managed close to its source; (*v*) The architecture should provide a mechanism to aggregate profile data and policies from different sources, supporting a flexible and fine-grained conflict resolution mechanism; (*vi*) The architecture should rely on an advanced system for privacy protection which allows the user to precisely control the partial sharing of his profile data; (*vii*) The architecture should provide a configurable mechanism for 'intra-session' adaptation based on real-time update of certain profile data (e.g., location).

Clearly, efficiency should be taken into account when evaluating different solutions, even if efficiency requirements may vary based on the considered service.

2.2   Architecture Overview

The specification and implementation of a full-fledged architecture satisfying all the requirements illustrated above is a long-term goal. The contribution illustrated in this paper is a first step in this direction. We present an architecture where three main entities are involved in the task of building an aggregated profile, namely: the user with his devices (called *user* in the rest of the paper), the network operator with its infrastructure (called *operator*), and the *service provider* with its own infrastructure. A Profile Manager devoted to manage profile data and policies is associated with each entity and will be called *UPM*, *OPM*, and *SPPM*, respectively. In particular, (*i*) The UPM stores information related to the user and his devices. These data include, among other things, personal information, interests, context information, and device capabilities. The UPM also manages policies defined by the user, which describe the content and the presentation he wants to receive under particular conditions; (*ii*) The OPM is responsible for managing attributes describing the current network context (e.g., location, connection profile, and network status); (*iii*) The SPPM is responsible for managing service provider proprietary data including information about users derived from previous service experiences. Clearly, the architecture, including conflict resolution mechanisms, has been designed to handle an arbitrary number of entities (e.g., profile managers owning context services).

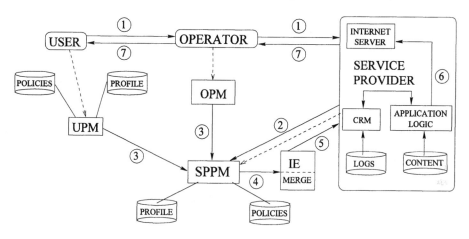

Figure 1. Architecture overview and data flow upon a user request

Figure 1 provides an overview of the proposed architecture. We illustrate the system behavior by describing the main steps involved in a service request: *(1)* A user issues a request to a service provider through his device and the connectivity offered by a network operator; *(2)* The service provider queries its Profile Manager (SPPM) to retrieve the profile information needed to perform adaptation; *(3)* The SPPM queries the UPM and the OPM to retrieve profile data and user's policies; *(4)* The SPPM then forwards collected and local profile data and policies to the Inference Engine (IE); *(5)* The IE first merges profile data; then, it evaluates service provider and user policies against the merged profile, resolving possible conflicts. The resulting profile attributes are then returned to the Service Provider; *(6)* These attribute values are used by the application logic to properly select content and customize its presentation; *(7)* Finally, the formatted content is sent to the user.

2.3 Profile Management and Aggregation

In the following we explain the mechanism of profile management, and address the issue of how to aggregate possibly conflicting data in a single profile.

2.3.1   Profile representation

In order to aggregate profile information, data retrieved from the different profile managers must be represented using a well defined schema, providing a mean to understand the semantics of the data. For this reason, we chose to represent profile data using the Composite Capabilities/Preference Profiles (CC/PP) structure and vocabularies [19]. CC/PP uses the Resource Description Framework (RDF) to create profiles describing device capabilities and user preferences. In CC/PP, profiles are described using a 2-level hierarchy; attribute values can be either *simple* (string, integer or rational number) or *complex* (set or sequence of values, represented as rdf:Bag and rdf:Seq respectively). CC/PP attributes are declared in RDFS vocabularies. In addition to well known CC/PP-compliant vocabularies for device capabilities like UAProf [24] and its extensions, our framework assumes the existence of vocabularies describing information like user's interests, content and presentation preferences, and user's context in general. Clearly, there are several issues regarding the general acceptance of a vocabulary, the privateness of certain server-side attributes, and the uniqueness of attribute names. In this paper, we simply assume there exists a sufficiently rich set of profile attributes that is accessible by all entities in the framework. We also simplify the syntax used to refer to attributes avoiding to go into RDF and *namespace* details.

2.3.2   Profile aggregation and conflict resolution

Once the SPPM has obtained profile data from the other profile managers, this information is passed to the IE which is in charge of profile integration (Step 4 in Figure 1). Conflicts can arise when different values are given for the same attribute. For example, the UPM could assign to the *Coordinates* attribute a certain value x (obtained through the GPS of the user's device), while the OPM could provide for the same attribute a different value y, obtained through triangulation. In our architecture, resolution of this kind of conflicts is performed by the Merge submodule of the IE. In order to resolve this type of conflict, the Service Provider has to specify resolution rules at the attribute level in the form of priorities among entities. Priorities are defined by *profile resolution directives* which associate to every attribute an ordered list of profile managers, using the *setPriority* statement. This means that, for instance, a service provider willing to obtain the most accurate value for user's location can give preference to the value supplied by the UPM while keeping the value provided by the OPM just in case the value from the UPM is totally missing. Continuing the above example, the directive giving higher priority to the user for the *Coordinates* attribute is:

setPriority Coordinates=(UPM,OPM)

Profile resolution also depends on the type of attribute. With respect to attributes of type Bag, the values to be assigned are the ones retrieved from all entities present in the list. If some duplication occurs, only the first occurrence of the value is taken into account (i.e., we apply the union operation among sets). Finally, if the type of the attribute is Seq, the values to be assigned to the attribute are the ones provided by the entities present in the list, ordered according to the occurrence of the entity in the list. If some duplication occurs, only the first occurrence of the value is taken into account.

2.4   Policies for Supporting Adaptation

As anticipated in the introduction, policies can be declared by both the service provider and the user. In particular, service providers can declare policies in order to dynamically personalize and adapt their services considering explicit profile data. For example, a service provider can choose the appropriate resolution for an image to be sent to the user, depending both on user preferences and on current available bandwidth. Similarly, users can declare policies in order to dynamically change their preferences regarding content and presentation depending on some parameters. For instance, a user may prefer to receive high-resolution media when working on his palm device, while choosing low-resolution media when using a WAP phone. Both service providers and users' policies determine new profile data by analyzing profile attribute values retrieved from the aggregated profile.

2.4.1   Policy Representation

Each policy rule can be interpreted as a set of conditions on profile data that determine a new value for a profile attribute when satisfied. A policy in our language is composed by a set of rules of the form:

If C_1 And ... And C_n Then Set $A_k=V_j$

where A_k is an attribute, V_j is either a value or a variable, and C_i is either a condition like $A_i=V_l$ or *not* A_i with the meaning that no explicit nor derived value for A_i exists. For example, the informal user policy:

"When I am in the main conference room using my palm device, any communication should occur in textual form"

can be rendered by the following policy rule:

"If *Location*='MConfRoom' **And** *Device*='PDA' **Then Set**
PreferredMedia='Text'"

2.4.2   Conflicts and resolution strategies

Since policies can dynamically change the value of an attribute that may have an explicit value in a profile, or that may be changed by some other policies, they introduce nontrivial conflicts. They can be determined by policies and/or by explicit attribute values given by the same entity or by different entities. We have defined conflict resolution strategies specific for different conflict situations. While a complete description of possible conflicts and of the solutions implemented in our architecture is beyond the scope of this paper (see [4] for further details), here we just mention the basic technique. We implement conflict resolution strategies by transforming the logical program defined by the policy rules. Transformations basically consist in the assignment of a proper *weight* to each rule and in the introduction of negation as failure. In the resulting program, each rule with a generic head predicate A and weight w is evaluated only after the evaluation of the rule with the same head predicate and weight $w+1$. When a rule with weight w fires, rules with the same head predicate having a lower weight are discarded. The weight assignment algorithm ensures that the evaluation of the program satisfies the conflict resolution strategies, and a direct evaluation algorithm can be devised that is linear in the number of rules.

3.   SOFTWARE ARCHITECTURE

An illustration of the software modules which have been developed is shown in Figure 2. There are two distinct data flows, which correspond to profile modifications and service requests, identified by Sequence I and II, respectively.

The local proxy (C) is an application running on the user device which adds custom fields to the HTTP request headers, thus enabling the SPPM to locate the user's ID and the URIs of his UPM and OPM. Currently, the local proxy is developed in C# (see Figure 3-A) and can be executed over the .NET (Compact) Framework. The UPM, OPM and SPPM consoles (B, P, Q) are browser-based web applications, which allow to modify profile attributes on the UPM, OPM and SPPM repositories. The Service Provider Application Logic module (E) is the component which delivers the profile- and context-dependent service to the user. The application logic implementation depends on the type of service to be delivered; the implementation of the application logic for the prototype web application we developed is briefly described in Section 4.

Besides managing local profiles and policies, the SPPM retrieves data from the remote profile managers and from its own repositories and feeds them to the Merge (I) and IE (J) modules. The integrated profile is returned via SOAP to the service provider application logic. The Merge module (I) receives from the Business Logic EJB (H) the profile resolution directives and the objects representing the remote profiles. Attribute values are retrieved from profiles using RDQL, a query language for RDF documents implemented by the Jena Toolkit [17]. The integrated profile is built by applying the service provider profile resolution directives, as explained in Section 2. Finally, the object representing the integrated profile is forwarded to the Inference Engine module (J), together with the set of user and content provider policies, and profile resolution directives.

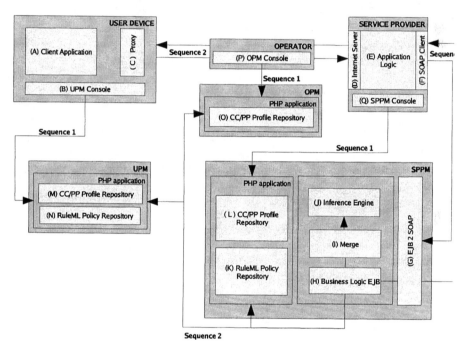

Figure 2. The developed software modules

Before starting the evaluation phase, the IE module modifies the logic program (composed by facts retrieved from the integrated profile, and policies) in order to apply the conflict resolution strategies described in Section 2. User and service provider policies are represented in RuleML [5]. The evaluation of the logic program is performed using Mandarax, an open source Java package for deductive rules. Mandarax is designed as a backward reasoning engine, and supports negation as failure, which is needed in our case to implement the conflict resolution mechanism. The output of the derivation process is a result-set in which every row contains a value of an attribute. These values are used to update the Java object representing the integrated profile, which is returned to the EJB (F).

Our planned technology for the Profile Managers includes the adoption of an RDF server such as Joseki [18]. However, at the time of writing, the profile repositories (L, M, O) are a collection of simple files in CC/PP format. Policy repositories (K, N) are a collection of RuleML files which describe the user and service provider policies.

Figure 3. Some screen-shots of the web application prototype

4.   AN ADAPTIVE PROXIMITY MARKETING SERVICE

In order to test our software architecture we developed a set of prototype services. In this section, we illustrate a web-based adaptive proximity marketing service. Its main goal is to provide targeted, location-aware *advertisements* about sales on items contained in a user's personal shopping list. For example, if the user's shopping list includes a specific camera model and the user is walking on a street where a shop has that camera on sale, the service will list an appropriate geolocalized ad on the user's device, possibly linked to multimedia content details. While we are not the first to consider such a service, our emphasis is on adaptation based on user and service provider policies. Advertisements are chosen and ranked by considering not only the personal shopping list, but other profile data such as the user's location, interests, and action context. Users can be either paying or non-paying service subscribers. Non-paying subscribers may also receive *unsolicited advertisements* regarding items which are not on their shopping list. The choice of items for unsolicited advertisements can be driven by standard CRM software as well as from aggregated profile data. The service currently implemented is browser-based, and provided on a per-request basis (i.e., it is a pull service). The service is activated by accessing a specific web page, and the delivery of content is performed by the Cocoon programming framework [10]. Upon each request, the service returns a web page with the list of ads, which is automatically refreshed after a certain period of time. This time is dynamically set server-side based on aggregated profile data, and communicated to the (micro) browser using a META element.

Table 1. An excerpt of policies

Policy	Owner
(1) If *DeviceType* = 'PDA' Then Set *MediaQuality* = 'High'	user
(2) If *AvailableBandwidth* < 56kbps Then Set *MediaQuality* = 'Low'	service provider
(3) If *UserSpeed* = 'Slow' Then Set *RefreshTime* = '15min'	service provider
(4) If *UserSpeed* = 'Fast' Then Set *RefreshTime* = '3min'	service provider

Table 2. An excerpt of profile resolution directives

Profile Resolution Directive
(5) *setPriority AllowRecommandations = (SPPM, UPM)*
(6) *setPriority Coordinates = (UPM, OPM)*
(7) *setPriority MediaQuality = (SPPM, UPM)*
(8) *setPriority UserSpeed = (UPM, OPM, SPPM)*

In order to show some of the profile resolution directives and policies which determine service adaptation, we report one of the test cases we have considered: An hypothetical user is browsing around a hypothetical town with a PDA in his hands. We appropriately divided the town into bi-dimensional cells identified by a pair of coordinates, further assuming that some of the cells are covered by a GPRS connectivity service, while others by a more efficient WiFi HotSpot service. Movements of our user and context changes are simulated. The service needs to continuously adapt to user's changes of context. The screen-shots in Figure 3 show how different ads are displayed depending on the user's location and time of the day. In addition, the presentation is properly adapted to the user's device capabilities and available bandwidth. The adaptation parameters are set by the IE module, upon the evaluation of policies declared by the user and by the service provider. For instance, we suppose the user declared policy (1) in Table 1 to request high-quality multimedia content when using his PDA. Similarly, service providers can declare policies for determining content and presentation directives. A possibly conflicting policy (2) is declared by the service provider, stating to deliver low-quality multimedia contents when the available bandwidth drops below a certain threshold. The refresh rate of the service is determined by policies (3) and (4). In particular, policy (3) determines a long refresh interval when the user is moving slowly, while policy (4) shortens the refresh interval when the user is moving fast.

The firing of policy rules may depend on the aggregated profile obtained by the Merge module, which in turn relies on profile resolution directives. We remind that this kind of directives can only be specified by the service provider. Some profile resolution directives are given in Table 2. For instance, directive (8) is intended to solve conflicts due to different estimations of the user's current speed given by different entities. The service provider gives higher confidence to the value provided by the UPM, since speed can be estimated precisely by user-side sensors (e.g., supplied by car appliances or GPS-enabled devices). If no value for speed is given by the user, the value provided by the operator (if present) is taken into account; otherwise, the value inferred by the service provider analyzing the history of the user's location is chosen.

5.   RELATED WORK

Many research groups and companies have been working, at different levels, to provide effective solutions for service adaptation and personalization in a multi-device and mobile environment. In the following, we report on the efforts we consider closer to our work. Our approach is similar to the one underlying DELI [8] and Intel *CC/PP SDK* [6]. However, our framework provides a finer control on profile aggregation, and includes a policy mechanism. Various other architectures address the problem of service adaptation in mobile environments [2, 7, 9, 11, 14, 21]. The distinguishing feature of our architecture is that in our case the adaptation process is driven by the evaluation of distributed profile data and policies which are stored on and handled by modules in the trusted domain of their data source. For example, the Houdini framework [14] provides a mechanism of rule evaluation against user context information that is similar to ours. However, policy rules in [14] are specified by users only and stored on and handled by a single module. Since efficiency is a major concern in their applications this module is in the domain of the service provider. Moreover much less emphasis is given to conflict resolution issues.

We claim that our framework is able to support a wide range of context-aware applications, which can profitably exploit it for adapting and personalize their services to users. Even focusing on the domain of the application described in this paper, the number of related works is large (e.g., [12, 15, 23]). In particular, the ViaVis' Proximity Marketing allows users to personalize the reception of advertisements in terms of their location, time and content. Again, a main difference in our service is that profile data and user preferences are not stored and managed at the service provider, but kept in the user trusted domain (at the UPM). This has several advantages especially when multiple services need to access overlapping portions of profile data (centralized updates, privacy control). Moreover, our solution provides users with a richer set of personalization parameters, which allow for a better definition of user contextual situations and a finer personalization of the service.

6.   CONCLUSIONS AND FUTURE WORK

In this paper we presented a framework supporting adaptation and personalization of mobile Internet services. We illustrated the software architecture adopted for its implementation, and a prototype service used as a test-bed. Even if the main components of the framework are consolidated, various extensions and enhancements are possible and already foreseen. In particular, our profile technology can be meaningfully coupled with various content-based services and recommendation systems. Thanks to our framework, these systems can exploit both the explicit rules expressed as preferences by users, and the information regarding the context the users are immersed in. Moreover, various interesting works exist which are focused on gathering information about the user and its environment on the basis of sensors (e.g., [1, 22]). We believe that the integration of numerous sources of profile data (i.e., sensors) and related processing modules in our framework would be a natural and promising research direction.

REFERENCES

[1]   AmbieSense. European project # IST-2001-34244. http://www.ambiesense.com/

[2]   P. Bellavista, A. Corradi, R. Montanari, and C. Stefanelli. Context-aware Middleware for Resource Management in the Wireless Internet. *IEEE Trans. on Software Engineering*, 29(12):1086–1099, IEEE, 2003.

[3]   C. Bettini, S. Jajodia, X. Wang, and D. Wijesekera. Provisions and obligations in policy rule management. *Journal of Network and Systems Management*, 11(3):351–372, Kluwer, 2003.

[4]   C. Bettini and D. Riboni. Profile Aggregation and Policy Evaluation for Adaptive Internet Services. In *Proc. of The First Annual International Conference on Mobile and Ubiquitous Systems: Networking and Services (Mobiquitous)*, 2004.

[5]   H. Boley, S. Tabet, and G. Wagner. Design Rationale of RuleML: A Markup Language for Semantic Web Rules. In *Proc. of the first Semantic Web Working Symposium*, pages 381–402, 2001.

[6]   M. Bowman, R. D. Chandler, and D. V. Keskar. Delivering Customized Content to Mobile Device Using CC/PP and the Intel CC/PP SDK. *Intel Technical Report*, Intel, 2002.

[7]   K. H. Britton, R. Case, A. Citron, R. Floyed, Y. Li, C. Seekamp, B. Topol, and K. Tracey. Transcoding. Extending e-business to new environments. In *IBM Systems Journal*, 40(1):153–178, IBM, 2001.

[8]   M. Butler. DELI: A DElivery context LIbrary for CC/PP and UAProf. *External Technical Report HPL-2001-260*, HP, 2002.

[9]   H. Chen, T. Finin, and A. Joshi. Semantic Web in the Context Broker Architecture. In *Proc. of IEEE International Conference on Pervasive Computing and Communications (PerCom2004)*, pages 277-286, IEEE, 2004.

[10] The Apache Cocoon Project. Apache Software Foundation. http://cocoon.apache.org

[11] C. Efstratiou, K. Cheverst, N. Davies, and A. Friday. An Architecture for the Effective Support of Adaptive Context-Aware Applications. In *Proc. of the International Conference on Mobile Data Management*, pages 15–26, IEEE, 2001.

[12] ELBA: European Location Based Advertising. European project # IST-2001-36530. http://www.e-lba.com/

[13] B. Grosof. Prioritized Conflict Handling for Logic Programs. In *Proc. of Symposium on Logic Programming (ILPS)*, pages 197-211, 1997.

[14] R. Hull, B. Kumar, D. Lieuwen, P. Patel-Schneider, A. Sahuguet, S. Varadarajan, and A. Vyas. Enabling Context-Aware and Privacy-Conscius User Data Sharing. In *Proc. of the International Conference on Mobile Data Management*, pages 187–198, IEEE, 2004.

[15] IMAP: An innovative Interactive Mobile Advertising Platform. European project # IST-2001-33357. http://www.imapproject.org/imapproject/hmain.jsp

[16] S. Jajodia, P. Samarati, M. L. Sapino, and V. S. Subrahmanian. Flexible Support for Multiple Access Control Policies. In *ACM Transactions on Database Systems*, 26(2):214–260, ACM press, 2001.

[17] Jena 2 - A Semantic Web Framework. http://jena.sourceforge.net/

[18] Joseki - The Jena RDF server. http://www.joseki.org

[19] G. Klyne, F. Reynolds, C. Woodrow, H. Ohto, J. Hjelm, M. Butler, and L. Tran, editors. Composite Capability/Preference Profiles (CC/PP): Structure and Vocabularies 1.0, W3C Recommendation, 15 January 2004. http://www.w3.org/TR/2004/REC-CCPP-struct-vocab-20040115/

[20] J. Krogstie, K. Lyytinen, A. L. Opdahl, B. Pernici, K. Siau, and K. Smolander. Mobile Information Systems - Research Challenges on the Conceptual and Logical Level. In *Proc. of ER'02/IFIP8.1 Workshop on Conceptual Modelling Approaches to Mobile Information Systems Development*, pages 1-13, Springer, 2002.

[21] S. Riché and G. Brebner. Storing and Accessing User Context. In *Proc. of the International Conference on Mobile Data Management*, pages 1-12, IEEE, 2003.

[22] D. Terdinam. Soon, Marketing Will Follow You. Wired News, 2003. http://www.wired.com/news/technology/0,1282,61597,00.html

[23] ViaVis Mobile Solutions Inc. http://www.viavis.com

[24] User Agent Profile Specification. WAP-248-UAProf. http://www.wapforum.org/

ANALYSIS OF MOBILE COMMERCE PERFORMANCE BY USING THE TASK-TECHNOLOGY FIT

Kun Chang Lee[1], Sangjae Lee[2] and Jin Sung Kim[3]
[1]*School of Business Administration, Sungkunkwan University, Seoul 110-745, Korea,*
leekc@skku.ac.kr

[2]*Department of E-Business, Sejong University, Seoul 143-747, Korea, kt_sjlee@hanmail.net*

[3]*School of Business Administration, Jeonju University, Jeonju, Jeonbuk 560-759, Korea,*
kimjs@jj.ac.kr

Abstract: The rapid growth of investments in mobile commerce (M-commerce) to reach a large and growing body of customers, coupled with low communication costs, has made user acceptance an increasingly critical management issue. The study draws upon the task-technology fit (TTF) model as its theoretical basis and its empirical findings to pragmatically explain the key factors that affect the performance and user acceptance of M-commerce. A total of 110 usable responses were obtained. The findings indicate that the task, technology, and individual user characteristics positively affect task-technology fit and M-commerce usage. The task-technology fit and M-commerce usage are the dominant factors that affect M-commerce performance. The result points out the importance of the fit between technologies and users' tasks in achieving individual performance impact from M-commerce. This paper identifies pertinent issues and problems that are critical in the development of M-commerce.

Key words: Mobile, M-Commerce, Task-Technology Fit (TTF)

1.   INTRODUCTION

Mobile commerce is an emerging discipline that involves mobile devices, middleware, protocols, and wireless networks. Internet-based M-commerce has received considerable attention because of its potential organizational impact. Various business communities have announced plans for M-commerce enhancements in business transactions, as mobile telephony now allows the potential platform for unprecedented penetration of the mobile communication services. In addition, a great number of organizations have used mobile communication services and M-commerce for business purposes in order to stand a better chance of achieving their competitive advantage. For instance, NTT DoCoMo, Vodafone, Verizon, Sprint PCS, and AT&T Wireless provide "cyber-mediation" and great efficiency in supplies and marketing channels through mobile commerce. The benefits of an M-commerce include: more efficient payment systems, reduced time to market new products and services, improved market reach, and customization of products and services (Barnes, 2002; Senn, 2000).

M-commerce applications involve transmitting payment details, requesting information, receiving specific content, or retrieving status information over mobile communication devices. For instance, airlines are now developing technology that will alert passengers, especially frequent fliers, to schedule changes, seat upgrades, and so on, through wireless devices. Recently, the electronic commerce applications provided by mobile communication services include mobile information agents (Mandry et al., 2001; Omicini and Zambonelli, 1998), online kiosks (Slack and Rowley, 2002), government applications (e.g., online selling by the postal service and web-based electronic data interchange in trade applications) and direct online shopping, such as Internet-based (or web-based) shopping malls and Internet-based stock markets. Travel-related and hobby-related sites that provide leisure information are also among the common websites available through mobile communication services. Since 1997, when cyber trading was first allowed, there has been a continuous growth in Internet-based stock trading systems through mobile communication services in Korea. Electronic cyber trading was utilized by Korean securities companies in processing more than 50% of all transactions in 1999. In two or three years, it is predicted that more than 80% of all transactions will be done over the Internet (Moon and Ahn, 1999).

In the US, the current rush in using wireless communications was triggered by the US Federal Communication Commission's auctioning of personal communication-service spectrum space (Senn, 2000). The collaboration of both the public and private sectors has facilitated the development of mobile commerce.

In Korea (Republic of), public organizations, such as the Ministry of Information and Communication, and the Ministry of Industry Resources, and private organizations sponsored by the government, such as Korea Telecom, Dacom, and SK-Telecom, have provided the basic telecommunications infrastructure. Private sector organizations include retailers, banks, stock investment companies, system integration companies, and entertainment companies. The development of M-commerce in Korea is clearly an innovation in the way commercial transactions between businesses and consumers are conducted. Among the three distinct identifiable classes of EC applications (Applegate et al., 1996) – business-to-customer, business-to-business, and intra-organization – M-commerce deals with the business-to-customer class. M-commerce provides a web presence with information about a company, product, or service, and facilities for purchasing, which may be online or conventional. M-commerce also provides another web presence that has information on specific matters, such as entertainment, real estate, or financial investment, and encourages potential customers to spend while using such information.

The objectives of this study were: (1) to develop a TTF model for M-commerce performance, (2) to examine the direct effect of these determinants by using a structural equation model, and (3) to test measurement and its structural models.

2.   TTF AND M-COMMERCE PERFORMANCE

IT adoption and usage is a phenomenon in its own right (Davis, 1989; Mathieson, 1991; Moore and Benbasat, 1991; Thompson et al., 1991; Hartwick and Barki, 1994). Researchers have studied the impact of users' individual beliefs and attitudes on usage behavior (DeSanctis, 1983; Fuerst and Cheney, 1982; Srinivasan, 1985), and how these individual beliefs and attitudes, in turn, influenced various external factors, such as the technical design (Benbasat and Dexter, 1986; Dickson et al., 1986; Malone, 1981), the type of system development process used (King and Rodriguez, 1981), user involvement in system development (Franz and Robey, 1986), and the nature of implementation such system (Vertinsky et al., 1975).

Studies linking technology and performance employed user attitudes and beliefs to predict the degree of utilizing current information systems. From the Diffusion of Innovation perspective (Tornatzky and Klein, 1982), researchers suggested a variety of factors that affect IT adoption and usage: innovation (Hoffer and Alexander, 1992; Moore, 1987), individual users (Brancheau and Wetherbe, 1990), and communication channels (Nilikanta and Scammell, 1990).

The literature suggested the task and its impact on system usage or user performance. A technology was more useful if it provided features that fit the requirements of a task (Culnan, 1983; Daft and Macintosh, 1981). At the organization level, researchers have linked "fit" and utilization (Cooper and Zmud, 1990; Tornatzky and Klein, 1982). At the individual user level, a "system/work fit" construct has been proposed as a critical determinant in managerial electronic workstation use (Flyoid, 1986). The impact of data representation on performance is dependent upon its fitness with the task (Benbasat et al., 1986; Dickson et al., 1986). Kim (1988) suggested that the performance of a sub-unit of IS was determined by its coordination modes, but was contingent upon the task in terms of task predictability, problem analyzability, and task interdependence. Raymond, et al. (1994) investigated the correlation between technology-structure fit and organizational performance based on the contingency theory. Lai (1999) suggested that the performance of IS professionals was dependent upon the CASE-task fit. The IS developers' performance would be more effective when the CASE tool was compatible with the IS and the corresponding task contexts.

The link between "cognitive fit" and performance has been supported by laboratory experiments (Jarvenpaa, 1989; Vessey, 1991). Decision-making performance slowed down as the mismatches between data representations and tasks demanded additional translations between data representations or decision processes (Vessey, 1991). This was based on the cost-benefit perspective, which asserted that individuals weighed benefits (impact on correctness, speed, and justifiability) and costs (mental effort on information acquisition and computation), before they chose a strategy for processing the information in decision-making (Goodhue, 1995; Creyer et al., 1990). Information systems positively affected performance when functionality met the task requirements of users. There existed a more general "fit" theory of tasks, individual user characteristics, and performance (Goodhue, 1988).

TTF has been defined as the extent to which technology functionality matched task requirements and individual user abilities (Goodhue, 1995). A number of researchers have proposed that performance would result from task-technology fit. Organizational structure contingency theories that proposed the organization's structure must "fit" its organizational context to have some similarity to TTF (Goodhue, 1995). While TTF is at the individual level, the structural contingency theory is at the organizational level.

3. INDIVIDUAL USER CHARACTERISTICS, TTF, AND PERFORMANCE

Goodhue (1998) suggested the basic model of TTF with moderating effects. This model suggested the different information systems functionalities required by users for a certain task, which then served as the basis for a "task-technology fit" instrument. The instrument thus measured the degree to which an organization's information systems and services were meeting the information needs of its managers. In this research model, we should focus on the construct known as individual user characteristics. Goodhue (1998) assumed and validated a hypothesis that the task characteristics and individual user characteristics directly affected TTF. In addition, they "moderated" the strength of the link between specific characteristics of information systems and users' evaluations of those information systems. Therefore, we could determine how individual user characteristics affect the performance of TTF and users' satisfaction with those information systems. Figure 1 shows Goodhue's TTF model (1998).

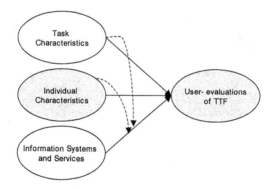

Figure 1. The basic model of TTF

Individual user characteristics, as suggested by Goodhue (1998), were defined as the user's ability in managing information systems. In this point of view, we focused on end-user ability. Therefore, we found Lee, et al.'s causal model (1995) helpful. In the study, they suggested the relationship among the end-user's ability, information system acceptance, training, and effectiveness. The heart of this research focused on the end-user's ability to affect system utilization, information system (IS) acceptance, job satisfaction, and over-all IS satisfaction. Figure 2 represents these relationships.

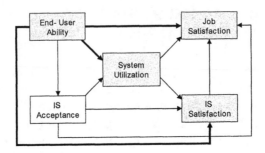

Figure 2. A causal model of end-user training

Baldwin and Rice (1997), similar to this research, suggested a research model based on individual user characteristics and performance. Baldwin and Rice (1997) suggested that the individual user characteristics of securities analysts influenced their use of information sources and communication channels. Figure 3 presents the model of the proposed relationships among individual, institutional, source/channel, and outcome variables.

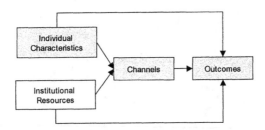

Figure 3. Baldwin and Rice (1997)'s research model

In these researches, we could conclude that many researchers had considered individual user characteristics as an important construct to enhance information systems' utilization and performance, and users' satisfaction. Therefore, we combined the above-mentioned researches into our research model, which was based on individual user characteristics, system utilization, performance, and TTF. In the next chapter, we will be presenting our research model.

4. RESEARCH MODEL

Our research model concerning relationships among variables is developed and presented in Figure 4. The research model addresses the application of the TTF model to M-commerce.

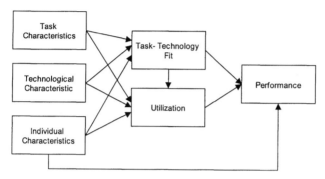

Figure 4. Research model

This study mainly deals with the updated version of the TTF model for M-commerce, as the studies concerning a knowledge management issue in the context of the TTF model are rare. The ultimate goal of M-commerce is to derive user benefits. From multiple vantage points, task, technology, and individual user characteristics are indicated as fundamental and distinct constructs that are influential in determining TTF, the utilization of M-commerce, and M-commerce performance. Hypotheses used in this study were summarized as follows:

H1: **Task characteristics directly affect TTF in M-commerce.**
H2: **Technology characteristics directly affect TTF in M-commerce.**
H3: **Individual user characteristics directly affect TTF in M-commerce.**
H4: **Task characteristics directly affect the utilization of M-commerce.**
H5: **Technology characteristics directly affect the utilization of M-commerce.**
H6: **Individual user characteristics directly affect the utilization of M-commerce.**
H7: **TTF directly affects the performance of M-commerce.**
H8: **The utilization of M-commerce directly affects its performance.**
H9: **Individual user characteristics directly affect the performance of M-commerce.**
H10: **TTF directly affects the utilization of M-commerce.**

The task, technology, and individual user characteristics all affect the utilization of M-commerce, as well as TTF. In addition, TTF affects the utilization of M-commerce. M-commerce should be used comprehensively to support user tasks, individual users, and upper-level management, and to facilitate the widespread transfer of the technology to other departments in the organization. The user's needs, as well as the task requirements, must be satisfied to attain the system objectives through the integration of information with external networks. Internal applications, such as accounts payable and receivable systems, may be efficiently processed in conjunction with an M-commerce system. The rapid and accurate transmission of shipping notices to the production department is critically important in eliminating the need for a large inventory of safety stocks. To compress cycle time and improve data integrity for the rapid transmission of data, the supplier's computers must be integrated with that of the customer's.

The "utilization of mobile communication services" indicates the extent to which M-commerce is used and spread throughout an organization. The IS success model by DeLone and McLean (1992) suggested that IS usage is positively related to other measures of IS success, such as user satisfaction, and individual and organizational impact. However, it has also been argued that system usage and perceived system effectiveness may not always be positively interrelated (Srinivasan, 1985). For instance, the extent of usage would be a misleading indicator of success if the system were considered as a service rather than a product developed to help managers to perform more effectively (Ginzberg, 1978), or if the system were implemented as a reaction to the influence of external parties (e.g., industry associations, government, etc.). There might be no alternative, but to use that system to effectively complete the task. Furthermore, the utilization of M-commerce, as a measure of M-commerce success, only makes sense when system implementation is voluntary, rather than compulsory. The growing use of M-commerce through requests by external influential companies or industry influences makes it an inappropriate surrogate for M-commerce success.

TTF and the utilization of M-commerce affect M-commerce performance. Innovation is implemented over a long time, while adoption is a single event. IS implementation is an organizational effort directed toward diffusing information technology within an organization (Cooper and Zmud, 1990). After an organization has formally adopted an IS, its implementation has to proceed comprehensively within the organization to start reaping benefits. The IS should be integrated to support the widespread transfer of its technology to various applications, which could then significantly redesign the business process (Premkumar et al., 1994). The full potential of the IS could be realized as the advocates of its implementation (or innovation) gain wider acceptance (Swanson, 1994). This could not be obtained by merely automating the process of transaction or the communication procedures. IS implementation would tend to be increasingly more elaborate with additional business functions, as users' needs are identified and met by various extensions and enhancements. Organizations might derive full benefits from an inter-organizational system (IOS) by expanding external services and electronic links to attain economies of scale (Vitale, 1985).

The positive effects of IS implementation on performance have been consistently proven. For example, the integration of information collected through EDI with internal IS applications has been asserted as a critical factor for system effectiveness and efficiency (Iacovou et al., 1995; Premkumar et al., 1994). The integration of M-commerce with internal applications could lead to better customer service and improved inter-firm relationships because rapid and accurate information were provided to customers. The adoption and implementation of M-commerce may impose significant one-time costs on an organization, as its internal systems must be adjusted to allow an interface with its trading partners. It would be difficult to obtain significant benefits from a costly change in business processes unless volume has reached a level sufficient enough to warrant change. The transaction volume should be large enough to cover the initial high investment cost, and then reduce administrative costs. The goals of many M-commerce users include increasing sales and replacing paper documents and verbal-based commerce methods with online transactions, thus reducing order costs and cycle time. These aims would not be achieved without a substantial shift in the use of the system, which would be possible with the use of high TTF. M-commerce users could obtain only transitional benefits after moving only a limited portion of their total transactions to the new system.

5.   METHODOLOGY

Data for this research were collected through interviews with M-commerce managers. Each respondent was asked a series of questions under a structured interview format. Each interview lasted approximately an hour.

The structured interview was the primary data collection method. Target respondents were selected as follows: Persons, who were employed in companies that used M-commerce extensively, were identified. From publicly available company databases (through the Chollian network service), the companies that frequently contact customers in their business activities were selected. The employees of the companies were randomly contacted to assess their level of M-commerce usage.

Three hundred mails were sent by post, and 200 more were sent through E-mail. Two hundred fifteen replied, and among these, the respondents who used M-commerce more than once a month and transacted online for more than 10 minutes per month were selected. One hundred ten mails drew target respondents. The over-all response rate was high because participation in the survey was solicited through direct visits to M-commerce managers. Also, the objectives of the study were clearly explained to them.

The questionnaire was tested for validity and reliability. Content validity was established through a literature review on the Internet and IS implementation. The items were pre-tested with both practitioners and experts to enhance the content validity of the instrument. Several minor modifications were made based on feedback regarding the presentation of the survey and the clarity of several items. The survey was then deemed ready for actual respondents after no major comments were made.

Reliability and construct validity of the measures were evaluated using the Cronbach alpha and factor analyses. The three commonly employed rules to identify factors – a minimum eigen value of 1, simplicity of structure, a minimum factor loading of 0.5 – were followed (Hair et al., 1979). The items that failed the factor analysis were dropped.

The final principal component in the factor solution with a varimax rotation produced a five-factor solution that explained 70 percent of the systematic covariance among the scale items. All empirically derived factors had eigen values greater than one. Tables 1 and 2 show the descriptive statistics of the items and the results of the confirmatory factor analysis. The factor analysis and the reliability tests suggest that the factor structure of the variables is stable, and provide the evidence for the construct validity of the given measures.

Four items, which represent the complexity and understandability of the work process, measure the task characteristics. The items are adapted from Perrow (1967) and Withey (1993). The technology characteristics are measured by four items, which represent the perceived quality of mobile technology. The items are based on Hage and Aiken (1970), and Jarvenpaa and Ives (1991). The individual user characteristics are measured by five items, which intend to measure user attitudes toward the use of technology. TTF indicates fitness between task and technology. The 15 items for TTF are based on Goodhue and Thompson (1995), and represent perceived usefulness, ease of use, perceived benefits, and customer satisfaction. The utilization of M-commerce indicates the extent of the usage of M-commerce. The three items for the utilization of M-commerce are based on Davis et al. (1989), Thompson et al. (1994), and Trice and Treacy (1988).

Three items measure the performance of M-commerce, based on Davis et al. (1989) and Goodhue and Thompson (1995). The three items represent the extent of improving work effectiveness and efficiency from using M-commerce.

Table 1. Descriptive statistics of variables

Variables (Constructs) & Sub-constructs		Item	Description	Mean	STD
Task characteristics		TC1	M-commerce requires very simple knowledge to use. is	4.4	1.2
		TC2	The complex decision making process is not necessary to use M-commerce.	4.5	1.1
		TC3	Users need not think deeply when using M-commerce.	4.5	1.1
Technology characteristics		TE1	M-commerce facilitates the communication between people.	4.4	1.3
		TE2	The procedure of functions in M-commerce is very obvious.	4.2	1.2
		TE3	M-commerce excels other technology in providing and retrieving information.	4.1	1.3
Individual characteristics		IC1	Users are familiar with using M-commerce.	3.7	1.4
		IC2	Users have appropriate knowledge to use M-commerce.	3.9	1.3
		IC3	Users generally use M-commerce frequently.	3.6	1.4
		IC4	M-commerce helps users find the right information.	3.9	1.4
TTF	Perceived usefulness	PU1	The work performance will be improved by using M-commerce.	4.1	1.5
		PU2	The work productivity will be improved by using M-commerce.	4.3	1.5
		PU3	The work efficiency will be improved by using M-commerce.	4.4	1.5
		PU4	M-commerce is very useful in performing work process.	4.3	1.5
	Ease of use	EU1	It is very easy to do business through mobile commerce.	4.2	1.4
		EU2	It is very easy to manage M-commerce.	4.1	1.3
		EU3	It is very easy to use M-commerce.	4.1	1.3
	Perceived benefit	PR1	Mobile commerce is very friendly way to buy goods and service.	4.2	1.3
		PR2	M-commerce helps better control business process.	4.1	1.3
		PR3	M-commerce helps efficiently manage business process.	4.3	1.3
		PR4	M-commerce is a convenient way to do business.	4.5	1.3
		PR5	M-commerce is a useful way to do business.	4.6	1.3
	User satisfaction	SA1	Users are generally satisfied with the service provided by M-commerce.	3.9	1.2
		SA2	Users are generally satisfied with the technology of M-commerce.	3.8	1.2
		SA3	Users are generally satisfied with the way of doing business through mobile commerce.	3.9	1.2
Utilization		UT1	Users consider using M-commerce very positively.	4.3	1.4
		UT2	It is a very good decision to use M-commerce.	4.2	1.2
		UT3	Users are willing to use M-commerce continuously.	4.3	1.3
Performance		PI1	M-commerce has a strong and positive influence on the user work process.	4.0	1.3
		PI2	M-commerce greatly contributes to the improvement of user work process.	4.0	1.3
		PI2	Users will use M-commerce to improve work performance.	4.1	1.3

Table 2. The results of confirmatory factor analysis

Variables	Item	FL	CR	VE	NFI
Task Characteristics	TC1	0.608	0.95	0.85	1.00
	TC2	0.856			
	TC3	0.819			
Technology Characteristics	TE1	0.989	0.89	0.81	0.91
	TE2	0.843			
	TE3	0.497			
TTF	SA1	0.550	0.98	0.77	0.90
	SA2	0.443			
	SA3	0.538			
	EU1	0.756			
	EU2	0.741			
	EU3	0.833			
	PR1	0.698			
	PR2	0.645			
	PR3	0.745			
	PU1	0.658			
	PU2	0.527			
	PU3	0.580			
	PU4	0.538			
Utilization	UT1	0.826	0.95	0.87	1.00
	UT2	0.915			
	UT3	0.887			
Performance	PI1	0.800	0.94	0.84	1.00
	PI2	0.825			
	PI2	0.625			
Individual Characteristics	IC1	0.719	0.96	0.85	0.99
	IC2	0.877			
	IC3	0.617			
	IC4	0.794			

* FL: Factor Loadings, CR: Composite Reliability, VE: Variance Extracted

6.   RESULTS

Table 3 shows that the selected respondents are predominantly in the ages of 20~30, male, college graduates, and have annual salaries ranging from 100 to 300 thousand dollars. The respondents are fairly diverse in terms of age, educational background, job, and salary. This result is in line with the fact that innovative customers are more likely to use M-commerce due to the Internet's global connectivity, improved market reach, low communication and purchasing costs, and creation of new market opportunities. Table 4 suggests the correlation analysis of variables.

This study tests the structural relation between variables using LISREL. LISREL provides several advantages over other multivariate techniques. First, it can validate a causal link, rather than showing a mere empirical association among variables. It can also express intricate causal links, including recursive or non-recursive relations, among latent variables to better characterize real-world processes. These links help the development of a theory (Blalock, 1969), but these same relationships cannot be tested by other multivariate techniques.

Table 3. Demographic profile of samples

	Categories	Count	%	Job	Categories	Count	%
Sex	Male	73	66	Job	Public officer	3	3
	Female	37	34		Employee of private company	53	48
Age	20-30	42	38		Specialized job (doctor, lawyer, etc.)	46	42
	30-40	59	54		Student	4	4
	40-50	6	5		Others	4	4
	50-60	3	3	Wage	Less than 1000 $	8	7
Education	High school	10	9		100-200 thousand $	47	43
	University Student	9	8		200-300 thousand $	49	45
	College graduate	60	55		300-400 thousand $	2	2
	MS or PhD	31	28		400-500 thousand $	3	3
					500-1000 thousand $	1	1

Table 4. Correlation analysis (** p <0.01)

Variables	TC: Task characteristics	TE: Technology characteristics	IC: Individual characteristics	TTF	UT: Utilization	PF: Performance
TC	1					
TE	0.0942	1				
IC	0.0160	0.4935**	1			
TTF	0.3178**	0.4477**	0.2959**	1		
UT	0.3459**	0.4670**	0.3792**	0.7425**	1	
PF	0.2479**	0.4977**	0.3983**	0.6396**	0.7148**	1

The structural model is represented in Figure 5. The latent variables are enclosed in circles or ellipses. A one-way path between variables indicates a hypothesized direct effect of one variable upon another. If there is no arrow or link between two variables, it means that one variable does not have a direct effect on another.

The chi-square is 7.108 for the given model. The model's goodness of fit index is 0.979, which is a measure of the relative amount of variables and co-variances of the model. The adjusted goodness of fit is 0.888. The root mean square residual is 0.039, which is the average of the residuals. These measures of overall fitness indicate the explanatory power of the model.

Significant causal coefficients are found in the path: from task characteristics and technology characteristics to TTF; from task characteristics and individual user characteristics to utilization; from individual user characteristics, TTF, and utilization to performance; and from TTF to utilization. TTF and the extent of high utilization of M-commerce have led to the improved performance of the system. The results support hypotheses 1, 2, 4, 6, 7, 8, 9, and 10.

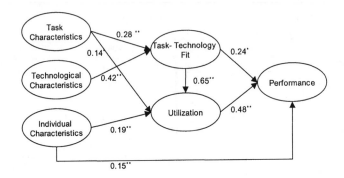

Figure 5. Causal path model (* p < 0.05, ** p < 0.01) Chi-square = 7.108, p = 0.130, GFI = 0.979, AGFI = 0.888, NFI = 0.973, RMSR = 0.039

The positive influences of individual user characteristics, TTF, utilization, and performance indicate that an individual's progress in handling its business transactions through M-commerce is related to an increase in sales and improvement in customer service. Further, the use of sophisticated functions and services (e.g., ordering processes and authentication services) is related to the extent of perceived usefulness, benefit, customer satisfaction, and system profitability. The extent of providing TTF is directly related to ease of use and customer satisfaction. Companies provide information mainly to satisfy customers' needs to know the task and technology characteristics, which help improve customer service.

7.   CONCLUDING REMARKS

The research findings offer significant academic and practical contributions in planning M-commerce. They provide practical value for evaluating M-commerce in terms of whether they fit the user's tasks, which means the functionality of technology must correspond to the task requirements of the user. IS practitioners can explain why a planned system may not be fully acceptable to users, take corrective measures to improve the acceptability of M-commerce, and determine ways to improve M-commerce adoption and its proper level of technological sophistication in order to increase business impact. Based on the results in this study, user acceptance of M-commerce can be improved when developers put their limited implementation resources to act on users' attitude toward M-commerce, and check whether TTF is appropriate or not. One way to improve TTF is to adopt a participatory design process for M-commerce.

The results point out that in order to truly exploit the latent large-scale operational and strategic potential benefits of M-commerce, business firms need to plan systematically and pursue a more extensive implementation of M-commerce via an increase in the TTF and in the utilization of M-commerce transactions. Expanding sophistication of user functions through integrated services, and making systems user-friendly also contribute to increased sales through M-commerce. Customer service can be improved by better access to information, availability and quick response to changing customer needs, faster information retrieval and delivery systems, and increased volume of information output. In general, these findings regarding the relationships among TTF, M-commerce utilization, and performance support the large body of research that focuses on the relationship between IS implementation and performance (Mahmood & Mann, 1993; Weill, 1992).

Mobile commerce in Korea is still in its embryonic stage. The vast majority of mobile commerce service has been around only in the last few years. Many Korean companies consider M-commerce as a strategic information technology that alters the ground rules by which businesses interact with their consumers. Not enough has been understood about the real impact of this rapidly evolving phenomenon, particularly in terms of differentiating between impact and hype concerning the Internet. The results of this study can improve our understanding of the factors affecting M-commerce success.

A majority of companies use M-commerce as a medium for online selling and as a means to attract more customers. The average level of system sophistication, however, is generally low. This shows that many firms still significantly use other means of communication, such as faxes and phones, when their information exchange and processing can be handled through the increasingly convenient mobile communication services. Also, they still do not have integrated internal applications. This is interesting in light of past predictions that more exchanges between firms and customers would be made possible through electronic communication technologies due to more reliable communication networks.

This study supports the positive influence of the use of M-commerce on individual user performance. The mobile service providers should know subscriber demands, and develop the corresponding services, user interfaces, and mobile Internet settings. Increasing M-commerce volume can replace traditional means of commerce, and supports various business transactions through the Internet. M-commerce businesses must expand their connections with customers through the Internet in order to increase system profitability and improve customer service. Sophistication in system functions, including authentication of services and integration with internal applications, raises the benefits of reduced system operation and maintenance costs, and increased sales and profitability. If firms can provide information on their products and services in less time, they will have the ability to make better managerial decisions sooner, allowing them to react more quickly to threats and opportunities in the marketplace. M-commerce should be successfully assimilated into the work behaviors of target businesses early for them to realize its vast potential. Given the early stage of Internet use and the low extent of M-commerce implementation, future research should investigate on a long-term basis the impact of M-commerce on corporate outcome. Although M-commerce adoption among various industry sectors has been growing, high diffusion levels have yet to be reached.

This study may be a starting point for future M-commerce implementation studies. Future studies should include items that will reflect either "quality of web information" or "quality of web page/site design" of M-commerce ventures, and examine appropriate design characteristics related to M-commerce performance. The research findings suggest a need for future studies that will examine the internal and external environmental factors of an organization (e.g., top management support, size, compatibility, competitive intensity, and government support), which influence the implementation of M-commerce. This will help identify factors that may influence consumer views toward the desirability of online shopping. Further, the research results should be verified by other methods, such as using data collected in other countries, or by utilizing longitudinal data. M-commerce in Korea is developing rapidly. Its expansion largely depends on external pressures, such as government policy and regulation, and influential trading partners. With the results reflecting the state of M-commerce in Korea, they may be limited to generalizing M-commerce results in other countries. Any attempt to generalize the findings among M-commerce systems operating in different environments must be undertaken with care and caution. The results of this study may only be reflective of the unique characteristics of Korean M-commerce companies.

ACKNOWLEDGEMENTS

We would like to express our gratitude to Korean Research Foundation since this work was supported by Korea Research Foundation Grant (KRF-2003-042-B00047).

REFERENCES

Applegate, L.M. Holsapple, C.W., Kalakota, R., Radermacher, F.J., and Whinston, A.B., "Electronic commerce: building blocks of new business opportunity," *Journal of Organizational Computing and Electronic Commerce*, 6 (1), 1996, 1-10.

Bailey, M.N. and Lawrence, R.Z., "Do We have a New Economy," *The American Economic Review*, 91(2), 2001, 308-312.

Baldwin, N.S. and Rice, R.E., "Information-seeking behavior of securities analysts: individual and institutional influences, information sources and channels, and outcomes," *Journal of the American Society for Information Science*, 48, 8, 1997, 674-493.

Barnes, S.J., "The mobile commerce value chain: Analysis and future developments," *International Journal of Information Management*, 22(2), 2002, 91-108.

Benbasat, I. and Dexter, A.S., "An investigation of the effectiveness of color and graphical presentation under varying time constraints," *MIS Quarterly*, March 1986, 59-84.

Benbasat, I., Dexter, A.S., and Todd, P., "An experimental program investigating color-enhanced and graphical information presentation: An integration of the findings," *Communications of the ACM*, 29, 11, November, 1986, 1094-1105.

Blalock, H.M., Theory Construction: from Verbal to Mathematical Formulations, Prentice-Hall, Englewood Cliffs, NJ, 1969.

Brancheau, J.C. and Wetherbe, J.C., "The adoption of spreadsheet software: Testing innovation diffusion theory in the context of end-user computing," *Information Systems Research*, 1, 2, 1990, 115-143.

Cho, N.J., "Internet business in Korea: the state-of-art," *Management and Computer*, September, 1999, 188-220.

Cooper, R.B. and Zmud, R.W., "Information technology implementation research," *Management Science*, 36 (2), 1990, 123-139.

Creyer, E.H., Bettman, J.R., and Payne, J.W., "The impact of accuracy and effort feedback and goals on adaptive decision behavior," *Journal of Behavioral Decision Making*, 3, 1, 1990, 1-16.

Culnan, M.J., "Environmental scanning: The effects of task complexity and source accessibility on information gathering behavior," *Decision Sciences*, 14, 2, April, 1983, 194-206.

Daft, R.L. and Macintosh, N.B., "A tentative exploration into the amount and equivocality of information processing in organizational work units," *Administrative Science Quarterly*, 26, 1981, 207-224.

Davis, F.D., "Perceived usefulness, perceived ease of use, and user acceptance of information technology," *MIS Quarterly*, 13, 1989, 319-339.

Davis, F.D., R.P. Bagozzi, and P.R. Warshaw, "User acceptance of computer technology: A comparison of two theoretical models," *Management Science*, 35, 8, 1989, 982-1003.

Dearle, A., "Toward ubiquitous environments for mobile users," *IEEE Internet Computing*, 2, 1, 1998, 22-32

DeLone, W. H. and McLean E. R.. Information systems success: The quest for the dependent variable. *Information systems Research*, 3 (1), 1992, 60-95.

DeSanctis, G., "Expectancy theory as an explanation of voluntary use of a decision support system," *Psychological Reports*, 52, 1983, 247-260.

Dickson, G.W., DeSanctis, G. and McBride, D.J., "Understanding the effectiveness of computer graphics for decision support: A cumulative experimental approach," *Communication of ACM*, 29, 1986, 40-47.

Fernandez, A., "The future of mobile telephony," Presentation to *Mobile Telephony and Communications*, Madrid, Spain May 2000, 22-23

Floyd, S.W., "A causal model of managerial electronic workstation use," *unpublished doctoral dissertation*, University of Colorado at Boulder, Boulder, CO, 1986.

Forrester Research, "USD7 trillion in e-commerce revenues by 2004," http://www.nua.ie/surveys/index.cgi?f=VS&art_id=905355736&rel=true, accessed 21, April 2003.

Fuerst, W.L. and Cheney, P.H., "Factors affecting the perceived utilization of computer-based decision support systems in the oil industry," *Decision Sciences*, 13, 1982, 554-569.

Franz, C.R. and Robey, C., "Organizational context, user involvement, and the usefulness of information systems," *Decision Science*, 17, 1986, 329-356.

Ginzberg, M.J., "Finding an adequate measure of OR/MS effectiveness," *Interfaces*, 8 (4), August 1978, 59-62.

Goodhue, D.L., "IS attitudes: Toward theoretical and definition clarity," *Database*, 19, 3/4, Fall/Winter 1988, 6-15.

Goodhue, D.L., "Understanding user evaluations of information systems," *Management Science*, 41 (12), December 1995, 1827-1844.

Goodhue, D.L. and Thompson, R.L., "Task-technology fit and individual performance," *MIS Quarterly*, 19, 2, June 1995, 213-236.

Goodhue, D.L., "Development and measurement validity of a task-technology fit instrument for user evaluations of information systems," *Decision Sciences*, 29, 1, Winter 1998, 105-138.

Hair, J.F., Jr., Anderson, R.E., Tatham, R.L., and Grablowsky, B.J., *Multivariate Data Analysis*. Tulsa, OK; PPC Books, 1979.

Hage, J. and Aiken, M., *Social Changes in Complex Organizations*, New York, Random House, 1970.

Hartwick, J. and Barki, H., "Explaining the role of user participation in information system use," *Management Science*, 40 (4), 1994, 440-465.

Haskin, D., "Analysts: Smart phones to lead e-commerce explosion," allNetDevices, http://www.allnetdevices.com/news/9911/991103ecomm/991103ecomm.html, 3, November 1999,

Hoffer, J.A. and Alexander, M.B., "The diffusion of database machines," *Data Base*, 23 (2), 1992, 13-20.

Iacovou, C.L., Benbasat, I., and Dexter, A.S., "Electronic data interchange and small organizations: adoption and impact of technology," *MIS Quarterly*, 19 (4), 1995, 465-485.

Jarvenpaa, S.L., "The effect of task demands and graphical format on information processing strategies," *Management Science*, 35 (3), March 1989, 285-303.

Jarvenpaa, S.L. and Ives, B., "Organization for global competition: The fit of information technology," *Decision Science*, 24(3), 547-480, 1991.

Kalakota, R. and Whinston, A.B., *Frontiers of Electronic Commerce*, Addison-Wesley Publishing Company, Inc, 1996.

Kim, K., "Organizational coordination and performance in hospital accounting information systems: An empirical investigation," *The Accounting Review*, 63 (3), 1988, 472-488.

King, W.R. and Rodriguez, J.I., "Participative design of strategic decision support systems: An empirical assessment," *Management Science*, 27, 1981, 717-726.

Korea Internet Information Center (KIIC), *Statistics of Internet Users*, www.nic.or.kr, 2001.

Lai, V.S., "A contingency examination of CASE-task fit on software developer's performance," *European Journal of Information Systems*, 8, 1999, 27-39.

Lee, S.M., Kim. Y.R., and Lee. J.J., "An empirical study of the relationships among end-user information systems acceptance, training, and effectiveness," *Journal of Management Information Systems*, 12, 2, Fall 1995, 189-202.

Mahmood, N.A. and Mann, G.J., "Impact of information technology investment: An empirical assessment," *Accounting, Management, and Information Technologies*, 3 (1), 1993, 25-32.

Malone, T.W., "Toward a theory of intrinsically motivating instruction," *Cognitive Science*, 4, 1981, 333-369.

Mathieson, K., "Predicting user intentions: Comparing the technology acceptance model with the theory of planned behavior," *Information Systems Research*, 2 (3), September 1991, 173-191.

Mandry, T., G.Rohm, A.W., "Mobile agents in electronic markets: Opportunities, risks, agent protection," *International Journal of Electronic Commerce*, 5 (2), 2001, 47-60.

Moon, H.J. and Ahn, J.H., "Enhanced competitive edge through cybertrading system: A case of Daishin Securities Co., Ltd," *Information Systems Review*, 1 (2), 1999, 1-20,.

Moore, G.C., "End user computing and office automation: A diffusion of innovations perspective," *INFOR*, 25 (3), 1987, 214-235.

Moore, G.C. and Benbasat, I., " Development of an instrument to measure the perceptions of adopting an information technology innovation," *Information Systems Research*, 2 (3), 1991, 192-222.

Nielsen, J., "Graceful degradation of sclalble internt services, WAP: Wrong approach to portability," *Alertbox*, www.useit.com/alertbox/991031.html, 31 October 1999.

Nilikanta, S. and Scammel, R.W., "The effect of information sources and communication channels on the diffusion of innovation in a database development environment," *Management Science*, 36 (1), 1990, 24-40.

Omicini, A. and Zambonelli, F., "Co-ordination of mobile information agents in TuCSoN," *Internet Research: Electronic Networking Applications and Policy,* 8 (5), 1998, 400-413.

Perrow, P., "A framework for the comparative analysis of organization," *American Sociological Review,* 32(2), 1967, 194-208.

Premkumar, G., Ramamurthy, K., Nilakanta, S., "Implementation of electronic data interchange: an innovation diffusion perspective," *Journal of Management Information Systems,* 11 (2), 1994, 157-186.

Raymond, L., Pare, G., and Bergeron, F., "Matching information technology and organizational structure: An empirical study with implications for performance," *European Journal of Information Systems,* 4, 1994, 3-16.

Reynolds, F., Hjelm, J., Dawkins, S., and Singhal, S., "Composite capability / preference profiles (CC/PP): A user side framework for content negotiation," *W3C Note,* http://web4.w3.org/TR/Note-CCPP/, 1999

Senn, J.A., "The emergence of M-commerce," *Computer,* p.148-150, December 2000.

Slack, F. and Rowley, J., "Online kiosks: The alternative to mobile technologies for mobile users," *Internet Research: Electronic Networking Applications and Policy,* 12 (3), 2002, 248-257.

Srinivasan, A., "Alternative measures of system effectiveness: associations and implications," *MIS Quarterly,* 9, September 1985, 243-253.

Strategy Analytics, "Strategy analytics forecasts $200 billion mobile commerce market by 2004," http://www.wow-com.com/newsline/press_release.cfm?press_id=862, accessed 10, July 2000.

Swanson, E.B., "Information systems innovation among organizations," *Management Science,* 40 (9), September 1994, 1069-1092.

Thompson, R.L., Higgins, C.H., and Howell, J.M., "Personal computing: Towards a conceptual model of utilization," *MIS Quarterly,* 15 (1), March 1991, 125-143.

Thompson, R.L., Higgins, C.A., and Howell, J.M., "Influence of experience on personal computer utilization: Testing a conceptual model," *Journal of Management Information Systems,* 11(1), 1994, 167-187,.

Tornatzky, L.G. and Klein, K.J., "Innovation characteristics and innovation adoption-implementation: A meta-analysis of findings," *IEEE Transactions on Engineering Management,* 29 (1), February 1982, 28-45.

Trice, A.W. and Treacy, M.E., "Utilization as a dependent variable in MIS research," *Data Base,* 19(3/4), Fall/Winter 1988.

Varshney, U., "Multicast support in mobile commerce applications," *Computer,* February 2001, 115-117.

Varshney, U. and Vetter, R., "A framework for the emerging mobile commerce applications," *Proceedings of the 34th Hawaii International Conference on System Sciences,* 2001.

Müller-Veerse, F., "Mobile Commerce Report," Durlacher Corp., London, http://www.durlacher.com/ downloads/mcomreport.pdf, accessed 2002.

Vertinsky, I, Barth, R.T., and Mitchell, V.F., "A study of OR/MS implementation as a social change process," In R.L. Schultz & D.P. Slevin (eds.), *Implementing Operations Research/Management Science,* American Elsevier, New York, 1975, 253-272.

Vessey, I., "Cognitive fit: A theory-based analysis of the graphs vs. tables literature," *Decision Sciences,* 22 (2), Spring 1991, 219-240.

Vitale, M.R., "American Hospital Supply Corp.: the ASAP system," *Harvard Business School Case,* Services No. 9-186-005, Harvard University, Boston, 1985.

Wearden, G., "UK mobile phone users hits 40 million," http://www.zdnet.co.uk/news/2001/0/ns-20014.html, accessed 2 February 2001.

Weill, P., "The relationship between investment in information technology and firm performance: A study of the valve manufacturing sector," *Information Systems Research,* 3 (4), 1992, 307-333.

Withey, M., Daft, R.L., and Cooper, W.H., "Measures of Perrow's work unit technology: An empirical assessment and a new scale," *Academy of Management Journal,* 26(1), 1983, 45-63.

USER-CENTRED DESIGN OF MOBILE SERVICES FOR TOURISTS
A Case Study on Student Work on Mobile Design

Franck Tétard, Erkki Patokorpi and Vaida Kadytė
Institute for Advanced Management Systems Research, TUCS, Åbo Akademi University, Datacity B, FIN - 20520 Turku, Finland

Abstract: In recent years, mobile technology has developed fast in Europe. We have the basic hardware but the content, in the form of services, is often missing or unattractive to the consumer. Tourism is an industry in which mobile services should be especially valuable to the user but so far few mobile applications have been successful in the market. Mobile services are said to suffer, among other things, from poor usability. The user-centred design (UCD) approach, which is widely applied in the design of mobile services and applications, is supposed to remedy this defect. We assigned 5 groups of international, advanced level Information Systems students the design of a mobile service for tourists while applying the UCD approach. We analysed and evaluated their design process as well as the prototype. Our objective is to find out how the UCD design process guided their work: What difficulties there were in the application of the UCD? Does the UCD set some undesirable constraints to design work?

Key words: mobile services; user-centred design; technology education; tourism.

1.   INTRODUCTION

In the last few years, a lot of attention has been paid to the potential impact of mobile technology in all walks of life. Mobile technology brings services to people on the move where and when those services are needed. Mobile technology enhances, among other things, personalisation, the freedom of movement, localisation and collaboration. The next few years will be crucial as a major shift will take place in terms of infrastructure

(WCDMA, broadband wireless access, GPS), mobile devices (3G devices) and the features of future applications. Presently, however, most mobile applications and services are still in a tentative state.

One application area of mobile technology is tourism and related services. Because tourists are by definition on the move and usually in unfamiliar surroundings, the concept of providing personalised information and services to tourists through their personal mobile devices is appealing. The tourism industry is still looking for the killer application which will be adopted by everyone and at the same time will deliver the promises of personalisation. The problem is how to design a service for the many in a market, which has a quite segmented customer base.

In a design problem area where customer needs are likely to be fragmented, it is generally suggested that one applies a user-centred design (UCD) approach. The UCD pays special attention to user needs, incorporating them into usable designs. In 2004, it will be technically possible to develop mobile applications with an extended set of features (compared to what we are used to now): audio, video, positioning and localization features, as well as interactive features (multimodal to some extent). This extended set of features has raised the expectations of application developers, service providers, network operators and the consumers (primary users) alike.

In this paper, we discuss the applying of the UCD approach to the design of mobile services for tourists, on the basis of the course work of international advanced level students of Information Systems. We are primarily interested in finding out how the UCD design approach guides the design process and its outcome. Three issues will be addressed: 1) How well the groups applied UCD? 2) How well the usability goals were attained? 3) Are there innate constraints in the UCD that lead to an undesirable design outcome?

2. USER-CENTRED DESIGN

2.1 User-centred design

User-centred design refers to the process of designing an information system (or any other artefact) with a user-centred approach, which implies extensive and coherent user involvement in the design process jointly with the designer(s) of the system. According to Norman (1986), user-centred design aims at designing systems, whose primary purpose is to serve the user and the user's goals, not to use a specific technology, nor to be an elegant piece of programming. For some other authors, the UCD is the design of a system based on requirements formulated by the users themselves, without any further involvement by users in the design process, except maybe at the evaluation stage where user involvement might be more frequent. There are probably as many definitions of the UCD as there are designers and researchers: the most important to remember is the emphasis on the exploitation of the user's knowledge and the involvement of the user in the design process.

One recurrent theme in the UCD is the concept of iterativeness. This is based on the insight that it is rarely the case that we capture the user requirements and provide a workable design the first time round, and that it takes several iterations to learn about the users and their requirements. Iterativeness is outlined as an important feature of the UCD processes in the ISO standard 13407. In addition to iterativeness, user focus and measurable usability are among the main driving principles of the UCD. Figure 1 illustrates the features of the UCD in a generic model.

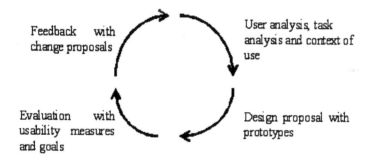

Figure 4. A UCD generic model

Of course, the UCD is not the panacea for system development, but it is a step towards more usable systems. The UCD has lacked evidence supporting its cost-effectiveness; however, recent empirical research indicates that the UCD can be successfully integrated with other system development models, outlining best practices for achieving this (see Jokela, 2001; TRUMP project, 2001). UCD shares common traits with the newest system development models, as these have evolved from the traditional waterfall development to evolutionary system development, which promote iterativeness, incremental development, and evolutionary design. These common traits ease the integration of the UCD with these models (Gulliksen et al., 2002).

UCD models are useful for representing the activities carried out during the UCD process, and for understanding how they relate to each other. We talk about "models" because there is not only one model that will capture the

UCD process. Each IT project has its own characteristics, and it can surely be said that there are as many UCD models as there are projects.

One relevant factor that can help us make a distinction between different UCD models is the level of user involvement. There can be different degrees of user involvement depending on the project's nature. UCD models with relatively low user involvement will tend to be based on extensive theoretical knowledge about the user. UCD models with high user involvement will tend to be based on accumulation (and the learning process associated with it) of knowledge about the user "in situation" and his context. Ethnographical methods and contextual design number among the techniques used in these models. Obviously, UCD models with low user involvement will rely much on expert knowledge, whereas high user involvement will require extensive use of human resources and will be time-consuming.

Another interesting dimension that can be used to compare UCD models is how active or passive users are, in respect with what happens in the UCD process. For example, a design process might involve the observation of thousands of users: in this case user involvement might be considered to be high because of the number of users, but it will remain passive user involvement, as users are not asked to contribute to the design. On the other hand, active user involvement can take place when a dozen of users formulate themselves requirements and design proposals. Here again, it is a matter of degree: the nature of the project will determine how active or passive users will be during the design process.

2.2   UCD and mobile services

Designing for mobile services is challenging. In most cases, designers have to deal with (i) devices and technology infrastructure with a limited capacity, (ii) high user expectations and (iii) short time-to-market. Also, designers often have to design for devices which do not yet exist on the market, or which have a limited customer-user base. This leads to a situation where product concepts are launched and do not meet adequately their goals (in terms of adoption rate, reach and revenue). It is believed that the UCD could offer solutions to these design problems: by designing mobile services with the user core needs as a starting point, one can increase the odds of services success when launched.

3. MOBILE TECHNOLOGY IN TOURISM

3.1 State of the art of mobile technology in tourism

Many scenarios have been created to illustrate the potential of mobile services for consumer market, with the tourism sector being among the most popular ones (see esp. Anckar 2002, p. 15; EC Statistics 2002). The nature of the content of tourism and cultural heritage services could open up numerous opportunities to the so-called third generation (3G) multimedia in various forms and situations. However, we must admit that the characteristics of the current technological infrastructure available for commercial use[3] cannot quite support the realization of such scenarios. Therefore mobile services and applications for consumers, including those for tourists, are still in their infancy. According to many industrial experts and consulting companies, the actual usage of 3G services is, at best, postponed until 2005.

Although the actors in a mobile commerce value chain learned from the wireless application protocol (WAP) services painful lessons about raising customer expectations they cannot fulfil, there is a necessary question to be asked again: will the services developed for the tourism sector really bring added value for the end user? More and more researchers (e.g. Groot and Welie, 2002; Carlsson and Walden, 2002) agree with the idea that the success of mobile services in general is rather a matter of creating 'killer values' than inventing 'killer applications'. It is crucial to know what things are perceived by the consumers to be valuable (Mobilocity 2001; Anckar 2002). However, due to a lack of empirical research it is not yet known what makes consumers adopt mobile services (Pedersen and Nysveen, 2003; Anckar, 2002). As the initial enthusiasm for everything mobile has by now simmered down, investors too, demand more concrete evidence than sheer technological novelty before they are willing to put their money in mobile applications or services. Presently, research on m-commerce has started to focus more on the consumers' expectations and intentions than on the theoretical or actual technological potentials. The education and training of mobile technology professionals should follow suit and pay more attention both to the creation of added value to the user and usability issues.

---

[3] With the exception of the city of London, the 3G networks in Europe are not yet available for commercial use. The Finnish operators Radiolinja and Sonera started their 3G network trials already in August 2001, but the commercial use of the 3G networks in Finland will start only when the technology needed is of the quality that customers are used to. Telia operator in Sweden will launch the 3G services commercially in March 2004.

3.2   Extant mobile tourist applications and systems

The design and usability of mobile services have been tested in a number of projects related to the development of mobile services for tourists: mobile cultural heritage, and tourism in general, has been a topic to which the community of mobile commerce professionals has paid a lot of attention. A short description of these projects is given below.

CHIMER (Children's Heritage Interactive Models for Evolving Repositories) is an EU project for studying tools and methods of mobile environment to encourage European schoolchildren's participation in building a living view of the cultural heritage of their villages, towns and regions. Models for wider applications, such as mobile cultural heritage tourism, are developed on the basis of didactic and organization expertise of teachers, museums, libraries and technical partners.

TellMaris is a project in which new technology is developed to support interaction with 3D maps to retrieve tourist information on mobile computers. Boat tourists travelling in the Baltic Sea Region are used as a case in point. TellMaris develops new means for search and retrieval of customised leisure information for the European citizen.

LoL@ (Local Location Assistant) is a demonstration of a mobile multimedia Tourist Guide. It accompanies visitors through the historical first district of Vienna, determines the user's position and provides a personal guided tour. LoL@ offers location specific content: multimedia tourist information, maps, and navigation.

CRUMPET project aims to implement, validate, and test tourism-related value-added services for nomadic users (across mobile and fixed networks). The project delivers a mobile system for tourists, which focuses on personalization and interaction facilities and uses intelligent agent technology. The system has among other things a route finder function and a geo-coding service (Schmidt-Belz *et al.* 2001).

Prototypes for mobile context-aware systems for tourists have been around for some time now. One of the first prototypes was the Cyberguide, which is intended for indoor and outdoor use and works on a variety of handhelds. The experiences from the prototype have given early insight into what services context-aware mobile technologies could offer for tourists (Abowd *et al.* 1996).

Another system with both indoor and outdoor components is the so-called REAL system developed at the University of Saarbrücken. REAL is a pedestrian navigation system which operates on different mobile devices, combining different types of location awareness technology, such as GPS and Bluetooth (Baus *et al.*, 2001).

MINERVA, tested in a Smithsonian museum in 1998, is an interactive museum tour-guide robot that guides people in the museum in an interactive manner (Thrun *et al.*, 1999).

The AudioGPS created by Holland and Morse (2001) is an audio interface coupled with the Global Positioning System (GPS). Instead of speech the system relies on non-speech sounds (i.e. spatial audio), which appear to come from the immediate surroundings through open stereo headphones. The AudioGPS is designed for sighted users but somewhat similar systems have been developed for the visually impaired.

4. EVALUATION OF STUDENT WORK ON USER-CENTRED DESIGN OF MOBILE SERVICES

4.1 Methodology

The study explores how 5 groups of international, advanced level Information Systems students applied the UCD approach to the design of mobile services for tourists. The work that the students conducted was carried out in a user-centred design course as a course project. They were given a broad description of the system that they should design (purpose, potential target user groups, technology to be used), and they were given freedom to choose any UCD methods that they thought were suitable.

This is a case study of the design work of the five above-mentioned student groups. Both the design process and the prototype are being analysed and evaluated. We present seven evaluation criteria by which we roughly sort the groups and their work. This rough analysis serves as a basis for a discussion on the benefits and shortcomings of the UCD model.

4.2 Assessment

We have outlined criteria by which we will evaluate the students' design work. The criteria derive from the UCD and IS research literature (e.g. Gulliksen *et al.*, 2002, Alter, 2002), and from our practical experience of applying the UCD to ICT design. The criteria are divided into three categories: the first category includes criteria about the involvement of users in the design process; the second category includes criteria about the business and technological knowledge that is needed to ensure the workability of the prototypes; and the third category includes criteria about the conceptualization of the prototype and its realisation from a design perspective:

- Degree of user involvement: the UCD promotes user involvement in the design activities. Involvement can vary depending on the types of projects (time and resources available): user involvement can vary between low involvement (experts or focus groups) and high involvement (large user population).
- Information sources used: how many sources have been used; what was the quality of the information sources; to which extent they have been fed into the design process.
- Business logic: to what extent the business potential has been considered.
- Technology and infrastructure: how well the existing technology (its features, constraints) has been investigated, and taken into account in the design process.
- Conceptual level: how the concept of the mobile service design problem has been defined. Do the student groups understand conceptually how the design meets user needs?
- Design level: how the design level supports the concepts defined above. Do the interaction styles chosen support effectively the service concept?
- Originality: the level of originality can vary between replication of existing designs (low originality) to innovative design proposals (high originality). An innovative design should not, however, compromise the objective of usability: "meets the user requirements in a successful way".

Having in mind a case study methodology, we used some rough statistical representations of data (low, medium, high) to depict the general results from the evaluation of prototypes.

Five groups, comprised of three students each, have carried out their project work and designed five different prototypes for mobile tourists. The UCD seems to give a great degree of freedom for subjects involved in the design process. Groups 1 and 3 followed the UCD guidelines more conscientiously, whereas groups 4 and 5 were applying the method to a lesser degree.

Table 1. Assessment of user involvement and use of information sources

	Degree of user involvement	Information sources
Group 1	Low: survey	Low: study materials
Group 2	Low: fictional user narratives	High: study materials, literature, and websites.
Group 3	High: interviews used for user profiling	High: study materials, literature, websites, methods documentation, benchmarking.
Group 4	Low: fictional user narratives	Low: study materials
Group 5	Low	Low: study materials

Group 3 has a high degree of user involvement and an extensive use of information sources; this reflects proper applying of a design process according to the UCD principles. Groups 1, 4 and 5 used sources only minimally and the degree of their user involvement, too, was low.

Table 2. Assessment of business logic and technology and infrastructure

	Business logic	Technology & infrastructure
Group 1	Considered but not integrated	Device mentioned. Infrastructure not considered
Group 2	Not considered	Device considered. Infrastructure not considered
Group 3	Not considered	Device considered. Infrastructure not considered
Group 4	Considered and integrated	Device not considered. Infrastructure not considered
Group 5	Not considered	Device not considered. Infrastructure not considered

Group 4 investigated possible business models and business knowledge, and integrated these throughout their design process. The rest of the groups paid little attention to business logic. No group did sufficiently take infrastructure aspects into consideration, nor use their knowledge about infrastructure to ensure the workability of the prototype.

Table 3. Assessment of conceptual level, design level, and originality

	Conceptual level	Design level	Originality
Group 1	Question & answer	Supports conceptual level	High
Group 2	Menu-based	Supports conceptual level	Low
Group 3	Menu-based	Supports conceptual level	Medium
Group 4	Menu-based	Supports conceptual level	Low
Group 5	Menu-based	Does not support conceptual level	Low

Conceptually, the prototypes are rather conservative (search and find); most prototypes were designed according to the prevailing interaction styles (menu-based interaction). One prototype deviated from the others by providing a concept promoting high learnability as a design objective. Most prototypes were designed consistently, providing proof that our groups had a good understanding of the basic design guidelines and their use. It was somewhat disappointing that none of the groups proposed a new concept that could be supported by future technology (this maybe reflects the fact that our groups did not investigate conscientiously enough the technology features of the devices that they were designing for).

4.3 Comparison of prototypes with state of the art mobile systems for tourists

Kray and Baus (2003) report a survey of mobile guides which have been proposed and commercialized. The mobile guides that they evaluate have been selected on the basis of the unique features that they offer or their influence in the field of mobile guides. Their evaluation is based on the following factors: the basic features offered (tourism-related services and positioning capabilities); the situational factors (context-awareness of the system); the adaptation capabilities to the physical and technical environment (for example, in case of network breakdowns, storage of information for later use, access to a scale-down version, etc.); the interface and user interaction modes (in terms of language support and multimodality); the system architecture. They claim that currently missing features of mobile guides are to be found in terms of situatedness, which is how the mobile guide adapts according to different situations such as user, context, and task status; addition of such features is believed to increase user experience and satisfaction. System adaptation is seldom implemented. According to Kray and Baus, it is also an open question whether mobile guides should adopt a client-server or multi-agent system architecture.

By comparing students' prototypes with the systems reported in Kray and Baus, we can see how the students' works position themselves in respect with existing state-of-the-art systems. Most of our students' works include basic features such as (i) information, guidance and reservation; these features are also found in the systems evaluated by Kray and Baus. On the other hand, positioning features were seldom considered. (ii) Situational factors were largely taken into account: four works included functionality to create user profiles and use the user profile information in the designed system. (iii) Adaptation capabilities were also taken into account in the prototyping of two systems: the prototypes included the possibility to store retrieved tourist information for later use, or to browse off-line tourist information content. The prototypes were (iv) not innovative at the design level: all systems allowed the use of only one language, and multimodality was not supported. In terms of (v) system architecture, there was a consensus that mobile tourist applications should use a client-server architecture, and be somewhat integrated with other services, such as reservation services.

5. DISCUSSION AND CONCLUSION

It is generally believed that the rapid development of mobile communication technology and the failure to introduce enduring mobile solutions for tourists call for a user-centred approach to design. Five student groups to inform the design, and to obtain an understanding of the mechanisms within the mobile tourism context applied the UCD approach. The advantage of having groups of advanced level students, which share the same design assignment, is that we can compare the design processes and the prototypes. In the real world this would be difficult to arrange.

In line with the principles of the UCD approach, the design problem is not something you get ready-made but an outcome of a long and iterative research process in which the user is involved. One group did not present any preconceived ideas about the design problem but followed the UCD procedure from the very beginning and fully, which shows especially in the degree of user involvement. The UCD is easy to apply because little preparation and background research is required, but this is also its weakness. The UCD proved to give results fast, which is important as the time-to-market for mobile services is short. At the same time the UCD is highly deceptive if one skips research into technology and infrastructure; the result will be conservative, even below state-of-the-art.

The students involved the intended users in the design work for instance through interviews, and also had access to expert guidance in the form of instructor and guest lecturer support. Apart from apprenticeship, training and education cannot escape certain artificiality, that is, an element of make-believe. Moreover, design work is often even in the real world artificial in the sense that the design outcome is frequently discovered to be a flop functionally, economically or in some other sense. We ourselves feel – and the students generally agree – that the course came fairly close to real-world design work. One informant who works as an interface designer said that he especially enjoyed the theoretical framework which helped him to gather and organize his thoughts about design work. Real as they may be, bad practices are not worth imitating. Our point here is that if closeness to the real world also has something to do with a good understanding of how things work, there may – to quote an old wisdom – be nothing as practical as a good theory.

The absence of business logic is a matter of concern in our sample of UCD design work. Tourists, as one group of users, will be willing to use mobile solutions only if these add value to them, are cost-effective and reliable. Business knowledge about how to gain the critical mass is necessary to make the applications financially attractive. Market research, too, in the promising but still little known mobile tourism sector is required. Unfortunately all of the student prototypes were lacking in this respect. In a real design process, getting to know your users requires usually generic market research. Firstly, market data must be gathered about different tourist segments and various needs associated with particular groups, and, secondly, generate ideas for future products and services that could fulfill their expectations. The user profiling is quite adequate for the design of such systems and some degree of generalisation is welcome to achieve economics of scale.

Most of the prototypes produced by the students were designed according to accepted guidelines. From a pure design perspective, the works are completed successfully; and, apart from a few minor design mistakes, an acceptable level of usability could be ensured. However, the lack of business logic consideration has compromised the expected utility of the prototypes. Utility, together with the ease of use, is an important adoption factor of new technology (Davis, 1989; Venkatesh, 2003). Often it is a matter of trade-off between utility and the ease of use. Most prototypes proposed ensured ease of use, but few actually proved to be useful in the sense of utility.

The course did not cover the whole product development cycle. It would be possible to extend the course work further to include prototype testing and a second cycle of design. However, the resulting amount of work would exceed the present limits of course work measured in study weeks.

In our case study, the UCD did not foster innovative use of technology. Innovative design can be defined as something that creates new practices that go beyond the everyday routines, rather than supports the existing practices in conventional tourism. One reason for a lack of innovativeness might be low user involvement and insufficient use of many sources of knowledge. For instance, the user involvement was usually focused on user requirements, whereas user grievances (bottlenecks in technology) did not receive enough attention. In many cases the designer was also a user in which case we can talk of participatory UCD. However, a user/designer cannot automatically be considered an expert. It is likely that a routine user of a system may become blind to some aspects of the system. Anthropologists are only too eager to confirm that an outsider often sees the routines of a culture far more sharply than the members of the culture themselves. Thus the importance of extensive user involvement and information retrieving from users as well as the use of (real) experts could be recommended.

Our case study of five groups of advanced level university students applying user-centered design indicates that the UCD is fast and easy to apply, but may tend to lead to conservative design outcomes.

REFERENCES

Abowd, G. D., Atkeson, C. G., Hong, J., Long, S., Kooper, R., and Pinkerton, M., 1996, Cyberguide: a mobile context-aware tour guide, *Baltzer Journals*. September 23:1–21.

Alter, S., 2002, *Information Systems: The Foundation of E-business*, 4th ed., Prentice Hall, New Jersey.

Anckar, B., Carlsson, C., and Walden, P., 2003, Factors affecting adoption decisions and intents in mobile commerce: empirical insights, in: Proc. of the 16th Bled eCommerce Conference, Bled, Slovenia, pp. 886–900.

Anckar, B., 2002, Contextual insights into the value creation process in E-commerce: antecedents and consequences of consumer adoption of electronic travel services, Åbo Akademi University, Turku, Grafia Oy.

Baus, J., Kray, C., Krüger, A., and Wahlster, W., 2001, A resource-adaptive mobile navigation system (April 22, 2003). Available at http://w5.cs.uni-sb.de/~krueger/papers/iui2002.pdf.

Carlsson, C., and Walden, P., 2002, Mobile commerce: a summary of quests for value-added products & services, in: Proc. of the 15th Bled eCommerce Conference, Bled, Slovenia.

Carrol, J.M., Rosson, M. B., Chin, Jr, G., and Koenneman, J., 1998, Requirements developments in scenario based design, *IEEE transactions of Software Engineering*, 24(12):1156-1170.

Davis, F. D., 1989, Perceived usefulness, perceived ease of use, and user acceptance of information technology, *MIS Quarterly*, September: 319-340.

European Commission, 2002, Statistics: tables / diagrams (January 7, 2002). Available at http://europa.eu.int/comm/enterprise/services/tourism/policy-areas/statistics.htm.

Groot, B., Welie, M., 2002, Leveraging the context of use in mobile service design, in: Proc. of the 4th International Symposium, Mobile HCI 2002, Pisa, Italy, Springer, pp. 334-338.

Gulliksen, J., Göransson, B., 2002, Användarcentrerad Systemdesign, Studentlitteratur, Lund.

Holland, S., and Morse, D. R., 2001, Audio GPS: spatial audio in a minimal attention interface, in: *Proc. of the 3rd International Workshop on Human-Computer Interaction with Mobile Devices*, M. Dunlop and S. Brewster, ed., IHM-HCI, Lille, pp. 28-33.

Jokela, T., 2001, Assessment of User-Centred Design Processes as a Basis for Improvement Action: an Experimental Study in Industrial Settings, Academic Dissertation, Dep. of Information Processing Science, University of Oulu, Oulu.

Mobilocity, 2001, Fundamentals of M-Business: White Paper, (May 6, 2003). Available at http://www.mobilocity.com/mi/Mobilocity_Fundamentals2001.pdf.

Kray, C., and Baus, J., 2003, A Survey of Mobile Guides, in: Proc. of the 5th International Symposium on Human-Computer Interaction with Mobile Devices and Services, Workshop on HCI on mobile guides, Italy.

Norman, D., 1986, *User Centered System Design*, Lawrence Erlbaum Associates, Inc., Hillsdale, New Jersey.

Pedersen, P. E., and Nysveen, H., 2003, Usefulness and Self-Expressiveness: Extending TAM to Explain the Adoption of a Mobile Parking Service, in: Proc. of the 16th Bled eCommerce Conference, Bled, Slovenia, pp. 705–717.

Schmidt-Belz, B., Mäkeläinen, M., Poslad, S., and Zipf A., 2001, Personalized and easy-to-use mobile services for tourists, (April 22, 2003). Available at http://www.emorphia.com/downloads/ubicomp-paper.pdf

Teo, T.S.H., and Pok, S.H., 2003, Adoption of WAP-enabled mobile phones among Internet users, Omega, *The International Journal of Management Science*, 31:483-498.

Thrun, S., Bennewitz, M., Bulgard, W., Cremers, A.B., Dellaert, F., Fox, D., Hähnel, D., Rosenberg, C., Roy, N., Schulte, J., and Schulz D., 1999, Minerva: a second generation museum tour-guide robot, (January 2, 2004). Available at http://www.ri.cmu.edu/pub_files/pub1/thrun_sebastian_1999_1.

TRUMP, 2004, Trial usability maturity process (January 7, 2004). Available at http://www.usability.serco.com/trump/trump/index.htm.

Venkatesh, V., Morris, M.G., Davis, G.B., and Davis F.D., 2003, User acceptance of information technology: toward a unified view, *MIS Quarterly*, 27(3):425-478.

A FRAMEWORK FOR ANALYZING MOBILE TELECOMMUNICATIONS MARKET DEVELOPMENT

Jan Damsgaard and Ping Gao
Department of Informatics, Copenhagen Business School, Denmark

Abstract: Current research focuses on the dynamics of mobile telecommunications market either from the perspectives of technology innovation or service adoption. However, because there is a mutual dependency between them, each perspective alone can only partly explain the pace and direction of change we currently witness in this market. This article combines them into one framework to pursue a holistic understanding of mobile telecommunications market innvoation. To test its explanatory power, we apply this framework to dissecting the case of China based on second-hand data. It concludes that our model enables a systematic description on the mutual influence of infrastructure innovation and innovation adoption that moves beyond unilateral accounts. Our framework also captures the interplay between mobile telecommunications market and the social network formed by interrelated providers, users and institutions.

Key words: infrastructure; innovation; mobile telecommunications; market.

1.   INTRODUCTION

Recent decades bear witness of the dramatic changes in mobile telecommunications technology and service. This phenomenon raises wide research interests as the availability and widespread adoption of advanced telecommunication technologies are linked to the economic potential of nations.

Generally people study the dynamics of mobile telecommunications market from two distinct perspectives, either technology innovation or service adoption. As examples of innovation studies, Edquist (2003) reports the results of a collection of papers that draw upon systems of innovation theory to investigate the innovation of Internet and mobile telecommunications technology. Choudrie et al (2003) provides an example of using institutional theory, specifically the model of King et al (1994), to analyze the role of government in promoting the broadband technology diffusion. There are also a lot of research efforts to explain the adoption of mobile telecommunications by users (see e.g. Pedersen et al., 2003), for which Diffusion of Innovation theory (Rogers, 1995), Theory of Reasoned Action (Ajzen, 1980) as well as its extensions like Technology Acceptance Model (Davis 1989) serve as major analytical tools.

Mobile telecommunications market is built upon networked-technologies and infrastructure. Its transformation involves evolutionary innovation in one technology paradigm like 2G, and the revolutionary transition from one paradigm to the next for example from 2G to 3G (Muller-Veerse, 2000). We argue that technology innovation or service adoption perspectives alone can only partly explain the mobile telecommunications market change. In this article we combine the two perspectives into one framework to pursue a holistic understanding of mobile telecommunications market innvoation.

This paper is organized as follows. In the second section we review innovation and adoption theories and their applications in studying telecommunications market innovation. The third section describes our framework, and the research questions it may address. In the fouth section we dissect four cases based on data from literature, which may preliminarily justify the explanatory power of our model. The last section derives conclusion, and discus the limitations and future work.

2.   INNOVATION AND ADOPTION TRAITS

In literature there have been two major ways to understand the market development, either from infrastructure innovation or adoption of innovation perspectives. These two perspectives are condensed in Table 1.

Table 1. Summary of infrastructure innovation and innovation adoption perspectives

	Infrastructure innovation	Innovation adoption
Key Drivers	Innovation of infrastructure and technology	User value
Unit of analysis	Networks of organizations, diverse communities, different institutional actors	Users

	Infrastructure innovation	Innovation adoption
Viewpoint of diffusion	Longitudinal process that stretches over a considerable amount of time and space	Single point or short period
Key theoretical references	Institutional theory (King et al, 1994); Network economics (Arthur 1989, 1990; Van de Ven, 1993); Systems of innovation (Dosi et al, 1988; Edquist, 1997)	Diffusion of innovation theory (Rogers, 1995; Tornatzky and Klein, 1982); Theory of Reasoned Action (Ajzen, 1980)
Typical examples	(Choudrie et al, 2003; Edquist, 2003)	(Anckar and D'Incau, 2002; Pederson et al, 2003)

2.1   Market Market development as a result of innovation adoption

An innovation is an idea or concept that is new to the unit of adoption that autonomously can decide to adopt or refrain from doing so. In line with diffusion of innovation theory (DOI), the transformation of mobile telecommunications market is the result of technology and service adoption by the users. DOI identifies four elements that characterize a successful diffusion process of an innovation: 1) an innovation and its characteristics, 2) that they are communicated through specific channels 3) to the members of a social system 4) over time. General factors that have been found to influence adoption include adopter characteristics, the social network, the communication process, the characteristics of the promoters, and the innovation attributes which include triability, relative advantage, compatibility, observability and complexity (Rogers, 1995).

Theory of Reasoned Action (TRA) and its extensions like Technology Acceptance Model are another set of theories that address technology adoption (Ajzen, 1980; Davis 1989). Like DOI, these models predict diffusion of innovation over time and space by associating a set of variables with an adoption outcome (Wolfe, 1994). Often people incorporate DOI theory with these models to find the best mix of innovation characteristics that increases adoption. Accordingly, scholars have applied adoption models to explain diffusion with a small set of factors, like relative advantage, compatibility, complexity, management support, champion, size, centralization, and technical sophistication (Tornatzky and Klein, 1982).

Overall, the technology adoption tradition is founded on a desire to explain individual adoption decisions within the adopting unit. The adoption population is assumed relatively homogeneous with well-defined boundaries. The adoption decision is usually considered an atomic event, and the implementation stretches over limited time (months rather than years). Learning is seldom involved after the adoption, and not considered as a part of the adoption process (Lyytinen and Damsgaard, 2001). In current literature adoption models have remained popular means to explain adoption of mobile service (Anckar and D'Incau, 2002; Pederson et al., 2003).

2.2   Market development as a process of infrastructure innovation

In general, although the traditional adoption theories have provided many useful insights to understanding the diffusion of technological innovations in the past, recent empirical studies of the diffusion of complex, networked information technology like B2B infrastructure point out its limitations (Lyytinen and Damsgaard, 2001). The diffusion of a technology is not only a consumer matter or "user-pull". It also depends on the "technology-push" which should take into account the characteristics of technology. Two technological characteristics are in particular essential in understanding the infrastructural features of telecommunications technology: its reliance on standards, and its networked properties with strong network effects (Arthur, 1990). Meanwhile, the researchers should not only emphasize user adoption issue but also take into account the roles of broader mobile telecommunications market stakeholders including for example equipment vendors, network operators, content providers, government, and intra-governmental organizations in promoting the market innovation. Institutional theory (King et al., 1994), systems of innovation theory (Dosi et al, 1988; Edquist, 1997), and network economics (Arthur, 1989, 1990; Van de Ven, 1993) have been used to tackle these social and technological problems. Significantly different from DOI and other adoption theories, these theories emphasize infrastructure traits of mobile telecommunications market innovation.

Institutional theory. The institutional theory analyzes the necessary involvement of institutions in promoting infrastructure innovation and the market transformation. From this perspective, the innovation of mobile telecommunications infrastructure will be possible only if coordinated action takes place, for which institutions play an important role. Institution encompasses relevant legislative and regulative bodies and associated scientific communities (Van de Ven, 1993). The institutional measures of building an infrastructure include mobilizing bias around the technology, educating potential adopters, setting common standards, and influencing the operator to choose networks (King et al., 1994). The deployment of mobile infrastructure has been examined from the institutional perspective. For example, drawing upon the model of King et al. (1994), Choudrie et al. (2003) describes generic institutional measures that further innovation production and diffusion in Korean broadband market.

Systems of innovation. The mobile telecommunications market is socially constructed. The researchers should not only focus on the users from an adoption perspective, but also study the roles of other stakeholders in promoting the diffusions. The technology innovation must be based on the establishment of an ecologic social system that is characterized by the efficient cooperation between different actors based on a specific business model (Star and Ruhleder, 1996). Hence the study of innovation and diffusion of complex technological systems, like mobile telecommunications infrastructure, must involve the theory of systems of innovation (Edquist, 1997), which allows the researchers exploring the social network around the technology instead of focusing on marketing strategies and changes in consumer behavior. There have been some efforts of drawing upon systems of innovation theory to investigate the innovation of Internet and mobile telecommunications technology (Edquist, 2003).

Network economics. The logic of adoption rationale is captured by the concept of network externalities (Oliva, 1994). In general, the usability of a networked technology increases with the number of adopters. This means that the benefit of being an early adopter can be relatively low compared to being a "laggard". Network externalities make it beneficial to postpone adoption until most partners have adopted and a network has been formed. This is especially true when there are several competing and incompatible alternatives (Shapiro and Varian, 1999).

Under the condition of positive network externalities once the number of adopters reaches a certain level the diffusion process will self-evolve rapidly until a saturation point is reached, or a better innovations disturb the balance. The stability and static nature of an established infrastructure comes at a price after the technology trajectory is locked-in to a certain path (Arthur, 1989). The lock-in effects can seriously slow down the innovation of technology. Often established monopoly infrastructures stand as insurmountable barriers to the adoption of new (and more advanced) technologies. As an example, Damsgaard (2002) applies network economics to analyze the development of Internet portal market.

3. DYNAMICS OF INNOVATION AND ADOPTION: A FRAMEWORK

We challenge current work that generally treats the mobile telecommunications market change from either infrastructure innovation or innovation adoption perspective. Based on specific sets of theories, both perspectives offer plausible explanations as to why a complex social-technological system diffuses (Table 1). Yet we argue these two fundamental perspectives are not exclusive but complement, and they are interdependent not separate. The innovation adoption drives the infrastructure innovation and vice versa. A self-enforcing spiral of mutual re-enforcement of both infrastructure innovation and innovation adoption can unfold under favoriate circumstances. We next will build a model that combines the individual adoption decision with infrastructure innovation (Figure 1).

First, mobile telecommunications services are based on complicated technologies where the mobile phone itself is just a small fraction of the various components that need to be in place for the proper operation and use of the technologies. Examples of components are applications, services, networks, handsets, standards. These interdependent components together comprises a sophisticated infrastructure (Muller-Veerse, 2000). The mobile telecommunications market is built upon this infrastructure. In other words, the infrastructure supports a series of technology applications and enables different sorts of services for the potential adoption of the users. From diffusion of innovation perspective it is clear that individual users will only adopt a technology insofar it is perceived superior to not to adopt it (Rogers, 1995). This is as perceived by the potential adopters based on the fit between the technology's immediate properties like usability and accountability, and adopters' characteristics for example education and financial background, gender and age etc (Ajzen, 1980). In return, the situation of user adoption on services and technology influences the innovation of infrastructure so that appropriate services can be offered. Mobile telecommunication infrastructure is emergent in nature and it is not only built but also grown (Ciborra, 2000). As an example, GSM system started with major providing voice communications. Afterwords SMS services was enabled. As this service is provided through control channel which means it does not involve additional cost for the operator hence a low price has been set for its consumption, and at the same time it is convenient to use for customers, it turned to be a welcomed service. This encouraged the operators to extend SMS to business field, and promoted the market to move from 2G to 2.5G that was capable of providing better data services. Hence, as we have argued above, the change of mobile telecommunications market covers the issues of both infrastructure innovation and innovation adoption. These entities are depicted in the top part of Figure 1.

The interrelance between infrastructure innovation and innovation adoption can get proof from network economics. Because a telecommunications service is dependent on a supporting infrastructure the analysis on user adoption must be expanded to take networked properties, standard depended features, and institutional arrangements into account. For networked technologies, each individual adoption decision affects the value of using the technology. It adds one vote in favor of a technology. This creates a positive feedback loop directly linked to the actual adoption and consequently it must be incorporated into the diffusion analysis (Arthur, 1990). The continuous growth of the complex technology also changes the properties of the innovation as perceived by the potential adopters. It lowers adoption risks and creates a bias towards the technology. It also guarantees stability of the promoted technology, triggers learning and thereby reduces costs. At the same time, the emergence of the infrastructure lowers the knowledge threshold to adoption and reduces the complexity of the technology (Attewell, 1992). The infrastructure also invites technology providers to produce standard compliant products and services. In combination, this shifts the innovation's properties in favor of adoption. Meanwhile, the infrastructure that favors adoption can over time become an inertia that constrains innovation (Van de Ven, 1993). Hence, whilst the market becomes firmly established it locks the technology properties into a certain trajectory (Arthur, 1989). The innovation is thus a process of path dependency and path creation. This explains why in most countries the mobile telecommunications markets have been transformed from 2G to 3G via a phase of 2.5G technology, and why for 3G system there are two major international standards existing in parallel that are respectively based on two 2G systems used now.

Second, the market transformation involves a social system, which is composed by interrelated providers, users and institutions as is depcited in the lower part of Figure 1. In the light of King et al. (1994), here institutions cover government and public authorities, trade and industry associations, and standard setting bodies. Furthermore, there is an interplay between market innovation and social system. On the one hand, as the industry evolves and the market matures there are varied providers involved according to technological requirement. For example, in 2G market the network operators alone control the market, but for 3G market there exists a provider community composed by manufactures, network operators, service providers, content providers, and service aggregators etc. Firms will carve out their specific roles and create firm-specific value chains. Depending on their specific resources and core competencies, players will position themselves differently, resulting in different overall value systems (Maitland et al., 2002). On the other hand, the three groups of actors work together to promote the market innovation. A specific actor may participate in and influence the market in different ways. For example in 2G system the regulators in general enacted a license through a "beauty match" method, but for 3G market several countries preferred bidding and charged a large sum for one license. As another example, in 2G market the network operators was dominant, but in 3G market it is supposed that the content providers are the "kings" (Muller-Veerse, 2000).

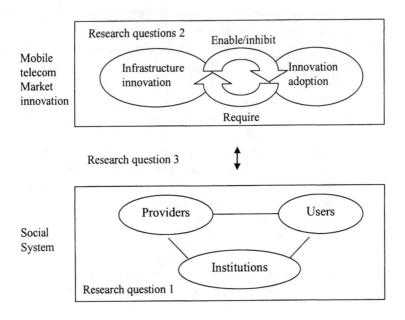

Figure 1. A framework for analyzing mobile telecommunications market innovation

Figure 1 provides a framework for us to capture and explain mobile telecommunications market innovation. According to it we should examine the interrelated action and actor layers of the market. The framework facilitates answering the following questions.

1. What actors is the social system composed of? What are the characteristics of their interactions in the social system? What are their roles in the mobile telecommunication market innovation?

2. How does the mobile telecommunications market transform? How do the infrastructure innovation and innovation adoption co-depend? What is the role of path dependence and path creation for infrastructure innovation and innovation adoption?

3. How does the social structure determine the market development, and in return how does the market development situation influence the characteristics of the social system?

4.   A CASE STUDY

Our framework is suitable to study mobile telecommunications market innvoation, for example the transformation from 2G to 3G. Our concern is with highly complex processes that take several years to unfold. The longitudinal case study method is well suited to capture the richness and complexity of these processes (Holmes and Poole, 1991; Yin, 1994). Following Glaser and Strauss (1967) that researchers need to consider their theoretical purpose in selecting cases, we use China as our data source. In the global scale China offers an interesting case to study. China has the largest GSM network in the world. But its 2.5G market size is very small. Most parts of China's mobile telecommunications market will move from 2G to 3G directly. Now the government is organizing pilot tests on different 3G standards so as to decide 3G licenses.

Our framework is designed for an in-depth longitudinal case study, for which we have not finished the fieldwork yet. In this section we limit our aim to using secondary data to demonstrate the explanatory power of our framework, and hereby seek the necessity to improve it. We also want to solicit guidance for using it in field study in the future. We select our data source from a recent issue of Communications of The ACM (Yan, 2003), which provide a concise but comprehensive description on the mobile telecommunications market innovation in China. By "comprehensive" we mean that ideally the selected papers cover the three themes described by our framework, including the interrelated processes of infrastructure innovation and innovation adoption, as well as the social network around these processes. We dissect the papers and code their data according to our framework. Table 2, 3 and 4 condense our analysis.

Table 2. Mobile telecommunications market development

Market development	
Adoption	An advanced but less user-friendly technology like WAP is not necessarily more commercially viable than basic but easy-to-use ones like SMS
Innovation	Monternet is a system of innovation. WAP fails to form a system of innovation
Dynamics	Generally adoption and innovation are treated as two independent traits of iMode diffusion. It mentions that the success of SMS leads operator to launch Monternet

Table 3. Social system for market development

Social system	
Providers	Cooperation between China Telecom, HP, content providers
Users	Addressed
Institutions	Not mentioned
Interplay between social system and market innovation	The operator and a vendor jointly construct an infrastructure called Aspire, and in return the Aspire platform shapes the relation between the operator, service providers, and content providers

Table 4. Research questions addressed in case paper

	Research questions addressed
Question 1	It has identified the operator, content providers and vendor as major actors, and analyzed their interaction and specific roles
Question 2	It provides a static picture on SMS and WAP diffusion from innovation and adoption perspectives. SMS is an example that adoption influences innovation
Question 3	It has examined interplay between market and social system in the case of Monternet

4.1   Case description

One key argument of the author is that "an advanced but less user-friendly technology like WAP is not necessarily more commercially viable than basic but easy-to-use ones like SMS" (Yan, 2003, p. 84). In China SMS usage volume increased from 126.7 million messages in the first half of 2000 to 40.69 billion messages in the first half of 2003. The author attributes the success of SMS to six factors: 1) It is an economical way to communicate; 2) It is useful in special circumstances, like in a conference when its use will not disturb others; 3) It is better at expressing certain information than verbal media, like delivering greeting on Chinese New Year; 4) It is more suitable for broadcasting information; 5) The Chinese users are reluctant to leave voice messages; 6) It is a tool to distribute jokes and adult humor among subscribers, which are prohibited in the public media. In contrast, the diffusion of WAP is a failure. In contrast, only 2% of Chinese subscribers access Internet via a WAP phone, which is the lowest percentage of the Asia-Pacific economies. This is due to that WAP uses WML language for programming content hence it creates a big switching cost for content providers. As a result the content is limited. Meanwhile WAP runs over circuit-switched networks with low transmission speeds and per-minute charging, which makes it have a very limited value for the users.

The Monternet program introduced by China Mobile from November 2000 plays a key role for the booming of mobile data communications based on SMS. Known as the "one-stop shop, China-wide service" arrangement, it allows information service providers to access the operator's mobile network at any place and time to provide nation-wide services. Following iMode, it has a simple revenue sharing model between the operator and content providers, which is that China Mobile keeps 9% of traffic revenue. In order to facilitate Monternet, in 2000 China Mobile set up a subsidiary called Aspire with Hewlett-Packard that owns 7% of the company. Aspire built the Mobile Information Service Center (MISC) to serve as the common platform for all of China Mobile's mobile Internet services. It was installed on the basis of the distributed structure of China Mobile's provincial operating subsidiaries. A unified MISC platform provides mobile subscribers with mobile data-roaming capabilities throughout China. MISC also provides a uniform data interface open to third-party service providers, through which standard network information, including billing, is provided. Segregating service platforms from basic mobile communication services ensures that all mobile communications networks developed through the platform migrate smoothly when they are upgraded to 2.5G and 3G networks, making them truly forward-compatible networks. Monternet generated an overwhelming response from service providers. As an illustration, by the end of 2000, more than 500 had joined. Especially after China Mobile upgraded the circuit-switching network to a packet-based network, more advanced mobile value-added services like MMS are now available. As a result the mobile data communications market has kept a fast development.

4.2   Case analysis

The six factors for the market success of SMS fall in the category of user adoption. Moreover, this paper attributes the fast development of SMS to Monternet program, which presents a successful case of systems of innovation. Furthermore, the author attributes its development to the efficient interplay between technology innovation and the social system: the operator and a manufacture cooperate to construct an infrastructure called Aspire, and in return the Aspire platform shapes the relation between the operator, service providers and content providers.

The failure of WAP has been explained from adoption perspective that claims that it has limited user values because of low transmission speeds and per-minute charging method. From the innovation perspective content providers hesitate to participate in the market because of high switching cost, and as a result the system of innovation has not been formed.

It has mentioned that the success of SMS encourages the operator to launch Monternet. Unfortunately in this paper has not deeply examined the interrelation between the innovation and adoption processes argued by our model. By inference, as SMS is welcomed by the user, it encourages the operator to invest in technology innovation, which in return promotes the continuous fast development of SMS and other related mobile data communications services. However, for the case of WAP such a cycle of efforts does not exist. This paper is purely a description without any theoretical support. Yet, obviously the facts it gives can be better interpreted using our framework.

5.   DISCUSSION AND CONCLUSION

As Barnes and Huff (2003, p.84) have observed in studying iMode market in Japan: though technology adoption theories help us understand how characteristics of technology, factors underlying the behavioral norms, and industry features have driven the rapid market development, it needs a comprehensive framework to explain how these factors together forge market innovation. In this paper we move one step towards this aim. Our framework integrates adoption and innovation perspectives. It calls for a dynamic description on the process of innovation and adoption, and a focus on the interrelation of these two processes. It encourages disclosing the interplay of mobile telecommunications market innovation and its social systems. Our framework enables the researchers to have a systematic description on a diffusion issue. It offers a higher explanatory power compared with a traditional innovation or adoption theory.

We have used the case of China to justify our framework. We find the case paper only addresses part of the questions that should be covered by our model (see section 3). It notices that adoption and innovation are necessary perspectives to analyze a diffusion process, and observe social systems are an important dimension to analyze a diffusion process. However, basically it omits the interplay between social systems and market development, and interrelation between adoption and innovation. Their analyses are static in nature.

One conclusion is that our model has a high explanatory power to analyze the diffusion of mobile technologies. Currently we are drawing upon this model to engage in an in-depth field study on mobile telecommunications market development in different countries including China. We aim to generate market innovation patterns by comparing the answers of different countries to our research questions enumerated in section 3. Moreover, following the principle of dialogical reasoning we will rationalize the present theoretical assumptions about mobile telecommunications market innovation as the data collection moves forwards. During this process, we open the opportunities of improving our model so as to make it generally applicable to studying other networked technologies (Klein and Myers, 1999).

ACKNOWLEDGEMENT

This research was conducted as a part of Mobiconomy project at Copenhagen Business School. Mobiconomy is partially supported by the Danish Research Agency, grant number 2054-03-0004.

REFERENCES

Ajzen, I. *Understanding Attitude and Predicting Social Behavior,* Prentice-Hall, 1980.

Anckar, B., D'Incau, D. "Value Creation in Mobile Commerce: Findings from a Consumer Survey", *Journal of Information Technology Theory and Application,* (4:1), 2002, pp. 43-64.

Arthur, W.B. "Competing Technologies, Increasing Returns and Lock-in by Historical Events", *Economic Journal,* 99, 1989, pp. 116-131.

Arthur, W.B. "Positive Feedbacks in the Economy", *Scientific American,* (262:2), 1990, pp. 80-85.

Attewell, P. "Technology Diffusion and Organizational Learning: the Case of Business Computing", *Organization Science,* (3:1), 1992, pp. 1-19.

Barnes, S.J., Huff, S.L. "Rising Sun: iMode and the Wireless Internet", *Communications of the ACM,* (46:11), 2003, pp. 79-84.

Choudrie, J., Papazafeiropoulou, A., Lee, H. "A Web of Stakeholders and Strategies: A Case of Broadband Diffusion in South Korea", *Journal of Information Technology,* (18.4), 2003, pp.281-290.

Ciborra, C.U. *From Control to Drift: the Dynamics of Corporate Information Infrastructures,* Oxford University Press, 2000.

Damsgaard, J. "Managing an Internet portal", *Communications of the AIS,* (9:26), 2002, pp. 408-420.Davis, F.D. "Perceived Usefulness, Perceived Ease of Use, and User Acceptance of Information Technology", *MIS Quarterly,* (13:3), 1989, pp. 319-340.

Dosi, G., Freeman, C., Nelson, R., Soete, L. *Technical Change and Economic Theory,* 1988.

Edquist, C. *Systems of Innovation: Technologies, Institutions, and Organizations,* 1997.

Edquist, C. *The Internet and Mobile Telecommunications Systems of Innovation,* UK: Edward Elgar, 2003.

Funk, J.L., Methe, D.T. "Market- and Committee-based Mechanisms in the Creation and Diffusion of Global Industry Standards: the Case of Mobile Communication", *Research Policy,* 30, 2001, pp. 589-610.

Glaser, B.G., Strauss, A.L. *The Discovery of Grounded Theory: Strategies for Qualitative Research,* New York: Aldine Publishing Company, 1967.

Holmes, M., Poole, M.S. "The Longitudinal Analysis of Interaction", in *Studying Interpersonal Interaction,* B. Montgomery and S. Duck (eds.), New York: Guilford, 1991.

King, J.L., Gurbaxani, V., Kraemer, K.L., McFarlan, F.W., Raman, K.S., Yap, C.S. "Institutional Factors in Information Technology Innovation", *Information Systems Research,* (5:2), 1994, pp. 139-169.

Klein, H. K., Myers, M.D. "A Set of Principles for Conducting and Evaluating Interpretive Field Studies in Information Systems", *MIS Quarterly,* (23:1), 1999, pp. 67-93.

Lyytinen, K., Damsgaard, J. "What's Wrong with the Diffusion of Innovation Theory"? in *Diffusing Software Product and Process Innovations,* M.A. Ardis and B.L. Marcolin (eds.), Kluwer Academic Publishers, 2001, pp. 173-190.

Muller-Veerse, F. *Mobile Commerce Report,* London: Durlacher Research Ltd, 2000.

Oliva, T.A. "Technological Choice under Conditions of Changing Network Externality", *The Journal of High Technology Management Research,* (5:2), 1994, pp. 279-298.

Pedersen, A.F., Andersen, K.V., Jelbo, C. "The Paradox of the Mobile Internet: Acceptance of Gadgets and Rejection of Innovations", *Proceedings of 16th Bled eCommerce Conference*, 2003.

Rogers, E.M. *Diffusion of Innovations,* New York: The Free Press, 1995.

Shapiro, C., Varian, H.R. *Information Rules: A Strategic Guide to the Network Economy,* Boston, Mass.: Harvard Business School Press, 1999.

Star, S.L. and Ruhleder, K. "Steps toward Ecology of Infrastructure: Design and Access for Large Information Spaces", *Information Systems Research*, (7:1), 1996, pp. 111-134.

Tornatzky, L.G., Klein, K.J. "Innovation Characteristics and Adoption-Implementation", *IEEE Transactions on Engineering Management,* (29:1), 1982, pp. 28-45.

Van de Ven, A.H. "A Community Perspective on the Emergence of Innovations", *Journal of Engineering and Technology Management*, (10,) 1993, pp. 23-51.

Wolfe, R.A. "Organizational Innovation: Review, Critique and Suggested Research Directions", *Journal of Management Studies*, (31:3), 1994, pp. 405-431.

Yan, X. "Mobile Data Communications in China", *Communications of the ACM,* (46:12), 2003, pp. 81-85.

Yin, R. K. *Case Study Research: Design and Methods,* Thousand Oaks, CA: Sage, 1994.

FINITE SEGMENTATION FOR XML CACHING

Adelhard Türling and Stefan Böttcher
Faculty of electrical engineering, computer science and mathematic, Fürstenallee 11, D-33102 Paderborn, Germany, Email: Adelhard.Tuerling@uni-paderborn.de, stb@uni-paderborn.de

Abstract: XML data processing often relies on basic relations between two XML fragments like containment, subset, difference and intersection. Fast calculation of such relations based only on the representing XPath expression is known to be a major challenge. Recently XML patterns have been introduced to model and identify handy subclasses of XPath. We present the concept of ST-pattern segments that uses sets of adapted tree patterns in order to describe a finite and complete partitioning of the XML document's data space. Based on such segmentations, we present a fast evaluation of XML relations and show how to compute a set of patterns for an optimal segmentation based on frequent XPath queries.

Key words: mobile databases; XML; query patterns; XPath; caching.

1.   INTRODUCTION

Whenever XML data is exchanged, processed and cached on computers within a network, data management meets new challenges. For example, in networks of resource-limited mobile devices, efficient usage of data storage and data transportation over a wireless network is a key requirement[10-12]. In such a network, a common situation is that a client queries for data of a dedicated source. Within such a network, it may be of considerable advantage to share and exchange cached XML data among several neighboring clients, compared to a solution where data is only transferred between each requesting client and a dedicated server. One of the main new challenges in such a data sharing scenario is the organization of the data space which is shared among the clients. This includes specifying how the data space can be divided into handy segments, how to profit from distributed data according to these segments, and how cooperative usage in a network can enhance data processing. A basic challenge of fragmentation is to identify a finite set of atomic XML fragments for cooperative usage. Whether or not data segments have to be requested in order to fulfill an operation, must be decided by data processing components on the fly, without losing time for extensive intersection tests and difference fragment computations on XML data. To enable collaborative use of a so called segmentation, we identify two requirements for the segmentation's atomic data units, namely the segments. Firstly, segments can be easily (re-)joined and identified (minimal operating costs). Secondly, most query results can be represented by such segments or joins of such segments with little or no dispensable offset (fitting granularity). Obviously there is a conflict between the requirement of a fitting granularity and the need of a finite and collaboratively accepted segmentation. We address this area of conflict and show how to find an optimal segmentation based on access frequency analysis of XML patterns.

The remainder of our paper is organized as follows. In Section 2, we propose to expand the common definition of patterns towards what we call ST-pattern and give a short introduction in the main features and properties. In Section 3, we show in detail how to use the most frequent patterns as a base to decompose the data space into disjointed segments. In Section 4, we discuss related work. And within section 5, we present the summary and conclusion of our contribution.

```
<!ELEMENT car EMPTY>
<!ATTLIST car
    name CDATA #REQUIRED
    year CDATA #REQUIRED
    price CDATA #REQUIRED
    type (truck | convert | limo)
#REQUIRED
>
<!ELEMENT contact EMPTY>
<!ATTLIST contact
    name CDATA #REQUIRED
    image CDATA #REQUIRED
>
<!ELEMENT offer (seller, car+)>
<!ELEMENT offers (offer+)>
<!ELEMENT seller (contact+)>
<!ATTLIST seller
    town CDATA #REQUIRED
>
```

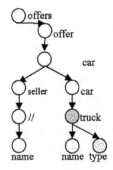

Figure 1. Example DTD   *Figure 2.* Example for ST-pattern

2. FOUNDATION AND ST-PATTERN

In this section, we shortly review the concept of DTD graphs and XML patterns. We introduce *search-tree patterns* (short ST-pattern) based on additional nodes namely *split nodes* that partition a node's child set. We use ST-patterns as logical data descriptions for data processing that are easy to handle and that allow a good degree of granularity. We here withhold the formal and complete definition of ST-pattern and their operations due to page limitation and refer to future publications. Instead, we give some examples and an overview of properties.

2.1 Definition of the DTD graph

DTDs are schema definitions for XML documents. As long as the DTD is acyclic, such a DTD can be rolled out and represented as a tree. Each element, text-node and attribute occurring in such a DTD is converted to a node in the DTD graph. The parent-child relation (and the attribute-relation) between the elements and the attributes of a DTD are represented by directed edges within the DTD graph. A DTD graph for the DTD of Figure 1 can be seen in Figure 3. In a DTD graph, a '*' is concatenated to a node's label to indicate that the DTD allows the occurrence of that node at that position in an arbitrary quantity, e.g. for car, offer and contact. Ignoring the special annotation '*', a DTD graph can also be seen as an XML pattern.

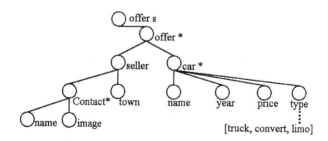

Figure 3. Example DTD graph

2.2 XML patterns

XML tree patterns are used in the context of XML as expressions that describe XML fragments. These patterns can be seen as tree models for XML queries. Nodes of a pattern can be labeled with any tag name, the wildcard '*' or the relative paths '//', where '*' indicates any label and '//' represents a node sequence of zero or more interconnected nodes. Directed edges represent parent → child relations. These edges must correspond to relations defined in a DTD, e.g. fulfill the restriction of a single incoming edge for each node, to be valid according to the given DTD. Furthermore, we use the same terminology for patterns as used for XML documents. For example, we call all nodes that can be reached by outgoing edges the node's children, the incoming edge leads to the node's parent, all children of a node are in sibling relation and the transitive closure of all nodes reached by outgoing (incoming) edges is called the set of descendent (ancestor) nodes.

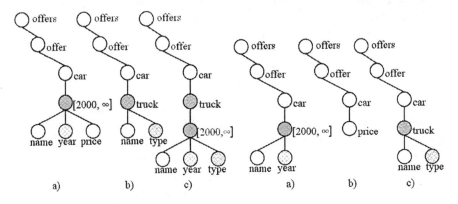

Figure 4. Pattern c) is the intersection of the two ST-patterns a) and b).

Figure 5. The 3 most frequently accessed patterns.

2.3   ST-patterns

In contrast to basic XML patterns[9], *ST-patterns* are restricted to rooted patterns because they describe XML fragments that correspond to absolute XPath expressions. In addition, we introduce a new node type called *split node* which contains simple selection information as used in XPath filters. As an example in Figure 2, the additional nodes labeled 'truck' and 'type' restrict the pattern to cars of type truck. Such patterns support a minimal subset of possible filter expressions known from XPath, just enough to describe the granularity required. With the DTD given in Figure 1, an XPath query which asks for car-offers of type 'truck' and which is interested in car-names and available car-sellers could be:

offers/offer/*[@type='truck' or self::name()='seller']//@name.

Figure 2 shows the corresponding ST-pattern. We call an XML data-fragment that is selected by an ST-pattern the fragment related to a pattern or for short, *pattern fragment*.

2.4   Operations and properties of ST-patterns

Split nodes are of a specific comparison type and contain specific decision criteria. We distinguish between two types of split nodes: *range-based* and *equality-based* split nodes. See Figures 4a and 4b. Split nodes are related to two nodes in the ST-pattern. The two related nodes are called *split parent* and *reference node* (short ref. node). The ref. node must be a leaf node in the pattern. In our examples throughout the paper, we visualize a split node and its ref. node with an identical texture where the split node is gray and the ref. node is white, indicating that the ref. node must fulfill the split node's decision criteria. The split parent is the first node on the ref. node's ancestor-axis in the pattern that is marked as multiple occurring in the DTD graph. This relation indicates that the sub fragment represented by this split parent is constrained by the split node. The `contact`, `offer` or `car` node might be split parents in our example. A split parent's sub decision tree can have multiple split nodes, which follow a predefined tree-level-based order. We call the complete sub tree of a split parent, its *sub decision tree*.

We define two ST-patterns to be space equal, if they describe the same pattern fragment for a given DTD and for any XML document valid to that DTD. The two operations *compress* and *extend* are used to space equally transform ST-patterns e.g. for normalization purposes.

The three operations *union*, *intersection* and *difference* map two given ST-patterns onto a resulting ST-pattern. For any valid XML document, the resulting ST-pattern describes a pattern fragment that is equal to the result of the given operation applied to the pattern fragments of the two operands.

See Figure 4c as an example for an intersection of the patterns 4a and 4b. We say that two ST-patterns are disjointed, if for every pair of corresponding leaf nodes that they have in common, (1) the two nodes must be ref. nodes and (2) the split nodes they belong to have no overlapping decision criteria.

Evaluating operations on ST-patterns can be done by adapting fast XML match algorithms. Similar to the more complex XPath expressions, ST-patterns are used to select fragments of an underlying XML document and thereby address the document with a fine granularity. For example, any ST-pattern can be split into two patterns, where each of the resulting patterns addresses a fragment with about half the size of the fragment the original patterns addressed. Thus, any fragmentation granularity can be achieved.

3.   SEGMENTATION

In Section 2, the definition and some operations for ST-patterns have been introduced. Now we show how these patterns can be used to organize fast XML data processing. Therefore we reconsider that every ST-pattern (based on the DTD) represents a pattern fragment in an XML document (usually in an underlying XML database).

We use pattern fragments as atomic data items in any data processing. In addition, a pattern fragment belongs to a specific pattern segmentation. A pattern segmentation represents a complete decomposition of the whole underlying schema S and is based on the given DTD tree. Beyond the DTD tree detail level, a schema S might even be decomposed by additional equations or ranges on specified node values to support specific requirements. In this section, we shape the requirements for segmentations and show how they are constructed relying on ST-patterns.

3.1   Requirements for a fitting segmentation

It is elementary for the success of data processing to find the appropriate set of patterns which represents the segmentation. Their corresponding pattern fragments are the atomic data units our XML processing is based on. Thus, the patterns shall represent fragments that are handy in the following sense: For a given XPath request, it shall be easy to find the optimal set of patterns where the union U of those patterns relates to an XML fragment that is the smallest possible superset of the XML fragment represented by the XPath request. The parts of the fragment related to U, that are not needed to answer the XPath request, should be minimal or none for frequent requests. We call these parts *clipping offsets* of patterns corresponding to an XPath request. Data transfer overhead caused by the segmentation must be minimal and come out as a clear advantage compared with savings based e.g. on caching.

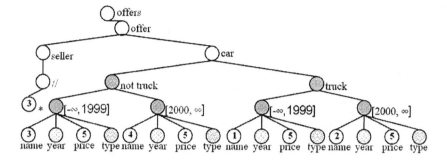

Figure 6. Colored schema graph (numbers represent colors)

3.2 Pattern segmentation

Formally, we define:

A *pattern segmentation* S is a set of pair-wise disjointed ST-patterns {p_1, p_2, ... , p_n}where the union of all p_i results in a pattern $P_{complete}(S)$ representing the whole data space, e.g. given by the corresponding DTD. The graph representation of $P_{complete}(S)$ is called the segmentation's schema graph. Notice that the DTD graph is a valid schema graph. In general, there are many different valid segmentations for a single schema graph. For the DTD graph, the DTD's pattern itself as well as S = {//*} are valid segmentations with |S| = 1. Figure 8 shows a segmentation with five patterns, Figure 6 shows the corresponding schema graph. To encode the specific segmentation in a schema graph, we introduce colored schema graphs. For example in Figure 6, the numbers inside the nodes represent their colors. All leaf nodes that are not ref. nodes have an associated color identifying the pattern in the segmentation they belong to. The following has to be proven to verify that a set of ST-patterns S is a segmentation:

- For each pair of patterns in S, the intersection test shows that they are disjointed.
- $P_{complete}(S)$ must be space equivalent to the underlying DTD's pattern.

3.3 Glue nodes and the ID constraint

As the set of ST-patterns of a segmentation are pair-wise disjointed, the pattern fragments they describe, describe a pair-wise disjointed partitioning of the XML document's leaf nodes. For a given segmentation, a major requirement is to guarantee that the union, intersection and difference of any two patterns of the segmentation can also be applied to their related XML fragments. Thus, we have to assure to track the pattern fragments' relationships to each other. In the context of XML trees, one-to-one and one-to-many relationships are supported[4]. For example, in the segmentation of Figure 8, the segment defined by pattern p_3 has a one-to-many relationship to all other segments. The segments defined by the patterns p_1, p_2, p_4, p_5 all have a one-to-one relationship to each other. We define some multiple occurring nodes from the DTD to be *glue nodes* which we require to have a unique key attribute. If the DTD doesn't support the required IDs they can be added in a preprocessing step. We don't have to apply the union, intersection or difference operation to the pattern fragments directly. It is enough to calculate the operations on the corresponding pattern and to use the resulting pattern as a filter for a joined pattern fragment. To guarantee that any two pattern fragments can be joined, we use pairs of IDs and references. In our small example, the car node and the offer node are both glue nodes and as the DTD does not support ID attributes for them, we have to provide additional ID attributes. To identify a segmentation's glue nodes, each pair of patterns of the segmentation is tested. A pair's glue node is the first multiple occurring node they have in common in the colored schema graph starting at the patterns' leaf nodes. Based on the glue node's ID, any relationship between XML fragments that correspond to a segmentation's patterns can be joined. In our example, the fragment corresponding to the pattern p_3 can be joined with any fragment corresponding to pattern p_2 up to p_5 (one-to-many relationship), by using the offer ID as a join criterion. Fragments corresponding to the patterns p_1, p_2, p_4, p_5 can be joined by using the car ID as a join criterion (one-to-one relationship). As we see, the number of glue nodes is bounded by the amount of multiple occurring nodes, but can be smaller and is segmentation dependent. For example, the multiple occurring contact node is not a glue node, since it is not needed to join pattern fragments.

> **Input**: given DTD graph
> Sorted list of most frequent query patterns L= $\{q_1,…, q_n\}$
> **Initialize**:   S = $\{//*\}$
> Ref. node order: O = $\{\emptyset\}$
> Max. node index: I_{max} = const. (e.g. 2)
> Clip tolerance T = const. (e.g. 0.9)
> Max |S|: $|S|_{max}$ = const. (e.g. 100)
> 10   For each q_i in L do {
> 11   For each p_j in S do {

---

[4] XML supports special id/id_ref attributes to support n to n relations. Our techniques support such relationships but are not optimized for them.

```
12   If intersect (qᵢ, pⱼ) ≠ Ø  {
13       p_temp1 = compress (intersect (qᵢ, pⱼ))
14       p_temp2 = compress (difference (qᵢ, pⱼ))
15       If (max_amount_split_node_series(p_temp1) < I_max ) and
16       (max_amount_split_node_series(p_temp2) < I_max ) and
17       ((size(pattern_fragment (p_temp1) / size(pattern_fragment (pⱼ) < T)) or
18       (size(pattern_fragment (p_temp2) / size(pattern_fragment (pⱼ) < T)))  {
19           remove pⱼ from S
20           if              not           contained(S_temp1.newRefNode,O)
add(S_temp1.newRefNode,O)
21           if              not           contained(S_temp2.newRefNode,O)
add(S_temp2.newRefNode,O)
22           add(S_temp1, S)
23           add(S_temp2, S)
24   } }
25   break if |S| >= |S|_max
25   }
```

Figure 7. Segmentation algorithm

3.4   Construction of the finite pattern segmentation

The amount of different patterns corresponding to a non-recursive DTD is already finite, if split nodes are not used, because there is a finite set of possible patterns for each set of edges. A pattern with the maximum amount of edges and nodes is the DTD graph itself. As we introduce split nodes, we have to constrain the size of segmentations by a threshold $|S|_{max}$. The value of $|S|_{max}$ correlates with the granularity of the segmentation and must be adjusted application-context dependent, considering DTD complexity and the amount of represented data. In order to keep the pattern set of a segmentation finite, we restrict the amount of segments in a segmentation to a fix maximum $|S|_{max}$. For example, for the DTD graph given in Figure 3, a valid segmentation with $|S| = 5$ is shown in Figure 8. Additionally we might constrain the depth of sub decision trees to limit the segmentation's schema graph complexity and the amount of ref. nodes in a single pattern.

A good solution to establish a fitting segmentation is to analyze the access frequency to certain tree patterns and to build a segmentation according to the most frequently accessed pattern. Our algorithm is based on that concept and takes a sorted list L of the most frequent requests as input. The resulting segmentation can guarantee that any of the requests in L can be answered exactly by joined pattern fragments of the segmentation. The algorithm of Figure 7 creates such a segmentation. Starting with an initial segmentation S = {//*}, it splits patterns until $|S| = |S|_{max}$. For each frequently requested pattern q_1 of L, it has to be checked with which of the exiting patterns p_i in S it intersects (line12) and for each intersecting pattern p_j the intersection and difference has to be calculated (lines 13, 14). Thereafter, each such p_j is removed from S, and the segments intersect($q_{i,}$, p_J) and difference($q_{i,}$, p_J) are added to the segmentation (lines 19, 22, 23). The ref. node order simply correlates with the sequence in which they are first referenced by a split node (lines 20, 21). Iterating the above steps, we keep the set of patterns in the segmentation disjointed and thus the segmentation valid. Figure 8 shows a possible resulting segmentation for $|S|_{max}=5$. Constructing a segmentation according to the presented algorithm, patterns that are used to answer frequent requests are in general very specific and represent a small segment of the XML document. In comparison, infrequently requested patterns are in general more unspecific in the sense of conglomerations and are related to bigger segments in the XML document.

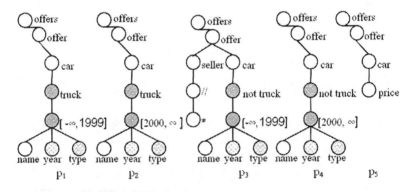

Figure 8. A pattern segmentation for the given DTD

3.5   Thresholds

In addition, the algorithm provides the two thresholds I_{max} and T to adjust the basic segmentation algorithm (lines 15 to 18).

The threshold I_{max} constrains the amount of descendent sequenced split nodes in the resulting patterns. Using this threshold can compensate two drawbacks. First, such sequences can expand a schema graph's sub-tree exponential. Since the schema graph is the 'construction plan' for any further data processing, transmitting and fast processing of the schema graph are important operations and a rather compact graph is preferred. Second, such series result in related XML fragments that are in a one-to-one relation which need to have ID nodes as introduced in 3.3. T is a threshold that corresponds to the degree of acceptable clipping tolerance. Since the transmission of a slightly bigger pattern fragment is acceptable, this threshold can prevent unneeded granularity. For this threshold, it is important to take the related pattern fragment's size in the XML document into account, rather than just to stick to the pattern's relative fraction of the schema graph. As mentioned, both thresholds must be set up according to the application's domain. The algorithm of Figure 11 creates the valid segmentation shown in Figure 8 for the input $L = \{5a, 5b, 5c\}$, $T=1$, $I_{max} = 2$ and the given DTD.

3.6   Mapping from and to XPath

In general, applications based on XML access XML fragments by XPath expressions. Mapping such an XPath query to patterns of a finite segmentation is easy. Since all patterns of the segmentation are disjointed, we just have to identify which patterns contribute to the result. Therefore, we represent the colored schema graph as an XML document and query it with the given XPath expression. Each color in the result represents a contributing pattern and the join of the related pattern fragments is the minimal superset of the XML fragment selected by the given XPath expression. If after joining the exact result is needed, the obtained superset can be queried by the standard XPath evaluation engine, e.g. a SAX filter. Mapping from ST-patterns to XPath is even simpler. Each node of a pattern represents a node-test, each edge a child-axe and each split node a conjunctive-filter-criterion of its split parent in a corresponding XPath expression.

3.7   Segmentation in application context

As seen in Section 3.5, a fitting segmentation, e.g. for the system introduced in Section 2, can be calculated in a preprocessing step. Thereafter, the colored schema graph, e.g. in number scheme representation form, can be published. Even more, we suggest adapting the segmentation continuously according to query behavior, if the overall clients' focus changes. For example, think of a train schedule where the focus changes naturally with elapsing time. In such cases, an update of the colored schema graph and the information about some invalid pattern segments has to be distributed. A centralized technique, that keeps track of focus changes, is to let the client send the original XPath expression with the request towards the server. The server or an intermediate caching server can analyze the query, can match it with the requested pattern, and can calculate the amount of data that is not needed in the answer-pattern fragment. This information can be used in order to identify inefficient segmentations and can thereby lead to an adjustment of the segmentation and a reduced response. Cache management for server and client can use the colored schema graph as index structures for lookups and store the pattern fragments in joined form in their memory. Thus, finding the set of missing and locally available segments can be done fast by querying the locally available colored schema graph.

As the originator of a request joins the pattern fragments as they arrive, the IDs introduced in Section 3.3 are used for accurate matching of any two pattern fragments using join optimization concepts[17, 18]. Any cache server contributing more than one segment can even send its pattern fragments in joined form to reduce calculation overhead and transmission of redundant ref. nodes in one-to-one relations. An alternative solution to the usage of filters to obtain the exact answer to the last XPath request as introduced in Section 3.7, is to mark nodes during the join process as 'not belonging to the current request' and thus defining a temporary view.

As well as changes in the segmentation, updates in XML documents must be propagated. A simple solution could be a master server that coordinates updates and distributes the list of effected pattern fragments to indicate that they are outdated. Since ST-patterns guarantee that their decision criterions (the ref. nodes) are included in the pattern fragment, finding and updating affected patterns can be performed in a decentralized manner and thus only a moderate amount of communication between master server and any cache server is needed. For example, after updating an outdated value, the client can decide whether the changed node still belongs to the original pattern or belongs to a different pattern and can publish that information.

3.8   Properties of finite segmentations

Besides the properties of ST-patterns discussed in Section 2, patterns of a finite segmentation have some properties which make them perfectly suitable for XML data processing. As seen in Section 3.6, it is easy to find the set of needed patterns to answer any query. The found set is optimal, since all patterns in the segmentation are disjointed. The algorithm of Figure 7 finds a finite segmentation providing pattern fragments that answer frequent queries with no or minimal clipping offset. With finite segmentations, we have the instrument to build fast data processing modules for XML data. As discussed in Section 3.6, the use of ID nodes in coexisting pattern fragments with one-to-one relations turn out as no disadvantage, since they are transferred and stored redundancy free, if accessed in common. The additional IDs introduced to manage union-, intersection- or difference-joining of pattern fragments are an acceptable overhead compared to the achievable savings, e.g. with finite segmentation caching.

4. RELATED WORK

Tree patterns are well known in the context of XML data processing and especially used to improve query response times. To search frequent XML tree patterns in XML documents[8] is a widely adapted technique and is used for various applications, ranging from indexing optimal access paths[1-3] to the formulation of various classes of XML queries[4,5]. We follow these approaches, as we use frequent access tree patterns to achieve optimization goals. With the latter two approaches, we have in common to use tree patterns to specify subclasses of queries. Tree patterns represent the tree-structure of XML query languages like XPath[6] or XQuery[7], and are treated separately from regular expressions also found in such queries. In the context of querying and maintaining incomplete data, Abiteboul[20] shows a solution for XML data. The presented incomplete data trees are similar to our colored schema graphs, in that they use conditions on the elements' data values and are based on DTDs. Different to our approach, their incomplete tree is used for fast calculation of missing parts in a single client.

In comparison to all these approaches, we use tree patterns to identify sets of pattern fragments and include some information also found in regular expressions and handle them in a search tree manner. A caching strategy based on frequently accessed tree patterns is introduced in Yang[9]. We extend the approach of classical patterns presented in Yang[9] to ST-patterns including predicate filters, which enable us to express finer XML granularity. Our approach also differs in that we support cooperative caching by sets of pair-wise disjointed patterns.

A different approach for XML caching is to check whether cached data can contribute to a new request by testing the intersection of cache entries and an XPath query[16] and thereafter compute difference fragments as partial results[19]. Such tests are known to be NP-hard for XPath expressions[13, 15] and difference computations are known to be resource consuming. In comparison, our approach focuses on efficient computation and thereby requires only minimal resource consumption.

5. SUMMARY AND CONCLUSIONS

We expect finite pattern segmentation to be a solution for splitting a huge XML document into handy atomic units to support fast data processing based on simple and fast intersection and containment decisions, e.g. in the area of cashing, replication or query processing. The drawback of using normalized data units is a clipping offset caused by answering a request by a slightly bigger superset. This is acceptable, since frequent requests can be answered with minimal or no clipping offset based on a well adjusted preprocessed segmentation. Especially in the area of mobile data processing, it is important to minimize communication costs and preserve the mobile client's resources. Besides communication resources, we keep shared CPU resources to a minimum because costly intersection or containment tests are reduced to simple lookups. In the context of collaborative data processing, it is important that participating clients interact and interchange data based on a set of predefined data units. Otherwise, advantages of collaboration will be consumed by adjusting and comparing (slightly) different data objects.

Currently we implement a mobile peer-to-peer approach which will use finite segmentation caching for any data exchange. In our further research, we address the challenge of segmentation adoption and update propagation for the overall system. Adapting ST-patterns towards dependent patterns, not containing the decision criteria, and distributed query processing[17, 18] based on ST-patterns, seem to be further promising steps. We use these search tree patterns (ST-patterns) to model virtual schema expansion which we intend to discuss in detail in future publications. Our solution is especially tailored to adapt to context switches in query behavior supporting, e.g., a fine granularity in hot spot areas.

REFERENCES

1. Chin-Wan Chung, Jun-Ki Min, Kyuseok Shim: APEX: an adaptive path index for XML data. SIGMOD Conference 2002: 121-132 [DBLP:conf/sigmod/ChungMS02]
2. Torsten Grust: Accelerating XPath location steps. SIGMOD Conference 2002: 109-120
3. Raghav Kaushik, Philip Bohannon, Jeffrey F. Naughton, Henry F. Korth: Covering indexes for branching path queries. SIGMOD Conference 2002: 133-144
4. Shurug Al-Khalifa, H. V. Jagadish, Jignesh M. Patel, Yuqing Wu, Nick Koudas, Divesh Srivastava: Structural Joins: A Primitive for Efficient XML Query Pattern Matching. ICDE 2002
5. Nicolas Bruno, Nick Koudas, Divesh Srivastava: Holistic twig joins: optimal XML pattern matching. SIGMOD Conference 2002: 310-321
6. J. Clark and S. DeRose. XML Path Language (XPath) version 1.0 W3C recommendation, 1999.
7. D. Chamberlin, D. Florescu, J. Robie, J. Simon, and M. Stefanescu. XQuery: A Query Language for XML W3C working draft, 2001.
8. L. H. Yang, M. L. Lee, W. Hsu. Mining Frequent Query Patterns in XML. 8th Int. Conference on Database Systems for Advanced Applications (DASFAA), 2003.
9. Liang Huai Yang, Mong-Li Lee, Wynne Hsu: Efficient Mining of XML Query Patterns for Caching. VLDB 2003: 69-80
10. Stefan Böttcher, Adelhard Türling: XML Fragment Caching for Small Mobile Internet Devices. Web, Web-Services, and Database Systems 2002: 268-279
11. Franky Lam, Nicole Lam, Raymond K. Wong: Efficient synchronization for mobile XML data. CIKM 2002: 153-160

12. Douglas B. Terry, Venugopalan Ramasubramanian: Caching XML Web Services for Mobility. ACM Queue 1(1): (2003)
13. Jan Hidders: Satisfiability of XPath Expressions. DBPL 2003: 21-36
14. Georg Gottlob, Christoph Koch, Reinhard Pichler: XPath Query Evaluation: Improving Time and Space Efficiency. ICDE 2003: 379-390
15. Georg Gottlob, Christoph Koch, Reinhard Pichler: The complexity of XPath query evaluation. PODS 2003: 179-190
16. S. Böttcher: Testing Intersection of XPath Expressions under DTDs. International Database Engineering & Applications Symposium. Coimbra, Portugal, July 2004.
17. Yanlei Diao, Michael J. Franklin: Query Processing for High-Volume XML Message Brokering. VLDB 2003: 261-272
18. Alan Halverson, Josef Burger, Leonidas Galanis, Ameet Kini, Rajasekar Krishnamurthy, Ajith Nagaraja Rao, Feng Tian, Stratis Viglas, Yuan Wang, Jeffrey F. Naughton, David J. DeWitt: Mixed Mode XML Query Processing. VLDB 2003: 225-236
19. S. Böttcher, Adelhard Türling: Caching XML Data for Mobile Web Clients. International Conference on Internet Computing IC'04, Las Vegas, USA, Juni 2004.
20. Serge Abiteboul, Luc Segoufin, Victor Vianu: Representing and Querying XML with Incomplete Information. PODS 2001 [DBLP:conf/pods/AbiteboulSV01]

FACTORS INFLUENCING THE DESIGN OF MOBILE SERVICES

Michael Amberg, Jens Wehrmann and Ralf Zimmer
Chair for Business Information Technology, University of Erlangen-Nuremberg, Lange Gasse 20, 90403 Nuremberg, Germany. Telephone: +49-911-5302-800; Fax: +49-911-5302-802, Email: {michael.amberg; jens.wehrmann; ralf.zimmer}@wiso.uni-erlangen.de

Abstract: Due to emerging technologies and a high speed of innovation the planning and development process of mobile services is highly dynamic. Numerous failures of mobile services emphasise the need for a comprehensive analysis of all relevant influencing factors. A widely accepted understanding of the number and type of factors to be analysed during the development of mobile services does not exist.

  This paper provides a theory based framework that helps to identify a balanced set of relevant influencing factors. For this purpose the contribution of different scientific approaches is examined. By combining these approaches a framework for the classification is derived within a two step process. First experiences confirmed its suitability for the systematic classification of factors influencing the design of mobile services.

Key words: Classification of Influencing Factors; Theory Based Classification Framework; Design of Mobile Services

1. MOTIVATION

Mobile services for end-users (e.g. messaging, navigation, yellow pages, chats) are more and more influencing our private life. The Gartner Group estimates the annual turnover for mobile services in 2005 to be more than 32 billion US$ with a rapidly growing trend in the future[1]. In contrast to the development of regular end-user products the development of mobile services is characterised by a permanent and frequent appearance of new technologies. This makes the planning and development process of mobile services highly dynamic[2].

Potential end-users often do not recognize the added value or are not willing to pay the price for a specific mobile service. Even extensive marketing campaigns do not lead to a satisfying dissemination and revenue of a broad spectrum of mobile services. As a consequence mobile services are often not developed any further, marketing campaigns are stopped or the services are displaced.

Böcker and Kotzbauer empirically verify the positive coherence between systematic planning of an innovation and its success[3]. Influencing factors that are not adequately considered may lead to an incomplete or incorrect specification of mobile services. As any misinterpretation affects all following phases of development, the analysis and planning process is particularly important for the design of a mobile service[4,5].

To support these processes scientific approaches help to manage the existing complexity. Models that especially focus on mobile services and regard the identification of influencing factors are not established. According to this lack of suitable approaches this paper discusses different approaches for an identification of influencing factors in a two step process. Chapter 2 presents four basic dimensions for a classification of influencing factors. Chapter 3-6 discusses a sub-division for each of these dimensions. Chapter 7 summarises the results, chapter 8 gives an outlook.

2.   CLASSIFICATION OF INFLUENCING FACTORS

For a systematic planning process there is a need for a comprehensive, complete and disjunctive classification of influencing factors of mobile services. Regarding the state of the art literature leads to several classifications that either provide an abstract overview or regard parts of the entirety of influencing factors more detailed. These detailed approaches do not identify concrete influencing factors in general, but provide classifications with a level of abstraction that is regarded as appropriate for identifying influencing factors for specific mobile services.

The combination of general and detailed approaches leads to a two step process for the classification of influencing factors of mobile services[6]. In a first step general dimensions can be identified. In a second step these dimensions can be subdivided to permit the identification of tangible influencing factors of mobile services.

In the first step mobile services can be divided into the four dimensions *Structure*, *Process*, *Outcomes* and *Market*[6,7]. This classification traces back to several approaches that identify the first three dimensions for a systematic service engineering[8-11]. Taking external dependencies of mobile services into account these dimensions can be extended by the fourth dimension *Market*[7]. Amberg et al. give a detailed overview of current state of the art approaches[6].

The *Structure* dimension describes the required input factors for the service development[12]. The *Process* dimension represents all required processes during the product lifecycle[11]. The *Outcome* of a mobile service can be divided into procedural outcome and impact of the outcome[13,14]. The procedural outcome can be evaluated at the end of the service provision. The impact of the mobile service has a medium or long term character (continuous quality)[15]. Especially for mobile services the *Outcomes* focus on the result of the process from the end-user's perspective. This is significantly determined by the end-user's acceptance[16]. Thus, the dimension *Outcomes* is termed *Acceptance* in the following. The relevant actors of the mobile value chain are regarded in the *Market* dimension[4].

As a result of the first step the dimensions *Structure, Process, Acceptance* and *Market* classify the influencing factors completely and disjunctive. In the second step these dimensions can be subdivided into feasible sub-dimensions[6]. Chapter 3-6 discusses different approaches for a subdivision in detail. The choice of suitable approaches is based on the originality of approaches, the suitability for mobile services and a feasible level of abstraction.

3.   STRUCTURE DIMENSION

A mobile service can be defined as a combination of internal potentials and usage factors (resources)[5,17]. The *Structure* dimension focuses on the provision of mobile services i.e. the capability and willingness to combine internal potential factors to be able to provide a service[12].

Regarding theories that subdivide this dimension leads to a variety of different approaches. Significant models are McKinsey's *7-S Model* that focuses on change management and emphasises mutual dependencies of dimensions, Pfeiffer's *Five Factors Model* that is based on a procedural analysis of industrial processes in general and Porter's *Value Chain Model* that describes support activities for any kind of product or service. Most of the further approaches are derivates of Porter's *Value Chain Model* and do not offer additional perceptions for a subdivision of the *Structure* dimension.

McKinsey's *7-S Model* identifies seven significant elements of an organization: *Strategy, structure, systems, style/culture, staff, skills* and *shared values*. Any change in one of the elements affects all others[18].

Pfeiffer provides a *Five Factor Model* that describes the structural and procedural dimensions of industrial systems. It identifies the dimensions *input, personnel, organisation, technology* and *output*[19]. Porter's *Value Chain Model* identifies the activities *firm infrastructure, human resource management, technology development* and *procurement*. These so called support activities affect all processes along the entire value chain[20]. Figure 1 shows these approaches in an overview.

Approach	Dimensions	Summary	Suitability
7-S model (Mc Kinsey)	• Strategy • Structure • Systems • Style/Culture • Staff • Skills • Shared Values	Change management approach that divides an organisation into seven factors. Each change of one factor influences any other factors.	As information procurement and technology is not regarded, this approach is not directly appropriate.
5 Factors Model (Pfeiffer, et al.)	• Input • Personnel • Organisation • Technology • Output	Closed model for the structural and procedural description of industrial systems.	Cross sectional model that does not fit in the superior dimension structure (e.g. Output).
Value Chain Model, Support Activities (Porter)	• Firm Infrastructure • Human Resource Management • Technology Development • Procurement	Divides the support activities of an enterprise cross sectional. All Dimensions affect all processes of the primary activities along the entire value chain. Focuses primarily on manufacturing industry. Highly established.	Describes all relevant aspects of the structure dimension. Includes all relevant sub-dimensions of the other approaches.

Figure 1. Overview of Approaches for the Subdivision of the Dimension *Structure*

The dimensions of the *7-S Model* allow a detailed view on the characteristics of an organisation. Some aspects that are relevant for the provision of mobile services (e.g. technology and procurement) are not regarded. Pfeiffer's first four dimensions can be interpreted almost alike the dimensions identified in Porter's *Value Chain Model*. The additional element output is already subject of the *Acceptance* dimension. The supporting activities of the *Value Chain Model* include all relevant aspects of the other approaches. Even if Porter does not explicitly regard the specific characteristics of mobile services, a stronger focus of the procurement on information than on material goods is the only constraint[21].

Influencing factors for Porter's sub-dimension *Firm Infrastructure* are financial resources, organizational structure and brands. *Human Resource Management* contains factors like knowledge as well as the quantity and qualification of personnel. Regarding the sub-dimension *Technology Development* leads to influencing factors like IT systems, technical standards and experience with emerging technologies. In the sub-dimension

Procurement influencing factors like content acquisition, information retrieval and situation determinants can be identified. Figure 2 gives an overview on the four sub-dimensions of *Structure*.

Sub-Dimensions	Influencing Factors
Firm Infrastructure	• Organizational Structure (e.g. existing Structure) • Financial Resources (e.g. sufficient Ressources) • Brands (e.g. usable or transferable Brands)
Human Resource Management	• Knowledge (e.g. existing knowledge) • Personnel Quantity (e.g. manpower requirements) • Personnel Qualification (e.g. key qualifications)
Technology Development	• IT Systems (e.g. Servers, Content Management Systems) • Technical Standards (e.g. UDDI, WAP, UMTS) • Experience with the Integration of Emerging Technologies
Procurement	• Content Acquisition (e.g. Contacts, Relationships) • Information Retrieval (e.g. Information, News, Location Information) • Technical Procurement (e.g. Server, OS, DB, Software)

Figure 2. Influencing Factors and Examples in an Overview

4. PROCESS DIMENSION

A mobile service can be interpreted as an assessable process of internal and external interactions[11]. The internal interactions include the development of the mobile service. The external interactions refer to the participation of the end-user in planning, developing and providing mobile services.

According to Porter the overall value creating logic of the value chain with its generic categories of primary activities is valid in all industries. Although Porter's framework plays a central role it is challenged in resource-based critiques[22,23]. Considering the weaknesses of Porter's framework two alternative models for the value configuration, the *Value Shop* and the *Value Network*, can be discussed[24].

According to the *Value Shop Model* the value creation bases on the five dimensions *problem finding/acquisition, problem solving, choice, execution* and *control/evaluation*. Within these dimensions a firm relying on intensive technology is able to solve customer or client problems[24]. The *Value Network Model* considers the main dimensions *promotion* and *contract management, service provisioning* and *infrastructure operation*. This approach focuses on value creation in firms that rely on mediating technology to link clients or customers[24]. The primary activities of Porter's *Value Chain Model* describe the whole building process of products or services. Porter specifies the dimensions *inbound logistics, operations, marketing/sales, outbound logistics* and *after-sale service* as generic activities of the process. This approach originally focuses on manufacturing industries[20]. Figure 3 gives an overview of approaches for the subdivision of the *Process* dimension.

Approach	Dimensions	Summary	Suitability
Value Shop (Stabell, Fjeldstad)	• Problem-Finding and Acquisition • Problem Solving • Choice • Execution • Control/ Evaluation	Approach for value creation logic in firms that rely on intensive technology to solve a customer or client problem	Regards the stages of service provision; relevant aspects of the *Process* as information handling are not considered
Value Network (Stabell, Fjeldstad)	• Promotion and Contract Management • Service Provisioning • Infrastructure Operation	Approach for value creation logic in firms that rely on mediating technology to link clients or customers	Focuses on the value creation of MNO's; does not consider relevant aspects as customer care
Value Chain Model, primary activities (Porter)	• Inbound Logistics • Operations • Outbound Logistics • Marketing and Sales • After-Sale Service	Primary activities are directly involved in creating and bringing value to the customer. Approach focuses primarily on manufacturing industry	Regards all relevant influencing factors for the structure of organisations

Figure 3. Overview of Approaches for the Subdivision of the Dimension *Process*

As the *Value Shop Model* especially regards problem solutions it is suitable for analysing concrete aspects of mobile services but not for a profound classification of the *Process* dimension. Depending on the interpretation the value shop model can be regarded as a subset of Porter's primary activities[24]. The *Value Network Model* focuses on network providers. From the view of providers of mobile services the provision and operation take place at the same time[25]. For mobile service providers the contract management is not part of the provisioning process. Taking Bullinger and Schreiner's classification into account it has to be regarded in the *Structure* dimension[7].

Regarding mobile services the critiques of Porter's *Value Chain Model* have no effects on its suitability. The primary activities are appropriate to describe the different stages of value creation of mobile services. They are suitable for a detailed classification of the *Process* dimension. The only adaptation refers to the generally termed dimensions.

Particularly important for the sub-dimension inbound logistics is the handling of information. The outbound logistics can be reduced on service distribution as mobile services use only digital distribution channels. In addition after-sale service can be termed customer care.

Regarding the sub-dimension *Information Handling* the transaction standards and the handling of content and situation determinants can be identified as influencing factors. The sub-dimension *Technical Operations* includes influencing factors like service generation, reliability and situation dependency concepts. The analysis of the sub-dimension *Service Distribution* leads to co-operations, distribution concepts and access technologies. The sub-dimension *Marketing* contains factors like promotion, placement and price of a mobile service. Customer support, customer relations and service enhancement are influencing factors of the sub-dimension *Customer Care*. Figure 4 shows the five sub-dimensions and influencing factors of the *Process* dimension.

Sub-Dimensions	Influencing Factors
Information Handling	• Content Handling (e.g. Storage, Databases) • Transaction Standards (e.g. Interfaces, Technologies) • Handling of Situation Determinants (e.g. Location Information)
Technical Operations	• Service Generation (e.g. Databases, Content Management) • Reliability (e.g. Security, System Stability) • Situation Dependency Concepts (e.g. Location, Personalisation)
Service Distribution	• Co-operations (e.g. Portals, MNO's, SP's) • Distribution Concepts (e.g. Push, Pull) • Access Technologies (e.g. GSM, GPRS, UMTS)
Marketing	• Promotion (e.g. Advertisement, Public Relations) • Placement (e.g. Target Groups and Markets) • Price (e.g. Elasticity, Structure)
Customer Care	• Customer Support (e.g. Help Systems, FAQ's, Hotlines) • Customer Relations (e.g. Controlling, CRM) • Service Enhancement (e.g. Ideas, Adaptation Mechanisms)

Figure 4. Influencing Factors and Examples in an Overview

5. ACCEPTANCE DIMENSION

The end-user's acceptance is more and more regarded as a critical factor for the analysis and evaluation of mobile services[26]. The acceptance significantly depends on the end-user's perspective of the mobile service.

The *Technology Acceptance Model* (TAM) is a highly established model to evaluate the end-user's acceptance and considers the end-user's perception[27]. The *Compass Acceptance Model* is a model that explicitly regards mobile services. It extends *TAM* for general conditions that are not determined by the specific mobile service and has been approved in several projects[28]. Another concept that is focused on mobile services is Silberer's layer concept. It focuses on the customer satisfaction of mobile commerce applications. Other acceptance models (e.g. Goodhue, Degenhardt, Kollman) do not regard the specific aspects of mobile services.

According to Davis' *Technology Acceptance Model* the user acceptance is determined by the factors *perceived usefulness* and *perceived ease of use*.

It regards the acceptance of technologies in general[27]. The *Compass Acceptance Model* is a model for (re-) evaluating the end-user's acceptance for mobile services[26]. As an extension of *TAM* it subdivides the influencing factors of the end-user's acceptance into *perceived usefulness, perceived ease of use, perceived costs* and *perceived network effects*[28]. Silberer's *Customer Satisfaction Approach* considers the dimensions *hardware, transmission costs* and *mobile commerce application*. Regarding these dimensions experiences, expectations and the conformity of expectations can be examined[29]. Figure 5 gives an overview of approaches for the subdivision of the *Acceptance* dimension.

Approach	Dimensions	Summary	Suitability
Technology Acceptance Model (Davis)	• Perceived Usefulness • Perceived Ease of Use	Approach for the (re-) evaluation of the acceptance of mobile services from the end-user's point of view	Highly established; mobile services are not regarded explicitly
Compass Acceptance Model (Amberg et al.)	• Perceived Usefulness • Perceived Ease of Use • Perceived Costs • Perceived Network Effects	Approach for the (re-) evaluation of the acceptance of mobile services from the end-user's point of view that expands TAM for mobile services.	Approach especially for mobile services that regard all relevant sub-dimensions of this dimension from the end-user's perception.
Customer Satisfaction (Silberer et al.)	• Hardware • Transmission Costs • Mobile Commerce Applications	Regards experiences, expectations and the conformity of expectations along three layers.	Approach of conformity of expectations is suitable. Usability is not considered explicitly.

Figure 5. Overview of Approaches for the Subdivision of the Dimension *Acceptance*

The *Technology Acceptance Model* regards the acceptance in general and does not consider mobile aspects explicitly. As Silberer's *Customer Satisfaction Model* is technology driven, usability aspects are not regarded. The *Compass Acceptance Model* is specialised on the acceptance of mobile services. It contains all relevant aspects of the other approaches[26] and is approved for a subdivision of the *Acceptance* dimension[28].

Regarding the *Perceived Usefulness*, influencing factors like added value, emotions and the information quality are relevant. The sub-dimension *Perceived Ease of Use* contains factors like initial operation, usability of the service and terminal equipment. An assignment of influencing factors for the sub-dimension *Perceived Costs* leads to factors like monetary costs, transparency of costs and health concerns. The sub-dimension *Perceived Network Effects* identifies general conditions of mobile services[28]. Influencing factors that affect the mobile service indirectly are the network coverage, terminal equipment or the image. Figure 6 shows the four sub-dimensions of the dimension *Outcomes* in an overview.

Sub-Dimensions	Influencing Factors
Perceived Usefulness	• Added Value (e.g. Fun Factor, Information) • Emotions (e.g. Feeling of Independence) • Information Quality (e.g. Timeliness)
Perceived Ease of Use	• Initial Operation (e.g. Registration, First Configuration) • Usability Service (e.g. Intuitive Handling, Idle Time) • Usability Terminal Equipment (e.g. Display, Keypad)
Perceived Costs	• Monetary Costs (e.g. Purchasing Costs, Basic Rates, Usage Costs) • Transparency (e.g. Tariff Models, Cost per Minute/Request/Bit) • Health Concerns (e.g. Dangerous Radiation)
Perceived Network Effects	• Network Coverage (e.g. Dissemination, Roaming) • Terminal Equipment (e.g. Design, Size, Colour) • Image (e.g. Service as Status Symbol, Group Affiliation)

Figure 6. Influencing Factors and Examples in an Overview

6.   MARKET DIMENSION

During the early stage of the development of mobile services the consideration of the market plays an important role[4]. Current best practices for planning are often based on speculations about the market of mobile services[30]. This inadequate market orientation is a main reason for deficits in the development of services[31].

Regarding the market and its actors leads to Porter's *Five Forces Model* of competitive advantage that is highly established. Grove extended Porter's model by the sixth force *Complementors*. Regarding the telecommunication business Downes criticises this model due to adaptations to actual developments. He suggests a *Three Forces Model*. An alternative perception to classify this dimension is to regard the participants of mobile markets. Following this approach various models exist. These so called value chain models specify the actors in a varying level of abstraction. The *Wireless Value Chain* is a representative model that subsumes the relevant aspects as a superset.

For a classification of the *Market* dimension it has to be considered how promising the market and how competitive a service is. Porter terms this as competitive advantage[32]. He identifies *Competitors, Customers, Suppliers, Substitutes* and *Potential Competitors* as the five forces of competitive advantage. Grove enhanced this model with *Complementors* (e.g. Portals for Mobile Services) as a sixth force[33]. Downes regards these factors as inadequate for the consideration of digital services. Therefore he proposes the factors *digitalisation, globalisation* and *deregulation* as new forces for the determination of the competitive advantage in times of economical changes[34]. JP Morgan's *Wireless Value Chain* provides a detailed classification of actors of mobile business. It specifies the categories *equipment, networks, software* and *services*[35]. Figure 7 gives an overview of approaches for the subdivision of the *Market* dimension.

Approach	Dimensions	Summary	Suitability
6 Forces (Grove)	• Competitors • Complementors • Customers • Suppliers • Substitutes • Potential Competitors	Enhances Porter's 5 Forces Model with the power, vigor and competence of complementors that are highly relevant for mobile services (e.g. terminal equipment)	Regards all relevant influencing factors for the market of mobile services.
3 Forces (Downes)	• Digitalisation • Globalisation • Deregulation	Criteria for the considera-tion of services underlying economical trends	Criteria only valid in certain times; focuses on external influences on the market
Wireless Value Chain (JP Morgan)	• Equipment • Networks • Software • Services	Approach for structuring the players in Mobile Business.	Regards all relevant market players; does not consider competition (e.g. Substitutes)

Figure 7. Overview of Approaches for the Subdivision of the Dimension *Market*

The *Wireless Value Chain* provides all relevant actors of value creation in mobile business. As it does not consider competition explicitly, it is not directly applicable for a subdivision of the *Market* dimension. Downes' three forces clarify the difficulties in regarding the market and its players due to external influences. The actors itself are not directly considered. Grove's *Six Forces Model* provides all relevant aspects of competitive advantages for the market and contains all significant aspects that are regarded by the other models. Therefore the *Six Forces Model* appears to be an adequate approach for a detailed classification of the *Market* dimension.

The sub-dimension *Competitors* includes influencing factors like service providers, mobile network operators and hybrid products that are competing in the same market. Mobile devices, portals and independent payment systems can be assigned to the sub-dimension *Complementors*. An actual example for the influence of *Complementors* is the lack of UMTS devices for the European market. The sub-dimension *Customers* includes factors like requirements, quantities and properties of potential end-users. The sub-dimension *Suppliers* is influenced by mobile network operators (in their primary role as MNO, not as service provider), content providers and third parties (e.g. for billing or encashment). The sub-dimension *Substitutes* contains traditional "non mobile" products as well as emerging technologies and new approaches for the replacement of mobile services. Besides actual competitors new or already existing SP's or traditional enterprises may enter the market and have to be regarded as *Potential Competitors*. Figure 8 shows the six sub-dimensions of *Market*.

Sub-Dimensions	Influencing Factors
Competitors	• Other SP's that provide equal services • MNO's (in their role as SP) that provide equal services • Hybrid products (e.g. Service Combinations, Broadcast Information)
Complementors	• Portals and Platforms (Startpage of MNO or Intermediate) • Mobile Devices (e.g. Required Technologies) • Independent Payment Systems (e.g. PayPal, MoxMo)
Customers	• Requirements (e.g. Demands, Needs) • Quantity (e.g. Potential End-Users, Market Size) • Properties (e.g. Structure and Attributes)
Suppliers	• MNO's (Guidelines, Technology, Location Information) • Content Provider (e.g. Monopoles, Timeliness, Pricing) • Third Parties (e.g. Billing, Encashment)
Substitutes	• "Non Mobile" Products (e.g. Map instead of Navigation Service) • Emerging Technologies (e.g. Faster, Smaller, Better) • New Approaches (e.g. Automation instead of Mobile Service)
Potential Competitors	• Emerging SP's (e.g. Entrepreneurs) • Existing SP's (e.g. expanding existing services) • Traditional Enterprises (e.g. expanding with mobile strategies)

Figure 8. Influencing Factors and Examples in an Overview

7. FRAMEWORK

Initial point of this paper was the need for a systematic classification for identifying factors influencing the design of mobile services. As suitable approaches that directly address mobile services currently do not exist, different scientific approaches from nearby research disciplines were evaluated. By combining selected approaches a theory based framework for the classification of influencing factors was derived in a two step process. It identifies the four basic dimensions *Structure, Processes, Acceptance* and *Market*. For the subdivision of these dimensions, different approaches were selected and discussed. Based on this discussion sub-dimensions for the classification were derived. To evaluate the appropriateness of this classification representative influencing factors were identified for each sub-dimension.

For the dimensions *Structure* and *Process* Porter's *Value Chain Model* was applied. For the dimension *Acceptance* the *Compass Acceptance Model* was selected. For the subdivision of the *Market* Grove's *Six Forces Model* was used. Figure 9 shows the four dimensions and all sub-dimensions in an overview.

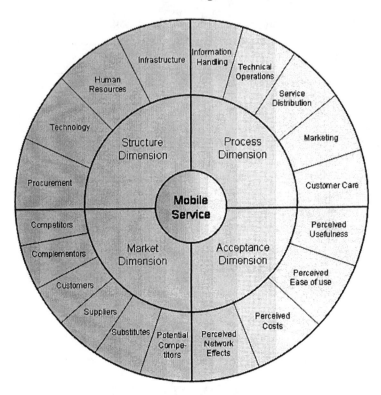

Figure 9. Classification of Influencing Factors

From the theoretical point of view, the derived dimensions appear suitable for identifying a balanced set of influencing factors. First experiences in the context of practical projects confirmed the suitability of the framework for the complete and disjunctive classification of influencing factors of mobile services.

8. OUTLOOK

The presented framework for the classification of influencing factors of mobile services is expected to lead to a significant improvement of the transparency of relevant influencing factors for the design of mobile services. Additionally, the framework can be applied for comparing and benchmarking different mobile services. Furthermore it can be used for planning (e.g. for the selection of mobile services in the early stages) or the controlling of mobile services during the product lifecycle. To prove its significance, the framework has to be challenged by an empirical validation.

Need for further research is seen in the qualitative and quantitative measurement of influencing factors. Especially the identification of suitable criteria, combinations between qualitative and quantitative criteria, weighting factors and the visualisation of results have to be regarded in the future. Furthermore the availability and suitability of methods for these aspects have to be analysed.

As a future target, the framework can be expanded for a support of appropriate measures considering effort and benefit for the evaluations of mobile services. Due to the general validity of the identified and selected approaches it is expected that the framework can be applied for services in general as well.

REFERENCES

1. Gartner Group: GPRS will not succeed until new Technologies are developed, Press Release, June 3, 2002.
2. Geer, R.; Gross, R.: M-Commerce. Geschäftsmodelle für das mobile Internet, Landsberg/Lech, 2001.
3. Böcker, F.; Kotzbauer, N.: Einflussgrößen des Erfolgs von Markteinführungen industrieller Produkte, Arbeitspapier 52 des Instituts für Betriebswirtschaftlehre der Universität Regensburg, Regensburg, 1989.
4. Lehner, F.: Mobile und drahtlose Informationssysteme. Technologien, Anwendungen, Märkte, Heidelberg, 2003.
5. Benkenstein, M.: Dienstleistungsqualität: Anpassungen zur Messung und Implikationen für die Steuerung. In: Zeitschrift für Betriebswirtschaft, 1993, 63. Jg., Heft 11, p. 1095-1116.
6. Amberg, M.; Wehrmann, J.; Zimmer, R.: Towards a Theory Based Identification of Influencing Factors for the Design of Mobile Services. In Aguilar, J. et al. (Eds.): Proceedings 10th International Conference on Cybernetics and Information Technologies, Systems and Application (CITSA), Florida, 2004.
7. Bullinger, H.-J.; Schreiner, P.: Service Engineering: Ein Rahmenkonzept für die systematische Entwicklung von Dienstleistungen. In: Bullinger, H.-J.; Scheer, A.-W.: Service Engineering – Entwicklung und Gestaltung innovativer Dienstleistungen, 2003, p. 51-82.
8. Donabedian, A.: Evaluating the quality of medical care. In: Milbank Memorial fund Quarterly, 1966, 44. Jg., Heft 3, Part 2, p. 166-203.
9. Ramaswamy, R.: Design and Management of Service Processes, Boston, 1996.
10. Deutsches Institut für Normung DIN: Qualitätsmanagement und Elemente eines Qualitätssicherungssystems. Leitfaden für Dienstleistungen DIN EN ISO 9004-2, Berlin, 1992.
11. Edvardsson, B.; Olsson, J.: Key concepts for new service development. In: The Service Industries Journal, 1996, 16. Jg., Heft 2, p. 140-164.
12. Corsten, H.: Dienstleistungsmanagement, München, 2001.
13. Grieble, O.; Scheer, A.-W.: Grundlagen des Benchmarkings öffentlicher Dienstleistungen. In: Scheer, A.-W. (Hrsg.): Veröffentlichungen des Instituts für Wirtschaftsinformatik, Nr. 166, Saarbrücken, 2000.

14. Donabedian, A.: The definition of quality and approaches to its assessment, explorations, quality, assessment and monitoring, Michigan, 1980.
15. Meyer, C.; Mattmüller, R.: Qualität von Dienstleistungen – Entwurf eines praxisorientierten Qualitätsmodells. In: Marketing – Zeitschrift für Forschung und Praxis ZFP, 1987, 9. Jg., Heft 3, p. 187-195.
16. Galletta, D. F.; Malhotra, Y.: Extending the technology acceptance model to account for social influence: theoretical bases and empirical validation. In: Proceedings of the 32nd Hawaii International Conference on System Sciences, 1999, p. 6-19.
17. Engelhardt, W. H.; Kleinaltenkamp, M.; Reckenfelderbäumer, M.: Dienstleistungen als Absatzobjekt. In: Veröffentlichungen des Instituts für Unternehmensführung und Unternehmensforschung, Arbeitsbericht Nr. 52, Bochum, 1992.
18. Peters, T.; Waterman, R.: In Search of Excellence, New York, 1982.
19. Pfeiffer, W.; Weiß, E.; Strubl, C.: Systemwirtschaftlichkeit: Konzeption und Methodik zur betriebswirtschaftlichen Fundierung innovationsorientierter Entscheidungen, 1994.
20. Porter, M. E.: Competitive Strategy: Techniques for Analysing Industries and Competitors, New York, 1980.
21. Amberg, M.; Wehrmann, J.: Effizientes Angebot von situationsabhängigen mobilen Diensten. In: Zeitschrift Industrie Management, 2003, Ausgabe 06/2003, p. 35-37.
22. Barney, J. B.: Firm resources and sustained advantage. In: Journal of Management, 1991, Vol. 17, p. 19-120.
23. Wernerfelt. B.: A resource-based view of the firm. In: Strategic Management Journal, 1984, Vol. 5(2), p. 171-180.
24. Stabell, C. B.; Fjeldstad, O. D.: Configuring Value for Competitive Advantage: on Chains, Shops and Networks. In: Strategic Management Journal, 1998, Vol. 19, p. 413 – 437.
25. Meiren, T.: Entwicklung von Dienstleistungen unter besonderer Berücksichtigung von Human Ressources. In: Bullinger, H.J.: Entwicklung und Gestaltung innovativer Dienstleistung. Tagungsband zur Service Engineering 2001, (IAO) Stuttgart, 2001.
26. Amberg, M.; Hirschmeier, M.; Wehrmann, J.: The Compass Acceptance Model for the Analysis and Evaluation of Mobile Information Systems. In: International Journal for Mobile Communications (IJMC), 2004, Vol. 2, N 3.
27. Davis, F. D.: Perceived Usefulness, Perceived Ease of Use, and User Acceptance of Information Technology. In: MIS Quarterly, 1989, Vol. 13, No. 3 (8/1989), p.319-341.
28. Amberg, M.; Wehrmann, J.: Benutzerakzeptanz mobiler Dienste. Ein Erfahrungsbericht zum Compass-Akzeptanzmodell, Arbeitsbericht Nr. 02/2003 des Lehrstuhls für Wirtschaftsinformatik III, Friedrich-Alexander Universität Erlangen-Nürnberg, Nürnberg, 2003.
29. Silberer, G.; Magerhans, A.; Wohlfahrt, J.: Kundenzufriedenheit und Kundenbindung im Mobile Commerce. In: Silberer, G.; Wohlfahrt, J.; Wilhelm, T. (Eds.): Mobile Commerce. Grundlagen, Geschäftsmodelle, Erfolgsfaktoren. Wiesbaden, 2002, p. 309 – 324.
30. Strebel, H.: Klein- und Mittelunternehmen in Technologie- und Innovationsnetzwerken. In: Schwarz, E.J. (Eds.): Technologieorientiertes Innovationsmanagement, 2003, p. 62-74.
31. Jenner, T.: Überlegungen zur Integration des Kunden in das Innovationsmanagement. In: Jahrbuch der Absatz- und Verbraucherforschung, 2000, 46. Jg., Heft 2, p. 130-147.
32. Porter, M. E.: Competitive Advantage. New York, 1985.
33. Grove, A. S.: Only the Paranoid Survive, London, 1988.
34. Downes, L.; Mui, C.: Unleashing the Killer App. Boston, 1998.
35. Parlett, T.: A Public Market Perspective: Recipes for Success, JP Morgan, 2000.

REPAIRING LOST CONNECTIONS OF MOBILE TRANSACTIONS WITH MINIMAL XML DATA EXCHANGE

STEFAN BÖTTCHER

University of Paderborn, Faculty 5 (EIM) - Computer Science
Fürstenallee 11, 33102 Paderborn, Germany

Abstract: Whenever applications running on mobile clients share XML data within a server-side database, some key requirements are optimized data exchange, transaction synchronization, and the correct treatment of lost connections during application execution. In order to reduce the costs for data exchange, it may be considerably advantageous when the client caches and reuses XML data of previous queries in comparison to delivering the same XML data from server to client repetitively. Furthermore, transactions synchronization has to provide not only the correct treatment of parallel updates, but has to also take into account lost connections. We present a solution for both problems, which combines an exchange of XML difference fragments with an optimized transaction synchronization technique for long transactions that is able to handle lost connections correctly.

Key words: Mobile databases; lost connections; XML; XPath; caching; optimistic synchronization; optimized data transferal.

1. INTRODUCTION

1.1 Problem origin

Whenever mobile clients access XML data which is stored in a server-side database, some of the major problems to be solved are data exchange, transaction synchronization, and lost connections during application.

A standard approach to handle lost connections within client applications that require access to server data, is that the client aborts the running application and restarts it when the connection is re-established. In comparison, our goal is that not all of the work of the client application is lost. Instead the application shall continue after the connection to the server has been re-established, and whenever possible the previous work of the client application shall be saved.

Furthermore, the possible occurrence of lost connections influences the way in which concurrent mobile transactions synchronize their access to a server-side database. Synchronization by 2-phase locking is not appropriate, as a client that loses its connection to the server during transaction execution prevents other client applications from accessing locked data for an unforeseeably long duration.

Finally, both repairing lost connections and correctly synchronizing transactions within mobile information systems rely on data exchange. Whenever small bandwidth connections are a bottle-neck for data exchange, it is preferable to reduce the data transfer required for repairing lost connections or for correct transaction synchronization, to a minimum. This includes reusing old query results still stored in a client's cache wherever possible, and transporting only the difference XML fragment not yet stored but required on the client, from the server to the client.

Our work has been motivated by the development of an XML based information system for e-learning, which uses XPath queries [14] within a client-server environment involving mobile clients. However, we regard the application field to be much broader, i.e. we regard our technique to be useful wherever XML database data has to be shared by applications running on mobile clients. Figure 1 shows our overall system architecture.

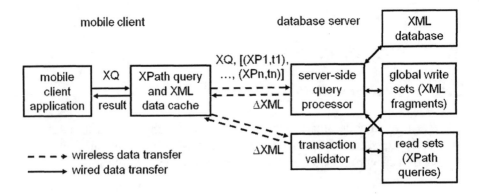

Figure 1. System Overview

1.2   System overview

As shown in Figure 1, a mobile client application does not access an XML database directly. Instead it communicates via a client cache for XPath queries and XML data, which has a wireless connection to a server-side query processor that accesses the XML database. The communication via a client cache and server-side query processor will be used to reduce data exchange and to repair lost connections in such a way that transaction synchronization is still correct. For the purpose of transaction synchronization, the mobile client's cache communicates with a server-side transaction validator. This validator synchronizes the mobile client's transaction – independent of whether or not it has been interrupted by a lost (and re-established) connection.

As low bandwidth is a key problem (at least for our application), we focus on sending small ΔXML fragments (also called XML difference fragments) from the server to the client for all three purposes: ordinary query processing, transaction synchronization, and data status checks after re-establishing a lost connection. In order to support the exchange of XML difference fragments, the client has to inform the server about which data is still stored in the client's cache. Within our system, the client informs the server about the results of previous queries (XP1, ..., XPn), the results of which are still in the client's cache. Furthermore, for each query result, the client stores a timestamp that indicates the last time when the query result was refreshed by a difference fragment from the server.

The server uses the previous queries and their timestamps to compute the actual difference XML fragment. Only this difference XML fragment has to be submitted to the mobile client. Thereafter, the client integrates the difference XML fragment with its previous query results. Finally the client uses its refreshed cache to answer the query. (In some cases it may even be possible that a client answers a query without any access to the server, based on the data of its cache alone. We outline this further in section 6.3 including the consequences for validation).

The same technique, i.e. submitting a difference XML fragment from the server to the client, is used at the end of each transaction. This difference XML fragment contains new values for outdated data that have been used within the client's transaction. If this difference XML fragment is empty, the client then knows that its transaction has been committed by the server. Otherwise, the client already has the new values of the outdated data and can restart the transaction using this fresh data.

1.3   Related work, focus of this contribution and problem definition

Our system as given above has to solve a variety of practical problems, including data and query caching, query processing, transaction synchronization and cache consistency checking, and handling lost connections. Within this paper, we present an optimistic transaction synchronization protocol, and we focus on the reduction of data exchange between server and client and on the treatment of lost connections.

While some contributions to mobile transactions relax or redefine transaction properties (e.g. [7]), we follow the argumentation of [6] and support the classical ACID properties. Like other approaches in mobile transactions (e.g. [4]), we combine validation with client side data caching, however we do not update the clients' caches by a server initiated broadcast, but leave the decision to refresh the read data up to the client. According to [1] and [12], this outperforms all other approaches to cache consistency in client/server architectures like ours, where application processing is performed at the mobile client.

Like other approaches to client-side data caching, we let the client reuse previous query results which are still in the client's cache. The server transfers only XML difference fragments to the client, i.e. that data which is needed but missing in the client's cache. We do not discuss how to compute the needed difference fragments and how to integrate these different fragments with the previous query results, as this is already described in [2]. Instead we focus on the data exchange required for transaction processing and transaction synchronization, and on the reuse of cached results in case of lost connections and transaction restarts.

Another problem excluded from this paper is how the client can check, without access to the server-side XML database, that a new XPath query XQ can be answered by using a cached previous query result described by an XPath expression XP. This is the case when XQ selects a subset of XP, independently of the state of the XML database, which can be proven by an XPath containment test. There are a variety of solutions proposed for XPath containment tests, e.g. [5,10,11], whereas our system uses an implementation based on query graphs [3].

One major problem solved in this paper is whether and how the client can continue a transaction which has been interrupted by losing the connection to the server. Another problem also discussed in this paper, is when and how cached query results of previous transactions can be reused. A related problem is to reduce the necessary data exchange from server to client when a transaction has to be restarted because of a synchronization conflict.

Finally, we investigate how to reduce the data transfer needed for synchronization purposes from client to server.

The remainder of this paper is organized as follows. Section 2 summarizes how difference fragments are computed at the server's side and how they are integrated with previous query results within the client's cache. Section 3 describes how the client reads and writes data and what are the options of the client with respect to the use of old data. Sections 4 and 5 focus on status check and synchronization issues. Section 6 describes how to treat transactions when repairing lost connections and outlines opportunities for cross transaction optimization. Finally, Section 7 contains the summary and conclusions.

2.   THE USE OF LOCATION INFORMATION FOR FRAGMENT INTEGRATION

In order to reduce the amount of data exchanged between client and server wherever possible, validation information, status check information, and answers to queries XQ are sent in the form of XML difference fragments from the server to the client. As XML difference fragments contain the XML data required but not yet stored in the client's cache, the server has to compute the XML different fragment, and the client has to merge it with previous query results stored in the client's cache.

Together with a query XQ, the client informs the server about the results of previous queries XP1, ..., XPn which are still stored in the client's cache. Given all these query expressions, the server computes the difference fragment that contains the answer to XQ but not the answer to XP1, ..., XPn.5

When the client shall merge an XML difference fragment with a stored fragment of previously retrieved data, it is essential for the client to know the position where the new fragment has to be inserted. This includes that the client has to know under which parent node and after which sibling node a fragment has to be inserted into the client's cache, such that parent-child relationship and sibling order in the client's cache reflect the relationships found in the server's XML database.

In order to solve this problem, we use a node numbering schema which is an extended version of the node number scheme presented in [2]. Our node

---

[5] Note that client and server can use and communicate query IDs instead of XPath expressions for describing previous query results. This would further reduce the size of data exchanged by the client and the server, but it would require the server to store the XPath expressions and the associated IDs for all previous queries.

numbering scheme assigns a sibling sequence number between 0 and 1 to each node and respects the sibling-order as follows. Whenever C1, ..., Cn are all the child nodes of the same node P and n>=2, then the sibling sequence number of Ci is less than the sibling sequence number of Ci+1 whenever Ci is a preceding sibling of Ci+1. Whenever a fragment is transferred from client to server, each node in this fragment is augmented with the sibling sequence number of the node. Furthermore, each fragment is augmented with the list of sibling sequence numbers of all its ancestors up to the root, called the root path of this fragment. This ancestor path to the root, containing all the sibling sequence numbers from the root to the node or fragment of interest, can be used by the client to find the correct position in its partial copy of the server's XML document. The same sibling sequence numbers are also used within the fragment stored in the client's query cache, such that query results retrieved from the server can be easily merged with the client's fragment.

3.   QUERY PROCESSING AND WRITE OPERATIONS AT THE CLIENT'S SIDE

In order to reduce client-server communication to an absolute minimum, the client works as long as possible with its own cache (with the exception of status check operations which are described below). This affects the way in which read and write operations are performed on the client as follows.

3.1   The client's local write set

The client's write operations are stored in a local write set in the client's cache. This local write set is transferred to the server at the end of the transaction. This reduces communication steps from client to server when the same XML fragment is changed multiple times within a client transaction (this is quite typical for experimental applications where data values have to be adjusted).

The client's local write set stores inserted and updated XML fragments together with their root paths which uniquely determine their position within the complete XML document. Furthermore, the client's local write set stores root paths to the deleted fragments of data for each of the client's delete operations. However, for the delete operation it is not necessary to transfer deleted fragments back to the server, i.e. the root paths to deleted fragments are sufficient in order to identify and locate fragments to be deleted from the XML database.

3.2   The client's options for query processing

Whenever a read or write operation is transmitted from the client application to the client's cache, the client's cache computes an XPath expression XQ that describes a sufficiently large fragment which contains all the data to be read or written, as described in [9]. For each query XQ, the client has the choice to use the following query processing algorithm (which is the default case), or to use the status check operation outlined below (which may be used after lost connections or for very old cached data).

3.3   The query processing algorithm of the client's cache

The client's query processing algorithm (Algorithm 1 outlined below) shows the procedure Client.query(XQ) that is called on the client cache for each query XQ that the client application submits. At first, the client collects the XPath expressions XP1, ..., XPn of previous queries, the results of which are still in the client's cache (line (2)). Then the client uses a containment test [3] in order to check whether or not the result of the query XQ can be computed from cached results of previous queries XP1, ..., XPn alone (line (3)). If this is the case, the query XQ is answered locally and no server interaction is needed (line (4)). Only if this is not the case (lines (5)-(11)), the query XQ is submitted to the server together with the list of previous queries, the results of which are still available in the client's cache. The server computes and returns an XML difference fragment of the data needed for answering XQ but not yet contained in the client's cache (lines (6)-(8)) by using a method described in [2]. Furthermore, the server determines which of the previous query results are needed to answer the current query XQ, such that the client can displace other query results whenever it needs memory space for the difference fragment received from the server. The difference XML fragment is merged into the client's cache as described in Section 2, such that the client cache contains a copy of the server's fragment for XQ (line(9)). Thereafter, the timestamp for XQ received from the server is stored in the client's cache (line (10)) for the purpose of transaction validation or status checks after re-establishing a lost connection. Finally (line (11)), the client's copy of the fragment for XQ is merged with the client's own changes (which are stored in the local write set). The resultant data is used within the client's application.

```
(1)     Client.query( XQ )
(2)     { collectPreviousQueries( XP1, ..., XPn ) ;
(3)     if ( XQ can be computed from results of previous queries
        XP1,...,XPn)
(4)     return localResultFor( XQ ) ;    // XQ can be answered locally
(5)     else // get the difference fragment required to answer XQ
(6)     {XMLnewFragment = getDifferenceFromServer(XQ,(XP1,...,XPn)
        ) ;
(7)     // loading the difference from server
(8)     // includes the replacement of fragments if necessary.
(9)     integrate( XMLnewFragment ) ;
(10)    XQ.setTimeStamp = XMLnewFragment.getTimeStamp();
(11)    XQ.applyLocalWriteSet() ;
(12)    }}
```

Algorithm 1: The client's main query processing algorithm

3.4   The client's commit request operation

The client informs the server about the intended completion of a transaction by submitting a commit request to the server at the end of each transaction. Together with the commit request operation, the client transfers its local write set to the server. Furthermore, the client informs the server about (further) previous query results that have been read from the client's cache as part of the actual transaction – together with the timestamp for each previous query result. Because we allow the client to reuse old query results even after lost connections and also from previous transactions, the server has to know which query results the client transaction relies upon, and at what time these query results have been retrieved.

The server answers the client's commit request with an XML difference fragment which returns new values of outdated data in the client's cache that the client has sent as part of its commit request. The XML difference fragment also identifies paths to deleted fragments. If this XML difference fragment is empty, the client then knows that the server has successfully validated the client's transaction. Otherwise, the client knows that its commit request has failed, and the client can merge the new values with its cache and restart the aborted transaction. In both cases, the client takes the timestamp returned with the difference XML fragment as the actual timestamp of the queries which were sent to the server as parameters of the commit request.

3.5 The client's status check request operation

As within the commit request operation, within the status check request operation the client informs the server about previous query results that have been read from the client's cache or are still in the client's cache – together with the timestamp for each previous query result. Again, the server answers the client's status check request with an XML difference fragment which returns new values of outdated data in the client's cache and which identifies paths to deleted fragments. If this XML difference fragment is empty, the client then knows that the previous query results are still up to date. Otherwise, the client knows which previous query results are not up to date. If the client has used this outdated data within the current transaction, the client knows that it has to abort the transaction. If however the XML different fragment contains only data which the client intended to use within the current transaction, the client can simply apply the difference fragment to its cache in order to replace the outdated data. Because the client has refreshed all the previous query results which have been checked, the client can continue with the current transaction.

Transactions can use the status check operation at any time in order to check the status of the cached data. This may be especially useful at the beginning of a transaction when the data to be read is known in advance and the previous query result containing this data has a rather old timestamp.

Again, the timestamp is actualized for every XPath query expression that the client used in the status check request operation.

4. THE SERVER'S IMPLEMENTATION OF THE STATUS CHECK

4.1 The server-side data structures: global write set and transaction's read set

The server's status check operation and the validation use the same data structures.

The global write set is an ordered collection of the local write sets of the successfully committed transactions. The local write sets within the global write set are ordered by timestamp. The value of the timestamp is from the time when the transaction has committed and thereby has added its local write set to the global write set.

XPath queries XQ submitted by the client are collected in read sets. The server maintains one read set per mobile client. The read set is an ordered collection of XPath expressions XQ which have been sent from the client to the server. A timestamp which indicates the last use of the XPath expression is associated to each XPath expression. The timestamp is updated every time a difference fragment for XQ is submitted to the client, caused by either a commit request, or a status check request operation, or an ordinary query.

Whenever there are too many fragments stored in the global write set, the server can displace some fragments starting with the fragments that have the oldest timestamp. As a consequence, the clients can not check the validity of their local data, if this local data has an older timestamp. Therefore, cached local data with a timestamp older than the oldest timestamp found in the global write set, is considered to be outdated.

4.2   Server-side status check operation

The server-side status check operation works as follows. Whenever a timestamp of a query received from the client is older than the oldest timestamp of a local write set stored in the global write set, then the fragment previously retrieved by this query is considered to be outdated and the complete new query result is transferred to the client. This is a special case in our approach, however note that the standard validation approach requires this amount of data transfer for each query.

Otherwise, the query is applied to each local write set fragment which is stored in the global write set and which has a timestamp that is newer than the timestamp of the query. Each XML fragment found in the global write set summarizes changes of the XML database caused by a concurrent transaction. The fragments describing changes of the XML database, which have occurred after the current transaction has read the database, are combined into a single difference fragment which is returned to the client as the result of the status check operation.

5.   VALIDATION BASED ON XPATH QUERIES APPLIED TO GLOBAL WRITE SETS

Our synchronization protocol is adapted to the specific needs of mobile clients which must synchronize their server access and which should provide a reduction in the data transfer between client and server. Our protocol differs from the conventional parallel validation protocol contributed by Kung and Robinson [8], in various aspects. The most obvious differences are that our synchronization protocol extends validation with time stamps, works on XML fragments, is predicative, i.e. it applies XPath query expressions to

XML fragments, and is adapted to the exchange of XML difference fragments.

5.1 An optimistic protocol with read phase, validation phase and write phase

Lost connections and a long duration of transactions require a non-blocking transaction synchronization protocol. Our synchronization protocol is optimistic in the sense that transaction execution is performed on the client's cache within a read phase and that the success of the client's read phase depends on a commit decision or a status check decision made by the server.

Within the read phase, the client only reads data from the server (or the client's cache) and writes data into its local write set. Therefore, a transaction abort during the read phase will never damage any data within the server-side database.

There are the following alternatives for how the client's read phase is terminated. First, the client can abort the transaction with an explicit abort operation. This may happen as a result of a client application program error, or when the client decides that a connection has been lost for a period of time which is too long. Second, an abort stops a transaction when a status check request returns the result that the current client transaction has read outdated data, i.e. data which meanwhile has been modified by a successfully committed concurrent transaction. Third, a commit request of the client invokes a procedure commitRequest(...) on the server which terminates the transaction, and during which the read phase of the client is terminated, the validation is performed and eventually a write phase is performed.

5.2 The server-side procedure commitRequest(...)

The server-side procedure commitRequest is outlined in Algorithm 2 below. The parameters are the local write set of the transaction, the XPath expression XPwrite which describes the fragment accessed by write operations (insert, update, delete) and a list of pairs, each of which contains an XPath query expression and a timestamp. The timestamp associated with an XPath query XP denotes the server-time when the last difference fragment for XP has been computed (or the time when the result of XP has been computed if there was only one access to XP).

```
(1)  diffXMLfragment commitRequest( writeSet, XPwrite, list((XP1,t1),…,(XPn,tn)) )
(2)  { < tv = getValidationTimeStamp( ) > ;    // critical section for end of read phase
(3)    diffXML = validation( XPwrite, tv, list((XP1,t1),…,(XPn,tn)) );  //validation phase
(4)    if diffXML.isEmpty( )
            {   // write phase: apply insert, update & delete operations to server-side DB
(5)             XMLdatabase . applyChangesOf ( writeSet ) ;    // modify DB
(6)             globalWriteSet.add( writeSet, currentTime( ) ) ; // update global write set
(7)        }
(8)    < signalEndOfTransaction > ;    // critical section for transaction is completed
(9)    return diffXML ;                              // inform client
(10) }
```

Algorithm 2: The server's implementation of commitRequest

The critical section within line (2) determines the end of the transaction's read phase and the beginning of the transaction's validation phase. As within the parallel validation contributed by Kung and Robinson [8], transactions are ordered according to their validation timestamp in the sense that newer transactions validate against older transactions, i.e. in case of a conflict the newer transaction is aborted and restarted.

The validation phase (line (3)) computes the difference XML fragment diffXML of outdated data as outlined below. If and only if this fragment is empty, the write phase, which consists of the following two parts, is performed. First, the client's modifications collected in the local write set are applied to the XML database (line (5)). Second, the local write set is added to the global write set, together with a timestamp (line (6)). Thereafter, the transaction is completed on the server-side (line (8)), and the resulting difference fragment is returned to the client (line (9)).

5.3   The predicative queries of the validation phase

Our validation protocol differs from the conventional parallel validation protocol contributed by Kung and Robinson [8], not only because we use XML fragments instead of database tuples for write sets and because we synchronize client transactions on a central server. Additionally, one key difference is that within our protocol, the server does not use sets of nodes or XML fragments as read sets, but instead uses the XPath expression submitted by the client in the read set. As the XPath expressions are usually considerably smaller than the read XML fragment, transferring these considerably smaller XPath expressions instead of the XML fragments allows a reduction in the data exchange from client to server. We consider this to be a competitive advantage in mobile clients that use small bandwidth connections to the server.

Our validation protocol applies XPath expressions of the validating transaction to XML fragments which have been collected in the write sets of older concurrent transactions. Similar to predicative validation [13], we use this as follows not only for read-write conflicts, but also for write-write conflicts.

With transactions To that are already completed when a validating transaction Tv enters its validation phase, Tv has to check only read-write conflicts, which is done as follows:

> For each XPath expression XPE in the read set of Tv:
> For each modified XML fragment MXF in the write set of To,
> If timestamp(XPE) < timestamp(MXF)
> differenceXMLfragment . add(XPE applied to MXF) ;

With an older transaction To2 that is validating concurrently to Tv (i.e. To2 enters its validation phase before Tv, but To2 is not completed at the time when Tv enters its validation phase), Tv has to check for write-write conflicts and for write-read conflicts. Since write expression set XPwrite (i.e. the second parameter of the procedure commitRequest(…) in Algorithm 2) contains all the XPath expressions which are used to write a fragment of the XML document, write-write conflicts can be checked together with write-read conflicts as follows:

> For each XPath expression XPE in XPwrite or in the read set of Tv:
> For each modified XML fragment MXF in the local write set of To2,
> differenceXMLfragment . add(XPE applied to MXF) ;

Note that all the computations of the validation can be performed with a usual XPath query evaluator, i.e. our approach does not need any additional tool. Additionally, this avoids the phantom problem, because conflicting insert and read operations are found by querying the inserted fragments. Note that the validation applies (read or written) XPath expressions to small modified XML fragments, i.e. not to the whole XML document.

Because the global write set consumes a limited memory, the oldest global write set entries are deleted when an overflow of this memory occurs. Therefore, a special treatment is provided for very old query results, i.e. query results that the client retrieved at a time t1 which was prior to the timestamp of the oldest entry that is still stored in the global write set. Whenever such an old query result has been used, it may be the case that global write set data has been deleted which is needed for validation. Therefore, validation regards these query results as outdated, i.e. validation fails and the results of these outdated queries or recomputed and transferred to the client.

5.4   Reducing the exchange of XML fragments for write operations of the client

When the client asks the server to commit a transaction, it transfers its local write set, i.e. a modified XML fragment containing only new values of inserted or updated nodes, to the server. As an additional parameter (the parameter XPwrite in Algorithm 2), the client sends an XPath expression that identifies the modified (inserted, updated or deleted) XML fragments to the server. Note however that it is not necessary that the client returns another modified XML fragment containing the old values of deleted or updated XML fragments to the server for two reasons. First, the XPath expressions sent to the server for the delete or insert operations are sufficient to identify those fragments of the server side XML document that have to be updated or deleted. Second, if the transaction validates successfully, the fragments to be updated or deleted have not been modified by a concurrent transaction. Therefore, the modified XML fragment containing old values can be computed simply by applying the XPath expression for delete or update to the server side XML document, just before the delete or update is applied to the XML document.

6.   TREATMENT OF LOST CONNECTIONS AND CROSS TRANSACTION SYNCHRONIZATION

6.1   Lost connections do not stop a running commit request

Lost connections after the client's call of commitRequest(...) do not interrupt the validation process because all the data required for the validation phase and an eventual write phase are already stored on the server. As soon as the connection is re-established the server can inform the client about the result.

A lost connection before the call of commitRequest(...) can never damage data of any other transaction, because changes on the XML fragment are made on local copies on the client and are not yet transferred to the XML document.

Note furthermore, that a lost connection during a commitRequest operation never violates or blocks concurrent transactions, i.e. the only client which is prevented from continuing its work is the client that has lost its connection.

6.2   The client's repair options after re-establishing a lost connection

The client has the choice between four different options after a lost connection is re-established. First, the client can ignore its work, i.e. it can abort the client application. Second, the client an abort and restart the interrupted transaction. Third, the client may decide to continue the transaction as if nothing happened. Fourth, the client may use the *status check* operation in order to be informed whether or not it is useful to continue the transaction with the current content of the cache.

Which of the four alternatives is most appropriate after re-establishing a connection, depends on the work the client has done (i.e. if the client has not done much work, it may decide to restart the transaction) and on the duration for which the connection was lost (i.e. if the time was short, the client may decide to continue as if nothing happened).

Note that whatever a client decides to do after re-establishing a connection, no other client has to take care of whether or not the connection was lost and whether or not it was re-established during a running transaction. Furthermore, no other client can be damaged or delayed, which we consider to be an advantage of the optimistic approach that we use.

6.3   Cross transaction optimization

Whenever a client which has used server data during a previous successful transaction also requires this data in a following transaction, the client has similar options to those in the case of lost connections. The client can either use a status check in order to be sure that the data is still correct, before it starts further work, or the client can optimistically use the previous query result without any further server interaction. In the latter case, the client's previous query results are checked within the validation phase. Again, which of the decisions is appropriate, may depend on the time since the commit of the last transaction, on the work the client transactions will have to do, and on the probability that the data is changed by a concurrent transaction. For example, general data like a customer name is very unlikely to change. Therefore, it is reasonable to reuse the data even if it is stored in the client's cache with a very old time stamp, instead of reading it again within a new transaction.

6.4   Optimized restart of transactions

Furthermore, the same options as mentioned for a successor transaction also apply to the restart of a transaction. However, as restarts directly follow an abort and because the difference XML fragment is returned to the client as the part of the commit decision, the client can integrate the difference XML fragment without an additional server access. Furthermore, the restarted transaction which operates on the modified difference XML fragment will most likely be successful (except for the rare case that the restarted transaction accesses a different fragment, or the case that other conflicting transactions perform their commit request operation in between).

Note however that in any case, the restart of a transaction requires significantly less data transfer from server to client.

7.   SUMMARY AND CONCLUSIONS

We have presented a combination of client-side caching and optimistic transaction synchronization which treat lost connections and reduce the amount of data being exchanged between client and server through a variety of optimizations.

Our system can treat lost client connections during transaction execution without disturbing the work of other clients, i.e. it has the following properties which make it suitable for mobile clients. On the one hand, whenever a client loses its connection to the server, no other client is blocked or may retrieve outdated data. Even the client transaction itself can proceed as long as it does not require data from the server, however it cannot commit. On the other hand, when a lost connection is re-established, the client can choose between different options. First, the client can restart the whole application. Second, the client can abort and restart the actual transaction within the application. Third, the client can perform a status check in order to find out whether the data it had used is still valid. Fourth, the client can continue the transaction as if nothing happened, i.e. the validation at the end of the transaction checks whether or not the transaction has to be aborted and restarted.

Which option is the best, depends on different parameters, e.g. how long a connection was lost and how much work a transaction has done when the connection is re-established.

Furthermore, our approach to transaction synchronization and repairing lost connections integrates well with a reduction of data exchange between server and client. Wherever possible, the server computes and transfers only an XML difference fragment instead of submitting a complete XML fragment. Difference XML fragments are used within data status checks, within restarts of transactions in order to replace outdated data, and for ordinary queries. The computation and transferal of difference fragments instead of complete query results may be even more advantageous when the

XML data has to be generated on the server-side (e.g. by a transformer) from a different data source. In this case, difference queries can be used in order to reduce the amount of data which has to be generated.

Although we have presented and developed our approach specifically for the needs of mobile XML database clients that rely on a small bandwidth connection to a server, the approach seems to be equally appropriate for other mobile XML database and information systems using optimistic transactions as well.

REFERENCES

[1]   Adya, A., Gruber, R., Liskov, B., Maheshwari, U.: Efficient Optimistic Concurrency Control Using Loosely Synchronized Clocks, ACM SIGMOD Int. Conf. on Management of Data, 1995.

[2]   Stefan Böttcher, Adelhard Türling. Caching XML Data for Mobile Web Clients. International Conference on Internet Computing IC'04, Las Vegas, USA, Juni 2004.

[3]   Stefan Böttcher, Rita Steinmetz. A DTD Graph Based XPath Query Subsumption Test. XML Database Symposium (XSym) at VLDB 2003, Berlin, September 2003.

[4]   Chung, I.-Y., Hwang, C.-S.: Transactional Cache Management with Aperiodic Invalidation Scheme in Mobile Environments. ASIAN 1999: 50-61.

[5]   Daniela Florescu, Alon Y. Levy, Dan Suciu: Query Containment for Conjunctive Queries with Regular Expressions. PODS 1998: 139-148.

[6]   Gore, M.M., Ghosh, R.K.: Recovery of Mobile Transactions. DEXA Workshop 2000: 23-27.

[7]   Ku, K.I., Yoo-Sung, K.: Moflex Transaction Model for Mobile Heterogeneous Multidatabase Systems. RIDE 2000: 39-46.

[8]   Kung, H.T., Robinson, J.T.: On Optimistic Methods for Concurrency Control. ACM TODS, 6, 2, 1981.

[9]   Amelie Marian, Jerome Simeon: Projecting XML Documents, VLDB 2003.

[10] Gerome Miklau, Dan Suciu: Containment and Equivalence for an XPath Fragment. PODS 2002: 65-76.

[11] Frank Neven, Thomas Schwentick: XPath Containment in the Presence of Disjunction, DTDs, and Variables. ICDT 2003: 315-329.

[12] Öszu, M.T., Valduriez, P.: Distributed Database Systems, 2nd Ed., Prentice Hall, 1999.

[13] Reimer, M.: Solving the Phantom Problem by Predicative Optimistic Concurrency Control, 9th VLDB, Florenz, 1983.

[14] XML Path Language (XPath) Version 1.0 . W3C Recommendation November 1999. http://www.w3.org/TR/xpath.

STRATEGIC PLANNING FOR MOBILE SERVICES ADOPTION AND DIFFUSION:
Empirical evidence from the Danish market

IOANNA D. CONSTANTIOU, JAN DAMSGAARD and LARS KNUTSEN
Department of Informatics, Copenhagen Business School

Abstract: This paper investigates mobile services adoption, diffusion and usage patterns in the Danish market. A similar empirical research was conducted during 2001 in Finland, Germany and Greece when mobile services were first introduced. This paper explores the impact of a set of attributes identified on that research in a more mature market context. Our objective is to confirm or reject and possibly expand the attributes that affect consumer behaviour in the long run, highlight the differences due to market evolution and observe the specific socio-economic characteristics of Danish market. We use an online survey that is based on the earlier research, but has been elaborated to address specific Danish market characteristics (e.g. the recent introduction of 3G services). The preliminary results offer indications on the evolution path of mobile services' market and highlight the accelerating adoption of mobile services.

Key words: mobile services; adoption and diffusion patterns; service usage; mobile shoppers.

1. INTRODUCTION

The availability and the plurality of mobile services are growing at a rapid pace in most countries around the world. As a stream of observations pertaining to the troubles of WAP, consecutive revisions of world 3G diffusion forecasts, and slow actual 3G uptake have emerged, scholars and practitioners have emphasized that technological advances and service availability do not automatically lead to widespread adoption and use (Baldi & Thaung, 2002; Funk, 2001). Moreover, in roadmaps for future research there are repeated suggestions that more efforts should be made at understanding issues and factors explaining adoption, acceptance and use of mobile services (Lyytinen & Yoo, 2002; Urbaczewski, Wells, & Sarker, 2002).

Most of the traditional diffusion of innovation literature (Rogers, 1995) would argue that the greatest benefits from a service belong to the first adopters and while the adoption proceeds, the relative advantage of being an early adopter diminishes. Moreover, traditional diffusion of innovation literature argues that latter argument is prominent in case of a company, which cannot sustain a competitive advantage based on a single technology, since others will imitate it and consequently achieve a similar advantage.

We argue that for mobile services the same logic cannot be readily applied. The greatest benefits from mobile services often come after their widespread adoption. For instance, in case of SMS, its value increases as the number of adopters increases due to network externalities. Most services become more readily available and better developed as the customer base increases. We have some indications from earlier studies of mobile services on the main attributes pertaining to adoption and diffusion. In this study we seek to confirm, reject and expand these factors by building a survey that incorporates earlier findings with current knowledge and local characteristics. In particular, we provide insight on the following question:

What factors explain and predict users' adoption and diffusion of mobile services?

The adoption of mobile services is not random. We believe that there is a certain order in which services are adopted and appropriated. Thus, the adoption trajectory forms a path that evolves under the influence of specific factors. By investigating the key attributes affecting adoption, diffusion and usage of mobile services it is possible to identify behavioural patterns pertaining to the specific market. The key players may use such patterns as an insight in strategic planning that enables them to increase their market share and maximise their profits. While the recent trends of GPRS services adoption are ambiguous, we witness that the use of some independent services (e.g. MMS) is increasing rapidly. On the contrary, transactional services, have not yet reached a critical mass of users.

This paper is organized as follows. Section 2 offers a brief review on related theoretical work to consumer behaviour of electronic and mobile business and highlights the results of a previous survey with similar objectives as well as the market trends of Danish mobile communications market. Section 3 presents the research methodology used, the demographic characteristics of the sample and the hypothesis tested. Section 4 presents part of the preliminary results and addresses the research question set.

Finally, section 5 concludes by underlining the main results and highlighting future research directions.

2. CONSUMERS' REACTIONS TO INNOVATIVE MOBILE SERVICES

2.1 Research in consumer behaviour of electronic and mobile business

Reviewing the business to consumer (B2C) e-commerce literature, it is clear that the majority of research efforts have focused on the Internet, rather on mobile telephony. As noted by Anckar & D'Incau (2002), our understanding of the real value-adding elements in mobile business is limited, in particular "the consumers' actual reasons – the primary drivers – for adopting and intending to adopt mobile services remain unclear". However, mobile business dynamics generate challenging research questions that enable building new theoretical frameworks as well as investigate managerial implications and emerging business opportunities.

Besides, B2C e-commerce, independent of the access device (e.g. PC, or mobile phone), has for any product, or service offering one generic but crucial objective: to satisfy consumers, create value and build strong relationships (Grönroos, 1997; Ravald & Grönroos, 1996) that are characterized by high level of loyalty, return patronage and bi-directional enthusiasm. In pursuit of in depth understanding, investigating consumer needs, wishes, preferences, attitudes, characteristics, and behaviours related to current and anticipated mobile phone use becomes invigorating for strategizing, development efforts and marketing. It is the authors' position that user surveys, constitutes a reliable method, which is particularly applicable when the purpose is to generate market data for comparison among broader categories of a population. Moreover, careful generation, dissemination and responsiveness of and to adequate survey data, can also guide organizations towards increased market orientation which in turn is connected to higher levels of organizational performance (Jaworski, Kohli, & Sahay, 2000; Jaworski & Kohli, 1993; Slater & Narver, 2000) and innovation (Baker & Sinkula, 2002; Han, Kim, & Srivastava, 2002; Hurley & Hult, 1998). Thus, current and future needs, existing consumers are a constituent group of significant importance in providing guidelines for the development of marketing and innovation strategies.

Online markets (either accessible through the PC, mobile phones or other wireless devices) constitute a channel for exchange which requires fundamental alterations in the purchasing behavior among customers. Therefore, a key task for e- and m-business is to find out who the actual and potential customers are (Turban et al. 1999). Along the same lines, Petrison et al. (1997) support that thorough knowledge of consumer behaviour, coupled with advances in technology, enable marketers to target customers on a more personalised, customised and segmented basis. However, consumer behaviour in mobile commerce has not yet been the subject of much research (Anckar et al., 2002; Pedersen, Methlie, & Thorbjørnsen, 2002).

The present study aims to contribute in the understanding of consumer behaviour in case of mobile services. To accomplish this aim we offer insight on consumer attitudes and behaviours towards mobile services based on the preliminary results of a survey.

2.2 The results of the previous survey

A study conducted in Finland, Germany and Greece as part of the MobiCom project (Vrehopoulos et.al. 2002, 2003) recorded the attitudes and perceptions of Internet and mobile telephony users in terms of new technology and services in mobile business (such as WAP, GPRS, purchases via mobile, etc). The study was based on a survey that was addressed to a self-selected sample of Internet users. This sample is representative of the most active segment of the market with respect to the adoption and use of new technologies. Among the survey findings, the cost of service, the the value of content and usability of the device emerged as key determinants of mobile commerce adoption and use. The latter determinant is also supported by Siau and Shen (2003). The survey led to important conclusions regarding the determinants of growth, the existing impediments as well as indications for appropriate strategic businesses responses.

In particular, besides the "killer-application" SMS, there were very few services used at a significant level. Among these services were information services (e.g. brokers) and mobile banking. Mobile services were mainly adopted due to their always and anywhere availability and the increased comfort they provided. New mobile services were diffused through social networks mainly by friends and colleagues. The Internet also played an important role as an information channel in the diffusion process. This finding was also supported by earlier research indicating that virtual communities might play a vital role in catalyzing mobile service use (Rheingold, 2003), (Kim, 2000).

The high access price was considered the main deterrent for adoption of new services. It is important to remind the reader that during 2001, data services in mobile devices were mainly supported by WAP. Moreover, high access prices might be attributed to the oligopolistic structures of the respective mobile operators' markets at that time. However, the survey results also indicated that mobile users were able to differentiate between the inflated connection fees and the charges for the actual mobile services. While the former were perceived as rather high, the latter were perceived as relatively low priced. Moreover, the key attributes affecting mobile services' market evolution were:

- Ease of use interface,
- Security,
- Customer service,
- Price,
- Personalization,
- Comfort of device.

2.3   The Danish market

The Danish market for mobile telephony and services has been chosen for the purpose of this research due to its considerable maturity vis-à-vis the other markets investigated in the previous survey. For instance, GPRS services have increasingly diffused and 3G services have recently been launched. This market context is expected to offer indications and generate insight on the attributes of mobile market evolution path.

In terms of operators, the Danish mobile telecommunications market can be characterized as an oligopoly where five key market players (TDC, Sonofon, Telmore, Orange, and Telia) are dominant. Despite the high concentration and oligopoly nature, this market exhibits high price competition, which can be attributed to specific market characteristics. First, new entrants (Telmore, CBB Mobile and Debitel) can purchase services from incumbent mobile operators and resell them to end users. These players operate in low cost margins and drive prices of communication services at lower levels. In addition, mobile operators are jostling to capture the segment of "younger" users and to stimulate demand for new mobile services (e.g. 3G video services and MMS). As these users have grown accustomed to the low prices on SMS and voice calls, this has generated a "mirroring effect" to the prices on MMS and 3G services. For example, extensive campaigns were launched during 2003 offering MMS for free; and for signing up to new 3G services, mobile users could obtain three months of unlimited and free access to most of the new mobile content offered by the mobile operator 3.

The demand side of Danish mobile communications market during 2003 showed high growth rates in terms of GPRS data transfer, SMS usage as well as MMS adoption. Statistics[6] reveal that the average 290,000 GPRS subscribers generated approximately 2.74 MB of traffic during the second

---

[6] from the Danish National IT and Telecom Agency

half of 2003. Comparing the first and second half of 2003, there was an increase of 105% in the number of GPRS subscribers that drove an increase of 145% in the download/upload GPRS rate. More impressively, the average mobile phone user sent more than 515 SMS in the second half of 2003. This is a 63% increase from the first half of 2003. Although the MMS rates are bleach vis-à-vis the SMS rates, the growth rates are not. From the some 500 000 MMS being sent over the Danish mobile infrastructure during the first half of 2003, this had increased by 355% to approximately 2,3 million MMS sent during the second half. It is also worth noting that the total minutes of voice calls placed from mobile networks increased some 10.4% during this period, while the corresponding numbers on fixed networks dropped 9%.

3.   METHODOLOGY AND SAMPLING

3.1   The Survey instrument

The survey instrument was first developed in English and then translated into Danish. It was pilot tested using the staff of a university department (25) where 50% had prior experience on mobile services usage. The questions were revised based on their feedback. Following the revision, the survey was launched on the Internet by utilizing an online software tool (SurveyMonkey[7]). The survey will run in Denmark from February to March 2004.

Miller and Dickson (2001) argue that on-line consumer behaviour research presents a new area of academic study in marketing. They also note that most of the work in this area has been done by practitioners and strongly encourage further academic research and learning from the data of on-line research. With 50.4 internet subscriptions per 100 inhabitants and Denmark being a leading nation in terms of e-commerce[8], the Internet was considered an appropriate medium for the survey as we aimed to obtain responses by users with experience of mobile phones, mobile services, and Internet services.

The survey instrument included questions on mobile communications' statistic, general demographics, mobile services adoption and diffusion processes, mobile services usage behaviour as well as Internet services usage behaviour and 3G services adoption process. Mobile users behaviour and usage patterns are investigated through eleven questions that include basic

---

[7] www.surveymonkey.com
[8] http://edition.cnn.com/2004/TECH/internet/04/20/world.online.ap/index.html

issues such as the use of more elevated services than SMS, knowledge on new technological solutions available in the market, but also more advanced issues such as the frequency of use for specific mobile services. Moreover, respondents are asked to reveal extent to which they agreed/disagreed with the key attributes that were identified in the previous survey. The items are rated by respondents on a scale of 1-5, where 1 represented "strongly disagree" and 5 "strongly agree". Furthermore, in this survey we investigate 3G services adoption process by collecting information on possession of a 3G mobile device, current usage pattern and preferences for existing services.

Finally, as an incentive we offered the respondents a chance to participate in the lottery of two popular mobile phones currently sold in the Danish market. We acknowledge that the incentive may attract early adopters that are interested in new technologies but may also decrease the quality of responses since some respondents may take part on the survey only to win the prize. The high number of respondents that already posses a similar device with the one offered in the lottery, lowers the negative impact of this effect.

3.2   The sampling

The sample size is influenced by Internet and mobile penetration as well as the advertising effort for the online survey. The sample is not representative of the total Danish population since it includes self-selective Internet users. However, the intense advertising campaign and the balanced mix of internet pages hosting links to the survey (e.g. information portal, and university website) have counterbalanced part of this shortcoming. Convenience sampling was used. The current sample size is comprised of 722 Internet users. According to Hair et al. (2000) and Kinnear and Taylor (1996), convenience sampling is suitable for the requirements of exploratory research designs like the present one. The demographic characteristics of respondents are presented in Table 1.

Table 1. Demographic Characteristics of the Samples

Demographic Categories	Range/Category	%
	18-31	64,2
Age Groups	32-40	20,4
	41-64	14,2
	65+	1,2

Table 1. (continued)

Demographic Categories	Range/Category	%
Gender	Male	49,3
	Female	50,7
Household Size (i.e. no. of members)	1	30,9
	2	35,7
	3	11,9
	4+	21,3
Monthly Gross Income of Household (in Euros)	0-1000	20,2
	1001- 2000	18,1
	2001 – 3250	13,5
	3251 – 5000	12
	5000 +	36
Education	Below High School Degree	6,7
	High School Degree	17,7
	College/University	45
	Postgraduate	30,6
Occupation	Employed in the commercial sector	5,8
	Executive / manager	3,4
	Computer Engineer	1,6
	Student	57,7
	Employed in the social sector	7,6
	Professional	1,5
	Technician / Engineer	2,4
	Academic / Educator	8
	Self-employed	1,3
	Employed in the public administration	3
	Other	7,7

3.3   The Hypotheses

The survey delves into the attitudes and behaviours of users with respect to mobile services, sources of influences and innovation. In this paper we investigate whether the identified key attributes of mobile services market evolution have changed in the relatively more mature market context for both mobile users and shoppers. The null (H_0) and the alternative (H_1) hypotheses are formulated as follows:

H_0: Danish mobile users and mobile shoppers attach the same importance to the identified set of attributes

H₁: Danish mobile users and mobile shoppers attach significantly different importance to the identified set of attributes

4.   PRELIMINARY RESULTS AND DISCUSSION

4.1   Data analysis

The majority of respondents own a mobile device. However, it should be mentioned that as the sample includes only Internet users, this finding should be interpreted with caution. The subscription type of mobile contract was chosen by 52.5% and prepaid by 47.5%. As far as the purpose of mobile use is concerned, the majority of respondents (55.5 %) use their mobile devices exclusively for private purposes.

Denmark seems to be a comparatively mature market in terms of mobile devices diffusion. 35% of the respondents reported that they have 4 to 6 years experience with mobile devices, and 28.2% have more than 6 years of experience. However, in terms of the age of handsets, it was found that the majority of Danish users (49%) owned their current mobile phone for less than one year. A considerable number of respondents reported that they would buy a new mobile device equipped with better color display (31%) and PC synchronization to access calendar and emails (26%). To our surprise, the least important criterion for buying a new mobile device under study is games (54%).

Finally, the majority of the respondents (55.2%) reported that their average daily calling time fluctuates between 0 to 5 minutes, and send between 6-20 SMS per week (33.9%), while most of respondents spend an average of 10 Euros as their monthly mobile phone expenditure (29%). This observation corresponds to the official statistics released by the Danish Ministry of Telecommunications and Innovation[9]. The decrease in daily calling time underlines the need for mobile operators to diversify their service offering and seek for new revenue sources. Moreover, it indicates that mobile users' attitude towards mobile communication as such has changed.

The previous indication may be explained by the responses on what is the most important reason for using mobile devices, which, was found to be the "independence of location and time" (61.3%). If this criterion is combined with the decrease in calling time, it indicates that mobile communication is perceived as a mean that enables contacting people and allows "reachability" anywhere, anytime. This emerging trend offers new business opportunities

---

[9] www.si.dk

to mobile operators for developing customized services that can be bundled with basic communication services. Moreover, other important criteria were "convenience" (47.6%), the "curiosity" (34.6%).

The most important criterion for Danish users on selecting a mobile operator was found to be the "low pricing scheme" (69.5%), which seems to stimulate the current price competition in communication services. Moreover, "good coverage" was evaluated as the second criterion (39.2%) and "operator' reputation" as the third (27.8%).

With respect to 3G services, their adoption is still at an embryonic stage. Only 8 respondents out of 722 are using 3G devices. The recently released official statistics on mobile traffic for the second half of 2003 also underpins this finding. The respondents' attitudes towards 3G services is explored by asking the respondents to choose a statement that best represents them. Whereas 49% of respondents stated 'no interest', 30% stated "interested but waiting for new devices and others' reactions". Although part of the respondents are interested in 3G devices and services, operators' prices and the devices available appear also to influence their attitude.

Furthermore, respondents were asked to report, which mobile services they mainly use. Table 2, provides details on the mobile services usage. However, it should be noted that a considerable percentage of mobile users have not used any of the alternative mobile services in the past (85%).

Table 2. Mobile Services Usage

Services	Sample
Banking and financial services	30
Shopping	7
Entertainment	35
Information and News	65
Travel booking	6
Ticket reservation	29

A major classification between mobile users (i.e., those that have not used any of the services included in Table 2 but have used GPRS data services like MMS and email)) and mobile shoppers (i.e., those that have used at least one mobile service included in Table 2) was made in order to investigate whether there are significant differences between the evaluations provided by each of these groups. In order to determine whether the two identified groups (i.e., mobile users and mobile shoppers) attach equal importance to the investigated variables *t*-Tests were used (Table 3).

The results of Tables 3 show that mobile users become more mature. In particular, mobile users and shoppers attach equal importance to the main attributes for mobile services adoption and diffusion, such as pricing, comfort of device, personalization, customer service and security, except of the "ease of use interface". These indications offer initial insight to mobile operators on how to develop their marketing strategies and address this market segment.

Table 3. t-Tests Results for Mobile Users versus Shoppers on mobile service attributes

	Means (1: Com. Unimportant – 5: V. Important)		t-Test for Equality of Means*			Hypothesis Testing
	Mobile Users 210	Mobile Shoppers 104	t	Sig.	p-value	
Ease of Use Interface	2,77	2,32	2,33	0,02	p<0,05	Reject Ho at α=0,05
Security	3,08	2,8	1,03	0,3	p>0,05	Cannot Reject Ho
Customer Service	3,21	2,87	1,51	0,13	p>0,05	Cannot Reject Ho
Price	3,86	3,67	0,74	0,46	p>0,05	Cannot Reject Ho
Personalisation	3,3	3,09	0,78	0,43	p>0,05	Cannot Reject Ho
Comfort of Device	3,4	3,58	-0,65	0,51	p>0,05	Cannot Reject Ho

*F-tests indicated equality of variance except of "price" and "personalization" attributes.

4.2 Evolution path of mobile service market

According to the results, included in Table 3, "price" remains the most important attribute for both mobile users and shoppers, implying that the cost of using mobile services is critical for their diffusion. It should be noted that this finding is in line with the results of similar studies discussed in section 2, which proved that "high price" constitutes one of the major obstacles towards mobile services diffusion.

Moreover, "comfort of device" was found to be the second most important attribute for both mobile users and shoppers. Mobile users become experienced and informed regarding the various mobile devices available in the market. Therefore, they seek devices that are "easy to use" when accessing mobile services. Apparently, the high sophistication of some devices that incorporate the latest technological advances makes them unattractive to mobile users that prefer easy and simple access to the new services. The recently released official statistics on mobile traffic for the second half of 2003 also underpins this finding, as less than 3500 persons had adopted the only 3G handset in the Danish market (e.g. the technologically sophisticated Motorola A920).

Furthermore, "personalization" and "customer service" were also found as important attributes for both mobile users and shoppers indicating the maturity of the Danish market where there are more experienced and informed consumers regarding the various mobile service providers and correspondingly the available mobile services.

On the contrary, "security" and "easy to use interface" were found to be relatively less important attributes for the respondents. As far as "security" is concerned, this does not keep pace with the fact that one of the most important reasons that Internet users do not shop through the Web concerns security issues. In addition, the issue of "easy to use interface" has not become unimportant, but has been "taken for granted" since new mobile handsets include more easy to use interfaces, and routine use tends to diminish the perception of difficulty. However, the difference between mobile users and shoppers, in the importance attached to this attribute may also indicate the users' difficulties on accessing mobile services.

Based on this discussion, it can be concluded that mobile users, which at the same time are Internet users (i.e., they used the Internet to participate in the online survey) are maturing rapidly. They should constitute a target segment for mobile service providers and their strategic marketing planning. Thus, marketing strategies should be customized to the characteristics of this emerging customer group towards satisfying their needs and preferences. For example, the promotional messages' content could underline the "comfort of device" attribute. Furthermore, different marketing strategies could be designed for mobile shoppers increase the usage of mobile services.

5.   CONCLUSIONS, IMPLICATIONS AND FUTURE RESEARCH DIRECTIONS

Consumer attitudes and behavioral patterns with respect to mobile services' attributes do not significantly differ between mobile shoppers and mobile users. Moreover, the demographic characteristics of these two groups are similar. This indicates that mobile services adoption in the Danish market is accelerating. The process can be enhanced by designing and offering customized marketing mixes tailored to the characteristics and needs of each target group. Mobile service providers can design their strategic marketing planning by using the provided findings in the customer analysis to identify the profile of their current and potential customers. To that end, the present study revealed some critical factors pointing towards acceleration of mobile services' adoption, as well as indicated to marketing experts should exploit the market potential of mobile users. Furthermore, the critical role of consumer behaviour research in the mobile industry was clearly justified.

Another, important parameter that this survey revealed is the different approach of mobile users towards communication services. In particular, mobile users do not spend a lot of time daily on voice services, but use them to contact people and coordinate personal activites. This emerging trend offers new opportunities to mobile service providers to design new mobile services that address it. However, there is a strong need to conduct in-depth consumer behaviour surveys focusing on such observations. It is also important to note that the dynamics of perceptions should be investigated by continuous market intelligence generation and dissemination for industry players to both respond to and better anticipate changes in preferences, needs and wants. For this, surveys are an adequate tool, but should be supported by qualitative research methods.

Further research can elaborate on the findings of this exploratory study and develop and test specific research hypotheses within conclusive research designs. For example, focus groups may be used to elaborate on the observation that mobile users do not heavily use communication services but appreciate the feeling of "anytime anywhere reachability" that is being offered. Moreover, experiments can be conducted to test hypotheses such as whether there are significant differences regarding mobile shoppers and users willingness to pay for specific mobile services. This type of research will provide direct managerial implications for mobile service providers and enable them to offer bundles of services for specific market segments. The authors of this paper currently study the social dynamics and price elasticity of two user segments in a field experiment. In the experiment there are a total of 50 people that are allocated new mobile phones and pre-paid SIM cards. The pre-paid card exceeds most peoples' current spending. We investigate how additional resources are allocated to various m-services as well as collect and analyse data in order to identify opportunities for versioning and bundling of mobile service.

ACKNOWLEDGEMENT

This research was conducted as part of the Mobiconomy project at Copenhagen Business School. Mobiconomy is partially supported by the Danish Research Agency, grant number 2054-03-0004.

REFERENCES

Anckar, B., and D'Incau, D. 2002, Value creation in mobile commerce: Findings from a consumer survey, *J. Information Technology Theory and Application*, 4(1): 43-65.

Baker, W. E., and Sinkula, J. M. 2002, Market orientation, Learning orientation and Product Innovation: Delving into the organization's black box, *J. Market-Focused Management*, 5: 5-23.

Baldi, S., and Thaung, H. P.-P. 2002, The Entertaining way to M-Commerce: japan's Approach to the Mobile Internet - A Model for Europe, *Electronic Markets*, 12(1): 6-13.

Funk, J. 2001, *The Mobile Internet: How Japan Dialled Up and the West Disconnected*, Kent, UK: ISI Publications.

Grönroos, C. 1997, Value-driven Relational Marketing: from Products to Resources and Competencies, *J. Marketing Management*, **13**(5): 407-419.

Hair, J.F.Jr., Bush, R.P. and Ortinau, D.J. 2000, *Marketing Research: A Practical Approach for the New Millennium*, McGraw-Hill International Editions.

Han, J. K., Kim, N., and Srivastava, R. K. 2002, Market orientation and organizational performance: Is innovation a missing link?, *J. Marketing*, **62**(4): 30-46.

Hurley, R. F., and Hult, G. T. M. 1998, Innovation, market orientation, and organizational learning: An integration and empirical examination, *J. Marketing*, **62**(3): 42-55.

Jaworski, B., Kohli, A. K., and Sahay, A. 2000, Market-driven versus driving markets. *J. Academy of Marketing Science*, **28** (1), 45-54.

Jaworski, B. J., and Kohli, A. K. 1993, Market orientation: Antecedents and consequences, *J. Marketing*, **57**(3): 53.

Kinnear, T.C. and Taylor, J.R. 1996, *Marketing Research: An Applied Approach*, 5th ed., McGraw-Hill, Inc.

Kim, A. J. 2000, *Community Building on the Web*, Peachpit Press Berkeley CA

Miller, T.W. and Dickson, P.R. 2001, On-line Market Research, *Int. J. Electronic Commerce*, **5**(3): 139-167.

Lyytinen, K., and Yoo, Y. 2002, Research Commentary: The Next Wave of Nomadic Computing, *Information Systems Research*, **13**(4): 377-388.

Pedersen, P. E., Methlie, L., B., and Thorbjørnsen, H. 2002, Understanding mobile commerce end-user adoption: a triangulation perspective and suggestions for an exploratory service evaluation framework. Procceedings of 35th Annual Hawaii International Conference on System Sciences (HICSS-35), Big Island, Hawaii.

Petrison, L., Blattberg, R.C., and Wang, P. 1997, Database Marketing – Past, Present and Fututre, *J. Direct Marketing*, **11**(4): 109-125.

Ravald, A., & Grönroos, C. 1996 The value concept and relationship marketing. European Journal of Marketing, **30**(2): 19-30.

Rogers, E. M. 1995, *Diffusion of Innovations*, 4th ed., New York: The Free Press.

Siau, K. and Shen, Z. 2003, Mobile Communications and mobile services, *Int. J. Mobile Communications*, **1**(1/2): 3-14.

Slater, S. F., and Narver, J. C. 2000, The positive effect of a market orientation on business profitability: A balanced replication, *J. Business Research*, **48**(1): 69-73.

Rheingold, H. 2003, *Smart Mobs – the next social revolution*. Persus Books Group Cambridge MA.

Turban, E., King, D., Lee, J., Warkentin, M. and Chung, M.H. 2002. *Electronic Commerce: A Managerial Perspective*, Prentice Hall – Pearson Education International.

Urbaczewski, A., Wells, J., and Sarker, S. 2002, Exploring Cultural Differences as a Means for Undertanding the Global Mobile Internet: A Theoretical Basis and Program of Research. Proceedings of 35th Annual Hawaii International Conference on System Sciences (HICSS), Big Island, Hawaii.

Vrechopoulos, A.P., Constantiou, I.D., Mylonopoulos, N, Sideris, I. and Doukidis, G. I. 2002, The Critical Role of Consumer Behavior Research in Mobile Commerce, *Int. J. Mobile Communications*, **1**(3):329-340.

Vrechopoulos, A.P., Constantiou, I.D., Mylonopoulos, N and Sideris, I. 2002, Critical Success Factors for Accelerating Mobile Commerce Diffusion in Europe, Proceedings of the 15th Bled E-commerce Conference, e-Reality: Constructing the e-Economy, Bled, Slovenia.

USING GROUP MANAGEMENT TO TAME MOBILE AD HOC NETWORKS

Malika Boulkenafed[1], Daniele Sacchetti[1], Valerie Issarny[1]

[1]INRIA-*Rocquencourt Domaine de Voluceau,*
Rocquencourt, BP 105,
78153 Le Chesnay Cedex,
FRANCE
{Malika.Boulkenafed, Daniele.Sacchetti, Valerie.Issarny@inria}-@inria.fr

Abstract   Mobile ad hoc networks (MANET) offer a convenient basis towards pervasive computing, due to inherent support for anytime, anywhere network access for mobile users. However, the development of applications over MANET still raises numerous challenges. One such challenge relates to accommodating the high dynamics of the network's topology. Group management appears as a promising paradigm to ease the development of distributed applications over dynamic, mobile networks. Specifically, group management takes care of assembling mobile nodes that together allow to meet target functional and non-functional properties, and of further making transparent failures due to the mobility of nodes. Various solutions towards group management over MANET have been investigated over the last couple of years, each targeting specific applications. Building upon such an effort, this paper introduces the design and implementation of a group service for MANET, which is generic with respect to the various attributes of relevance. Generic group management allows supporting various applications, as illustrated through groups dedicated to mobile collaborative data sharing.

Keywords: Ad hoc networking, group management, mobile environments, resource sharing.

Introduction

Mobile ad hoc networks (MANET) pave the way for pervasive computing due to inherent support for anytime, anywhere network access for mobile users. Nonetheless, the highly dynamic nature of mobile ad hoc networks poses tremendous challenges for the development of applications since the application's context keeps changing over time. One approach to master this complexity lies in the management of groups over MANET, i.e., applications execute on top of groups that manage the dynamic execution context, including mobility-related failures. There has been extensive research on group management and related group communication services in the context of fixed networks, with special emphasis on providing availability properties [16, 7]. However, proposed solutions cannot be applied directly to mobile wireless networks due to the network's highly dynamic topology [2]. This has led to adapt the management of group membership to the specifics of MANET.

Group membership is primarily defined according to the functional property to be achieved by the group, e.g., collaborative editing, sharing a computational load, increasing performance, providing fault tolerant service. In general, a member may leave a group because it failed, explicitly requested to leave, or is expelled by other members. Similarly, a member may join a group because it explicitly requests it or recovers from failure. A group membership protocol must manage such dynamic changes in a coherent way, i.e., all members of the group must have a consistent view of the group's membership despite failures [7]. The highly dynamic topology of MANET introduces additional complexity in the management of group membership because connections may be transient and partitioned networks may never be rejoined together. However, group membership for MANET may still be defined as for fixed networks, i.e., according to the functional property to be realized. In this case, it is considered that the MANET allows restoring lost connections using the underlying routing protocol. Solutions then lie in the adaptation of the group communication service to the dynamic topology of the network [11]. Such an approach does not adapt the system's functions to the specifics of the network but rather adapt the implementation of traditional distributed system functions. However, it is advantageous to revise the definition of group membership so as to integrate the connectivity dimension in addition to the functional one. This allows dealing with quality of service requirements by bounding communication latency [8] and/or supporting location-aware applications. Specifically, connectivity-constrained group membership enables managing a dynamic (sub-)network that is configured according to both connectivity constraints and the functional property to be implemented, while hiding mobility-induced link failures to applications [17]. Connectivity constraints may vary from 1-hop to multi-hop connectivity, where unbounded multi-hop connectivity corresponds to the aforementioned connectivity-unaware group membership addressed in [11]. Connectivity constraints may then be fixed according to the network's connectivity (i.e., number of hops) as in [17] or the respective geographical position of the group's members as in [14]. The definition of group membership may further be extended with integrity constraints (e.g., security constraints, size) [15].

In this paper, we provide a characterization of the attributes of group membership in ad hoc networks (Section 1), and then introduce the design of a group management service that is generic with respect to the elicited attributes (Section 2). We further assess the proposed service based on its theoritical complexity, its implementation in a middleware aimed at mobile computing (Section 3), and its usage for enabling pervasive computing scenarios relating to mobile collaboration and data management (Section 4). Finally, we conclude with a summary of our contribution and our future work (Section 5).

1. Attributes of Group Membership

We recall that groups are first defined with respect to a given functional property. We denote such a property by f. Without loss of generality, we assume that the property is offered by any node, as opposed to being an aggregation of some functions provided by grouped nodes. We use the Boolean function $support(x, f)$ to denote that node x offers function f. Note that f may characterize various features supported by nodes, and resembles to resources considered in resource discovery protocols [3]. Finally, we denote by G^f, a group realizing function f.

Network Model. We consider a WI-FI-based ad hoc network consisting of a set N of n nodes, and assume that every node x of N has a unique identifier $Id(x)$. However, we do not fix the routing protocol that is used. We further introduce the following functions to reason about the connectivity of nodes, for $x \in N$ and a time period T that is such that the network does not change over T.

- $Proximity(T, x, p)$ returns the geographical distance in meters between the location of x and geographical position p, during T.

- $Dist(T, x, y)$ returns the geographical distance in meters between the respective locations of x and $y \in N$, during T.

- $Connectivity(T, x)$ returns the set of all nodes of N with which x can communicate using the underlying network protocols, during T; note that due to the asymmetric nature of wireless networks in general, $y \in Connectivity(T, x)$ does not imply $x \in Connectivity(T, y)$.

- $DualConnectivity(T, x)$ returns the set of all nodes y of N such that $y \in Connectivity(T, x)$ and $x \in Connectivity(T, y)$.

- $Hops(T, x, y)$ returns the number of hops for communication between x and y for any y belonging to $Connectivity(T, x)$.

Location. We now define functions characterizing group membership with respect to constraints set on the relative location of member nodes.

- *Location-unaware* groups as, e.g., addressed in [11, 12], are defined solely with respect to the functional properties offered by the group members. Hence, $LocationUnaware(G^f)$ always holds.

- *Proximity-based* groups as, e.g., addressed in [14, 15], set that group members should be in a given geographical area, whose location may be fixed a priori or set relative to the position of group members. Let *pos* denote a referenced geographical position and *dist* let denote the maximal geographical distance that is allowed, we get:

$$Geo\_Prox(G^f, T, pos, dist) \Leftrightarrow \forall x \in G^f, Prox(T, x, pos) < dist$$
$$Relative\_Prox(G^f, T, dist) \Leftrightarrow \forall(x, y) \in G^{f2}, Dist(T, x, y) < dist$$

- *Bounded* groups are defined with respect to the number of hops separating node members as, e.g., addressed in [17, 18, 6], are defined in a similar way based on the maximal number of hops, noted *hops*, between nodes:

$$Bounded(G^f, T, hops) \Leftrightarrow \forall(x, y) \in G^{f2}, Hops(T, x, y) \le hops$$

Note that the above functions are not exclusive of each other and may be combined for the definition of a given group.

Openness. Group membership may be restricted to authorized nodes. We model such a constraint using the notion of *security domain*: a security domain S^f sets nodes of N that trust each other towards realizing function f. Practically, a security domain is managed by a trusted third party to which nodes may authenticate and register themselves; nodes then get a signed certificate that they may use to authenticate themselves with other nodes belonging to S^f. Secure group communication may further be enforced through the implementation of group key agreement within the group [4]. We get:

$$Closed(G^f, S^f) \Leftrightarrow \forall x \in G^f \Rightarrow x \in S^f$$

Connectivity. Group membership may require full, partial or even loose connectivity among nodes. In general, connectivity constraints may be combined with any of the aforementioned location-related constraints and may apply to both open and closed groups. Loose connectivity consists of relying on the connectivity enabled by the underlying network over time and thus does not impose any specific constraint. A fully connected group is further characterized by:

$$Connected(G^f, T) \Leftrightarrow \forall(x, y) \in G^{f2}, y \in DualConnectivity(T, x)$$

Partial connectivity is defined according to the client and server roles of nodes with respect to function f. We use the function $client(x, f)$, resp. $server(x, f)$, to denote that x is client of f, resp. server of f. We get:

$$Partial(G^f, T) \Leftrightarrow \forall(x, y) \in G^{f2}, server(x, f) \Rightarrow y \in DualConnectivity(T, x)$$

Note that $Connected(G^f) \Rightarrow Partial(G^f)$. Also, symmetric communication links may not be required between client and server nodes depending on the interaction patterns required by the application. However, we consider dual connectivity only, as this is the most common case for applications. The definition of partial connectivity with uni-directional reachability is further direct to infer. Finally, we enforce full connectivity among server nodes.

QoS Awareness. Group membership may further be constrained for the sake of enhanced quality of service, i.e., members of the group must meet a number of Quality of Service (QoS) attributes. Various QoS attributes may be considered. In particular, the following attributes appear to be the most dominant in the context of MANET [10]: reliability, security, performance and transactional behavior that relate to service-level attributes, and CPU load, memory, bandwidth and battery that relate to resource-level attributes. Then, a QoS-aware group may restrict group membership to nodes meeting the QoS attributes that are fixed for the group among the above. In addition, group membership may be constrained so as to limit the probability of a node leaving a group. For instance, exploiting the movement of nodes has been suggested as an additional criterion for integration within a group [17]. In general, disconnection of a node from a group may be due to the node's mobility and/or the node's resource scarcity. The former may be anticipated based on information on the node's movement, and the latter may be anticipated based on information about resource-level QoS attributes of the node [6].

2. Group Service Design

This section details the design of a group management service that is generic with respect to the above membership attributes. We further consider the following requirements for the service design: (i) The group management service must minimize resource consumption on mobile nodes, and in particular energy, requiring minimizing message exchanges. (ii) Group management cannot accommodate a centralized solution where a single node is responsible for managing the group, since the node may leave the group at any time. It is thus necessary to provide a decentralized solution. (iii) The group management service must mask the highly dynamic topology of the network to the application, requiring updating group membership accordingly. We distinguish three functions in group management:

- Discovering group members, i.e., discovering mobile nodes that are eligible for membership according to relevant membership attributes, i.e., location, openness and QoS-related constraints.

- Initializing the group, i.e., exchanging meta-data relevant to the group's functionality and further checking for global membership constraints, i.e., connectivity and QoS-related attributes.

- Managing the group's dynamics, i.e., updating group membership according to the dynamics of the network's topology.

2.1   Group Members Discovery

Each node maintains the list of all groups, $\{G^{f1}, \ldots G^{fn}\}$, to which it may belong. For each group, the node periodically runs a discovery process to locate peer nodes with which it may join. The discovery process consists of broadcasting a discovery message, *Disc*, towards nodes accessible in 1 hop, and dually handling *Disc* messages that are received. A *Disc* message embeds at least the name of the group and the Id of the sender. The discovery process is further customized according to the QoS-related, openness, and location attributes set for the group.

Prior to issuing a *Disc* message, every node checks compliance with respect to relevant local QoS-related attributes. In addition, in the case where membership is restricted to authorized nodes (i.e., $Closed(G^f, S^f)$ must hold), related discovery messages embed the signed certificate of the sender node, and transmitted data (but the group's identifier) are encrypted using the sender's private key given that the sender's public key is part of the sender's certificate.

Subsequent handling of discovery messages depends on the location constraints set for the group. If the group G^f is location-unaware, peer nodes that are discovered through receipt of relevant *Disc* messages are added to the local list of peer nodes, P^f. In addition, any *Disc* message that is received, for the given period, is broadcasted so that the message is eventually (assuming every two nodes of N are connected, possibly in n hops) received by nodes that are not accessible in 1 hop from the sender. If the group is proximity-based, *Disc* messages embed the geographical position (e.g., using embedded GPS function) of the sender and their handling is constrained by the enforced geographical and/or relative proximity. In the case of geographical proximity (i.e., $Geo\_Prox(G^f, T, pos, dist)$ must be enforced), a *Disc* message is sent only if the sender node is located in the targeted region. In the same way, nodes discovered through received *Disc* messages are included in the local list of peer nodes and further forwarded, only if their position meets the geographical constraint set for the group. Relative proximity (i.e., $Relative\_Prox(G^f, T, dist)$ must be enforced) is handled similarly; only *Disc* messages received from nodes whose position meets the enforced geographical constraint are processed by the receiver. Bounded groups (i.e., $Bounded(G^f, T, hops)$ must be enforced) are handled as for proximity-based groups; the only difference is that proximity is defined with respect to the number of hops instead of geographical position. The number of hops can be determined using the TTL (Time To Live) counter.

2.2   Group Initialization

The above decentralized process allows every node to discover its peers according to local QoS-related, openness and location constraints set for the group. However, setting the group requires further constraining group membership according to connectivity and global QoS-related constraints.

Note that decentralized management of location-unaware groups is only compliant with loose connectivity unless members of the group are fixed a priori and hence known by members prior to the discovery process. This restriction allows to bound the time taken by the discovery process. Precisely, the discovery phase is bounded according to the location constraints combined with the time taken for message exchange with the underlying network.

Once the discovery phase is terminated, the initialization phase establishes group membership so as to enforce required connectivity. This process is managed by a single node, called *leader*. The leader is a peer node whose *Id* is the greatest among all group members. Hence, based on its local list of peer nodes, P_n^f, for group G^f, every node n knows the group leader. Centralization of the initialization process via the leader allows minimizing the process' cost in terms of exchanged messages and thus of energy consumption. In addition, as detailed in the next section, the group leader is periodically changed within the group, so that the associated load is fairly distributed among nodes and the disconnection of the leader does not affect group management.

The role of the leader is first to check connectivity constraints. Thus, every node n sends its local list of peer nodes P_n^f to *its* leader l (i.e., $l \in P_n^f$ and $\forall x \in P_n^f : Id(x) < Id(l)$) using the *Join* message. Due to the partial connectivity inherent to wireless network, a node may be elected as leader by some nodes while not electing itself as leader. Thus, every node, even if it did not elect itself as a leader, handles incoming *Join* messages received within a given time period Δ that is set according to connectivity constraints combined with the time taken for message exchanges.

Consider first the case of full connectivity (i.e., enforcing $Connected(G^f, T)$). Let R^f denote the list of nodes from which l received a *Join* message over time period Δ, $G_l^f = P_l^f \cap R^f$, $I_l^f = \bigcap_{(j \in G_l^f)} P_j^f$ and $U_l^f = \bigcup_{(j \in G_l^f)} P_j^f$. In particular, I_l^f is the set of mobile nodes that discovered each other and meet the QoS-related, openness and location constraints of the given group. Also, note that $G_l^f \subseteq U_l^f$. Group membership is then established through comparison of the values of G_l^f, I_l^f and U_l^f. We distinguish three cases:

- If $G_l^f = I_l^f = U_l^f$, then all the peers of G_l^f have identical view on group membership. The leader then validates G_l^f as group membership, which is notified by sending the related *Group* message to all nodes of G_l^f.

- If $(G_l^f = I_l^f$ and $I_l^f \neq U_l^f)$ or $(G_l^f \neq I_l^f$ and $I_l^f = U_l^f)$ then nodes belonging to U_l^f but not to G_l^f do not meet location constraints with respect to the leader. In this case, the leader validates G_l^f as the group's membership and the nodes that are excluded are notified using an exclusion message.

- If $(G_l^f = U_l^f$ and $I_l^f \neq U_l^f)$ or $(G_l^f \neq U_l^f$ and $I_l^f \neq U_l^f$ and $G_l^f \neq I_l^f)$ then nodes belonging to I_l^f meet location constraints with respect to nodes belonging to G_l^f but some nodes belonging to G_l^f do not meet such constraints. It is then up to the leader to fix group membership (e.g., validates I_l^f as group membership).

Finally, in the case where a node receives a group membership message, while it already joined another group, it is up to the node to either ignore the message or change group.

Partial connectivity (i.e., enforcing $Partial(G^f, T)$) requires ensuring that every client node is connected to every server node. We further require all the server nodes to be fully connected. The client or server role is made known to peers during the discovery process. The group membership is then established as above, except that the leader is elected among server nodes only, and that group membership is set with respect to partial connectivity requirement.

QoS-related constraints on group membership may also lead to exclude peers from the group in the case global attributes cannot be met. Currently, we set the constraint as a maximal number on group members, provided that dedicated QoS management should be implemented within the group according to the function f that is provided (e.g., see Section 4 for an example).

In the case where the group is closed, the initialization process is further complemented with a group key agreement (GKA) protocol so as to establish a shared secret among the group's members. The secret will then be used to encrypt any message subsequently exchanged within the group. There exist various such protocols in the literature for Internet-based systems. The interested reader is referred to [4] for an overview and analysis of GKA protocols aimed at groups of resource-constrained nodes that require minimizing resource consumption.

Initialization of the group additionally depends on the specific functionality of the group, possibly leading to exchange additional data among group members. Basically, relevant data are piggybacked in the *Join* message sent to the leader, which combine and forward them to group members when issuing the message validating group membership.

2.3   Managing the Group Dynamics

Group management over MANET requires to take into account the highly dynamic topology of the network, i.e., mobility-induced changes in group membership, in a way that is transparent to applications. Changes are detected during the discovery and initialization phases. However, the related processes cannot be run continuously due to the resource consumption that they induce. We thus propose to make periodic the process of group maintenance, where the period is dynamically adapted according to the rate of changes within the group, as initially proposed in [5] and outlined below.

The period is initially set to a given value T and is then dynamically adapted according to the past behavior of the embedding group (which may be a single node in the case of a singleton group). Let t be the current time, T' and T be the last two periods, and $\Gamma = \frac{C^{prev}}{C^{last}}$ with C^{last} being the number of changes over the last period (i.e., over $[(t - T), t]$) and C^{prev} being the number of changes over $[(t - (T'+T)), (t-T)]$. Then, if Γ is greater (resp. smaller) than one, the value of T should be increased (resp. decreased) for the next period because the group has been changing less (resp. more) frequently over the last period than it changed over the previous period. The new value of T then becomes equal to: $T \times \Gamma$.

Upon expiration of period T, each node belonging to the group runs its local discovery process (§2.1) in order to detect possible changes in group membership. Due to the periodic discovery process, nodes (and even distinct groups) that may join together according to constraints set for group membership may not run the discovery process at the same time. It is then up to the groups' leaders[1] to synchronize their respective discovery process in order to join together.

The node elected as leader within a group changes periodically in accordance with period T, due to the leader's possible mobility but also to distribute the load for group management among group members. We recall that the election of the group leader is decentralized (§2.2). Precisely, the leader is elected according to the following algorithm. Assuming node n belongs to group G^f, n keeps the list L_n^f of the nodes that were elected as leaders within the group, provided that $L_n^f = \phi$ if n belongs to a singleton group. Then, n includes L_n^f in its discovery message *Disc*. After the completion of the discovery process, every node n computes L^f as the union of L_n^f with the sets L_x^f embedded in the discovery messages received from all the peer nodes x. Then, n elects as leader the node that has the maximum *Id* from $P_l^f - L^f$, which is added to L_n^f. In the case where $P_l^f - L^f = \phi$, L_n^f is set to ϕ. As a result, all nodes of a group G^f elects the same leader in a decentralized way.

Mobility of nodes (i.e., joining or leaving the group) does not affect the election of the leader since the decentralized nature of the algorithm makes it independent of the group's dynamic. In addition, the leader role is significant only during the initialization phase. Hence, the leave of the leader affects group management only if it occurs during the initialization phase, leading

---

[1] In the case where the group is a singleton, the single member node is the group's leader.

Table 1. Cost of group membership in terms of exchanged messages.

Node	Management Phase	Sent	Received	Discarded
Creation of a group by joining n singletons				
Leader	Discovery	1	n-1	0
	Initialization	1	n-1	0
Peer	Discovery	1	n-1	0
	Initialization	1	1	n-2
p nodes join the group				
Leader	Discovery	1	n+p-1	0
	Initialization	1	n+p-1	0
Peer	Discovery	1	n+p-1	0
	Initialization	1	1	n+p-2

to effective update of group membership at the next period. In addition, our algorithm guarantees that a single leader exists during a period.

3. Assessment

The following first provides an assessment of our group management in terms of theoritical complexity, and in terms of group dynamics impact on applications, and then discusses the implementation of the group management service on the top of the WSAMI middleware aimed at mobile distributed computing.

3.1 Theoretical Complexity

Our group service is designed so as to minimize resource consumption on nodes. In particular, the number of exchanged messages to manage group membership is minimized through the introduction of group leader. Table 1 gives the number of exchanged messages for group management, considering specifically the creation of a group of n nodes and the update of a group with p joining nodes. Precisely, we give the number of messages that are sent[2], received and discarded, given management over an one hop ad hoc network and considering only nodes of the group. The theoretical complexity of group management is in $O(n)$ with n being the number of group members. The node designated as leader sends/receives more messages than the other group members. Hence, resource consumption is larger on the leader node. In particular, induced energy consumption for the leader node is 32.5% higher than the one for peer nodes [6], which is why it is crucial to periodically change the node acting as leader.

---

[2]For message broadcast, we set the number of emission to 1 and the one of reception to n.

3.2 Group Dynamics Impact

Changes occurring within a group are detected every period T. Then, group membership G^f viewed by nodes may be inconsistent with actual group membership if the value of period T is greater than the period during which the network's topology does not change. This may possibly affect the application's correctness, provided that we consider that applications are designed to execute over dynamic groups. Note that we further consider that only location-based and connectivity constraints (i.e., membership constraints parameterized by time period in Section 1) can be violated. While it may be the case that the certificate of a group member may expire during period T in the case of a closed group, this case is avoided by integrating within a group, only nodes that have a certificate that is valid for the duration of whole period T. In the same way, QoS-related attributes are provided with respect to the period T.

Various cases may be considered with respect to inconsistent group membership. If the composition of G^f (as viewed by group members) still meets the group's (location-based and connectivity) constraints with respect to actual group membership then this does not impact the application's correctness; it simply means that the application misses nodes that could join the group. If the composition of G^f no longer meets the group's constraints with respect to actual group membership, then we consider two cases:(i) Required connectivity may still be established although violating location-based constraints (e.g., connectivity now requires 3 hops while the group should be limited to nodes at a distance less than 2 hops). (ii) Required connectivity cannot be established. Although the former case leads to an application that is possibly not correct with respect to some non-functional property for some period less than T (e.g., the group is bounded to fixed maximum response time), it does not affect the functional correctness of the application. On the other hand, the latter case possibly leads to message loss, and hence may affect application's correctness. Various solutions can be considered, e.g., using a gossip mechanism as in [11], for reliable group communications, leading to the former situation. However, there is no guarantee about when the message will be delivered, which may happen subsequent to the end of the current period. We thus choose a simpler solution that is to report an exception to the application.

3.3 Implementation

We are implementing a prototype of our group management service within the WSAMI[3] middleware aimed at supporting pervasive computing/ambient intelligence applications over hybrid networks, which is being developed as

---

[3] Web Services for Ambient Intelligence.

part of the European IST OZONE project[4]. WSAMI builds upon the Web services architecture, hence allowing to benefit from the pervasiveness of the Web for mobile applications[5]. The base WSAMI middleware comprises the WSAMI core broker, enabling interaction among mobile Web services, and the ND service for naming, discovery and lookup that allows retrieving services according to the user's situation [9].

The WSAMI core broker provides communication functionalities to distributed services, and offers a development and deployment environment to service developers. The WSAMI development and deployment environment is based on the WSDL[6] and WSAMI languages. WSDL documents define service interfaces and instances, as specified by the Web Services Architecture. WSAMI documents define service composition (i.e., required services) and quality of service requirements (i.e., non-functional requirements more specifically related to security and performance). The WSAMI ND service serves discovering instances of Web services implementing a given WSAMI interface provided the URI of the corresponding document, and offers the following functionalities: (i) the management of a repository of local service instances; (ii) the location of remote service instances, which is based on the Service Location Protocol[7] (SLP); and, (iii) the handling of connector customization for enforcing quality of service. The WSAMI customizer document associated to the service is used to discover local and remote customizer service instances.

The Group Service is then implemented on top of the ND service, which is extended to discover the peer services that meet the constraints set for a given group. Precisely, the ND service is extended with the function $DiscPeer$, which takes as input: the URI of the WSAMI document defining the function provided by the group, and additional parameters relevant to the group's constraints (i.e., certificate if closed group, and any related location and QoS data). The Group Service is deployed on any node taking part in group management, and offers a $RegGroup$ (resp. $UnRegGroup$) function for registering (resp. canceling) participation to a given group. The $RegGroup$ function takes as input the functional specification of the group (i.e., WSAMI specification) provided that a corresponding service instance is locally deployed, together with membership constraints associated with the group. In addition, any group member must support the function associated with the leader, i.e., group initialization. Group management is then initiated following call to the $Activation$ function of the group service for the given group, further leading

---

[4]http://www.extra.research.philips.com/euprojects/ozone/
[5]http://www.w3.org/2002/ws/
[6]http://www.w3.org/TR/wsdl
[7]http://www.srvloc.org/

to group creation and periodic maintenance, as detailed in the previous section, until the *Desactivate* function is called.

4. Collaborative Data Sharing

This section discusses the implementation of a specific group, providing example of group management supporting pervasive computing scenarios. This example relates to mobile data management, where group management in MANET may be exploited to implement a shared data structure that aggregates the content made available on peer nodes, e.g., [17, 6, 13].

Group management is much suited to collaborative data sharing in the mobile environment; nodes that have access to common data may join together so as get access to related data located on peer nodes. This further supports mobile collaborative applications [1], where collaboration may be either synchronous or asynchronous depending on the degree of concurrent updates. Supporting mobile collaborative data sharing further subsumes the definition of adequate replication and coherency management protocols. In general, optimistic coherency management, where data are updated independently and updates propagated when connectivity allows, is the most appropriate for the mobile environment where disconnections are frequent. However, strong coherency management is much suited to synchronous collaborative applications and may be supported by mobile groups whose membership is constrained by the proximity of nodes (e.g., group bounded by 1 hop-connectivity used for P2P meeting-based applications) [5]. Regarding replication management, data that are accessed by a node should be replicated on that node due to possible disconnection, and preventive data replicas may further be created so as to anticipate the disconnection of a node that holds data of interest and hence increase data availability [6]. Based on the above, we define a group, called G^{Collab}, dedicated to synchronous, collaborative data sharing, which is based on the proposal of [5]. In this context, the security domain defines nodes that are granted access to a given shared data structure and is managed by the server that stores a reference copy of the data. Then, peer nodes in the communication range of each other may join within a group, instance of G^{Collab}, which supports synchronous collaboration through the implementation of strong coherency management. Asynchronous collaboration is further supported at the level of the overall security domain (i.e., distinct groups) through the implementation of optimistic coherency management.

Group design. Membership constraints (as detailed in Section 1) associated with the G^{Collab} group are then:

- $Bounded(G^{Collab}, T, 1)$, i.e., members of a group instance should be at a distance of one hop, since we primarily target meeting-based applications.

- $Closed(G^{Collab}, S^D)$, i.e., members of a group instance should be granted access to the shared data, as identified by membership to the given security domain S^D.

- $Connected(G^{Collab}, T)$, i.e., nodes within a group instance should be fully connected so as to allow P2P-based data sharing among all nodes.

The *Collab* function relates to providing access to data that are locally stored on all peer nodes belonging to the security domain S^D. More specifically, we consider that nodes share XML data as in the XMIDDLE middleware [13]. Hence, each peer node offers the DOM-based *Collab* service, which provides access to the local (most likely partial) copy of the XML tree that is shared by all members of S^D. Any mobile node belonging to S^D then stores locally a partial copy of the tree, according to previous access to the tree performed on the node.

Management of the G^{Collab} group allows for mobile nodes that are members of an instance of G^{Collab} to access parts of the shared tree that are either not locally stored or are not locally up-to-date, but are stored on peer nodes of the group instance. Precisely, group initialization (see §2.2) is customized so that peer nodes get aware of the overall (possibly partial) copy of the tree that is stored within the group. After peer nodes are grouped, the local XML trees get annotated with information about replicas available in the group. Note that a subtree that is not locally available is not replicated at initialization time; only information about available replicas in the group is stored. Upon access to data of the XML tree on a node, if the data is stored locally, the data is checked for coherency according to the strong coherency protocol that is implemented at the group level and then possibly updated, prior to grant access to the node. Otherwise, a local copy is obtained from the peer node that has the most recent data version, still according to the strong coherency protocol that is implemented.

Group implementation. Implementation of the above group management for synchronous, collaborative data sharing using our group service lies in the implementation of the DOM-like Web service *Collab* and its deployment on every mobile node that is willing to participate in collaborative data sharing. Each such node must further obtain a certificate associated with the XML tree it is granted access to. As in [5], we assume that a reference copy of any shared XML tree is stored on some highly-available, secure server from which a certificate can be obtained. Note that a node may be granted access to more than one XML tree; this is distinguished by providing different names for groups, i.e., a group is identified by the supporting function (*Collab* in our example) and unique name (e.g., name of the tree/project). The interface of the *Collab* service is similar to the one of DOM enriched with operations dedicated to group management according to the aforementioned membership constraints. Implementation of the service further inherits from the *Group* class, which specializes with functions dedicated to synchronous, collaborative data sharing (i.e., replication and coherency management as detailed in [5], which is adapted here to XML tree sharing). Access to a shared XML tree on a mobile node then relies on accessing the tree using the local *Collab* service instance, which transparently handles collaborative data sharing through related group management. Note that in the case where the node cannot join a group, the node is a member of a singleton group, accessing only data that are locally stored.

5.   Conclusion

Group management appears as a key middleware functionality for assisting the development of applications over MANET. Group management takes care of managing a dynamic sub-network on top of which the application executes towards implementing given functional and non functional properties. Group management over MANET has actually given rise to various studies over the last couple of years, each concentrating on specific applications. However, a distinctive set of key attributes may be identified for MANET-based groups, which may further be exploited to design a generic group service that is to be customized by applications.

This paper has presented the design of such a generic group management service. In a first step, we have introduced key attributes for group management over MANET, in particular based on applications published in the literature. Those attributes amount to setting membership constraints in relation with the location, connectivity, authentication and supported QoS of group members. We then have introduced a group service that is generic with respect to membership constraints, and realizes three basic functions: discovery of group members, initialization of the group, and management of the group's dynamics. Implementation of the generic group service has further been addressed in the context of the WSAMI middleware aimed at mobile distributed computing, which is based on the Web Services Architecture. Finally, we have presented an instance of group management that builds on our generic group service and allows supporting ambient intelligence scenarios for instance related to mobile collaborative work.

Acknowledgments

This work was partially funded by IST-2000-30026 OZONE project (http://www.extra. research.philips.com/euprojects/ozone/) and ACI COrSS (http://www.irit.fr/ CORSS/).

References

[1] L. Bartram and M. Blackstock. Designing portable collaborative networks. *ACM Queue*, 1(3), May 2003.

[2] C. Basile, M-O. Killijian, and D. Powell. A survey of dependability issues in mobile wireless networks. Technical report, LAAS CNRS, France, February 2003.

[3] C. Bettstetter and C. Renner. A comparison of service discovery protocols and implementation of the Service Location Protocol. In *Proceedings of 6th EUNICE Open European Summer School: Innovative Internet Applications*, 2000.

[4] R. Bhaskar. Group key agreement in ad hoc networks. Technical Report 4832, INRIA-Rocquencourt, France, 2003.

[5] M. Boulkenafed and V. Issarny. AdHocFS: Sharing files in WLANs. In *Proceedings of the 2nd IEEE International Symposium on Network Computing and Applications*, April 2003.

[6] M. Boulkenafed and V. Issarny. Middleware service for mobile ad hoc data sharing, enhancing data availability. In *Proceedings of the 4th ACM/IFIP/USENIX International Middleware Conference*, June 2003.

[7] G. Chockler, I. Keidar, and R. Vitenberg. Group communication specifications: A comprehensive study. *ACM Computing Surveys*, 33(4), December 2001.

[8] B. Hugues and V. Cahill. Towards real-time event-based communication in mobile ad hoc wireless networks. In *Proceedings of the 2nd International Workshop on Real-time LANs in the Internet Age*, July 2003.

[9] V. Issarny, D. Sacchetti, F. Tartanoglu, F. Sailhan, R. Chibout, N. Levy, and A. Talamona. Developing Ambient Intelligence Systems: A solution based on Web services. *Journal of Automated Software Engineering*, 2004, To appear.

[10] J. Liu and V. Issarny. Qos-aware service location in mobile ad hoc networks. In *Proceedings of the 5th IEEE International Conference on Mobile Data Management*, January 2004.

[11] J. Luo, P. Eugster, and J-P. Hubaux. PILOT: Probabilistic lightweight group communication system for mobile ad hoc networks. Technical Report IC/2003/35, EPFL, May 2003.

[12] J. Luo, J-P. Hubaux, and P. Eugster. PAN: Providing reliable storage in mobile ad hoc networks with probabilistic quorum systems. In *Proceedings of the 4th ACM SIGMOBILE Symposium on Mobile Ad Hoc Networking and Computing (MobiHoc)*, 2003.

[13] C. Mascolo, L. Capra, S. Zachariadis, and W. Emmerich. XMIDDLE: A data-sharing middleware for mobile computing. *Personal and Wireless Communications Journal*, 21(1), April 2002.

[14] R. Meier, M-O. Killijian, R. Cunningham, and V. Cahill. Towards proximity group communication. In *Proceedings of the 1st Workshop on Middleware for Mobile Computing (in Conjunction with Middleware'2001*, 2001.

[15] A. Meissner and S. B. Musunoori. Group integrity management support for mobile ad hoc communities. In *Proceedings of the 1st Workshop on Middleware for Pervasive and Ad Hoc Computing Computing (in Conjunction with Middleware'2003)*, 2003.

[16] D. Powell. Group communication. *CACM*, 39(4), April 1996.

[17] G-C. Roman, Q. Huang, and A. Hazemi. Consistent group membership in ad hoc networks. In *Proceedings of ICSE'2001*, 2001.

[18] S. Sha, K. Chen, and K. Nahrstedt. Dynamic bandwidth management for single-hop ad hoc wireless networks. In *Proceedings of the IEEE International Conference on Pervasive Computing (PerCom)*, 2003.

AD HOC SERVICE GRID
A SELF-ORGANIZING INFRASTRUCTURE FOR MOBILE COMMERCE

Klaus Herrmann, Kurt Geihs, and Gero Mühl
Berlin University of Technology,
Institute for Telecommunication Systems - iVS,
EN6, Einsteinufer 17, D-10587 Berlin, Germany,
Tel: +49 30 314 25102, Fax: +49 30 314 24573,
Email: {kh, geihs, gmuehl}@ivs.tu-berlin.de

Abstract: The provisioning of location-specific services in medium-sized facilities like shopping malls, hospitals, and trade fares using WLAN access points or cellular phone systems has some drawbacks. It is rather inflexible or results in high running costs. We propose a new self-organizing infrastructure called *Ad hoc Service Grid* (ASG) that is based on a mobile ad hoc network to resolve these issues. In this paper, we define the necessary concepts, structures and components for realizing ASGs. We present our approach to building a Serviceware that enables an AGS to self-organize. We evaluate the effectiveness of our mechanisms for service migration, replication, and lookup based on simulation results.

Key words: Mobile services; Ad hoc Networking; Ad hoc Service Grid; Serviceware.

1.   INTRODUCTION

Providing wireless electronic services in public places becomes increasingly important for users and companies. Currently, there are essentially two alternatives for providing such services: IEEE802.11 (WLAN) access points can cover a limited area and let people gain access to the Internet. Cellular phone networks like GSM and UMTS provide ubiquitous access to global resources. However, it turns out that both WLAN and cellular phone networks fail to provide a valid coverage technology for local services at medium-sized locations such as shopping malls, hospitals, and construction sites which span areas of a few thousand square meters. Such locations are too large to be covered efficiently with WLAN. The main reason for this is that, in a standard setup, IEEE802.11 access points need to be wired to some networking infrastructure. Here, the paradox situation occurs that the wiring of several wireless access points costs large amounts of money. This was reported in 2001 by the company lesswire who covered a hall at the CeBIT fare with Bluetooth access points (Kraemer and Schwander, 2003). Other experiments with WLAN also resulted in the costs for wiring exceeding the costs of the wireless equipment by far. Moreover, wired access points limit the flexibility of the network since extending or restructuring the network is cumbersome.

The alternative of using mobile phone networks for service provisioning introduces another problem. The services that are subject to the coverage are in most cases local by nature. For instance, in a shopping mall a shop owner wants to provide a product information service, or a music store offers excerpts of current chart hits for download and lets the customer compose his own CD. Using these services requires communication between two parties at the same physical location (the shopping mall). However, using mobile phone networks implies global communication at a relatively high price and at a comparably low data rate (even with UMTS). Therefore, they seem inappropriate too.

Thus, there appears to be a gap between WLAN coverage and mobile phone network coverage, which cannot be served adequately by either of the two. The solution is a mobile ad hoc network (MANET). A MANET consists of devices that are equipped with a short range radio interface like Bluetooth. Two devices can only connect to each other if they are within each other's transmission range (usually between 10 and 100 meters). The devices may be mobile. Thus, the communication network among them is more or less dynamic. Connections may be setup and torn down frequently and there is no pre-existing infrastructure through which one device may connect to some other device reliably. Many different routing algorithms have been designed which enable two devices to communicate over a multi-hop route if they are not direct neighbors.

In this paper, we propose a new self-organizing service provisioning infrastructure called Ad hoc Service Grid (ASG) based on MANET technology (Giordano, 2002). ASG fills the gap between small-scale WLAN access points and global-scale mobile phone networks and presents a promising approach to the problem of covering medium-scale locations with local services. ASG uses MANET technology to connect individual PC-class devices (called Service Cubes) dispersed over the location. Together, the Service Cubes provide the basic infrastructure and the resources for service provisioning. The communication within this infrastructure is free of charge and at the same time the installation is quick and easy. The ASG also introduces a new way of service provisioning in terms of provider and client roles. In an ASG, these roles are not fixed. Multiple different providers should be able to provide their services to locally present users as indicated in the small shopping mall example.

The remaining paper is organized as follows: Section 2 presents an overview of the research work related to the ASG vision. In Section 3 we discuss the basic communication infrastructure that is based on ad hoc networking between autonomous Service Cubes. The notion of Location-specific Services is introduced in Section 4. Section 5 discusses the mechanisms and functions of a self-organizing Serviceware for ASGs in greater detail. The simulation results given in Section 6 for our service migration and replication mechanism and for our service lookup and discovery protocol prove the effectiveness of our approach. Finally, Section 7 concludes the paper and presents our research agenda.

2.   RELATED WORK

MANETs have originated from a military background. Recently, they have drawn much attention also in the civilian domain. Most people involved with MANETs assume that they consist of a group of mobile users that move relative to each other while trying to communicate. The question of service provisioning in MANETs has been studied especially with respect to two issues: Some research projects deal with the problem of optimally positioning a service on one of the devices in order to cover the largest possible number of the users (Li, 2001; Wang, 2001; Wang and Li, 2002, Lau et al., 2001). However, it remains questionable if this is a relevant problem at all since the authors only give a vague indication of the nature of the services and the scenarios they relate to. Other projects deal with the problem of designing service lookup protocols in MANETs (Cheng, 2002; Chakraborty et al., 2002). Again, the motivation for running a service on a resource-limited and battery-powered device of a mobile user remains unclear. Infostations (Goodman et al, 1997) are another approach to providing services in ad hoc networks. However, Infostations are not necessarily connected to each other. Instead, they represent islands covered by WLAN that may exchange information with mobile users passing by. These islands are connected in a logical sense by the users moving between them and by the information that may be exchanged indirectly via several users and Infostations. An area that has received some attention lately are Peer-to-Peer (P2P) services in MANETs (Datta, 2003; Klemm et al., 2003). The common ground that both P2P and MANETs build on is the lack of a hierarchy and predefined roles. There are no dedicated servers and clients. Instead, every node in the network acts as a server and a client at the same time. While this is an appealing approach for extending common P2P systems into the wireless world, such systems do not seem to have any potential for service provisioning on a commercial level, because the resources available through mobile devices are very scarce and the expected dynamics in a network purely made of mobiles is too high.

To the best of our knowledge, applying the MANET technology in a more conservative way to supply an alternative service provisioning infrastructure has not been subject to research yet.

3.   COMMUNICATION INFRASTRUCTURE

The basic communication infrastructure of Ad hoc Service Grid consists of so-called *Service Cubes*. Service Cubes are devices that offer computational resources comparable to standard personal computers. They need a power supply and can connect to each other over a short-range wireless network interface (e.g. Bluetooth). At a facility that is to be covered with wireless services, a number of Service Cubes are dispersed and automatically set up an ad hoc network (Figure 1). This network provides two things:

1. An access infrastructure that connects all the Service Cubes, and
2. A distributed pool of resources (the Service Cubes themselves) to host value-added services.

As opposed to existing wireless service provisioning infrastructures, in an Ad hoc Service Grid there is no real distinction between the access infrastructure and the system running the services. The whole infrastructure is modular with the Service Cubes providing networking *and* computing resources. The ASG follows a philosophy we call *Drop-and-Deploy*: A new Service Cube can be added to the network by simply putting it in an appropriate position (within communication range of at least one other Service Cube) and switching it on. The Serviceware that we envision recognizes the new resource and integrates it into the ASG. The aim is to reduce the overhead associated with planning, installation, and maintenance. The MANET technology is the key to this Drop-and-Deploy feature.

Users access the services via their own handheld device. A network connection to the nearest Service Cube is established automatically, and the user is provided with a list of available services. If the Service Cube network is dense enough, the user is always connected to at least one Service Cube, and thus, able to access the ASG's services while he moves through the location.

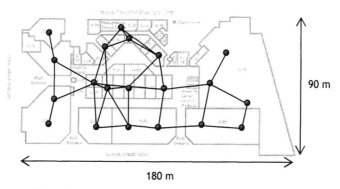

Figure 1. Example of an ASG Network in a shopping mall.

4. LOCATION-SPECIFIC SERVICES

The term *Location-based Service* is used to describe services that capture the user's current position and present content pertaining to this position. These services do not enable the user to interact with his current location in any way. The ASG, in contrast, offers *location-specific services*. Such a service allows the user to interact with his current environment. It is provided *by* the location instead of *on behalf of* the location (as with location-based services). Thus, a typical location-specific service runs locally (e.g. in the shopping mall) and can be used by users in close proximity. It is provided by a local party. For example, in a shopping mall, the operator could provide a *navigation service* that helps visitors in finding the right shop. Shop owners might offer *product information services*. A music store might offer music clips for free and let customers compile and purchase their own CD.

The ASG presents a model that is quite different from classical service provisioning architectures. Most notably, the increased flexibility implies that the roles of the participants are somewhat blurred. To clarify things, we introduce three basic roles:

- The *operator* is an institution (a single person or a group of people) that is responsible for administering the location or facility that is subject to service coverage.
- *Providers* are parties that are locally present at the facility. They may potentially provide electronic services to others (e.g. individual shop owners in a mall). Providers are divers and only loosely coupled.
- *Customers* are temporarily visiting the facility and are potential users of provided services. Customers are also called *clients* or *users* in this paper.

Basically, all three groups may offer and use location-specific services. Albeit, the ASG infrastructure implicitly assumes that customers will be at the receiving end of service provisioning in most cases.

5.   A SELF-ORGANIZING SERVICEWARE

Like existing Grid technology, an Ad hoc Service Grid provides the resources and the control structures necessary for accomplishing diverse tasks in a distributed, collaborative fashion. However, classical Grid tasks consist of calculations with a limited life span that need to be processed as quickly as possible and produce a (partial) result that is returned to the client. In contrast to this, in an Ad hoc Service Grid the tasks are services which typically run over a longer, indefinite period of time. Moreover, these services normally have extensive interactions with numerous users.

The ASG changes dynamically when new Service Cubes are added or existing ones are moved or removed. Thus, maintaining a global view on the overall system state is difficult. Additionally, dynamically changing usage patterns (dictated by mobile clients) necessitate an ongoing adaptation process in order to optimize the resource usage. Managing the ASG manually is therefore inappropriate. Allocating resources statically, i.e. installing services on fixed nodes will result in suboptimal resource usage since a proper initial placement of services will most likely become suboptimal when usage patterns change. The service might end up running on a node that is far away from the bulk of interested clients resulting in excessive overhead as messages are routed through the entire network.

Because of the Service Cube dynamics, the lack of an overall system view, and the changing usage patterns, the ASG has to organize many aspects of the service provisioning on its own, without manual intervention. It has to be *self-organizing*.

We aim to encapsulate the bulk of self-organization tasks inside a software layer that we call *Serviceware*. It is based on the middleware MESH*Mdl* (Herrmann, 2003) which is specifically tailored to self-organizing applications in MANETs. It employs mobile agents (Picco, 2001) and asynchronous communication based on Tuple Space technology (Gelernter, 1985; Ahuja, 1986). Every client device and each Service Cube runs a MESH*Mdl* Engine that is able to execute application components (mobile agents) and provides asynchronous communication via a MESH*Mdl* *Event Space* (special enhanced realization of the Tuple Space paradigm in MESH*Mdl*). Data items in this Space (also called *Entries*) can also be sent to remote devices via a multi-hop routing infrastructure. ASG services are implemented as mobile agents, and thus, are able to move between Service

Cubes if necessary. The three basic mechanisms used for dynamic service distribution are:

- *Migration*: Moving a service from one Service Cube to another. In most cases this is done to reduce the distance between clients and a service replica.
- *Replication*: Creating a replica of a service and migrating the original service instance and its new replica to different Service Cubes. This is necessary if an existing replica in unable to handle the local request load and if traffic patterns imply that high volumes of requests come in from different directions.
- *Recombination*: Removing a dispensable service replica and possibly merging its state into another replica. Due to dynamic changes, two or more service replicas in the same vicinity may end up serving a small number of clients. This excessive service capacity causes suboptimal resource usage. Thus, these service replicas may recombine into one single instance.

In the following subsections, we explain some of the core functions provided by the Serviceware in more details.

5.1   Network Clustering

To enforce a structure on the amorphous ad hoc Service Cube network and to implement basic networking functions, we adapted the clustering algorithm published by Basagni (1999). It partitions the Service Cube network into clusters, each having a cluster head node. As a consequence, every *ordinary node* has exactly one *cluster head* and the cluster heads are distributed evenly over the whole network. Cluster heads provide core Serviceware functions while ordinary nodes carry value-added services. Thus, the cluster assigns basic roles to the nodes in terms of service provisioning and introduces a separation of concerns.

Based on the clustered structure, we implemented a routing algorithm that is based on *Dynamic Destination-sequenced Distance Vector Routing* (DSDV) (Perkins and Bhagwat, 1994). Since the Service Cube network is not very dynamic, this simple algorithm is adequate. Clusters define subnetworks with the cluster head serving as a router. Thus, only routes between the cluster heads need to be set up. Each node is assigned a node address consisting of the node ID and its cluster head ID. This overlay network is used to route *Entries*, messages used by MESH*Mdl* for inter-agent communication (Herrmann, 2003), between different Service Cubes.

While classical distributed systems hide the network structure and issues like routing from the applications, the ASG Serviceware takes a different approach. To render the Serviceware self-organizing, structural information about the network and the message flow is vital. Indeed, the flow of requests from clients to services is an important stimulus for adaptation that enables, for example, the adequate placement of services replicas inside the ASG. Thus, we implement routing at the Serviceware layer to make this information accessible. The clustered structure must be perceivable for the Serviceware since it decides about the higher-level functions provided by a Service Cube.

5.2   Service Replication and Migration

A core function of the ASG Serviceware is to accept the installation of new services at an arbitrary Service Cube and move it to a Location that provides the necessary resources for its execution. The overall goal is to balance the computational load on the set of available Service Cubes and to minimize the networking load on the ad hoc communication network. Both can be achieved by dynamically allocating Service Cubes to services (i.e. by making services mobile) and by replicating services. Figure 2 depicts the combination of service migration and replication. Please note that the squares do not necessarily stand for individual clients, but rather for client request hot spots (i.e. Service Cubes that receive a high number of requests).

We have developed an algorithm for *service migration and replication* that lets a service migrate gradually towards the direction of the highest client request traffic. If the service receives a high number of requests via different network connections (see Figure 2b), it replicates and the two replicas move towards the directions of highest request traffic.

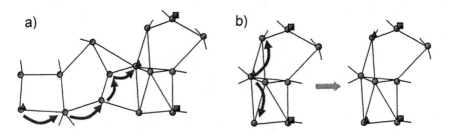

Figure 2. a) Moving services (depicted as triangles) towards the centers of client requests (indicated by squares) and b) service replication.

The algorithm executed for a service on node s_0 is defined as follows:

Let $S = \{s_1, \ldots, s_n\}$ be the set of neighbor nodes of s_0 via which s_0 has received requests for the service. Let S be in descending order with respect to the number of requests $m(s_i)$ received from s_i. Let T_A be the *adaptation threshold* and let T_M denote the *migration threshold*. T_A is measured in *requests per time unit* and indicates the volume of incoming requests that will trigger an adaptation. An adaptation can either be a migration (the service moves to a neighbor node) or a replication (the service clones itself and the two replicas are moved to different neighbor nodes). T_M is used to decide which of the two actions is to be invoked. Finally, let R be the set of currently active service replicas and let L_R be the maximally allowed number of replicas. The algorithm in Figure 3 is used to achieve the autonomous distribution of services.

1: **if** $|S| > 0$ **and** $m(s_1) \geq T_A$

2:     **if** $\left(|S| = 1 \text{ or } \dfrac{m(s_1)}{m(s_2)} > T_M \right)$ **and** $m(s_2) < T_A$

3:         migrateTo(s_1);

4:     **elsif** $|R| < L_R$

5:         replicateTo(s_1, s_2);

6:     **endif**

7: **endif**

Figure 3. Autonomous service distribution algorithm.

The algorithm is periodically executed in parallel by all active service replicas. In line 1 the algorithm checks if there have been any requests at all ($|S| > 0$) and if the number of requests received from the top sender has reached the adaptation threshold ($m(s_1) \geq T_A$). The *if* statement in lines 2 to 6 decides whether a migration or a replication should be executed. If we have only one sending neighbor ($|S| = 1$) or the ratio of the number of messages sent by s_1 over the number of messages sent by s_2 exceeds the migration threshold $\left(\dfrac{m(s_1)}{m(s_2)} > T_M \right)$ we will migrate to s_1, except, if the number of messages received from second highest sender s_2 also exceeds the adaptation threshold. The later case covers the situation that the service receives a high volume of requests via two different neighbors which should results in a replication. Note that if the ratio of received messages exceeds the replication threshold, s_1 is forwarding considerably more requests than s_2. If there is no indication for a migration, then the *elsif* statement is executed. It checks whether the maximum number of replicas has already been reached. If this is not the case, then a replication is triggered. The information about the number of currently active service replicas is maintained by the distributed lookup service that is explained in the next section. This information yields an approximation of the replica count. The results of simulating this algorithm in a network of 100 Service Cubes is presented in Section 6.

5.3   Service Lookup and Discovery

In the ASG, established service lookup protocols like that of Jini (Sun Microsystems, 2001) fail because services are mobile. We have developed a lookup service that can handle service mobility. The basic idea is to position a lookup service at every cluster head node in the network. Thus, at every Service Cube, clients and service replicas always have a lookup service within one-hop distance. A moving service can always easily notify its local lookup service about its new location. However, propagating such a change to the other lookup services without causing a broadcast storm on the network is not as easy. We have developed a *reply-driven signaling protocol* that minimizes the use of update broadcasts and uses a combination of piggybacking and message snooping in order to reduce the message overhead. Whenever a new service replica is started, it registers with its nearest lookup service. This service broadcasts the existence of the new service to all lookup services (running on cluster heads). If a registered service replica moves, client requests arriving at its old location are redirected locally to its new location by the Serviceware. Information about this redirect is stored in the request. The receiving service copies this meta information into its reply and sends it back to the client. As the reply is routed back, the nodes on this route *snoop* the redirect information stored in the reply and update their own lookup services with the new location of the service. Thus, the information about the service migration is propagated along the reply paths to all the clients and eventually reaches the clients themselves. The efficiency and effectiveness of this protocol is investigated in Section 6.

Initial service discovery is also done via the distributed lookup service. A nearby client can request a list of service instances that are running close to its location.

6. SIMULATION RESULTS

The migration and replication (MR) algorithm and the distributed lookup service have been implemented in a simulation environment to evaluate their effectiveness. Figure 4 depicts the reduction in the number of overall messages being transmitted in the network as the MR algorithm is executed. The two graphs in this figure represent two experiments with different service lookup strategies that will be explained below. In the context of service migration and replication, the striking property of both graphs is the downward trend and the fact that the overall network traffic is reduced by approximately 50% when the algorithm is applied.

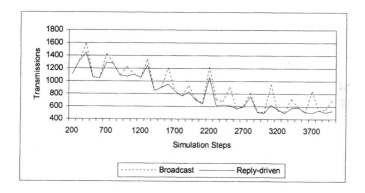

Figure 4. Overall transmitted messages for different lookup signaling strategies.

While the service is being replicated, the load is distributed over the individual service replicas. This is shown in Figure 5: It takes the service about 1300 steps to move to the *center of the network* (in terms of client requests). Then it starts replicating (replications indicated by vertical lines) and the replicas attract the requests that originate nearest to them. Consequently, the load is shared among them and effectively balanced within the network. Thus, the load on the individual services reduces.

The effect of the lookup service signaling protocol on the overall number of messages transmitted is shown in Figure 4. The Figure compares it with a broadcast protocol that simply broadcasts updates to all lookup services. It can be seen that the overall reduction in transmitted messages is still achieved. Thus, the new lookup signaling protocol proves to be effective and clients still find the services nearest to them. At the same time, the broadcast bursts caused by the simple protocol are avoided.

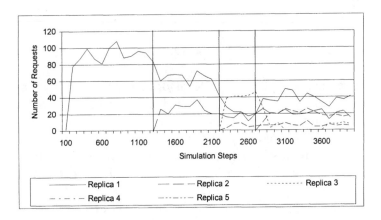

Figure 5. Reduction in per-service load as services move towards clients and replicate.

The reply-driven lookup signaling protocol reduces of the number of transmitted messages at the cost of some lookup services not receiving the correct information directly. Figure 6 depicts the fraction of lookup services that hold the correct information over time. While the broadcast protocol achieves 100% correctness shortly after every service migration, the reply-driven protocol slowly converges towards full correctness as the number of service replicas, and thus replies, increases. The services temporarily holding incorrect information have no clients in their local vicinity. If a new client arrives in such a location, it sends its requests to a wrong destination. However, the forwarding protocol will redirect them to the new location of the service and upon receiving a reply, the information in the lookup service will be corrected. This form of *lazy update* suits the nature of the ASG very well since trying to maintain overall correctness is costly and unnecessary.

7. CONCLUSIONS AND FUTURE WORK

In this paper we have introduced a new infrastructure for providing facility-specific services to mobile users. We argue that Ad hoc Service Grids are able to fill the gap that is observable between small-scale WLAN access point systems and large-scale mobile phone systems. We presented our vision of an Ad hoc Service Grid and pointed out the possible structures and concepts necessary for the realization of the infrastructure. We have evaluated our current work on *service migration and replication* as well as a *distributed lookup and discovery service* for the ASG Serviceware. The simulation results demonstrate that decentralized control mechanisms can be employed for the self-organization of ASG services. These mechanisms are based on the flow of user requests through the network and indicate that this stimulus can be used to trigger self-structuring behavior in the ASG.

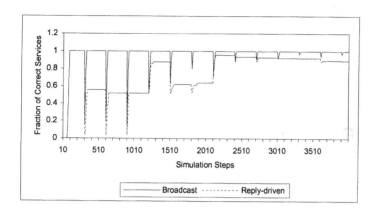

Figure 6. Fraction of lookup services holding correct information as a function of time.

Our current research efforts are directed towards refining the presented mechanisms. Moreover, we are developing concepts that allow stateful services to maintain data consistency among their replicas despite their mobility.

Realizing the Ad hoc Service Grid vision takes efforts from other fields. Is has to be pointed out that especially the basic ad hoc networking support provided by current standards is not sufficient. Furthermore, indoor positioning is an issue.

REFERENCES

Ahuja, S., Carriero, N., and Gelertner, D., 1986, Linda and friends, *IEEE Computer*, pp. 26–32.

Li, B, 2001, QoS-aware Adaptive Services in Mobile Ad-hoc Networks, In: *Proceedings of the Ninth IEEE International Workshop on Quality of Service (IWQoS 01)*, also Lecture Notes in Computer Science, Springer-Verlag, Vol. 2092, pp. 251-268, Karlsruhe, Germany.

Basagni, S., 1999, Distributed Clustering for Ad Hoc Networks, In: *Proceedings of the IEEE International Symposium on Parallel Architectures, Algorithms, and Networks (I-SPAN)*.

Chakraborty, D., Joshi, A., Yesha, Y., Finin, T, 2002, GSD: A Novel Group-based Service Discovery Protocol for MANET, In: *Proceedings of the 4th IEEE Conference on Mobile and Wireless Communications Networks (MWCN'02)*.

Cheng, L, 2002, Service advertisement and discovery in mobile ad hoc networks, In: *Proceedings of the Workshop on Ad hoc Communications and Collaboration in*

Ubiquitous Computing Environments, in conjunction with the ACM 2002 Conference on Computer Supported Cooperative Work, New Orleans, Louisiana, USA, November 16-20, 2002.

Datta, A, 2003, MobiGrid: P2P Overlay and MANET Rendezvous - A Data Management Perspective, In: *Proceedings of CAiSE 2003 Doctoral Symposium.*

Gelernter, D., 1985, Generative Communication in Linda, *ACM Transactions on Programming Languages and Systems*, 7(1):80--112, Jan. 1985.

Giordano, S., 2002, Mobile ad hoc networks, In *Handbook of Wireless Networks and Mobile Computing*, ed. I. Stojmenovic. John Wiley & Sons. 2002.

Goodman, D.J., Borras, J., Mandayam, N.B., and Yates, R.D., 1997, INFOSTATIONS : A New System Model for Data and Messaging Services, In: *Proceedings of IEEE VTC'97*, vol. 2, pp. 969-973, Phoenix, AZ. May 1997

Herrmann, K., 2003, MESHMdl – A Middleware for Self-Organization in Ad hoc Networks, In: *Proceedings of the 1st International Workshop on Mobile Distributed Computing (MDC'03)* May 19, 2003. Providence, Rhode Island USA.

Klemm, A., Lindemann, C., and Waldhorst, O., 2003, A Special-Purpose Peer-to-Peer File Sharing System for Mobile Ad Hoc Networks, In: *Proceedings of the IEEE Semiannual Vehicular Technology Conference (VTC2003-Fall)*, Orlando, FL, October 2003

Kraemer, R., and Schwander, P., 2003, Bluetooth based wireless Internet applications for indoor hot spots: experience of a successful experiment during CeBIT 2001, *Computer Networks*, vol. 41, no. 3, 2003

Lau, W. H. O., Kumar, M., and Venkatesh, S., 2001, A Cache-based Mobility-aware Scheme for Real-Time Continuous Media Delivery in Wireless Networks, In: *Proceedings of the 2001 IEEE International Conference on Multimedia and Expo (ICME2001)*, August 22-25, 2001, Waseda University Tokyo, Japan

Perkins, C. E., and Bhagwat, P., 1994, Highly dynamic destination-sequenced distance-vector routing (DSDV) for mobile computers, In: *Proceedings of SIGCOMM 94*, pages 234–244, August 1994.

Picco, G. P, 2001, Mobile Agents: An Introduction, *Journal of Microprocessors and Microsystems*, vol. 25, no. 2, pp. 65-74, April 2001.

Sun Microsystems, 2001, Jini Architecture Specification. Version 1.2. December 2001

Wang, K. H., 2001, Adaptive Service Provisionings in Partitionable Wireless Mobile Ad-Hoc Networks, M.S. thesis, University of Toronto, Department of Electrical and Computer Engineering, October 2001.

Wang, K. H., Li, B, 2002, Efficient and Guaranteed Service Coverage in Partitionable Mobile Ad-hoc Networks, In: *Proceedings of IEEE INFOCOM 2002*, Vol. 2, pp. 1089-1098, New York City, New York, June 23-27, 2002.

APPLICABILITY OF AN INTEGRATED ADOPTION MODEL
to an Adoption-Resistant M-Business Technology

Steve Elliot*and John Muller

School of Business, University of Sydney NSW 2006 Australia, s.elliot@econ.usyd.edu.au
*corresponding author, Ph: +61 2 9036 9347
Technical Director, Interacct Solutions Australia, johnmuller@optusnet.com.au

Abstract: Business is applying mobile technologies in the attempt to address its problems and to realize its opportunities at such a rate that researchers have difficulty maintaining their contact. Absent general models that can provide some assistance, business has few sources of impartial assistance. This paper aims to better assist organizations seeking to successfully adopt and to implement m-business innovations by testing the applicability of a general purpose e-business adoption model with a worst-case, adoption-resistant example of m-business technology. The Integrated Adoption Model was successfully applied to capture the complexity of the industry innovation and to identify major drivers and inhibitors of m-business success. Implications for practitioners and researchers are discussed.

Key words: Adoption model; M-Business; adoption factors.

1.   INTRODUCTION

Consumer demand for mobile phone 3G services remains unclear. Still and video photography are interesting novelties but do not appear to provide a sustainable base for demand. The interface remains difficult to use. Ease of access is limited with the small screen and complex keyboard manipulations required. Meanwhile, the demand for data services is significant if packaged correctly. "Operators are now promoting bundles of easy-to-use services, rather than endlessly going on about complicated technology. Colorful menus enable users to download games and ring-tones, read news updates, and send and receive photographs and small video clips" [26].

The technology for interactive, session-based data applications that are instantaneous in connection and delivery is contained within most Global System Mobile (GSM) networks and is available to nearly all GSM handsets. Unstructured Supplementary Service data (USSD) was built into the GSM standard as a means of transmitting information or instructions over the signalling channels of a GSM network. The fact that it uses the network's signalling channels makes USSD similar to SMS. But the vital difference between the two is that SMS is a store and forward service whilst USSD is session based. USSD was originally intended to provide set-up or cancelling for services like call forwarding. The capability of USSD to provide data services, however, remains virtually unknown and apparently resistant to adoption. It is the cellular industry's 'best kept secret' [10].

This paper initially provides an overview of adoption theory as applied to e-business and m-business noting the diversity of findings and then reviews an integrated adoption model (IAM) based on 30 implementations of B2C e-business in six countries; the design of the research project is explained; the detail of an m-business innovation utilizing USSD technology is examined; the industry experience is then compared with the IAM; and implications for theory and practice discussed.

2.   THEORETICAL OVERVIEW

Electronic Commerce presents the potential opportunity for strikingly different business ventures as well as radically new ways to run existing business. New technologies may be harnessed by organizations to help them to achieve competitive advantage; to transform relationships with customers, suppliers and business partners; to empower global business; and to redesign their organizations. In short, Electronic Commerce may result in fundamental changes to current business practice.

Despite industry enthusiasm for Electronic Commerce, a major impediment to its widespread adoption is seen to be uncertainty within organizations as to how to address the challenges it presents. Uncertainty about how and why organizations and individuals decide to adopt (or not to adopt) Electronic Commerce exists also at a theoretical level [12].

Electronic Commerce provides a rich field for academic research. Studies have included: technology platforms; business challenges; management approaches; emergent organizational forms; and social and macro-economic impacts. This level of variety indicates both diversity and the degree of fragmentation. The danger of misinterpretation of a phenomenon by researchers undertaking narrow investigations into Electronic Commerce has been highlighted by Peter Keen [12].

Research into IS innovation has been conducted predominantly at individual, departmental and organizational levels. Innovations studied include: personal work stations; spreadsheets; information centers; IT outsourcing; database management systems; automatic teller machines (ATMs); and electronic supermarket scanners. The focus in these studies has been predominantly on innovation by individuals within organizations. Much of the innovation literature is actually concerned with diffusion of the innovation throughout an organization rather than initial adoption into an organization, i.e., innovation at a strategic level. The literature dealing with adoption of technological innovation includes two major areas: intention-based models (which focus on behavioral aspects of innovators) and innovation models (focusing on innovation characteristics and processes).

Extensive research has been conducted on the applicability of intention-based models of innovation, which are grounded in theories of social psychology. These models include the Theory of Reasoned Action [2] and the Theory of Planned Behavior [1]. Of primary interest is the Technology Acceptance Model (TAM) [6]. TAM contends that the sole determinant of use of technology is the intention of the user, based on perceptions of the ease of use of the technology and of its usefulness. This model has been independently tested and commended for its parsimony and applicability. A major disadvantage is that TAM excludes the possibility of influence from institutional, social and personal control factors [13, 28]. Implications of these omissions are considered below. Kwon and Zmud's (1987) proposed Five Forces model of innovation and Scott-Morton's (1991) MIT90's framework both acknowledge the significance of environmental issues [15, 25].

A major influence in innovation literature is the work of E.M. Rogers [23]. Rogers locates adoption factors in individual, organizational and environmental groupings and sees the capability to distinguish between innovations of critical necessity to identify why some innovations are successful and some are not. "The usefulness of research on the attributes of innovations is mainly to predict their future rate of adoption and use" [23]. Rogers (1995) suggests the bulk of research conducted on innovations has been concerned with identification of differences between adopter groups with comparatively little regard for differences in characteristics of innovations. He provides a typology of characteristics for use in evaluation of an innovation: relative advantage; compatibility; complexity, and; trialability. All are considered influential in innovation and adoption.

Rogers' 1995 work identifies attributes of innovations, adoption processes and adoption decision approaches for organizations. Rogers considers that: "Innovations are not initiated on the spur of the moment, nor by a single dramatic incident, nor by a single entrepreneur" [23]. While Rogers does examine organisational characteristics such as attitude toward the individual leader, internal organisational characteristics and external characteristics of the organisation, he does not address the influence of organisational issues such as adequacy of resources available, nature and culture of the organisation and the qualities of the organisation's leadership, other than attitude to change.

Rogers work has been criticized for producing dimensions 'as universally relevant as possible' but which were so abstract that they may not be easily applied [5]. In a separate study, Rogers' attributes, processes and approaches have been compared with implementations of smart-card based Electronic Commerce and, in general, found not to reflect the levels of complexity and diversity found in practice [7]. Theory of the adoption of Information Systems has been mostly concerned with intra-organizational adoption rather than at the inter-organizational level necessary for Electronic Commerce. Traditionally, organizations have needed to concern themselves only with their own requirements for Information Systems. Increasingly, however, pressures from Electronic Commerce necessitate that these intra-organizational systems are closely integrated between, and capable of operation across, several organizations. The implications of inter-organizational systems on the adoption and diffusion of Information Technology are a substantial increase in complexity at planning, requirements definition, design, development and implementation stages. Pressures to conform to external requirements may result in a period of externally imposed radical change to current practice. Operationally, inter-organizational systems represent a completely new set of challenges for both technical and business staff.

Elliot and Loebbecke (2000) suggest that within a single innovation, individuals with very different roles and objectives are involved and these individuals may be in conflict. This potential for conflict between adoption factors raises the importance of further empirical investigation of multi-organizational adoption.

Environmental issues are those external to the organization and innovation. The necessity for increased attention to contextual and cultural factors has been identified by several authors [4, 17].

Calls have been made for convergence of the major areas of adoption theory: innovation and intention. Moore and Benbasat (1996) developed a tool for the study of initial adoption of innovations by individuals in organizations. This tool integrated the intentions-based models and innovations literature, including the Theory of Reasoned Action and the perceived characteristics of innovations [21].

Adoption theory is mute in an area that appears to be of critical importance to Electronic Commerce: the consumer [12, 14]. The role of consumers in adoption of Business to Consumer Electronic Commerce appears significant from both empirical and theoretical perspectives. The importance of consumers' attitudes to successful adoption of Electronic Commerce has been documented in several studies (e.g., [11]) but has little incorporation into adoption theory.

Reference must be made to the discipline of marketing for consideration of consumer issues relating to adoption of new technological products [29]. Boyd and Mason (1999) propose a two-stage conceptual model of how consumers' evaluation of product category attractiveness affects adoption decision-making [5]. The first stage of their model (intention forming) proposes three key antecedents of consumer adoption: characteristics of the individual (e.g. personal needs), communications (e.g. advertising, publicity and distribution) and attractiveness of the product category (influenced by product, firm and market related attributes) These antecedents are referred to collectively as extrabrand attributes. The second stage captures the brand-choice process. These two stages relate to Rogers (1983) decision and implementation stages of the innovation decision process. A key contribution is the importance of attractiveness as an antecedent of adoption and the implications of attractiveness for firms. 'Managers can improve an innovation's chances of success by influencing the level of the factors they can change and knowing the implications of the factors they cannot change' [5].

Consumers have been found to rely on categories of information when evaluating innovations into: product information (e.g. key benefits, variety, complexity, switching costs, relative advantage, perceived risk); company information (e.g. corporate reputation, firm size, age) and market information (market size, competitive structure, distribution channels and an aggregation of individual firm attributes) [5, 20]. Bell et al (1975) suggest that 'attraction may be a function of the seller's advertising expenditure and effectiveness, the price of his product, the reputation of the company; the service given during and after purchase, the location of retail stores and much more' [3].

The Bell et al (1975), Moore (1995) and Boyd and Mason (1999) studies of consumer attributes also highlight product and innovation attributes e.g. price / cost, key benefits, variety, complexity, switching costs, relative advantage, perceived risk); company information (e.g. corporate reputation, firm size, age) and market information (market size, competitive structure, distribution channels and an aggregation of individual firm attributes). Boyd and Mason (1999) also highlight a frequently overlooked issue of changing consumer perceptions in line with product development.

Much research studying innovations assumes innovations remain unchanged over their life. They suggest a more realistic approach recognizes that the innovations change over time and, as a result, consumer perceptions and evaluations can also be expected to change. Extrabrand attributes were found to be primarily: cost and key benefits.

Satisfaction with product offerings has been found to be a primary driver of overall customer satisfaction. Quality of customer service (financial statements and IT-enabled services) is also important but of varying impact across different customer categories. Functionality had the largest impact on satisfaction with quality of automated service delivery. - 'Customers seem to be receptive to the potential benefits offered by an electronic system, such as speed and convenience, provided it addressed all their trading needs and was easy to use.' [14].

In a challenge to utilitarian models of technology adoption (e.g., TAM) consumers purchasing home Personal Computers (PCs) were found to be most strongly influenced by social outcomes (e.g., increased status from having the latest technology) and hedonism (applications for fun) rather than other anticipated benefits [29].

Further challenges to existing theory have arisen, not so much from consumers but due to dynamically developing technologies. Lyytinen and Yoo (2002) question traditional assumptions underlying IS research and stress the difficulty of using traditional models to predict adoption successes. The increasing influence of disruptive technologies has been found to be dealt with poorly by IT innovation theory. Disruptive technologies are those that transform existing products, services and business practices, thereby destroying existing competencies [24] and breaking down existing rules of competition [18].

An examination of the literature was made in search of a multi-dimensional research framework that might cater for the diversity of research findings through more holistic consideration of the innovation, environment, organization and consumer. Three models which incorporate the significance of environmental issues were identified: Kwon and Zmud's (1987) proposed Five Forces model of innovation, Scott-Morton's (1991) MIT90's framework of forces supporting organizational transformation which is of lesser direct relevance, and Elliot's (2002) Integrative Adoption Model for Business to Consumer Electronic Commerce. Kwon and Zmud's model ignores consumers, being limited to innovation, organizational, and environmental factors [15]. Elliot's model, consisting of the factors shown in Table 1 was drawn from IS, management and marketing disciplines and tested internationally through examination of 30 B2C implementations in six countries [8].

No comprehensive model was found to focus on m-business although research into particular aspects of m-business adoption using specific adoption theories abound. Lawrence et al (2003) find Rogers' Diffusion of Innovation model to be applicable to Bluetooth technology. Based on a survey of 1253 bank customers Suoranta et al (2003) identify drivers of mobile banking (accessibility, independence, immediacy of service and cost savings,) and inhibitors (poor ease of use including slow transmission speed and insufficient guidance, and service malfunction) [27]. Supporting Venkatesh and Brown's (2001) work, Pedersen and Nysveen (2003) examined adoption of a mobile parking service, finding TAM with a modification to incorporate self-expressiveness to be applicable [22].

2.1   Factors in an Integrative Adoption Model for Business to Consumer Electronic Commerce ([8].

2.1.1   Environmental factors:

* Market (uncertainty, competition, concentration, funding, acceptance, channel conflict)
* Inter-organizational imperatives (degree of integration of core business functions required across organizations)
* Infrastructure (legal, regulatory, technical, financial, delivery)
* Cultural and international

2.1.2   Organizational factors:

* Strategic adopter (for organizational level adoption, this includes the characteristics of the founder(s) / CEO / Champion, eg qualifications, relevant prior experience, capability to determine a business vision, willingness to explore the potential of the Internet, capability to review and revise business models and strategies in response to market)
* Strategic motivation (inspiration from Internet pioneer, business threat or perceived opportunity)
* Business model(s) and strategies (realistic business models and effective business strategies)
* Skills (at strategic, tactical and operational levels)
* Individual employee (education, tenure etc),
* Structural (specialization, formalization),
* Task (uncertainty, autonomy, variety etc)
* Roles / functions (inter-organizational)

2.1.3   Innovation factors:

- Compatibility, complexity, relative advantage, trialibility, observability, usefulness, ease of use,
- Distinguishing characteristics / features (website characteristics based on the CEC Web Evaluation Framework)
- Perceived costs : benefits (to the firms)

2.1.4   Consumer factors:

The major benefit factors of Internet shopping include:
- Convenience in purchasing "anytime, from anywhere, to anywhere".
- Cost savings through lower prices.
- Availability of products
- Quality of products
- Increased range of products.
- Responsiveness in product delivery, eg "instantaneous distribution of digital products & services".
- Increased customisation, eg "capability to treat customers as individuals".
- Major consumer concern factors leading to unsatisfactory experiences include:
- Security
- Uncertainty about delivery
- Uncertainty about products
- Purchase procedures / ease of use / usability
- Poor levels of service
- Costs

Additional consumer factors include the demographic profiles of customers for particular firms and products, consumers' abilities to purchase on-line and their opportunity to do so.

3.   RESEARCH DESIGN

This paper aims to better assist organizations seeking to successfully adopt and to implement m-business innovations by testing the applicability of a general purpose theoretical e-business adoption model with a current industry example of m-business. The example was selected as a worst case representation – an adoption-resistant m-business technology.

The scope was to establish key factors that promote or inhibit the adoption of implementations of m-business. Factors were examined at the level of: the innovation; each major participant in the transaction process (i.e., providers and consumers); and the market or environment. All components of the transaction cycle were examined, from information provision to payment and exchange. Key research questions are:

1. *Which organisational factors influenced provision of m-business services and how?*
2. *What characteristics of the implementations influenced proposal and acceptance of that innovation?*
3. *What drives consumers to, or inhibits consumers from, performing m-business transactions?*
4. *Which environmental factors influence adoption and how?*
5. *Is a general purpose model of e-business adoption able to adequately represent a current example of m-business practice?*

This paper aims to extend current theoretical and empirical understanding of the drivers of and inhibitors to m-business adoption. This research is exploratory. The research questions are broadly based, addressing separate areas of research: provider, innovation, consumer and environmental factors. Primary and secondary data were collected by one of the authors, a principal involved throughout the project. A major strength of this examination is that the factors influencing implementation success were assessed comprehensively in a single, consistent and integrated study.

4. M-BUSINESS INNOVATION

This section describes details of an innovative application of an existing but overlooked technology. USSD was built into the GSM standard as a means of transmitting information or instructions over the signalling channels of a GSM network. As will be seen, USSD has the technical capacity to provide superior performance to popular SMS-based services or over-promoted WAP-based services but remains little used.

Originally, USSD allowed only for one-way communication between a handset and the network but USSD phase 2 supports interactivity; two-way communication between the user and the network for many services or forms of content. While it is not possible to bill for USSD services directly, text sent via USSD to a customer could result in them making a billable call and a USSD request made by a customer could trigger an SMS to be sent to them, for which a charge could also be levied.

USSD can enable services that look remarkably similar to WAP and can utilise SMS, but have benefits over both technologies. It is ideal for menu based services, although for single-use USSD services it can be quick and easy to use since the 'string' (e.g., #222#) can be entered from the phone's home screen. Nokia claims that USSD can be up to seven times faster than SMS in carrying out a two way transaction given the instantaneous nature of its session-based environment. It is also a lot quicker than WAP [10]. In short, it is a technology that appears resistant to adoption and implementation.

Interacct Solutions is an Application Service Provider specializing in mobile telephony. The firm had previously operated successfully in South Africa and had developed technical expertise and capability in development and operation of USSD-based services. Interacct's co-founder opened a business development office in Australia in 2001.

Firms were approached to identify potential interest in USSD. The national telco, Telstra, decided to support a trial application, provided it had a specified commencement and completion date as it did not want to make an open ended commitment. The forthcoming Rugby World Cup (RWC) in 2003 was agreed to be an ideal test application since it was likely to raise interest, had preset start and end dates and presented no anticipated technical challenges. The service would provide RWC SMS alerts, live score updates, results & fixtures, TV schedules, polls, RWC news and team news. The application was assigned the USSD code 176.

4.1   Organisations in the RWC value chain

The RWC application required multiple organizations for its implementation. Telstra provided telecommunications services. SEMA operated a USSD Gateway (SS7 protocol) to provide capability. Interacct Solutions developed the application and operated application servers that provided functionality. Interacct used Http / XML over TCP/IP links to TWI. Authentication was by IP address under the contract between Telstra and TWI. TWI was the content provider contracted to Telstra to provide feeds of RWC scores, news etc. [9]. TWI, the television arm of IMG, is the largest independent producer, packager and distributor of sports programming in the world. TWI also represents the television rights and distributes programming for some of the world's most prominent sports and cultural organizations.

4.2   Customer operation instructions

As discussed in section 2, functionality and ease of use have been shown to be critical elements in consumer acceptance of an innovation. Instructions for the RWC service's customer operation provide some insight into its usability. Customers key #176# [send] on their mobile handset and receive a menu screen of Telstra's once off welcome, how to instructions and some Terms &Conditions. To reply to any screen they:

1. *press the "answer" button*
2. *2. key in the number of their selection (1 in the case of the first screen)*
3. *3. press "send".*

Customer instructions weren't explicit but if they didn't manage to reply within a limited period (between 15 and 40 seconds) the system would cancel the session and they would have to try again. Once they had accepted these once off first time screens they would only see the main menu on future calls.

4.3   Innovation processes

Interacct initiated discussions with Telstra approximately four months before the RWC. Agreement was reached within a month. Telstra setup two teams to implement the pilot application; technical and business. The technical issues were straightforward: identify and manage changes required to the Ericsson network system that would support a USSD call (this service was not previously used by Telstra for application services); contract with SEMA to provide USSD gateway services, develop and implement USSD application and interface with TWI and SEMA. The systems developments and modifications were completed three weeks prior to the RWC start.

A pre-tournament portal was launched to help develop interest and to test the system operation. There was no charge for the information presented by the system. On the start day, the test server at Interacct was switched to the live system. Interacct resourced for 24/7 service delivery with round-the-clock backup and technical support. The server and system provided to be very stable. By the end of the RWC, support had been reduced to a weekly check of the server.

If the technical issues were simple, the business issues were challenging. Some business intentions conflicted with technical requirements. Since the technology was previously unused by Telstra the capability to bill customers had to be established. SMS charges are based on message delivery but since USSD is session based there are no messages to be monitored. The business decision was to charge for information provided in response to a request and then to close the session so if customers wanted additional information then they needed to initiate a new request.

The definition of requirements was more business than technical. Fortunately, Telstra had a specification for mobile applications (Application Requirements Document about 100 pages) that provided clear specifications for screen size and format, message format etc. Otherwise, the development would have taken much longer while all these matters were negotiated.

One major challenge related to the contract. Since this was a totally new service, the legal department required customers to specifically accept the terms and conditions of the revised contract before they could use the system. Reducing the contract terms and conditions to fit into two mobile phone screens with a maximum of 182 characters (accessed by scrolling) represented a significant challenge. Mobile phones with the traditional small screens can display a maximum of 17 characters on each of six lines (102 characters) without scrolling. The legal department initially insisted that the first screen displayed the terms and conditions. Subsequently, they were placed in a sub-menu for customers to review after they had accepted them by proceeding from the first screen. The terms and conditions screens were full of text and this broke all the rules for effective design of user interfaces on mobile phones.

The business case came down to the types of messages, format, response, how to terminate the session what to bill for and what was free. Menu screens and static information were free. Any data obtained from TWI was charged for. The business issues took about six weeks to resolve. The Marketing department wanted to encourage customers to browse on the system since every request for information would result in an additional charge. Engineering had a different view.

Engineering requirements were a major inhibitor. USSD messages utilize spare capacity in a GSM network's signaling channel. This channel is used to manage SMS services. The Engineering department was concerned that a high level of utilization of this capacity might impact on SMS services and so they specified rigid technical requirements. These included a maximum response time for any screen (including the first terms and conditions screen) of 15 seconds, although this was later extended to 20 then 40 seconds. A maximum duration of 70 seconds for the session was permitted after which the session was cancelled. Engineering's concern about possible network congestion since the system was not configured to cope with USSD traffic should have been catered for as #176# use developed. The network software was designed to dynamically re-configure itself based on load.

One week after RWC was completed the service was discontinued. A Post Project Review was conducted by Telstra and Interacct to consider their experiences. Perhaps as a result of the restrictive technical and operational specifications, the RWC trial did not attract the anticipated volume of customers. USSD's potential as a source of innovative services with a secure revenue stream was, however, assured provided the engineering concerns could be addressed.

5.   DISCUSSION

This paper aims to better assist organizations seeking to successfully adopt and to implement m-business innovations. While adoption factors and processes are a rich source of research in the m-business space, much of the work focuses narrowly on the characteristics of a particular m-business technology with little effort to generate a broader framework applicable to a range of mobile technologies and applications. Such a narrow focus raises the possibility that the nature of m-business precludes application of a general e-business adoption framework.

This possibility was explored through comparison of a general purpose Integrated Adoption Model to an arguably worst-case application - an adoption-resistant m-business technology. USSB technology is cited as having superior performance to SMS and WAP services but has been consistently overlooked by mobile telecommunications service providers.

As can be seen in Table 2, the Integrated Adoption Model was successfully applied to capture the complexity of the m-business innovation, identifying major drivers and inhibitors of success.

5.1   Factors in adoption of an M-Business Innovation (adapted from [8])

5.1.1   Environmental factors:

- Market (strong support from RWC fans seeking details on matches)
- Inter-organizational imperatives (highest degree of integration of core business functions required across organizations since the service operated in real time in sessions lasting 15-40 seconds)
- Infrastructure (legal, regulatory, technical, financial, delivery – all applicable)
- Cultural and international (reliance on strong sporting culture in Australia and international visitors attending RWC)

5.1.2   Organizational Factors

- Strategic adopter (not apparent)
- Strategic motivation (perceived opportunity for all parties)
- Business model(s) and strategies (realistic business models and effective business strategies)
- Skills (at strategic, tactical and operational levels to enable service delivery)
- Individual employee (not apparent),
- Structural (both specialization of skills and formalization of Application Requirements Specification),
- Task (uncertainty of technical impact, autonomy of business partners)
- Roles / functions (inter-organizational specialisations).

5.1.3   Innovation factors

- Compatibility with existing network and consumer handsets, complexity of functions reduced to simple activities, relative advantage over fixed location services or radio broadcasts due to results being continually available, trial completed, observability apparent, usefulness to customers, ease of use problematic,
- Distinguishing characteristics / features (specific features available including SMS alerts, live score updates, results & fixtures, TV schedules, polls, RWC news and team news)
- Perceived costs: benefits (contractually implemented).

5.1.4   Consumer Factors

The major benefit factors of RWC #176# included:
- Convenience in accessing RWC information "anytime, from anywhere, to anywhere". (key benefit)
- Cost savings through lower prices (not applicable)
- Availability of information (key benefit)
- Quality of service (limited capacity)
- Increased range of products (not applicable)
- Responsiveness in service delivery, e.g. "instantaneous distribution of digital services" (key benefit)
- Increased customisation, eg "capability to treat customers as individuals" (not applicable)

Major consumer concern factors leading to unsatisfactory experiences include:
- Security (not expressed)

- Uncertainty about delivery (not expressed)
- Uncertainty about products (not expressed)
- Purchase procedures / ease of use / usability (major disadvantage)
- Poor levels of service (major disadvantage)
- Costs (not expressed)

Additional consumer factors include the demographic profiles of customers (rugby fans), consumers' abilities to obtain mobile services and their opportunity to do so (both applicable).

Key research questions raised in this project were:

1. *Which organizational factors influenced provision of m-business services and how? Table 2 shows six of the eight Organizational factors were found to be applicable.*
2. *What characteristics of the implementations influenced proposal and acceptance of that innovation? All three Innovation factors were found to be applicable.*
3. *What drives consumers to, or inhibits consumers from, performing m-business transactions? Nine of sixteen Customer factors were found to be applicable.*
4. *Which environmental factors influence adoption and how? All four of the Environmental factors were found to be applicable.*
5. *Is a general purpose model of e-business adoption able to adequately represent a current example of m-business practice? The finding on research question 5 is resoundingly affirmative.*

A study of this m-business adoption narrowly focused on the specific technology or the organizational characteristics of the telco (or even on all organizations in the value chain) or the environmental circumstances or on the customers in isolation would have been unable to capture the range of issues integral to this m-business innovation and, therefore, would be unable to adequately explain its resistance to adoption. The implications of this paper for both theory and practice are clearly that even disruptive technologies may be better explained through application of multi-factor, comprehensive research models and that these will provide better guidance for organizations than a tightly focused examination of a specific technology.

This implication is open to challenge since it represents the findings of a single case. Yin (1994) suggests a single case design may be appropriate where it represents a critical test of current theory; where the case is extreme or unique; or where the case can provide revelatory insights [30]. The RWC case does not claim any of these states, just that it might adequately serve as an indication to m-business researchers that multi-application and multi-technology models of adoption may be applicable to m-business applications. Theory and practice alike benefit more from development of broadly-based models of adoption that reflect comprehensive representations of business activities than narrowly focused technology-specific models. Otherwise, theory may have little to offer organizations seeking to successfully adopt and to implement m-business innovations

REFERENCES

[1]. Ajzen, I. (1991) 'The Theory of Planned Behavior' Organizational Behavior and Human Decision Processes (50), pp. 179- 211.

[2]. Ajzen, I. and M. Fishbein. (1980) Understanding Attitudes and Predicting Social Behavior. Prentice-Hall, Englewood Cliffs, NJ.

[3]. Bell D.E., Keeney R.L. and Little J.D.C. (1975) 'A Market Share Theorem', Journal of Marketing Research. May, pp 136-141.

[4]. Benbasat I. And Zmud R.W. (1999) Empirical research in Information Systems: The practice of relevance' MIS Quarterly, 23,1. March, 3-16.

[5]. Boyd T.C. and Mason C.H. (1999) 'The link between attractiveness of 'extrabrand' attributes and the adoption of innovations'. Academy of Marketing Science Journal, Greenvale. Vol 27, No. 3, pp 306-319.

[6]. Davis F.D. (1989) Perceived usefulness, perceived ease of use, and user acceptance of Information Technology, *MIS Quarterly*, Vol. 3, No. 3, pp 319-340.

[7]. Elliot S. and Loebbecke C., (2000) 'Theoretical implications of adopting Interactive, Inter-organizational Innovations in Electronic Commerce.' Journal of Information Technology & People - special issue on Adoption & Diffusion of IT. Vol. 13 Nr. 1, pp 46-66.

[8]. Elliot S. (ed) Electronic Commerce: B2C strategies and models. John Wiley Series on Information Systems, Chichester UK, February 2002. pp 291-326

[9]. Interacct Solutions www.interacctsolutions.com

[10]. IMG www.imgworld.com/areasofbusiness/twi

[11]. Jarvenpaa S.L. and Todd P.A. (1997) Consumer reactions to electronic shopping on the World Wide Web. *Interl Journal of Electronic Commerce,* 1, 2, (Winter), 59-88.

[12]. Keen P.G.W. (1998) "Puzzles and Dilemmas: An agenda for value adding IS research". Keynote presentation at European Conference of IS. France. 5 June.

[13]. King J.L., Gurbaxani V., Kraemer K.L., McFarlan F.W., Raman K.S. and Yap C.S., (1994). "Institutional factors in Information Technology innovation". *Information Systems Research.* Vol. 5, Nr. 2, pp 139-169.

[14]. Krishnan M.S., Ramaswamy V., Meyer M.C. and Damien P. (1999) 'Customer Satisfaction for Financial Services: The Role of Products, Services and Information Technology' Management Science, Vol. 45, No. 9, September, pp 1194-1209.

[15]. Kwon T.H. & Zmud R.W., (1987) Unifying the Fragmented Models of Information Systems Implementation, in Boland R.J. & Hirscheim R.A. (eds) *Critical Issues in Information Systems Research*. John Wiley & Sons. Chichester.

[16]. Lawrence E. Culjak G. and Injam S. 'M-Enterprise technology: Diffusion of Innovation Awareness, Adoption and Uptake' in Giaglis G.M., Werthner H., Tschammer V. and Froesch; (eds) The Second International Conference on Mobile Business, Austrian Computer Society 2003, pp 15-26.

[17]. Lyytinen K. And Damsgaard J. (2001) 'What's wrong with Diffusion of Innovation Theory?' in Ardis M.A. and Marcolin B.L eds. Diffusing Software Product and Process Innovations'. Kluwer Academic Publishers Boston.

[18]. Lyytinen K. and Rose G. 'The disruptive nature of IT innovations. MISQ, Vol 27, Nr 4, December 2003, pp 557-595.

[19]. Lyytinen K. and Yoo Y. 'Research Commentary: The Next Wave of Nomadic Computing' Information Systems Research Vol. 13 Nr 4, Dec. 2002, pp 377-388.

[20]. Moore G.A.(1995) Inside the Tornado. Harper Business, New York.

[21]. Moore G.C. and Benbasat I. (1996) Integrating diffusion of innovations and theory of reasoned action models to predict utilization of IT by end-users. in Kautz K. and Pries-Heje J. (eds) *Diffusion and Adoption of Technology*. Chapman and Hall, London.

[22]. Pedersen P.E. and Nysveen H. 'Usefulness and Self-Expression: Extending TAM to explain the Adoption of a Mobile Parking Service'. Proceedings of 16th Bled Conference, 2003.

[23]. Rogers E.M. (1962, 1983, 1995) *Diffusion of innovations*, The Free Press, NYork

[24]. Schumpeter J. The Theroy of Economic Development. Harvard University Press. Boston. 1934

[25]. Scott Morton M.S., (1991). ed *The Corporation of the 1990s: Information Technology and Organizational Transformation*. Oxford University Press. New York.

[26]. Standage T. 'Crunch time for 3G' from The Economist, The World in 2004.

[27]. Suoranta M., Mattila M., Munnukka J., 'Technology-based Service Products – A study on the drivers and inhibitors of mobile banking' in Giaglis G.M., Werthner H., Tschammer V. and Froesch; (eds) The Second International Conference on Mobile Business, Austrian Computer Society 2003, pp 187-199.

[28]. Taylor S. and Todd P.A. (1995) Understanding Information Technology usage: a test of competing models, *Information Systems Research*, Vol 6, pp 144-176.

[29]. Venkatesh V. and Brown S. 'A longitudinal investigation of Personal Computers in the Home: Adoption determinants and emerging challenges' MISQ, Vol. 25 Nr. 1, March2001, pp 71-102.

[30]. Yin R.K. (1994) Case Study Research: Design and Methods, 2nd Ed. Sage Publications Thousand Oaks Calif

PROVIDING PREMIUM SMS SERVICES FOR MOBILE PHONES
Usability based on networks of user - developer relationships

Petter Nielsen and Jo Herstad
University of Oslo, Department of Informatics, Norway

Abstract: In this paper we argue for the need to expand from a perspective on a single user - developer relation in designing usability to a perspective on usability as dependent on a multi-layered and distributed network of relations between multiple and diverse actors. Based on an empirical study of the successful premium SMS services for mobile phones in the Norwegian market we make explicit the user – developer relationships related to usability in a service providing context. We describe this context with a network perspective based on the specific concepts of value networks (Stabell and Fjellstad 1998). This rich analytical perspective appreciates the critical aspects of the service providing context and provides support in solving the primary usability challenges related to premium SMS services.

Key words: Premium SMS services; usability; value networks; user – developer relationships.

1.   INTRODUCTION

From a system development perspective premium SMS services for mobile phones are rather simple and mundane. The focus of this paper is to introduce a different perspective on these services, making explicit new, important and indeed motivating challenges for system developers. To make these issues explicit we discuss the nature of the service providing context, the challenges of designing usability in this context and how these challenges should be appreciated and handled.

In general premium SMS services are under-researched and the concept of mobile services is in itself vaguely defined (Sørensen et al. 2002). What we can expect from these services is also still an open question (Carlsson and Walden 2002). Premium SMS services and their related business models have had a certain attention in M-commerce conferences (for example Anckar and D'Incau 2002; van de Kar et al. 2003). These contributions do however primarily focus on describing state-of-the art services and business models. They do not focus on how services are provided, the constituencies of the networks they are based on and how usability challenges are handled.

In 1997, premium SMS services for mobile phones were in Norway solely developed and provided by mobile network providers. Today, the situation is a different one as premium SMS services are based on a network of actors making up the final service to the end-users (mobile phone subscribers) with the required usability. These services are not only enabled by the transportation of content from the content producers to the end-users, but also services supporting acquisition, aggregation, market-wide-access, advertising, copyright handling etc. The system developers engaged in developing and providing these services do however have inadequate support in current system development methods. These methods are primarily supporting the technical development of software as packages, and not providing services within a context where there is more than one given user – developer relation, relations that have to be created and continuously maintained to create the necessary usability for the end-user.

In this paper we contribute with insights in a relatively novel context for system development. As this context involves a different nature of relations between users and developers, it also requires new approaches to usability design. Introducing and showing the appropriateness of using the concepts of value networks (Stabell and Fjellstad 1998) as an analytical lens, we suggest one approach to make visible and appreciate the critical factors within this context.

The research reported here is based on interviews conducted by one of the authors during 2003 and 2004. Interviews were held with the two mobile network providers in Norway as well as with 6 different content providers. Four interviews were in addition to this held with influential governmental agencies. All interviews were recorded and fully transcribed. The interviews were open-ended, but had a focus on the various actors' roles as well as the usability challenges they were struggling with related to providing premium SMS services.

We have structured this paper as follows. First, the concepts of value networks are introduced as an analytical lens to understand the context of providing premium SMS services. Next, based on our empirical research we describe the provision of ringtones for mobile phones, the network the usability of ringtones builds on and the actors it involves. Finally, we draw conclusions on how the insights provided in this paper can contribute to the provision of premium SMS services in the service provision context.

2.   VALUE NETWORKS

Some of the aspects related to developing premium SMS services and usability fit neatly into the prevailing system development methods and approaches. Typically, this is related to the relative disadvantage of phones with their small screens, limited bandwidth and processing capacity and cumbersome input interface, as well as the challenge of preparing the content in an appropriate format (discussed by for example Hjelm 2000; Tarasewich 2003). However, meeting the usability challenges with this approach is not necessarily sufficient. As consumption of premium SMS services usually is triggered by impulse, usability is also close related to how the impulse is turned into consumption. First, when the impulse is triggered the necessary information to order the service must be simple and easily available for the end-user. Second, the acquisition process must run smoothly and not require a cumbersome registration process as not to obstruct the impulse. Within this context, usability can only be enabled by agreements between e.g. mobile network providers, content providers and media windows providing services to each others. By this constellation, usability can be achieved in the sense that the need for relative complex instructions for and process of service consumption is avoided.

These challenges are brought by the service providing context and materialize in a distributed and fragmented network of service provision and a multiple of user – developer relations. As a design recommendation we suggest an analytical lens to support the analysis and understanding of this context as well as how usability to the end-user can be provided.

To identify and make explicit the actors, their relations and the services they provide related to premium SMS services, we suggest using the conceptual framework of value networks developed by Stabell and Fjellstad (1998). The framework provides analytical support for appreciating a network of actors and their indirect mediation of relations through service provisioning. The concept of mediation in particular appreciates the actors (mediators) that bring together actors that complement each others, as for example mobile network providers mediating between the content providers and the end-users.

Value networks are composed of actors mediating between other actors, typically as providers and users of services. The network is thus not the constellation of the actors, but the mediating services they provide. The primary activities of such a value networks are: network promotion and contract management, service provisioning and network infrastructure operations (Stabell and Fjellstad 1998). Network promotion and contract management are the activities of bringing new actors to the network and governing contracts related to service provisioning and charging. Service provisioning is the provision of the mediating links, as well as billing through the measurement of network usage. Network infrastructure operation is maintaining the infrastructure necessary to handle requests of the actors.

The concept of value networks in particular provides us with two important conceptual tools supporting our analysis and appreciation of provision of premium SMS services. First, it makes us focused on the networked nature of and multiplicity of mediators and their mediations in the network. Second, it makes explicit the challenges of the central activities necessary to build and maintain the network necessary to create usability and provide premium SMS services *per se*. With such a perspective we understand successful provision of SMS services, in particular related to usability, as a result of a dispersed network of services and service providers. Designing usability thus becomes the activities of creating and maintaining this network.

3.   NETWORKS, SERVICES AND USABILITY

Ringtones is one typical example of the networked nature of premium SMS services. Ringtones are primarily made available for the end-user by mobile network providers providing acquisition services, composed of billing and transportation services. However, other services such as copyright handling (by NPRS[10] in Norway), mobile service subscription and advertising through media windows such as TV-shows and magazines, are equally important for the usability of ringtones for the end-user. With a value network perspective, there is not only one group of users, and actors can both appear as users and service providers from different perspectives in the network of relations (figure 1).

We may be led to understand ringtones as based on as a simple indirect mediating structure between content providers and end-users by the mobile network providers. However, the provision of premium SMS services is not simply built on one exchange relationship or one value chain, but on several levels of mediating services in a network of value chains (Stabell and Fjellstad 1998). We thus draw a more complex, but also more encompassing picture of the network of mediating services and relations between actors in figure 1. We at the same time stress that this picture should be interpreted as our initial conceptualization of a network that is very much in change with actors entering and leaving the network.

---

[10] Norway's Performing Rights Society

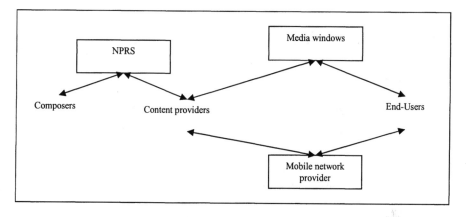

Figure 1. A value network of mediating relations

Providing the required usability of ringtones would not have been feasible without the acquisition services provided by the network providers, the advertising with instructions for how to order the ringtones provided by the media windows and the handling of intellectual property rights by NPRS. Even if service providers tend to see their role as the primary in the network, the complementary nature of the whole network makes all the actors and their mediating roles and provision of services a necessity in the network.

3.1 From developing a system to providing one service in a network of services

In this paper we ask for a change of focus from the system perspective to the service perspective in system development (e.g. Dahlbom 2003). In particular, a service perspective points at the nature of service provision as ongoing interactions between service providers and users. Within this context, exemplified by premium SMS services, the content services are complementary to network services that again are enabled by infrastructure services, as e.g. acquisition and access services. In the case of premium SMS services, the usability for the end-users is the result of reducing the complexity by media windows displaying the content and how to order it, the various mobile network providers coordinating common prizing and access numbers while also taking care of the billing.

When engaged in providing premium SMS services, a single system or interface focus makes little sense related to creating usability for the end-users. Usability and the end-user' experience is based on the combination of a range of systems and services. As system developers, we may find our selves in the middle of this network and without any direct relation to the end-user, even if we are making up the total usability. But only together, the various systems, services and relationships enable the provision of premium SMS services with the required usability. The basic prerequisite for the creation of such a network is for the various actors understand their role as well as appreciate the roles and the value of the other actors in the network.

3.2   Multiplying the gaps and redefining the role of mediators

Based on a common appreciation of the networked nature of premium SMS services, the relationships making up the network of mediators can be developed and maintained.

Raising the concerns about the lack of involving end-users in system development and the consequences for usability, Grudin (1991) introduced a framework describing how various system development contexts affect the user - developer relationship. The contexts discussed by Grudin are primarily based on when users and developers are identified during the development process, as in: Contract development, product development and in-house development. Describing in detail how conditions for user participation vary across these contexts, Grudin illustrate a range of mediators that bridge the gap between users and developers that occurs in the different contexts, both in time as well as space. These mediators, as for example domain experts or consultants, are however to be continually re-examined as they are only indirect and not as effective as direct user – developer interaction when designing usability.

Providing premium SMS services exemplifies another context for user – developer relationships. This context and the relationship between users and developers do at the same time challenge the framework developed by Grudin on three critical issues.

First, successful provision of premium SMS services is not solely based on one actor, but rather builds on a network of actors, services and mediators. Thus, providing services is not built on one, but multiple of user - developer relationships. The challenges for system developers are thus not only to develop systems and services, but also to develop and maintain these relations. Within this process, the responsibility and ability to provide usability becomes fragmented among the different actors, and there is no focal point where the totality of usability is coming from. Usability is not primarily a design or construct, but a result of the assembly of a range of different services

Second, even if Grudin questions whether it is possible to pin down in time when users and developers are known to each others, the project timelines he discusses are of a linear nature. Providing services, however, builds on a range of mediating services, services developed with multiple and overlapping timelines. If these projects are not coordinated, different actors may end up in a "chicken and egg" debate (discussed by for example COM 2002; Funk 2001). Without a close relationship between the various service providers, they will mutually be engaged in a highly complex and unpredictable context. On the other hand, providing incentives such as attractive revenue share models will engage other actors and facilitate coordinated timelines.

Third, in the contexts described by Grudin mediators bridge the gaps between users and developers, even if not as efficient as with a direct user – developer relationship. In providing services, mediators also play a very important part of the value network. For the final product; premium SMS services in our case, these different actors all contributes to usability. However, in our context mediators are the very substance of providing services – not only a stopgap and a substitute to bridge a gap a temporarily, but a permanent part of the design. Mediators are not conduits for usability information and inputs, but are equally important in providing usability themselves.

3.3   The changing role of the system developer

As the responsibility for providing the network of services is distributed, system developers related to providing of premium SMS services will be situated in one of the nodes in a network of services. Their role will first be to develop, maintain and provide the necessary "technical" service level to enable the network of mediations as well as enrolling the potential customers. Second, system developers have to make sense of, appreciate, engage and enroll the associated actors and layers of mediating networks that are necessary to make up the complete network. These other actors do at the same time not necessarily have their mediating network up and running, at the same time as they will follow their own agenda and nurture their own interests. Their different interests and agendas may or may not be in conflict, and may or may not promote and enable a successful network of services. Third, to overcome these challenges system developers must develop and promote a business model that is attractive for other actors to engage in and further invites to innovation.

According to this perspective there is much more than only one user – developer relationship. And the challenges for system developers are not only to engage with the end-users of premium SMS services to increase the usability of the system, but basically to understand who their users are. Further, system developers must understand their own role as users in a network that only as a whole provides usability of premium SMS services.

4.   CONCLUSION

One fundamental challenge for providing premium SMS services is usability. However, usability related to these services is not primarily the design of their appearance on the mobile phone. Creating and maintaining relationships among the various and complementary service providers becomes the most central issue to develop usability even if including end-users in the process does not become less significant. Rather, the complex network of actors involved will question who should engage in and be responsible for the relationships with the end-users.

Providing premium SMS services is a complex endeavor. Taking the issues we have discussed in this paper seriously reveals new challenges for system development, as well as it brings new perspectives on what a service consists of. More than technology, services are built on a network of mediating services enabled by relations between a range of different actors. To capture the dynamics of these networks we have suggested analyzing and describing the context with the concepts of value networks. Then, it becomes evident that the challenge for system development is simultaneously to analyze, appreciate and take these networks seriously, and to enroll other actors necessary to make up a complete network. To enable this shift, we extend our perspective from the simple user - developer relation and the single project timeline, to also include those mediating relations that enable the provision of services and how they can be maintained over time.

In this paper we have describe a context that includes a range of user - developer relationships. We have shown the importance of engaging users in the development of services, but users from one perspective are developers from the other. As system developers, we will thus find our selves in different places in the network and with different roles at different times. While end-user involvement still is a necessity to accomplish the network, system developers are also the users. How to appreciate the users, to what extent to involve them and on who' terms is, however, an open question.

A focus on creating, handling and maintaining these kinds of relations has not been a part of system development methods and agendas. Whether this new context and perspective should involve new system development models is an open question, and it has not been the scope of this paper to provide a full fledged approach or methodology to handle this challenge. Our contribution is rather describing one case where we have shown the necessity of a network perspective and to guide system developers to look at their roles from a different perspective when they develop and provide premium SMS services.

REFERENCES

Anckar, Bill, and Davide D'Incau. 2002. "Value-Added services in Mobile Commerce: An Analytical Framework and Empirical Findings from a National Consumer Survey." in HICSS-35. Hawaii: IEEE.

Carlsson, Christer, and Pirkko Walden. 2002. "Further quests for value-added products & services in mobile commerce." Pp. 715-724 in ECIS 2002. Gdànsk, Poland.

COM. 2002. "Digital Content for Global Mobile Services: final report." Brussels: European Commission: Directorate-General Information Society.

Dahlbom, Bo. 2003. "From users to consumers." Scandinavian Journal of Information Systems 15: 105-108.

Funk, Jeffrey Lee. 2001. The Mobile Internet: How Japan dialed up and the West disconnected. Kent, UK: ISI Publications.

Grudin, Jonathan. 1991. "Interactive Systems: Bridging the Gaps Between Developers and Users." IEEE Computer 24: 59-69.

Hjelm, Johan. 2000. Designing wireless information services: John Wiley & Sons, Inc.

Nielsen, Petter, and Ole Hanseth. 2003. "Enabling an Operator-Independent Transaction Model for Mobile Phone Content Service Provision Through the Open CPA Platform." Pp. 344-353 in Proceedings of the Workshop on Standard Making: A Critical Research Frontier for Information Systems, edited by John L King and Kalle Lyytinen. Seattle, WA.

Stabell, Charles B., and Øystein D. Fjellstad. 1998. "Configuring value for competitive advantage: On chains, shops, and networks." Strategic Management Journal 19.

Sørensen, Carsten, Lars Mathiassen, and Masao Kakihara. 2002. "Mobile Services: Functional diversity and Overload." in New Perspectives On 21st-Century Communications, edited by K. Nyiri. Budapest, Hungary.

Tarasewich, Peter. 2003. "Wireless Devices for Mobile Commerce: User Interface Design and Usability." in Mobile Commerce: Technology, Theory and Applications, edited by Brian E. Mennecke and Troy J. Strader. Hersey US: Idea Group Inc.

van de Kar, Elisabeth, Carleen F. Maitland, Uta Wehn de Montavlo, and Harry Bouwman. 2003. "Design guidelines for Mobile Information and Entertainment Services: based on the Radio538 ringtunes i-mode service case study." in 5th international conference on Electronic commerce. Pittsburg, Pennsylvania: ACM.

AUTOPOIESIS & MOBILE TECHNOLOGY ADOPTION:
The case of wireless collaboration

Robert Kay and Michael Er
Department of Information Systems, University of Technology, Sydney

Abstract: Highly complex collaborative systems often present contexts where the use of wireless enabled technologies could provide numerous benefits. The adoption of such technologies has proved extremely difficult, however. This paper explores issues of technology adoption from an autopoietic perspective in order to explain the success and failure of two case study examples of wireless technology adoption. This discussion will be used to propose a new view on technology adoption for wireless collaborative systems

Key words: Autopoiesis, user adoption, collaborative systems

1.   INTRODUCTION

To date the use of mobile communication technologies to assist individuals more efficiently undertake a collaborative task is growing at a rapid rate.

This paper will examine two case study contexts where the use of mobile collaborative technologies had been attempted with mixed results. The results, of this empirical work will be examined using autopoietic theory as a framework for understanding the dynamics involved with changing the work process to incorporate wireless technologies.

Autopoietic theory is a biological systems theory, that describes the rules and processes through which individuals relate to the environment, undertake cognition and develop language. It will be argued that if the implications of autopoietic theory are accepted, then the success of radical changes to collaborative business processes, involving wireless technology require that the software, hardware and the existing work processes of the user are considered as a single system.

2.   METHODOLOGY

The case studies involved up to 4 semi-structured interviews with users and developers of the systems. Subsequently a further four semi-structured interviews were conducted with construction site staff to ascertain their attitudes towards the adoption of new technologies on building sites. Interviews lasted on average for 1 hour, and a standard set of questions applied in order to ensure that the interviews covered the same key topics and issues. Interviews were audio recorded on a digital recorder and transcribed for subsequent analysis. A thematic analysis of the issues and benefits was undertaken.

3.   CASE STUDY 1: RESTAURANT MOBILE ORDERING SYSTEM

The Restaurant Mobile Ordering System utilized mobile PDA technology in order for table staff to take orders for meals in the restaurant and communicate these orders with bar and kitchen staff. Prior to the introduction of the system, a 'traditional' restaurant ordering process had been employed. The waitress/waiter, using paper note pads, wrote down client's drink and meal orders. Initially, table staff would record drinks orders from clients and verbally passed these on to bar staff for preparation, before returning to the table with the order. On return, meal orders were taken by table staff and handed to the kitchen staff who would cook the meal. Table staff retained the original order with the kitchen receiving a carbon copy. When orders were ready a bell was rung and table staff would deliver the order to the client. On finishing the meal, the floor staff would present the clients with the bill and the payment process takes place.

The restaurant owner, in an attempt to improve customer service, decided to replace the hand written order taking process with a wireless network framework, incorporating the use of wireless enabled PDAs for the table staff. "What I really wanted to achieve was improved customer service. The table staff were spending too much time running back and forth between the bar and the kitchen when ideally they should be waiting on the customers.

The PDAs mean that they can stay on the floor for a greater percentage of the time" (Restaurant owner, 28/7/03).

The hardware underpinning the system included: "...wireless enabled PDA's (personal digital assistants) which are used as a replacement to the order pads." (Restaurant owner, 28/7/03) The PDA's had an interface similar to the menus used by the customers with cascading screens allowing table staff to select the items for consumption, the quantity and any special requests to do with that order. The PDAs also allowed orders to be changed at any stage. "The PDAs connect to the restaurant's wireless network through two wireless access points." (Restaurant developer, 28/7/03) The wireless protocol utilized by this system is IEEE 802.11. This protocol allowed connectivity to a "printer located in the kitchen and the till system located at the bar". "It also connects to a database server which stores all processed orders." (Restaurant developer, 28/7/03). The software used on the PDAs was a proprietary package purchased by the restaurant and as such the basis of the system was created from an "off the shelf" product. As such, the base system, prior to adaptation and adoption by the restaurant, had undergone a rigorous (but generic) development process. Prior to testing the system, the manager "organized a meeting with all staff, including the table, bar and kitchen staff." (Restaurant owner, 28/7/03). In this meeting the proposed system was explained to staff and they were given the opportunity to participate in the design process, providing feedback about any concerns with regards to the automating of their work and specific user issues which needed to be considered. It is important to note that the system was relatively uncomplicated, only requiring the development of an interface for the restaurants menu and order forms, and no further modification to the already existing systems of the restaurant.

The restaurant manager acknowledged that the system provided almost instant benefits to the business, with further unexpected benefits emerging over time. The benefits described by the restaurant owner and manager were as follows:

- Greater accuracy in the orders produced: "...we now have fewer misinterpretations compared with the written orders form."(Restaurant owner, 28/7/03). This was achieved through the use of check boxes on the PDA interface with the consequence that there was less chance of misinterpretation by kitchen and bar staff (and therefore less incorrect orders).
- Improved record keeping: "...all orders are recorded to a database server"(Restaurant developer, (28/7/03) via the wireless network. There is no need to double handle the information, in the form of subsequent data entry from the hand written notes. This resulted in a reduction of recording time, associated cost benefits and improved data integrity.

- Improved customer service: The waiter / waitress no longer needs to physically move between the table service area and the kitchen or bar. This allows more time for waiting on the customer. It also has the added benefit of providing table staff a greater opportunity to sell more items such as drinks and desserts.
- A quicker response time to variations in customer orders: The use of the PDAs has also allowed for faster interaction between table staff and bar / kitchen staff. For example, "if a customer wants to know how their order is progressing then the waiter can make the query from the PDA and tell them more or less straight away."(Restaurant developer,28/7/03),

Interestingly, the restaurant owner did not perceive any issues associated with the system's introduction. "No, not really, in the beginning we only had two PDAs, which was not enough but now we have four which has addressed that." (Restaurant owner,28/7/03)

4.   CASE STUDY 2: MOBILE HOSPITAL WARD SYSTEM

The Mobile Hospital Ward System is being developed to access information in the patient records used by doctors on their ward rounds. The previous system required doctors to download information regarding a patient from the patient records of different departments (such as radiology or pathology) when appropriate. These documents were downloaded to create a paper-based hard copy, early in the morning prior to the doctors conducting their rounds. A number of collaborators could contribute to the patient record including several doctors (various specialists as well as the attending doctor), nurses, different medical departments as well as other medical consultants such as physiotherapists. It is important to note that there was no shared database between these collaborators and each was able to update information in the patient record at any point in time. This created a problem, in that if an update was made whilst a ward round was in progress, the doctor would not have access to that information until the end of the round, which could take up to 3 hours. The potential therefore existed for the doctor to make an incorrect / uneducated diagnosis in the absence of the most up to date information.

To address this issue, the case study hospital began trialing a wireless system that would allow doctors to access the up-to-date information whilst on their rounds. The system included a wireless enabled Tablet PC, which allowed the user to just write their reports using a sensor pen, access data as well as providing the availability of a keyboard. IEEE 802.11b was used as the protocol for data transfer to allow access to the patient records. The same graphical user interface as the ward's desktop PC appeared on the tablet. As such the interface was exactly the same as the one used to download patient information.

The development of the system included a long consultation process with the users. Training sessions were also organized however, no doctors attended. It is interesting to note that the system did not at the time of the interview, allow doctors to update the patient records and this process remained paper-based. The hospitals CIO suggested "…changes to the work process could only be achieved in small steps…" (Hospital CIO,12/9/03) and as such functionality was purposefully limited

Unlike the restaurant example described above, this system did not meet with a high level of success in terms of user adoption. The observed outcomes of this system include the following points:

- The system had been in use for approximately one month. At the time of implementation only one out of the three doctors on the ward had used the system. The doctor who had used the new system had only used it once and then returned to the traditional method. As such, document access was still undertaken using the old process.
- The system was perceived to be a useful tool by both the developers and users (even though they weren't using it).
- A key issue was security of the equipment. "Unless nailed down any piece of equipment will walk out of here (be stolen)."(Doctor 3, 12/9/03) This point significantly contributed to the poor success / adoption of the system, as neither nurses or doctors felt prepared to take responsibility for it if it was stolen during their round.
- The users / doctors were familiar with the technology, having to interface with a computer to download patient information.
- Access to the laptop was restricted to the doctors. The doctors believed that "if everyone else (administration, nurses etc) had access to the laptop then the system wouldn't be available for our use (by the doctors)." (Doctor 2, 12/9/03/03)
- Having tried the new system (once), one doctor returned to the old system because he felt "more comfortable with it" (Doctor 3, 12/9/03)

Although the system had been created in consultation with its users, the doctors continued to use the paper based system. It should be stressed however that this application was in an ongoing trial period and as such the potential existed for many of these issues to be addressed so that a more thorough evaluation of the system's benefits may be undertaken in the future.

5.   A BRIEF OVERVIEW OF AUTOPOIESIS

Autopoietic theory is a biological systems theory developed by Maturana and Varela (1980) to provide explanations of the characteristics of living systems, as opposed to non–living systems. The processes and rules that underpin an autopoietic system's operation, provide the basis for explanations of the nature of human behaviour, cognition, the development of language and to some extent the characteristics of social system behaviour (Kay, 2001). In the context of this research project, the particular aspects of autopoietic theory that we are interested in relate to the process through which the individual relates to their environment and learns over time. The key concepts involved here are operational closure, structural coupling and structural drift and the development of consensual domains. Due to space limitations it is not possible to describe these concepts in any detail and readers are referred to Maturana and Varela (1980;1992) for a comprehensive discussion of the theory.

As an individual experiences ongoing interactions with the environment, an individual will experience what Maturana and Varela describe as a structural drift, or a gradual change to the structure of their nervous system. When these interactions become 'recurrent', autopoietic unities (humans) can become structurally coupled. This means there is a history of recurrent interactions leading to a structural congruence between the two people. Structural coupling is not limited to intersubjective relationships only but relates to all recurrent interactions in the environment of the individual and as such relates to the way in which the individual interacts with technology.

Importantly, in the context of a collaborative system, language is an example of higher level structural coupling, or what Maturana and Varela would describe as a consensual domain. A consensual domain is "…a domain of arbitrary and contextual interlocking behaviours" (Mingers, 1995,pp78) Within a consensual domain two individuals would be able to observe the attribution of meaning to common events and undertake coordinated actions. This is manifest in organisations where particular words, metaphors or language emerge to describe a shared understanding of a situation and coordinate particular activities unique to the environment of that workplace.

Work practices represent a unique form of consensual domain in the sense that where multiple people are involved, their actions require a level of coordination in order to satisfactorily complete the task at hand. As a consequence all coordinated activities are slow to develop and require considerable investment in time as individuals co-adapt with the new consensual domain of operation.

6.   INTERPRETATION OF RESULTS & CONLUSION

The two case studies discussed above present examples of both a successfully implemented system and one that was having difficulty in being accepted. Even though both systems involved considerable consultation with users during their development, the system being applied in the hospital context was failing to demonstrate a level of acceptance that would achieve critical mass. Corresponding with this lack of critical mass was a failure to see any substantive change in the work practices of the ward. This failure would not appear to be due to inadequacies in the functionality either of the hardware or the software provided. The key distinguishing feature between the restaurant and the hospital related to the degree of change required in the work process itself. The use of PDAs in the restaurant environment did not represent a significant departure from the original information input process. The PDA had a very similar look and feel both in terms of function and size to the notepads the table staff had used before. If considered from an autopoietic perspective, there was no significant change made to the consensual domain or pattern of behaviours of the participants in the system.

Conversely, in the hospital example, doctors were required to undertake an extra activity in the form of accessing information whilst "on the job" rather than before. By having already collected the information prior to seeing the patients, the doctors had some opportunity to prepare for their meetings. By accessing this information 'on the job', the whole order of activities had changed .with an associated impact on other processes, including the way the doctors interacted with patients for example, their thought processes in terms of how they manipulated the data, even the way in which they moved around the ward. Given the extensive training involved in becoming a medical practitioner, the patterns of doctor/patient interaction used, develop over a long period and a complex process of socially interrelating, diagnosing, monitoring and recording of information (either mentally or physically). Arguably, because more complex operations and the consensual domains associated with them take longer to develop, the behaviours associated with them are more deeply ingrained into the structure of the individual and therefore a greater level of resistance to change would be expected within a consensual domain of this type.

The obverse is also true when considering the restaurant implementation. In the restaurant the activities or work practices of the floor staff were relatively simple, requiring little training and only minimal manipulation of data in order to get the job done, as such the work practices were less ingrained and the level of resistance not as great.

These observations have a number of implications when considering the implementation of a wireless collaborative system:

- Firstly, where the work practices that are to be affected involve consensual domains of action that have taken a long time to develop, change agents should expect a higher level of resistance to the implementation.
- Secondly, where higher resistance is expected, then it is likely that a greater number of changes to the work environment will be required in order to overcome the resistance. These may include changes to things like the reward system, the regulatory environment or the organisational structure. These additional changes would require the reconstruction of a variety of consensual domains, but would also be associated with considerable stress and uncertainty as the new patterns of interaction settle.
- Thirdly, as much as possible the process by which users both access and update information needs to closely mimic their existing work practice, in terms of physical activity and cognitive process if, given the time and economic constraints of many work places, the technology is to be rapidly adopted and successfully implemented.

Future research will aim to explore these observations in more detail, in order to gain a better understanding of the factors underpinning the successful adoption of wireless collaborative technologies.

REFERENCES

Kay, R. (2001). 'Are Organizations Autopoietic? A Call for New Debate', *Systems Research & Behavioural Science*, vol. 18, no. 6, 461-477.

Maturana, H. & Varela, F. (1980). *Autopoiesis and Cognition: The Realization of the Living*. BSPS, vol. 42, Reidel Dordrecht, Holland.

Maturana, H. & Varela, F. 1992. *The Tree of Knowledge*, Shambala Press Boston.

Mingers, J. (1991). 'The Cognitive Theories of Maturana & Varela', *Systems Practice*, vol. 4, no. 4, pp. 319-338.

Mingers, J. (1995). *Self Producing Systems: Implications and Applications of Autopoiesis*. Plenum Press, New York.

INVITING NEW PLAYERS TO THE MULTIMEDIA M-COMMERCE ARENA
An approach to enhance the current M-Commerce business model with regard to emerging DVB-T networks

Stefan Figge and Kai Rannenberg
Chair for Mobile Commerce and Multilateral Security, Johann Wolfgang Goethe-Universität Frankfurt a. M., Gräfstraße 78, D-60054 Frankfurt a. M., Germany, E-mail: [stefan|kai] @whatismobile.de

Abstract: Digital Video Broadcasting (DVB) using the same terrestrial infrastructure (DVB-T) as traditional analogue television has become a mature technology with a growing number of users. Different activities have been started (e.g. DVB-H) in order to apply that infrastructure for distributing multimedia content and interactive services to mobile devices. DVB (i.e. the television industry) and 3G mobile networks (i.e. the mobile telecommunications industry) are therefore becoming competitors from a value proposition point of view. On one hand there is the television industry with its close relation to the movie and media industry as well as its often advertising based business model. On the other hand there is the mobile telecommunications industry with its focus on direct revenue models for data and services (referred to as M-Commerce), targeting on mobile subscribers. The paper will show that currently the television industry applies different business models more flexibly than the mobile telecommunications industry does. Looking at the likely upcoming competition between the both industries, the paper proposes an approach to expand the business model that is currently applied in the mobile telecommunications industry in order to make it competitive against broadcasted mobile multimedia services. As research in progress the paper addresses the question, which concepts could be applied in order to redesign the current M-Commerce business model for the sake of higher user adoption.

Key words: Mobile multimedia; M-Commerce; business models; 3G; digital television.

1.   INTRODUCTION

Up to now Mobile Network Operators (MNO) and television companies have hardly any interdependencies in terms of markets or value chains. Due to current technological convergence it is likely that this situation is going to change and will most probably end up in making mobile phones und mobile TVs competitors when it comes to the mobile distribution of mobile multimedia services. For these services third generation mobile cellular networks (3G) are commonly regarded to be the technological foundation (UMTS Forum, 2001), while market analysts have hardly shown interest in current developments in the area of digital video broadcasted by using the terrestrial infrastructure (DVB-T) which in most countries already exists for analogue broadcasting (DVB Project Office, 2003a).

For the current market situation, in which the value proposition of M-Commerce services and digital television is becoming increasingly similar, the paper proposes a new business model for Mobile Network Operators to allow the application of indirect revenue models in order to expand the set of applicable business models for multimedia M-Commerce services. The proposed business model is based on the concept of a mobile usage situation that constitutes a dynamic mobile identity. The so called situation description allows a time-specific view on that dynamic mobile identity and enables Mobile Service Providers to judge and value mobile customer relationships with regard to their business relevance. By that a new implementation approach for indirect revenue models is explored in the context of mobile telecommunication markets.

The paper is structured as follows: In the next section the terms business model and mobile multimedia service are defined. In section 2 the current situation in mobile service provisioning is introduced. The German market is taken as an object for investigation, while most of the results are also valid in a European perspective. In section 3 an approach for the mobile telecommunications industry is presented to expand the current business model. Finally, section 4 concludes the paper and provides an outlook on future issues.

1.1   Business Models

The business model concept is a common research topic in economic literature (Timmers, 1998; Osterwalder et al., 2002; Pigneur, 2002; Faber et al., 2003). Nevertheless, an agreed ontology providing a meta-model for designing business models and defining the building blocks has not been achieved. For the purpose of this paper a business model comprises value proposition, revenue model and architecture for value provisioning. The value proposition describes the utility generated for clients and business partners. The revenue model defines income channels and pricing models, while the architecture for value provisioning describes the way the involved parties are arranged in the value chain.

This paper focuses on a new revenue model by introducing new revenue sources for mobile multimedia services. As a revenue model is understood as an essential part of a business model, the paper is accordingly introducing a new business model. This also applies as the proposed revenue model implies changes in terms of the value proposition generated.

1.2   Mobile Multimedia Services

A mobile multimedia service (as potential bearer for value propositions within business models) in the context of this paper shall be defined as a digital mobile data application that is distributed via a wide area wireless data network to a mobile terminal while providing enough bandwidth to enable simultaneous video and audio streaming. By that definition applications based on data bearers like Wireless LAN, Bluetooth, analogue television or GSM are meant to be excluded.

There are two technical distribution paradigms that can be applied for mobile multimedia service provisioning: Point-to-point and Broadcasting (Tanenbaum 2003, p. 14). While point-to-point addresses the communication between two communication partners, broadcasting in the first step allows a one-to-many communication as any party in reach is able to receive data that is sent. These distribution paradigms immediately affect service provisioning in 3G (i.e. point-to-point) and television networks (i.e. broadcasting). Due to the necessary identification in point-to-point networks, accounting, billing and charging is easier in 3G infrastructures than in broadcasting networks. In broadcasting networks, lacking an obligatory identification concept, indirect revenue models (e.g. based on advertising) are easier to apply and therefore the straightforward choice.

2.   CURRENT MOBILE MULTIMEDIA SERVICE PROVISIONING

2.1   Mobile Telecommunications Market

The German GSM market counted 64.8 million GSM subscribers at the end of 2003 being worth € 24 billion (Regulierungsbehörde für Post und Telekommunikation, 2004) of revenue through the delivery of mobile voice, messaging and data services. At the same time the high investments in mobile Internet and 3G infrastructures turned out to be related to the problem of missing billable and accepted M-Commerce applications. Revenues from mobile Internet, e.g. for the globally acting Vodafone Group, are commonly still less than 2% of the total revenue (Vodafone, 2004).

To increase usage and workload in terms of mobile Internet data, operators are currently marketing mobile service portals in the context of brands like i-mode, Vodafone live! or t-zones. Most applied revenue models are oriented towards the model introduced by i-mode in Japan (Bohlin et al., 2003) in which the MNO receives commission on revenues generated through the mobile service portal.

Concerning the architecture for value provisioning within this market it is a characteristic property that the MNOs have exclusive control over important assets (Camponovo and Pigneur, 2003), such as licenses or mobile network infrastructure. MNOs have only recently started to open these assets to third parties, referred to as Service Providers, for the sake of decentralised and specialised service provisioning. While the MNO focuses on providing an appealing entry point in the shape of the mobile service portal, Service Providers develop and offer several infotainment or entertainment services. The figure 1 illustrates value proposition and architecture for value provisioning currently applied for this market.

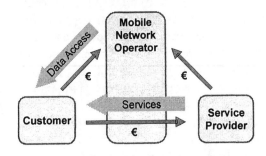

Figure 1: *Current provisioning of M-Commerce services*

The disappointing adoption of this service offering is often regarded to be due to the negative perception of aspects relevant for user acceptance such as usefulness, usability and especially costs by the user (Yom, 2002). The latter is caused by currently applied revenue models, where customers are solely addressed for paying mobile data traffic, which is the foundation of any mobile service. Hence, no mobile interaction can take place without the customer being charged. The user is therefore critically questioning the value of any mobile service and abstains from usage if this question is not clearly answerable. That leads to the current situation where only services providing an immediate, obvious value to the customer (e.g. the distribution of logos, ring tones etc.) are successfully brought to market. At the same time a huge number of promising applications such as advertising, couponing, customer care or loyalty applications, in which case not the customer but a company acting in a private customer market is the beneficial party, remain unmarketable.

2.2 Television Market

In contrast to mobile telecommunications the television industry, due to its history of many decades, can rely on globally well established markets. Applied business models comprise various forms of revenue models and reach from advertising, subscription, pay-per-view to transaction based. In Germany revenues from TV based advertising have been nearly € 4 billion (ZAW, 2003), almost the same amount came from television licence fees and around € 0.8 billion (Premiere, 2003) from Pay-TV subscribers.

Most TV stations rely on advertising based business models, as this is best suited for the anonymous one-to-many communication in broadcasting networks. In that sense, a TV station produces an appealing informative and entertaining programme to gain the highest amount of watchers. In the next step the contact to these watchers is sold as potential customer attention to companies in order to provide market communication (European Group of Television Advertising, 2004). The problem as with any other traditional mass media is that advertising in that way is not allocated efficiently and high spreading losses have to be accepted (Trommsdorf and Becker, 2001). At the same time it is not feasible for watchers to directly respond or interact. Figure 2 summarises the current business approach in advertising based television.

In terms of value proposition the current digitalisation of television in the shape of DVB provides not only a more efficient usage of infrastructure but also adds data applications to the traditional audio-visual channel. With technologies such as the Multimedia Home Platform (MHP) (DVB Project Office, 2003b) and a return channel watchers are able to download and use truly interactive applications on TV, e.g. electronic programme guides, through the broadcasting stream. On this foundation, traditional TV can be extended by applications enabling the user to fulfil commercial transactions and ending up in what is often referred to as T-Commerce.

At present there are several initiatives to roll out terrestrial DVB on a large scale. E.g. the German government is aiming at a full coverage of Germany by 2010 while first areas like Berlin are already being served (Deutsche TV-Plattform, 2003). With existing broadcast stations and each one sending several kilometres digital TV programmes become available nearly everywhere without the need for large equipment. At the same time bandwidth of several Megabits per second allows the distribution of digital multimedia content. While receiving digital TV programmes using a laptop PC and a PC card has been successfully presented (SCM Microsystems, 2003), the problem with even smaller devices and a form factor like a mobile phone is their limited computing and battery capacity. With DVB-H, a new DVB-T derivate for handhelds, these problems shall be solved (Nokia, 2003). Therefore mobile interactive digital television programmes will likely be available within a few years, and first solutions how to apply digital broadcasting networks to distribute multimedia applications and data have already been publicly presented (T-Systems, 2003).

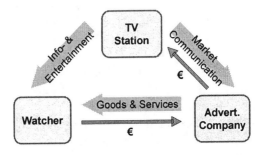

Figure 2: Current provisioning in advertising based television

The opportunities for TV stations are to extend their watcher base from a stationary audience at home to mobile people in cars, trains or any other place; a domain that is traditionally addressed by MNOs. At the same time television based data applications allow M-Commerce like service offerings. Reaching this stage, apparent media convergence will lead to a competition of business models and industries, namely the mobile telecommunications and the television industry.

3.   A NEW BUSINESS MODEL FOR 3G NETWORKS

As described in previous sections, the television industry comes along with a variety of business models, while the mobile telecommunications industry sticks with the one applied in the past. In a situation where both provide similar value propositions, the industry with more flexibility is likely to gain a competitive advantage. The business model described in the following is meant to extend the portfolio of business models MNOs can apply. In particular it enables a free-of-charge provisioning of mobile multimedia services and an indirect revenue model.

3.1   Situation Dependency in Mobile Networks

The model is based on meta-information available in most public mobile cellular networks. These networks are able to determine the user's identity as well as his or her position. This information is usually applied only to enable routing of calls or for billing purposes. The Situation Concept (Figge et al., 2003) is an approach for utilising this meta-data and is based on the idea that identity, position and the time of usage help to determine the user's current situation. The MNO describes the mobile usage situation of its customer by performing the tasks of determination, interpretation and provisioning.

At the time a mobile user requests a service through her or his mobile phone the MNO is able to *determine* the identity, position and time information from its network (e.g. in the case of a GSM cellular mobile network). The identity (i.e. the subscriber account) can be determined based on the Subscriber Identity Module (SIM), while the position can be derived based on the Cell-Of-Origin concept in which the position of base station related to user's current communication is determined. The local time can be determined by applying the derived position and the current, globally equal Coordinated Universal Time (UTC).

The technical references to these three situation determinants are used within the *interpretation* task to multilaterally add and extend it by more semantic information. To accomplish interpretation, databases with user specific as well as general information can be applied. These are acting as the underlying knowledge base and could comprise for instance personal preferences and settings to determine the personal life context (e.g. student, 29 years old, interests in sport etc.) as well as general geographic information or electronic calendars to determine information about the current spatial and temporal context.

To *provision* Service Providers with situation descriptions, it is necessary that the affected user has immediate access and control about her or his personal information, in order to be compliant with current data protection acts (European Commission, 2002). A personal privacy management platform as it is targeted by the European project PRIME (PRIME, 2004) is a necessity to ensure that provisioning of personal information like the situation description is accepted by the user. It could be implemented through customer self-administration applications already offered by nearly all MNOs through fixed Internet or voice access.

3.2   Sponsoring Mobile Customer Relationships

So far an application independent approach to derive mobile user situations has been presented. For the purpose to design a new revenue (i.e. business) model, a more specific application of situation descriptions is sponsoring mobile customer relationships.

Data transmission costs incur when using mobile services are making up for a significant share of the overall transaction costs while the transferred data itself does not provide an obvious benefit for the user. The Situation Concept can address this problem as it enables Service Providers to identify and to sponsor promising customer relationships. When a user is requesting a mobile service through the MNO's portal, the Service Provider compares the situation description with a defined target customer profile. If there is a certain conformity between the target profile and the situation description, the current user is regarded to be business relevant and the Service Provider covers incurring transmission costs (Figge and Schrott, 2003).

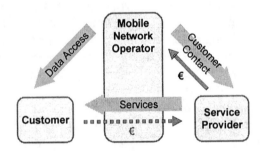

Figure 3: Sponsoring data access within situation dependent
mobile customer relationships

From an economic point of view the free-of-charge delivery of mobile multimedia services is reasonable, as the Service Provider can assume that the requesting customer is part of a targeted customer segment and will generate extra revenue at some stage of the business relationship. The MNO offers a new value proposition by allowing Service Providers to identify and acquire contacts to potential customers. In terms of market communication, the contacts may be used for advertising which is likely to be more cost efficient than traditional television broadcasting (Figge and Schrott, 2003). At the same time the mobile user as potential customer will have a higher acceptance to give attention to the content, as in the first place it is free-of-charge (i.e. no data transmission costs) and adapted to her or his personal situation.

Enabling new service concepts means to open up new players in the M-Commerce market and obtaining new source of revenue for MNOs. Instead of customers solely paying, companies in private markets are incorporated into the M-Commerce arena.

4. CONCLUSION AND OUTLOOK

Due to convergence of mobile telecommunications and television technology developments can be observed enabling the television industry to enter the mobile multimedia service landscape with relatively few investments and resources necessary. In order to develop a new value proposition for multimedia M-Commerce services a new approach for business models in the mobile telecommunications industry has been presented. It allows the application of indirect revenue models and therefore becomes a key opener to the huge market of advertising and marketing. It also provides the foundation to leverage the often discussed potential of ubiquitous computing, which is the determination and application of the mobile usage situation, with location and identity as some of its basic concepts.

An open question that will heavily influence the outcome of the 3G/DVB-T competition is what impact so called convergent networks will have on the development of mobile multimedia markets. By encompassing cellular and broadcasting networks to seamlessly form high speed mobile service provisioning platforms, as it is the research goal of the industry independent European project CISMUNDUS (Berg et al., 2003), MNOs as well as TV stations lose the exclusive control over the infrastructure involved. Suddenly market options and scenarios appear in which MNOs and TV stations form alliances to combine businesses and core competencies (Seite et al. 2003). This discussion will be very much influenced by strategic decisions of market players as well as regulation authorities and remains being worth a close observation.

REFERENCES

Berg, M., Butterfield, S., Cosmas, J., Casagranda, P., and Garrec, D., 2003, *CISMUNDUS: Convergence of Digital Broadcast and Mobile Telecommunications*, (2004-03-01); http://www.brunel.ac.uk/project/Cismundus/IBC2003vfinal.pdf.

Bohlin, E., Björkdahl, J., Lindmark, S., Dunnewijk, T., Hmimda, N., Hultén, S., and Tang, P., 2003, *Prospects for Third Generation Mobile Systems*, (2004-03-01); http://fiste.jrc.es/Pages/detail.cfm?prs=1110.

Camponovo, G., and Pigneur, Y., 2003, *Business Model Analysis Applied to Mobile Business*, Presented at the 5th International Conference on Enterprise Information Systems, Angers, France, April 23-26, (2004-03-01); http://inforge.unil.ch/yp/Pub/03-iceis.pdf.

Deutsche TV-Plattform, 2003, *Statement of „Deutsche TV-Plattform' on analogue/digital switchover to >DVB-T: Das ÜberallFernsehen<*, (2004-03-01); http://www.ueberall-tv.de/download/AG_DVBT2/Posi2Pap-E.pdf.

DVB Project Office, 2003a, *DVB-X White Paper*, (2004-03-01); http://www.dvb.org/documents/white-papers.

DVB Project Office, 2003b, *MHP - Multimedia Home Platform White Paper*, (2004-03-01); http://www.dvb.org/documents/white-papers/WP02%20(MHP).pdf.

European Group of Television Advertising, 2004, *The European Guide to TV Sponsorship*, (2004-03-01); http://www.egta.com.

Faber, E., Ballon, P., Bouwman, H., Haaker, T., Rietkerk, O., and Steen, M., 2003, *Designing business models for mobile ICT services*, Presented at the 16th Bled Electronic Commerce Conference, Bled, Slovenia, June 9-11, (2004-03-01); http://www.hec.unil.ch/businessmodels/papers/panelbled/PanelBled03_Faber.pdf.

European Commission, 2002, *Draft Directive on data protection and privacy*, (2004-03-01); http://europa.eu.int/information_society/topics/telecoms/regulatory/new_rf/index_en.htm.

Figge, S., Schrott, G., Muntermann, J., and Rannenberg, K., 2003, EARNING M-ONEY - A Situation based Approach for Mobile Business Models, in: *Proceedings of the 11th European Conference on Information Systems*, Naples, Italy, June 19-21.

Figge, S., and Schrott, G., 2003, 3G "ad" Work - 3G's Breakthrough with mobile Advertising, in: *Proceedings of the 8th International Workshop on Mobile Multimedia Communications*, Munich, Germany, October 5-8.

Nokia, 2003, *Press Release 2003-10-28*, (2004-03-01); http://press.nokia.com.

Osterwalder, A., Lagha, S. B., and Pigneur, Y., 2002, *An Ontology for Developing e-Business Models*, Presented at the IFIP DsiAge, Cork, Ireland, July 4.

Pigneur, Y., 2002, An Ontology for m-Business Models, in: *Conceptual Modeling - ER 2002*, Lecture Notes in Computer Science, Spaccapietra, S. et al., Tampere, Finland.

PRIME, 2004, *Privacy and Identity Management for Europe*, Project Leaflet, (2004-03-01); http://www.prime-project.eu.org/leaflet-pdf.

Regulierungsbehörde für Post und Telekommunikation, 2004, *Jahresbericht 2003*, (2004-03-01); http://www.regtp.de/imperia/md/content/aktuelles/jb2003.pdf.

SCM Microsystems, 2003, *Press Release 2003-08-27*, (2004-03-01); http://www.scmmicro.com/corporate/p_report.html?release=194&year=2003.

Seite, P., Launay, E., Levesque, T., and Martinez, G., 2003, *Terrestrial Broadcast and Mobile Telco Co-operation*, Presented at the IBC2003, Amsterdam, Netherlands, September 11-15, (2004-03-01); http://www.brunel.ac.uk/project/Cismundus/MobileBusModel2NGN.pdf.

Tanenbaum, A., 2003, *Computer Networks*, 4th ed., Prentice Hall, New Jersey.

Timmers, P., 1998, Business Models for Electronic Markets, in: *Electronic Markets – International Journal of Electronic Commerce & Business Media*, vol. 8, no. 2, pp. 3-8.

Trommsdorff, V., and Becker, J., 2001, *Werbekreativität und Werbeeffektivität – Eine empirische Untersuchung*, (2004-03-01); http://www.marketing-trommsdorff.de/forschung/werbekreativitaet_tu_berlin.pdf, 01-03-2003.

T-Systems, 2003, *Press Release 2003-08-29*, (2004-03-01); http://www.t-systems.de/TSIeng/cda/index_frame/1,3540,2108-869-2003-8--6229-0,00.html.

UMTS Forum, 2001, *A Reference Handbook for Portal Operators, Developers and the Mobile Industry*, Report 16, (2004-03-01); http://www.umts-forum.org.

Vodafone, 2004, *Press Release 2004-01-08*, (2004-03-01); http://www.vodafone.com/assets/files/en/KPI_Jan_2004_prl_FINAL.pdf.

Yom, M., 2002, Utility und Usability im Mobile Commerce, in: *Mobile Commerce*, Silberer, G. et al., Gabler, Wiesbaden, pp. 173-184.

Zentralverband der deutschen Werbewirtschaft – ZAW, 2003, *Werbung in Deutschland 2003*, Verlag edition ZAW, Bonn.

MOBILE PROCESS SUPPORT SYSTEMS
Experiences from a case study

Børge Haugset
SINTEF ICT, borge.haugset@sintef.no

Abstract: Work process support systems, both in the form of workflow systems and of more loosely structured systems have been widely developed and also to a large extent been taken into use in a large number of work situations. As computing is becoming both pervasive and nomadic, workers use of computing and communication services is less limited to solitary moments at an office desk. Thus it gets more and more important to provide mobile work process support systems. This paper presents experiences related to the development, introduction and evolution of such systems through results from a case study following phone engineers. The main conclusions from the study are that that smaller terminals not necessarily does the job better, computerised systems are not always better than paper-based systems, and that supporting nomadic work must be done in agreement with the overall work context.

Key words: Mobile Information systems applications in organizations; Interdependencies of mobile information technologies and organizational structures

1.   INTRODUCTION

A larger proportion of work is today done by what is termed the symbolic analyst (Thomson and Warhurst, 1998), whose work resources and work products are primarily symbol-structures. The proportion of such work is predicted to increase in the years to come, based on profound changes in business environments in connection to knowledge intensity, globalisation, and virtualisation. The main work pattern of the symbolic analysts is knowledge intensive projects often in dynamically networked organizations. Knowledge work, which is inherently cognitive rather than physical (Davis, 2002) will not be tied to the office only, but will consist of continuous collaboration, communication, and co-ordination on the fly among distributed actors (Bellotti and Bly, 1996; Luff and Heath, 1998). The modern knowledge worker works from many different locations (home, in the clients office, on a plane), using a variety of information processing devices based on what is available and practical at the time, including stationary PCs connected to a LAN or WLAN, portable PCs, and personal information appliances (PIA) including mobile phone and PDAs connected wirelessly to the network.

To address the needs of these types of workers (and of other workers whose work situation is inherently mobile), a number of solutions to mobile process support has been developed over the last years. Based on the visions of the impact of anytime/anyplace computing on increased productivity, one would expect these process support systems to already have had immense impact, and that even more revolutionary changes is to be expected as the 3G infrastructure (eventually) will be put into broad-scale operation.

Based on following the development, introduction and take-up of this type of system over a number of years in different organizational settings, we have found that rather than dramatically changing the organizations taking these kinds of systems into use, the changes in work practice seem to be more gradual and evolutionary.

We will in this paper present some of the overall findings from a case-study on the development, introduction and use of a mobile work process support solution. In the next section we present the case. Section 3 summarizes the main learning from the case study, whereas section 4 concludes the article with views for further work in this area.

2.   DESCRIPTION OF CASE STUDY

The results presented in this paper are collected on the basis of a case-study within work-process support for phone-engineers (Haugset, 2001).

In this case study, the researcher was doing a field study covering the introduction of two new mobile process support systems in a large telecommunications company in Norway. The study included interviews with engineers, their managers, and people working at the service centre, and following and observing the engineers as they were performing their task with support of the different systems.

According to Benbasat, Goldstein, and Mead (1987), a case study is an approach well suited when the context of investigation takes place over time, is a complex process involving multiple actors, and is influenced by events that happen unexpectedly. Our case satisfies these criteria. In deciding whether to use case studies or not, Yin (1994) encourages to evaluate the type of research question, the control the investigator has over the actual behavioural events, and how the case focuses on contemporary as opposed to historical events.

Yin (1994) states that the relevance of a single case study is high when the goal is to identify new and previously not researched issues, but when the intent is to build and test a theory, a multiple case study should be designed. At the start of the study there had not been reported much research within this area earlier, and a single case approach was chosen. Time and resource constraints also made this the most viable method.

The first interviews done were quite open, to get a broad understanding of the context of work. As for the later interviews and observations, these were more focused. The researcher observed, during 18 months, 6 engineers at work, each observation ranging from two hours to a full day. Furthermore, several phone interviews with engineers and interviews with other staff in the company were made. Based on this, a qualitative analysis was performed. Rather than making broad generalizations, the aim with the study was to pinpoint some factors that engineers think are important for performing their work. More in-depth studies should be performed in order to further generalize and support these findings.

A phone engineer is a common term used for those installing and maintaining the telecommunication network all the way to the end-user. The case-study focused on engineers delivering solutions to end-users and correcting errors. The work processes for these groups of tasks follow a similar overall pattern with or without a mobile work process support system. They need to establish or mend a line somewhere on the way to the customers' telephone outlet. They need information about where to go and what kind of job to expect. Occasionally they also need help from others, either from a service centre, or by other engineers.

The basis of each task is a work order which should contain all necessary information to perform the work. We followed the introduction and use of several mobile systems for following up work-orders, a previously paper-based process. The first system (*Dart*) was based on using a handheld device (introduced originally in 1998), whereas in the second one (*Advantex*), one used a portable computer that was placed in the engineers car (Haugset, 2001). Advantex was introduced in 2000, and a picture of a car with the Advantex system installed is shown in figure 1. The old paper-based work orders contained the same information that could be accessed by Dart and Advantex.

For paper-orders, the overall flow was as follows: A customer reported an order or an error to customer service, which forwarded this to the service-centre. The service-centre performed line-checks centrally, and established work orders for tasks that couldn't be done centrally. Each day, the engineers collected work orders (on paper) by going to the service centres. After each task was completed this was reported to the service centre before starting on the next task. This was done calling the centre on a mobile phone. The centre was also called for assistance, e.g. to perform line checks. The service centre performed final treatment of the order after it was reported fixed, billing the customer for the performed job.

In Dart, the major change was the all work orders were stored in a database, each task assigned to one of the engineers. At the start of the work-day, the engineer downloaded the work order and all the information about the task to his personal work tool, using their mobile phones as modems. The tasks were structured as HTML files, and accessed by an HTML viewer on the PDA. When a task was finished, the engineer was to report the job directly to the database by using the PDA. The people at the service centre also accessed this database.

Figure 1. A car with Advantex running on a laptop

When using Advantex the work flow was almost the same as in Dart. However, Advantex demanded a more interactive use. The engineer had to press a button to mark when he started working, when he got to the customer, and when he finished each job. A resource centre always knew where the different engineers are, and if an important fix in the network was needed, the engineer closest to the site could be dispatched to the site.

Common to both Dart and Advantex was that the engineer would no longer have to go to a central in the morning to pick up his work list; he could drive straight to the first job.

3. INSIGHTS AND LEARNINGS

Based on the knowledge gained from the field study, we now present some factors that are worth focusing on when introducing mobile work process support:

3.1 Smaller and more portable is not always better

One would easily be led to believe that a PDA containing all information on the work would result in satisfied engineers. They had access to up-to-date information at all times, without having to print out the tasks. In reality, however, this was not the case. The actual work flow for Dart turned out to be quite different from the intended flow.

Even if they are doing mobile work proper (moving around is an important part of their work, being both travelling and wandering (Kristoffersen & Ljungberg, 2000)), a higher degree of satisfaction was reported on the Advantex system where they used laptops situated in their cars. The dissatisfactions with the Dart system were many and important, leading to a different work ritual than initially envisioned. A small screen and tiny keyboard buttons combined with a slow processing speed and short-lived batteries on the PDA resulted in few people using it. Furthermore, the use of a mobile phone as a modem to upload and download work was tedious and unstable, often disconnecting so you had to try it again. As a result, some people downloaded all of the days work while having their breakfast, and uploaded the complete finished jobs. They chose to take their work home instead of using the Dart system as intended. A lot of people chose to call the service centre to describe their finished work, as they had done during the paper-based work situation. The time-consuming use of the PDA was seen as extra work they didn't see the usefulness of.

In Advantex, many of the problems of Dart were gone. Instead of a slow PDA they had access to a laptop. The laptops had their own modem, reducing the clutter with the mobile phone. As the laptop had more processing power than the PDA, the system only needed to send the data to and from the database, instead of the complete layout. The rendering of the data was done on the laptop in a graphical user interface. This reduced the time spent on downloading and uploading work.

The engineers' responsibilities were also enhanced, allowing engineers direct access to the database.

The larger machines were found to have more advantages than disadvantages, with better keyboard, faster processing, larger displays making it easier to have an overview of the different work-orders etc. This result was also linked to the next point:

3.2   Computerised is not necessarily better than paper-based

The case is an example of going from a paper-supported to a computer-supported process. For this to be efficient, the advantages of the new medium must be larger than the advantages of the old. Some problems related to the use of the system within the work environment were witnessed in the first system (Dart). The terminals did not work in cold and rain. Both in connection to this system and the version based on a portable PC, paper were still used a lot, even if it was explicitly discouraged due to security reasons. The workers used the traditional paper orders in a very flexible manner, jotting down additional information as they went along, and found this more flexible and surveyable than to input this on the PDAs. The engineers preferred copying notes from the Advantex laptop to a sheet of paper to bring into the customers building instead of bringing the H/PC inside. This is an example of the advantages regarding the micro-mobility of paper; paper is easy to use in many contexts and across contexts when necessary (Luff & Heath, 1998). Since the data collected as part of doing the job was normally only of interest to the engineer before reporting the job, it was sufficient for the overall organization that this was entered after the job was finished.

3.3   To support mobile knowledge work it is not sufficient to support the nomadic part of the work

At one of the service centres studied, in the original paper-based work process, the engineers met each morning at the main office to get their assignments before driving off to the different tasks. With the introduction of the computer-supported systems, this overall process was supposed to change. The engineers were meant to download their work assignments for the day from home, and drive straight to the first job. They were in fact explicitly forbidden to go to the office in the morning.

Most of the engineers, however, decided to meet half an hour before work usually started, some also met for lunch. In the meetings they sat down with a cup of coffee and a cigarette, and chatted about issues ranging from the prices of gasoline to today's work. They felt that they had a joint need in upholding this arena, regardless of the rules. Many engineers said they knew co-workers who were better in some fields than others, and they often called them if they got stuck on something. The community of practice (Wenger, 1998) supported by these meetings allowed for overhearing and joining colleagues' conversations, regarded as important in the learning process

(Bellotti and Bly, 1996). The nomadic part of the work, driving around in the city to install and fix telecom installations, was made easier by meeting in informal meetings, drawing on each others' experiences and practices.

The joint meetings also gave a larger visibility of the knowledge that the experts had, and thus higher self-esteem and pride in the job. One worker said *"You talk about your profession; you get something to be proud of."* This resembles what Orr describes as people telling each others *war stories* (Orr, 1996). As a phone engineer, being good is about showing skill. At the same time you teach the others what you have learnt.

The company had created a virtual meeting place on the Intranet, where engineers could ask questions and discuss issues with colleagues. At the time of the study very few people used this service. When asked why, one engineer thought it was because it was something completely different from asking a knowledgeable colleague a question while he is sitting beside you: On the Intranet you had to decide that *"Today I'll sit down and tell others about my experiences"*. The implicit communication at meetings had been suggested replaced by an explicit form of communication through the Intranet.

4. SUMMARY AND FURTHER WORK

This paper summarises some of the learning from following the development, introduction and evolution of a mobile work process support solution. It highlights that it is difficult to develop generic solutions within this area, and that such systems must fit the needs and characteristics of those using them. Further studies of similar introductions will enhance the value of the findings.

Our approach for future work within this problem-area will, in particular, be directed to the support of emergent non-routine work-processes, where systems supporting these tasks have unclear, inconsistent, and unstable user requirements, and where they can benefit to be accessible on a number of platforms. Traditional enterprise systems tend to be quite inflexible, hardly adaptable at runtime, and primarily support routine processes. Existing workflow management systems have typically been focused on dealing with exceptions and have thus offered some support for adaptive processes (Klein, 1998). These types of systems, however, have typically overlooked emergent processes, which seem to encompass an increasing part of knowledge workers' activities. On the other hand, only supporting the emergent work style of the individual is at times inefficient, because routine parts of the work can be prescribed and automated, and because sharing of explicitly defined work processes facilitates co-ordination, collaboration and communication between multiple parties. Thus there is a need for a balance between prescription and emergent representations.

REFERENCES

Bellotti, V. and Bly S. (1996): Walking away from the desktop Computer: Distributed collaboration and mobility in a product design team. *Proceedings of the CSCW'96*, Cambridge, MA, 1996, 209-218.

Benbasat, I., Goldstein, D. K. and Mead, M. (1987) "The case research strategy in studies of information systems" *MIS Quarterly* (11:3) p 369-386

Davis, G (2002): Anytime/Anyplace Computing and the Future of Knowledge Work. *Communications of the ACM* 45 (12).

Haugset, B. (2001): *Montøren og Terminalen* (The Phone Engineer and the Terminal, in Norwegian) M.Sc. Thesis, University of Oslo.

Klein, M. (1998) Workshop: *Towards Adaptive Workflow Systems, CSCW-98*, Seattle. Available on the Web at http://ccs.mit.edu/klein/cscw-ws.html 20040526.

Kristiansen, S. & Ljungberg, F. (2000). Mobility — From stationary to mobile work. In: Braa, K., Sørensen, C., & Dahlbom, B. (Eds.) *Planet Internet*, Studentlitteratur, Lund.

Luff, P. & Heath, C. (1998). Mobility in collaboration. In: *Proceedings of the CSCW-98*, Seattle, USA, 305-314

Orr, J. E. (1996) *Talking about Machines: an Ethnography of a Modern Job*. Cornell University Press

Thompson, P. & Warhurst, C. (1998). *Workplaces of the Future*. Macmillan Business

Wenger, E. (1998) *Communities of Practice: Learning, Meaning, and Identity*. Cambridge University Press.

Yin. R. (1994) *Case study Research*, 2nd ed. SAGE Publications.

ONE-HANDED MOBILE TEXT ENTRY
Evaluation of five-key text entry techniques

Frode Eika Sandnes
Faculty of Engineering, Oslo University College, P.O. Box 4, St. Olavs plass, N-0130 Oslo, Norway

Abstract: This paper addresses text entry techniques for miniature or wearable devices. Five keys are used for interaction control – one key for each finger. Tree approaches are examined: one dictionary-independent technique (multi-tap), a partially dictionary-dependent technique (tree-based) and a dictionary dependent technique (one-stroke). The study shows that users can type text at rates of up to 30 characters-per-minute after just 5 minutes of practice using the one-stroke approach. Although the proposed methods are slower than chord-based techniques they do not require the same amount of training that is required to acquire and maintain chording skills. Consequently, the proposed strategies are suitable for users that only type texts on a small device occasionally.

Key words: Mobile text entry; KSPC; chording; wearable computing; miniature devices.

1.   MOBILE TEXT ENTRY

The limited surface area offered by small devices only provides space for a few keys. There is also a trade-off between the number of keys and the size of the keys. Smaller keys are harder to use than larger keys and result in higher error rates as incorrect keys are more easily pressed accidentally.

Dictionary based text-entry techniques (King, 1995; Kreifeldt, 1989; Smith, 1971) have won wide commercial success due to their ease of use and fast text entry speeds. The market is dominated by the T9 system patented by Tegic, but other similar systems exist such as iTap and eZiText. Dictionary based text-entry allows text to be entered using close to one keystroke per character on phone keyboards.

Two and three key text entry systems were deployed on arcade game machines from the 70s. The user would pull the joystick to the left or right to cycle the alphabet (wheel-of-letters), or use rotator keys and press a select button to select the desired character when entering their names on high score lists. MacKenzie et al. (MacKenzie, 2002) has found that such text entry systems on average require 10.66 key-strokes per character for normal English text. In a different approach (Raghunath and Narayanaswami, 2002) the alphabet was split into two rings. The user could toggle between the two rings and then rotate the rings to obtain the desired character, i.e. one key is used to toggle between the two rings, one key is used to cycle forward in the rings and the final key is used to select a letter.

2.   5-KEY TEXT ENTRY

Five key text entry is has been around for over 100 years. The first five key text entry techniques were chord based keyboards originally used for mail-sorting applications (see the excellent survey of chord based text entry by Noyes (Noyes, 1983). Several studies addressing various aspects of five-key chord keyboards exist (Lehikoinen and Roykee, 2001; Rosenberg and Slater, 1999; Seibel, 1962; Kirchenbaum et al., 1986) and commercial chord keyboards include the Microwriter. Five-keys have also been proposed for use in stenograph typewriters (Beddoes and Hu, 1994).

The five keys allow 31 unique keystroke-patterns, or chords, to be entered (2^5-1) and thus allow the entire alphabet and more to be addressed. Although allowing for fast text entry rates, such systems have a high learning threshold, although (Gopher and Raij, 1985) claim that chording in principle is easier to learn than QWERTY touch-typing. The reason for this is probably the wide availability and familiarity users have with the QWERTY keyboard, and that most typists never have seen or tried a chord keyboard.

When Douglas Carl Engelbart invented the mouse in the 60'ies he originally visualized the mouse with five-keys allowing the users to type text using chords (Barnes, 1997). Although this particular detail of Engelbart's vision did not catch on, the idea of using five-keys is worthy of investigation due to the anatomy of the human body. Several strategies has been proposed for one-handed text-entry such as the ingenious half QWERTY keyboard (Matias et al., 1993). The principle of the half QWERTY keyboard is to transfer two-handed QWERTY typing skills using one hand on a special half keyboard. A totally different approach taken by (Isokoski and Raisamo, 2000) is to enter text in graphical patterns controlled by device independent north, south, east and west movements (i.e. four keys, mouse or joystick directions) to mimic the graphical shape one would handwrite a character. Finally, a class of five-key text-entry systems can be found on computer game consoles, for example the Nintendo Advance. Characters are organised into a two-dimensional wraparound mesh. This mesh is navigated by using four navigation keys (left, right, up and down) and select. This class of text entry systems are easy to learn and can be used with very little training.

3. METHOD #1: MULTITAP

The multitap approach is probably the simplest five-key text entry technique and is analogous to the multitap technique of the mobile phones. The alphabet is split into four groups and each group is mapped to one key. For example: 1: ABCDEF, 2: GIJKL, 3: MNOPQR, 4: STUVWXYZ, 5: [break-key] To enter a letter the user selects the key with the respective letter assigned and repeatedly taps the key until the desired letter is selected. Then the next character is entered and so forth. If two consecutive letters are from the same group the first letter is chosen pressing the break-key. For example, the expression "car_" is entered using 12 keystrokes. In general, the minimum number of keystrokes per character required to enter a character is $K_{a,min}=1$, the maximum number of keystrokes per character is $K_{a,max} = 9$, and the mean number of keystrokes per character for English $K_a = 3.47$. Note that the a subscript is used to denote the key entry component of the text entry procedure.

4. METHOD #2: TREE-BASED PARTIAL DICTIONARY TECHNIQUE

The tree-based technique is based on organising the characters of the alphabet into a five-way two-level tree, where characters are entered in two steps. In the first step the main category is selected and in the second step the desired character for the category is selected. The advantage of this technique is that usually K_a is constant, thus $K_{a,min}=K_{a,max}=K_a=2$. However, the problem is that such a tree only allows 25 leaf nodes (5^2) and there are 26 characters in the English alphabet. In addition a leaf node is required for the space character. The solution is to cluster less frequently needed characters with other characters. For example, by clustering p and q to the same leaf node and y and z to another leaf node we end up with exactly 26 leaf nodes including space. And words containing the clustered groups are resolved by the means of a dictionary. For example, the word "zen" is entered as follows:

```
0  (5)  [abcde fghij klmno pq-rstu vwx-yz_]
1  (4)  [..... ..... ..... ....... vwx-yz_]
2  (1)  [abcde fghij klmno pq-rstu vwx-yz_]y
3  (5)  [abcde ..... ..... ....... .......]y
4  (3)  [abcde fghij klmno pq-rstu vwx-yz_]ye
5  (4)  [..... ..... klmno ....... .......]ye
6  (5)  [abcde fghij klmno pq-rstu vwx-yz_]yen
7  (5)  [..... ..... ..... ....... vwx-yz_]yen
8  (?)  [abcde fghij klmno pq-rstu vwx-yz_]zen_
```

At the first step the fifth group is selected by pressing the fifth key, then the yz-group is selected by pressing the fourth key (it is the fourth subgroup within the group). Then, the first group is selected and the e character is selected from the group by pressing the fifth key. At step four the third group is selected by pressing key tree, and the fourth character in the group is selected by pressing the fourth key. Finally, space is retrieved by selecting the fifth character from the fifth group. The resulting word is either ``yen" or "zen", but "yen" is not in the dictionary and "zen" is selected. Thus, a total of 8 keystrokes are required to press the 4 character expression "zen" + space.

With the current configuration there will only be a small number of ambiguities for all valid sequences containing combined characters for English, i.e. $K_b \approx 0$. Note that the b subscript is used to denote the ambiguity resolution component of the text entry procedure. Another advantage of the approach is that only a small subset of the English dictionary is required, i.e. only the words containing the characters "p", "q", "y" or "z", or approximately 15,305 words (33.7% from a total of 45,392) which includes all grammatical variations.

5.   METHOD #3: ONE-STROKE DICTIONARY BASED

The idea behind the one-stroke approach is to assign several characters to the same key, enter a character by pressing the assigned key and resolve ambiguities by employing a dictionary. By brute force search the optimal partitioning scheme reveals the following character to key assignment. Namely, 1: ABCDE, 2: FGHIJKLM, 3: NOPQR, 4: STUVWXYZ, 5: space character.

For example, assume the user wants to enter the word "approximately". The user first presses key one since the letter "a" is in the first group. The next four letters "ppro" are all in the third group and the third group is pressed four times. Next the "x" is in the fourth group, selected with the fourth key and the "im" characters are both found in the second group. Next, the characters "ately" are in the first, fourth, first, second and fourth group respectively, activated with the corresponding keys. Finally, the space is retrieved by pressing the fifth key. The 15 character expression ``approximately" + space is unambiguous and retrieved with just 15 keystrokes.

For the one-stroke approach K_b=0.52 and $K_{b,max}$=1.33 respectively. Other interesting statistics regarding this technique is that there are 3.7 ambiguities on average and a maximum of 32 ambiguities.

Table 1. Results of the typing experiment. ikd = inter keystroke delay

Subject	Measure	MultiTap	Tree-based	One-stroke
Subject #1	Mean ikd	1.0	2.3	2.1
	Median ikd	0.5	1.4	1.2
	Mean chars/min	22.5	13.0	28.5
Subject #2	Mean ikd	0.76	1.62	1.97
	Mdian ikd	0.52	1.02	1.94
	Mean chars/min	27.2	18.6	31.1
Subject #3	Mean ikd	0.73	3.93	1.44
	Median ikd	0.24	2.13	0.55
	Mean chars/min	26.5	7.7	26.2

6.   EXPERIMENT

The three text entry techniques were implemented as part of a modular custom Java application framework. The applets where configured to accept key events from "a", "s", "d", "f" and "_" (space) keys representing the keys 1, 2, 3, 4 and 5 respectively. This configuration allows the user to touch type using the left hand.

Three subjects participated in the experiment. All the subjects were computer literate and capable of conventional QWERTY touch-typing at high rates.

Each participant was e-mailed a link to the experiment website. The tests were presented as a seven-step procedure. The entry page provided an overview of the experiment. The second page allowed the subject to practice the multi-tap experiment for five minutes, and the third page was dedicated to the typing experiment using the multi-tap technique with a duration of 15 minutes. A few lines of text to be typed were displayed at the bottom of the screen. Only a few lines are sufficient for such a short typing experiment as untrained typists are unable to type more. Pages four, five, six and seven were dedicated to practice and typing experiments for the tree-based technique and the one-stroke approach and the final page comprised a short questionnaire allowing the subjects to explicitly voice their opinions regarding the three methods.

Table 2. Results of the questionnaire. MT = multi-tap, TB = tree-based, OS = one-stroke.

Subject	absolute			relative		
	MT	TB	OS	MT/TB	MT/OS	TB/OS
Subject #1	3	0	4	0	4	5
Subject #2	1	5	4	5	4	1
Subject #3	4	0	3	0	2	5

7.   RESULTS

Tables 1 and 2 list the results of the experiment. Table 1 summarises the measurements of the typing experiment. The columns list the subject, the type of measurement and measurements obtained using the multi-tap, tree-based and one-stroke methods respectively. Three measurements are provided, the mean inter keystroke delay, i.e. the time between consecutive keystrokes, the median of inter keystroke delay (robust to outliers) and the characters typed per minute (including errors).

8.   DISCUSSION

Clearly, Table 1 shows that the one-stroke method results in the highest typing rates of 28.5, 31.1 and 26.2 characters-per-minutes for the three subjects, followed by the multi-tap method and finally the tree-based strategy.

The multi-tap method requires the least cognitive processing and is thus the easiest to use and the tree-based method requires the most cognitive processing and is the hardest to use. This is evident from inspecting both the mean and median inter-keystroke delay. For subject 1 the median inter-keystroke delay is 0.5 seconds while it is 1.2 seconds for the one-stroke method and as much as 1.4 for the tree-based method. Similar patterns can be seen for subject and 3, which has inter-keystroke delays of 0.24, 0.55 and 2.13 for the multi-tap, one-stroke and tree-based methods respectively. The results for subject 2 varies slightly as the inter-keystroke delay for the tree based method is shorter (1.02) for the tree-based than the one-stroke method (1.94) – yet the multi-tap method yields the shortest inter-keystroke delay of 0.52.

The measurements are also relatively consistent with the questionnaire assessments which are summarized in Table 2. All the subjects rate the one-stroke method highly, while only subjects 1 and 3 rate the multi-tap method highly. Instead, subject 2 rate the tree based method highly. When comparing methods against each other then subjects 1 and 3 prefer multi-tap over the tree-based method, while subject 2 prefers the tree-based method to multi-tap. Subjects 1 and 2 prefer the one-stroke method over the multi-tap method while subject 3 prefer the multi-tap method. Finally, subjects 1 and 3 strongly prefer the one-stroke method to the tree-based method, while subject 2 prefers the tree-based method. Clearly, the preferences of subject 2 differ from those of subjects 1 and 2 and this is also visible in the measurement data in Table 1 where subject 2 has a much shorter inter-keystroke delay for the tree-based method than the other two subjects. Perception of preference is somewhat linked to productivity and success using the methods, and subject 2 had an unusual skill using the tree-based method despite its cognitive complexity.

One of the subjects commented in the response e-mail that the multi-tap method was easy to use, but that one looses patience quickly using it. Further, the subject reported that the one-stroke method feels fast, however effort is required to look through the alternatives when typing an ambiguous word.

Clearly, the experiments show that although the multi-tap strategy has the highest KSPC it is still better than the tree-based method, which has a much lower KSPC – the main reason being the huge difference in cognitive difference between the two methods. The one-stroke has the lowest KSPC and also yields the highest keystrokes per character, but is still more cognitively difficult than the multi-tap method.

Clearly, all the methods discussed in this paper are much slower than chording techniques such as the chording glove (Rosenberg and Slater, 1999). In comparison, the chording glove allows users to type approximately 50 characters-per-minute after 80 minutes of practice and 95 characters-per-minute after 10 hours of practice. However, (Rosenberg and Slater, 1999) reports that it takes approximately 45 minutes to memorise the chords. Research also shows that such typing skills quickly deteriorate without practice and chording is therefore most suitable for frequent users of the technology. However, two of the strategies discussed in this paper can be used with acceptable typing speeds just after a few minutes of practice. The proposed strategies are therefore suitable for occasional users.

9. SUMMARY

Techniques for dictionary enhanced text input on miniature mobile devices with five keys are proposed, allowing text to be entered using one hand. Three methods were investigated – multi-tap, tree-based and one-stroke. The one-stroke method resulted in the highest typing rates of approximately 30 characters-per-minute and a theoretical KSPC of 1.52. The multi-tap method was measured to require the least cognitive load, while the tree-based method was found to be the least productive typing strategy with the highest cognitive difficulty. All the techniques allowed the subjects to type text after just five minutes of training, which is much less training time than what is required for chord keyboards.

REFERENCES

Barnes, S. B., 1997, Douglas Carl Engelbart: Developing the underlying concepts for contemporary computing. *IEEE Annals of the History of Computing*, 19(3):16-26.

Beddoes, M. P. and Hu, Z., 1994, A chord stenograph keyboard: a possible solution to the learning problem in stenography. *IEEE Trans. on Systems, Man and Cybernetics*, 24(7):953-960.

Bellman, T. and MacKenzie, I. S., 1998, A probabilistic character layout strategy for mobile text entry. In *Proceedings of Graphics Interface '98*, pp. 168-176. Toronto: Canadian Information Processing Society.

Gopher, E. and Raij, D., 1985, Typing with a two-hand chord keyboard: Will the qwerty become obsolete? *IEEE Trans. on Systems, Man and Cybernetics*, 18(4):601-609.

Isokoski, P. and Raisamo, R., 2000, Device independent text input: A rationale and an example. In *Proceedings of the Working Conference on Advanced Visual Interfaces AVI2000*, pages 76-83, Palermo, Italy, ACM.

King, M. T., 1995, Justtype. tm. – efficient communication with eight keys. In *Proceedings of the RESNA 95Annual conference*, Vancouver, BC, Canada.

Kirchenbaum, A., Friedman, Z., and Melnik, A., 1986, Performance of disable people on a chordic keyboard. *Human Factors*, 28(2):187-194.

Kreifeldt, J. G., 1989, Reduced keyboard designs using disambiguation. In *Proceedings of the human factors society 33rd annual meeting*.

Lehikoinen, J. and Roykee, M., 2001, N-fngers: A finger-based interaction technique for wearable computers. *Interacting with Computers*, 13:601-625.

MacKenzie, I. S., 2002, Mobile text entry using three keys. In *ACM proceedings of NordCHI02*, pages pp.27-34.

Matias, A. E., MacKenzie, I. S., and Buxton, W., 1993, Half-qwerty: a one-handed keyboard facilitating skill transfer from qwerty. In *Proceedings of the SIGCHI conference on Human factors in computing systems*, ACM press, pp.88 - 94.

Noyes, J., 1983, Chord keyboards. *Appl. Ergonoics*, 14(1):55-69.

Raghunath, M. T. and Narayanaswami, C., 2002, User interfaces for applications on a wrist watch. *Personal and Ubiquitous Computing*, 6:17-30.

Rosenberg, R. and Slater, M., 1999, The chording glove: A glove-based text input device. *IEEE Trans. on Systems, Man and Cybernetics*, **29**(2):186-191.

Seibel, R., 1962, Performance on a five-finger chord keyboard. *J. Appl. Psychol.*, **46**(3):165-169.

Smith, S. L., 1971, Alphabetic data entry via the touch-tone pad: a comment. *Human factors*, **13**(2):189-190.

MOBILE SUPPORT FOR COMMUNITY HEALTHCARE:
A JANUS VIEW

Carl Adams[1] and Tineke Fitch[2]

1ISCA, University of Portsmouth, UK, e-mail carl.adams@port.ac.uk; 2Healthcare Computing Group, ISCA, University of Portsmouth, UK, email tineke.fitch@port.ac.uk

Abstract: Mobile support, through powerful multimedia and communication devices, offers much promise to enhance the working environment. One area where substantial enhancements are possible, including considerable 'social good', is healthcare. The full infrastructure of the health systems can be brought to support the patient, irrespective of location. The role of community healthcare professionals could be considerably enhanced, enabling a fuller range of patient care to be provided in the community. However, applying such technologies are likely to have unforeseen consequences. This paper explores a 'Janus-faced' view of such technological changes to identify some of these unanticipated consequences. A case of district nurses in the UK is discussed, where technologies such as mobile phones are already being used. For the case, mobile technologies offer much potential, but this will require structural changes, not just in technology.

Key words: Mobile Applications; Mobile Services; Janus-faced; Community Healthcare.

1.   INTRODUCTION

Information systems using sophisticated mobile technologies offer much potential to enhance the working environment, particularly for groups working in remote contexts. Support for such professionals includes corporate information systems, network and communication infrastructure, and corporate databases. One area that seems ideal for such support is community healthcare. Community healthcare professionals visit patients in their own homes or health centres and collaborate with other support services to address pre- and post- primary healthcare, providing a key link between the patient/client and other health and/or social care services, such as housing, general practitioners, social workers and local hospitals. Community healthcare provides key support for vulnerable groups, such as the elderly, less mobile and newly born infants and assist often overstretched primary healthcare systems. For countries where the healthcare infrastructure is less well developed, community healthcare may be the only access to healthcare for much of the population.

Health and social care is a very lucrative market for developers of mobile systems, since significant proportions of GDP are spent on healthcare by national governments, and an increasing proportion of this is targeted at community healthcare (EOHCS 2002).

An examination of community healthcare in the South of England shows that mobile technology use is mainly limited to mobile phones and standalone equipment, however, trends point towards an almost inevitable increase in using more sophisticated mobile support. Governments want increases in efficiency, better communication, reduced bureaucracy and better patient care. Mobile technologies are identified as one way to achieve these by providing better support at point of patient care, providing better recording and monitoring capabilities and integrated communication facilities. However, we argue that before such move takes place we have to be aware of the implications which may be unforeseen and contrary to intended use. In this paper we explore such implications by developing a generic community healthcare case, based on existing practice, and applying a 'Janus-faced' analysis. Each area offering benefits may also yield malefic results. For instance, the aim to use mobile support to reduce bureaucracy may actually result in an increase in bureaucracy.

The paper is structured as follows: first a brief examination of current trends is provided, followed by the development of a generic case based on community healthcare in the South of England. The metaphor of 'Janus-faced' phenomenon is then examined and applied to the community healthcare case. The paper concludes with a discussion of some of the likely challenges of applying sophisticated mobile support in such environments.

2.   COMMUNITY HEALTHCARE, A GENERIC CASE

In the UK, healthcare is mainly provided by the National Health Service (NHS), a huge and complicated institution employing over one million people with an annual budget of around £42 billion (NHS, 2004). The NHS has seen major structural changes over previous years, often politically led, a process that is still continuing (DoH 1997, 1998, 2000, 2002, 2003; Wanless 2002).

District Nurses (DNs) and Health Visitors (HVs) work in patients' own homes after initial contact with general practitioners or after discharge from hospital, with the former assessing healthcare needs and developing appropriate packages of care for their patients, the latter helping people to achieve their potential for health and well-being.

The example developed is based on a pilot study of eight in-depth interviews with DNs, HVs and organizational support staff in fairly urban, including socially deprived, areas. The interviews lasted between 1 ½ and 2 hours and were conducted in the community over a period of two months; a larger study is planned in the near future. A set of open questions based around 5 categories including respondents' experiences of mobile computing/support technologies in general and in existing working practice. Questions also addressed the wider context, any negative experience of use and possible future uses. Responses were recorded and analysed within the context of the respondents' local working environments, thus enabling common themes to be identified.

The existing level of technology is likely to be based on mobile telephones. Existing management dilemmas include ensuring sufficient mobiles for each staff member on duty and having in place procedures to allow people to use their own mobiles when a staff phone is not available. Smaller weekend cover team staff may have a mobile phone each, yet busy main week schedules mean limited availability of mobile phones so staff may have to use their own. Typically there will be discussion on appropriate use of the mobile phone for work activities and bureaucratic processes for recording call activity and reimbursement of personal expenditure.

Although use of the mobile phone is not essential, it does contribute directly to efficiency targets. For instance, response targets are set for dealing with alerted and urgent calls. Without mobile phones HVs and DNs are not able to respond within the maximum time set out in the care protocols. Reduced travel time is yet another benefit, care staff returned to base to pick up referrals, whereas now they travel direct from one visit to the next after receiving the details via their mobile phones. In addition, community workers can telephone base to receive specific information on patient notes, if these are available.

Another "mobile" technology is digital cameras in wound care, where digital photos are attached to the patient's medical record, documenting their progress and condition. Data-pens are a further example and are used to record activity. Staff, patients and the care provided all have a unique barcode; these are swiped at the end of the visit, recording the interventions that have taken place. However, currently community staff can download information contained in the data-pens at base but retrieval in the field is not possible. Issues of current use include 'use protocols' such as what data can be stored on the mobile devices, what to do to reduce risk of theft and what to do in case of theft, practical issues such as recharging batteries practices and handing over the phones and other equipment in 'good condition' for the next set of users.

3.   A JANUS-FACED ANALYSIS

Technology is not always applied and used as expected. As Arnold (2003) notes: "Technologies of many kinds perform in ways that are ironic, perverse and paradoxical. That is to say, a certain technology applied in a certain way in a certain context may have consequences or implications of one kind, and may necessarily and at once be implicated in a contrary set of consequences." (Arnold 2003, p232)

Arnold, examining the effect of mobile phones on society uses the metaphor 'Janus-faced', based on the Roman deity Janus who was blessed and cursed with two faces pointing in opposite directions. Some examples given of technology performing in such a paradoxical manner include car brakes which are designed to slow cars down, and yet the more effectively brakes perform, the faster people drive their cars; antibiotics used to kill pathogens and reduce disease actually result in pathogens evolving into stronger stains resistant to antibiotics; heroin was recommended as a cure for morphine addiction but turned out to generate an even bigger addiction problem. (Arnold 2003, p234)

The concept of a technology paradox within the health service has been previously identified by Hebert (1998) while investigating healthcare provision in 5 community hospitals. As Hebert noted "results suggest that, for specific tasks, IT increased efficiency and productivity – a single employee was able to complete more tasks. However, this produced other consequences not predicted. Participants noted this change did not 'free up time' to spend with patients, but meant there were potentially more opportunities to provide services and more tasks to complete". Indeed, technology that was meant to increase quality of service to patients often resulted in less frequent and shorter contact between staff and patients, as staff time was increasingly taken up with computer-orientated tasks. Other unforeseen consequences were noted, including more 'visible' accountability, changes in roles and responsibilities and delineation between these, and a reduction in job satisfaction.

Arnold (2003) identifies conditions where the Janus-faced metaphor, incorporating notions of irony and paradox, are applicable:

"The performance of the socio-technical system gives rise to multiple implications or sets of implications, at least some of which pull in opposite directions towards contrasting conclusions.

These contrasting conclusions, implications, or binaries, are observed on the same axis of analysis, within the same conceptual frame, as it were.

And, these contrasting implications are not a result of error, to be resolved by better methods, but are co-dependent and co-productive, and are intrinsic to a full apprehension of the operation of the system." (p234)

Some of the challenges of more sophisticated mobile developments have already been discussed above. We analyse this further by applying the Janus-faced metaphor to the generic case, using the goals of parity, standards, increased collaboration and efficiency, reduced bureaucracy, meeting the growing expectations and demands, all of which affect the general quality of service for patients.

3.1   Parity of service: national versus local tensions

The potential of sophisticated mobile support enabling access to the full information infrastructure and support of the NHS would mean a consistent and comparable service across the UK. This would address the so called 'postcode lottery' phenomenon where people living in adjoining postcodes have access to different service levels. However, DNs operate within considerably different set of local resources and priorities. Current mobile use highlights some of the challenges of parity. Different centres use different mixes of technology, some using a pool of mobile phones and others relying more on DNs' own phones. There are differences even within the same Care Trust for alternative shifts. More sophisticated mobile support will add more complexity in the form of increased number of mobile devices and accompanying support mechanisms that have to be rolled out across the UK, which itself is likely to take considerable time to complete, possibly years. There is clearly potential for further inconsistent access to services throughout this transition period as well as local differences once it has been completed.

3.2   Standards: homogeneity versus heterogeneity

Standards are important in terms of integration of patient records and technology and this is accompanied by political and organizational challenges. Community healthcare is often at the forefront of the pull between the 'national' standards and aims driven by the centre and 'local' needs for partnerships, initiatives and collaboration. De jure standards may be imposed, forcing equipment and protocols down a particular route; at the same time, local de facto standards will develop through use, helped by the freedom of mobile devices, which are supposed to remove the shackles of geographic location and environmental limitations. National standards are likely to take considerable time to implement requiring developing a consensus from several different health authorities and different services with different aims and priorities. The array of local de facto standards will emerge more rapidly as the imperative of local needs and working practices evolve.

3.3   Increase in collaboration: interruption versus engagement

The need for better coordination and communication between different health and social care services is a powerful driving force for change, not least to address the needs of vulnerable groups. Sophisticated mobile support offers the potential of real-time communication and better coordination of schedules: social workers, doctors and health visitors can more quickly coordinate activity to address possible concerns with a vulnerable child-at-risk or an elderly person, even in real-time. Such real-time interaction increases interruption for the various service professionals. In addition, semi-automated activity (e.g. automatic synchronising of meeting diaries), could result in less individual control and engagement in the collaboration. Working practices are likely to change to accommodate more interruption, and the interruption is likely to be more insistent. Overall, the nature of collaboration is likely to change, possibly becoming shorter, more insistent and intrusive, less personal and possibly lacking the depth of existing collaboration.

3.4   Increased efficiency versus increased workload

Potential efficiency gains are usually argued along the lines that mobile support will offer benefits in automatic data entry and non-duplication of data/tasks, reduction in time (particularly in reducing the number of visits to hospitals for patients), and more efficient use of DN and other professional resources. However, examining what is likely to take place gives a different picture. Data entry is currently based on hand written elements and standalone bar code recording. More sophisticated automatic recording will require extra devices and their connection to a mobile communication device. This results in increased system complexity, such as work protocols to set up, connect, test and use of such devices, as well as general maintenance and care of such devices (eg cleaning pacing away in a reusable condition). Even before the DNs visit there are likely to be extra activities to ensure the equipment is in good condition for use by others, including mundane things like ensuring batteries are charged (as is the existing case with the mobile phone use). All these activities are likely to take extra time before and after visits as well as during a visit. As already identified, more sophisticated mobile applications requiring GP and other clinician input via mobile devices will involve substantial reengineering of processes for DNs, GPs and the clinicians. There are also likely to be a host of extra work protocols to be developed and adopted by the GPs and clinicians, including setting up, testing and auditing tasks. There may well be some efficiency gains but there will also be considerable increase in related supporting activities.

3.5   Bureaucracy: writing pens versus data-pens.

Existing use shows some bureaucratic challenges. Some of the paperwork has been reduced by the use of data-pens, where patient, condition, treatment and DN information can be swiped quickly by an electronic data-pen using barcodes. However, the time gained through this recording mechanism is lost when trying to retrieve the data, as that is only possible at base from particular workstations. Mobile telephones help DNs in their work but as there are not enough to go around, base need to keep track of which team take out what phone. In addition, whereas before DNs only had to check their medical equipment, they now need to ensure that on returning to base their enablers are re-charged, ready for the next day, in addition there is increasingly a requirement to record each of these activities. As discussed, some DNs have to use their personal mobile telephones while others use pool phones. In both cases there are bureaucratic processes to reimburse work calls made on personal phones and personal calls made on work phones. More sophisticated use of mobile support are likely to add further bureaucratic challenges. There are likely to be similar challenges with issuing and maintaining equipment. In addition, since there will be more service items to record and more people involved (e.g. GPs, clinicians) per visit the bureaucratic burden will increase. Initially, at least, there is likely to be a need to have back up recording activity until the system has proved robust. In a further perverse sense, the bureaucratic recording and auditing activity in patient care is likely to be mainly when something goes wrong, such as when a patient dies: Effectively confirming that the DN and other healthcare professionals have done a good 'job' when the patient dies!

Satisfying expectation and demand result in increasing expectations and demands.

Arnold (2003, p236) discusses Heidegger's notion of "technological enframing", whereby the technology works in such a way as to change the question through the answer. Because mobile telephones allow speedier referral visits, a quicker service is expected by patients. More sophisticated use will also change expectations. Because digital photographs, and videos can easily be sent to experts for a second opinion, the demand for second opinions and advice are likely to increase. As with other technology, in satisfying demand, the enabling mobile technologies are likely to increase the demands.

4.   SUMMARY AND CONCLUSION

It is clear that many community healthcare professionals, from the generic example, cannot do their community activity without some mobile technology support, such as a mobile telephone. More sophisticated support offers much potential to improve patient/client care in the community as well as efficiency benefits. Community healthcare professionals are generally open to such technologies, however, practical considerations and use protocols need to be addressed before the full benefits can be achieved. However, in considering the adoption of such technologies to address the issues and challenges in healthcare, we must not forget that new solutions bring new, additional problems that in turn will need resolution.

The generic example identifies the reengineering and process changes required to reach the potential benefits that the more sophisticated mobile applications offer. Although the challenges of reengineering are not trivial, the main challenges are not technical but at system level getting the different powerful stakeholder groups 'onboard'. The complexity of the task and the operating environment is considerable and still undergoing change (DoH 2003).

In addition, technology can result in paradoxical and ironic consequences. This has been demonstrated by applying the Janus-faced metaphor to the generic case of community healthcare. Along each of the dimensions where Governments seek improvements, such as parity, standards, collaboration, efficiency, bureaucracy, expectations, demands and QoS, there are doubts whether any net gains will be achieved. This is not to say that more sophisticated mobile application will not result in gains or even an overall net gain. Indeed, by applying such technology will change the needs of the patients, professionals and health service as a whole. Things will be able to be done that were not possible before. People will be treated, more quickly, for conditions in their homes that would have taken a hospital visit. Different support services will be able to coordinate activity to more quickly address the needs of a patient at risk. Overall there will be different demands on and for services and different ways of meeting those demands. Much of the change is going on anyway, such as development and integration of electronic patient records. However, as the Janus-faced analysis of the generic case shows, the challenges are considerable and there are doubts whether any of the expected potential benefits are achievable. A technology that is used to reduce bureaucracy may result in further bureaucratic activity. This paradoxical and ironic nature of technology needs to be considered when introducing it. Evaluating such new mobile developments calls for more understanding of the fuller unintentional and unforeseen consequences. Only then can we make an informed decision.

ACKNOWLEDGMENT

We would like to thank Professor David Avison for his kind support and constructive comments on earlier drafts of this paper.

REFERENCES

Arnold, M. (2003) On the phenomenology of technology: the "Janus-faces" of mobile phones. Information and Organization, 13,4, pp231-256.

DoH (1997) "The New NHS: Modern, Dependable" NHS White Paper, the Department of Health. Available online at
http://www.official-documents.co.uk/document/doh/newnhs/forward.htm Accessed July 2003

DoH (1998) "Information for Health 1998 – 2005. An Information Strategy for the Modern NHS" Department of Health. Available online at http://www.nhsia.nhs.uk/def/pages/info4health/forward.asp Accessed July 2003.

DoH (2000) "The NHS Plan, a Plan for Investment, a Plan for Reform." Department of Health. Available online a: http://www.doh.gov.uk/nhsplan/default.htm Accessed July 2003

DoH (2002) "Delivering the Plan." Department of Health. Available online at http://www.doh.gov.uk/ Accessed July 2003

DoH (2003) Keeping the NHS Local – A New Direction of Travel. http://www.doh.gov.uk/configuringhospitals/confighos.pdf Accessed July 2003.

EOHCS (2002), Healthcare Systems in Eight Countries: Trends and Challenges. European Observatory on Health Care Systems, LSE, London.

Hebert, M.A. (1998) Impact of IT on health care professional: changes in work and the productivity paradox. Health Services Management Research, 11, pp69-79.

NHS (2004) "The NHS explained". Available online at http://www.nhs.uk/thenhsexplained/how_the_nhs_works.asp#OPT Accessed March 2004.

Wanless, D. (2002). Securing Our Future Health: Taking a Long-Term View - the Wanless Report. HM Treasury, available online at http://www.hm-treasury.gov.uk/Consultations_ and_Legislation/wanless/consult_wanless_final.cfm Accessed July 2003.